THE BOOKSTORE

THE NEW INTERNATIONAL COMMENTARY
ON THE
OLD TESTAMENT

General Editors

R. K. HARRISON
(1968–1993)

ROBERT L. HUBBARD, JR.
(1994–   )

The Book of
ECCLESIASTES

TREMPER LONGMAN III

WILLIAM B. EERDMANS PUBLISHING COMPANY
GRAND RAPIDS, MICHIGAN / CAMBRIDGE, U.K.

© 1998 Wm. B. Eerdmans Publishing Co.
255 Jefferson Ave. S.E., Grand Rapids, Michigan 49503 /
P.O. Box 163, Cambridge CB3 9PU U.K.

Printed in the United States of America

02 01 00   7 6 5 4 3 2

Library of Congress Cataloging-in-Publication Data

Longman, Tremper.
The book of Ecclesiastes / Tremper Longman III.
p.   cm.
(The New international commentary on the Old Testament)
Includes bibliographical references and indexes.
ISBN 0-8028-2366-1 (alk. paper)
1. Bible. O.T. Ecclesiastes. — Commentaries.
I. Title.   II. Series.
BS1475.3.L66   1998
223′.8077 — dc21   97-24217
                                    CIP

To Dan B. Allender

CONTENTS

GENERAL EDITOR'S PREFACE

Long ago St. Paul wrote: "I planted, Apollos watered, but God gave the growth" (1 Cor. 3:6, NRSV). He was right: ministry indeed requires a team effort — the collective labors of many skilled hands and minds. Someone digs up the dirt and drops in seed, while others water the ground to nourish seedlings to growth. The same team effort over time has brought this commentary series to its position of prominence today. Professor E. J. Young "planted" it forty years ago, enlisting its first contributors and himself writing its first published volume. Professor R. K. Harrison "watered" it, signing on other scholars and wisely editing everyone's finished products. As General Editor, my hands now tend their planting, and, true to Paul's words, through four decades God has indeed graciously "[given] the growth."

Today the New International Commentary on the Old Testament enjoys a wide readership of scholars, priests, pastors, rabbis, and other serious Bible students. Thousands of readers across the religious spectrum and in countless countries consult its volumes in their ongoing preaching, teaching, and research. They warmly welcome the publication of each new volume and eagerly await its eventual transformation from an emerging "series" into a complete commentary "set." But as humanity experiences a new century of history, an era commonly called "postmodern," what kind of commentary series is NICOT? What distinguishes it from other similarly well-established series?

Its volumes aim to publish biblical scholarship of the highest quality. Each contributor writes as an expert, both in the biblical text itself and in the relevant scholarly literature, and each commentary conveys the results of wide reading and careful, mature reflection. Ultimately, its spirit is eclectic, each contributor gleaning interpretive insights from any useful source, whatever its religious or philosophical viewpoint, and integrating them into his or her interpretation of a biblical book. The series draws on recent methodological innovations in biblical scholarship, e.g., canon criticism, the so-called "new literary criticism," reader-response theories, and sensitivity to gender-based and ethnic readings. NICOT volumes also aim to be irenic in tone, summarizing and critiquing influential views with fairness while defending their own. Its list of contributors includes male and female scholars from a number of Christian faith-groups. The diversity of contributors and their freedom to draw on all relevant methodologies give the entire series an exciting and enriching variety.

What truly distinguishes this series, however, is that it speaks from within that interpretive tradition known as evangelicalism. Evangelicalism is an informal movement within Protestantism that cuts across traditional denominational lines. Its heart and soul is the conviction that the Bible is God's inspired Word, written by gifted human writers, through which God calls humanity to enjoy a loving personal relationship with its Creator and Savior. True to that tradition, NICOT volumes do not treat the Old Testament as just an ancient literary artifact on a par with the *Iliad* or the Gilgamesh Epic. They are not literary autopsies of ancient parchment cadavers but rigorous, reverent wrestlings with wonderfully human writings through which the living God speaks his powerful Word. NICOT delicately balances "criticism" (i.e., the use of standard critical methodologies) with humble respect, admiration, and even affection for the biblical text. As an evangelical commentary, it pays particular attention to the text's literary features, theological themes, and implications for the life of faith today.

Ultimately, NICOT aims to serve women and men of faith who desire to hear God's voice afresh through the Old Testament. With gratitude to God for two marvelous gifts — the Scriptures themselves and keen-minded scholars to explain their message — I welcome readers of all kinds to savor the good fruit of this series.

ROBERT L. HUBBARD, JR.

AUTHOR'S PREFACE

The book of Ecclesiastes has captured my attention, or gotten under my skin, for the past fifteen years. I was first attracted to it for academic reasons. At that time my attention was riveted to a number of Mesopotamian literary texts that formed the substance of my doctoral dissertation at Yale University.[1] As I will argue in the introduction, these texts bear a formal, structural similarity to the body of the book of Ecclesiastes.

However, as I read the book of Ecclesiastes closely, its content fascinated me. The sentiments of the main speaker of the book, a person given the name Qohelet, sounded incredibly modern. He expressed the uncertainty and anxieties of our own age. He is driven by the question, "Where can we find meaning in the world?" This issue is the fundamental one that all sensitive human beings must address.

But while the questions that Qohelet raised attracted me, his answers shocked me, coming as they do out from the midst of the sacred canon. "Meaningless," says Qohelet, "everything is meaningless." How does this perspective fit into the rest of biblical revelation? My commentary addresses this question.

It has taken me far longer than I had hoped to finish this commentary. Other projects, a few false starts, a discerning editor, and life have slowed me down. But I first of all thank God for allowing me the energy and time to complete the commentary.

Second, I wish to thank the late Professor Roland K. Harrison for the invitation to join the series. Professor Harrison died just before I submitted my first draft, so I regret not having the advantage of his feedback on my material.

Third, I extend my deep appreciation to Professor Robert Hubbard,

---

1. Since published as *Fictional Akkadian Autobiography* (Winona Lake, IN: Eisenbrauns, 1991).

who succeeded Dr. Harrison to the post of editor of the series. He has done a wonderful job working with a sometimes recalcitrant author, greatly improving the manuscript that the reader has before him or her. Dr. Hubbard was meticulous in his reading and guidance and has increased my respect and admiration for his scholarship and insight. For his benefit, however, I must admit that, while accepting the vast majority of his suggestions, I did not follow all his advice. Thus, he cannot be blamed for the remaining shortcomings of my analysis and presentation.

I wish to thank my colleagues in the Old Testament department at Westminster Theological Seminary for their support over the years it has taken to finish this work. Two of my colleagues are no longer here at the seminary. Ray Dillard died of a heart attack at the young age of forty-nine. He is greatly missed. Bruce Waltke, who has been an inspiration to many of us, left our faculty a few years ago and now teaches on the faculty at Reformed Theological Seminary in Orlando.

At the present time, my colleagues include Alan Groves, Doug Green, and Peter Enns. Thank you, my friends, for your friendship and support.

Over the past dozen years I have offered a doctoral course on the book of Ecclesiastes, allowing me to continue research during the semester. My students have never been afraid to disagree with their professor, and so this class has proved an excellent arena to try out my ideas and to refine or even discard them. The input of this class has been so important to me that I would like to thank the members of the seminar by name. Many of these former students are now professors in different parts of the world. Thanks go to Jack Brown, Lydia Brownback, Mark Bruffey, Mike Canham, Myung Sick Chung, Paul D'Angona, Martin Emmrich, David Freer, Ricardo Gouvea, Jin Kyu Kim, David Lee, John Makujina, Robert Mavis, Erika Moore, Phil Roberts, George Schwab, Adrian Smith, David Strabnow, Stephen Tan, Dean Ulrich, and Peter Yimbu.

As usual, I must extend special appreciation and love to my family. My wife, Alice, and my three children, Tremper (IV), Timothy, and Andrew, have borne with my preoccupations with great patience. I love them all.

This book is dedicated to Dan Allender, with whom I have traveled much of the path of life. Starting as boyhood friends playing junior and senior high school football together (among other things), we then attended Ohio Wesleyan University together. While there, we were both attracted to the mystery and promise of the Christian faith and decided to attend seminary. Not to be separated, we decided to go to Westminster. After seminary, Dan pursued a doctorate in psychology, while I went on in Old Testament. Recently, we have combined our two interests in a series of writing projects, which keep us in close contact. Dan's insight into the human condition and the Bible has stimulated much of my thinking about the book of Ecclesiastes.

ABBREVIATIONS

AB	Anchor Bible
ANET	J. B. Pritchard, ed., *Ancient Near Eastern Texts Relating to the Old Testament*. 3d ed. Princeton: Princeton University, 1969
AS	Assyriological Studies
ASTI	*Annual of the Swedish Theological Institute*
AUSS	*Andrews University Seminary Studies*
BASOR	*Bulletin of the American Schools of Oriental Research*
BDB	F. Brown, S. R. Driver, and C. A. Briggs, *Hebrew and English Lexicon of the Old Testament*. Repr. Oxford: Clarendon, 1959
BHK	R. Kittel, ed., *Biblia Hebraica*. 3d ed. Stuttgart: Württembergische Bibelanstalt, 1937
BHS	K. Elliger and W. Rudolph, eds., *Biblia Hebraica Stuttgartensia*. Stuttgart: Deutsche Bibelstiftung, 1967-77
BibSac	*Bibliotheca Sacra*
BKAT	Biblischer Kommentar: Altes Testament
BTB	*Biblical Theology Bulletin*
BZAW	Beihefte zur *Zeitschrift für die alttestamentliche Wissenschaft*
CAD	I. J. Gelb, et al., eds., *The Assyrian Dictionary of the Oriental Institute of the University of Chicago*. Chicago: Oriental Institute, 1956-
CBQ	*Catholic Biblical Quarterly*
CTM	*Concordia Theological Monthly*
EI	*Eretz Israel*
EQ	*Evangelical Quarterly*
ETL	*Ephemerides theologicae lovanienses*
Evan. Theol.	*Evangelische Theologie*
FOTL	Forms of the Old Testament Literature
GKC	E. Kautzsch, ed., A. E. Cowley, trans., *Gesenius' Hebrew Grammar*. 2d ed. Oxford: Clarendon, 1910
GTJ	*Grace Theological Journal*
HAR	*Hebrew Annual Review*
HKAT	Handkommentar zum Alten Testament

HTR	*Harvard Theological Review*
HUCA	*Hebrew Union College Annual*
ICC	International Critical Commentary
Interp	*Interpretation*
ITC	International Theological Commentary
JB	Jerusalem Bible
JBL	*Journal of Biblical Literature*
JETS	*Journal of the Evangelical Theological Society*
JJS	*Journal of Jewish Studies*
JNES	*Journal of Near Eastern Studies*
JQR	*Jewish Quarterly Review*
JSOT	*Journal for the Study of the Old Testament*
JSOTSup	*Journal for the Study of the Old Testament* — Supplement Series
JSS	*Journal of Semitic Studies*
JTS	*Journal of Theological Studies*
KAT	Kommentar zum Alten Testament
KB	L. Koehler and W. Baumgartner, *Lexicon in Veteris Testamenti Libros*
KJV	King James Version
MT	Masoretic Text
NAB	New American Bible
NASB	New American Standard Bible
NCB	New Century Bible
Neue EB	Die Neue Echter-Bibel
NIV	New International Version
NJB	New Jerusalem Bible
NKJV	New King James Version
NRSV	New Revised Standard Version
OTL	Old Testament Library
OTWSA	*Die Ou Testamentiese Werkgemeenskap in Suid-Afrika*
REB	Revised English Bible
SBLDS	Society for Biblical Literature Dissertation Series
SBLSCS	SBL Septuagint and Cognate Studies
SJT	*Scottish Journal of Theology*
TSF Bulletin	*Theological Students Fellowship Bulletin*
TWOT	R. L. Harris, et al., eds., *Theological Wordbook of the Old Testament*. 2 vols. Chicago: Moody, 1980
UF	*Ugarit-Forschungen*
VT	*Vetus Testamentum*
VTSup	*Vetus Testamentum,* Supplements
WBC	Word Biblical Commentary
WTJ	*Westminster Theological Journal*
ZAW	*Zeitschrift für die alttestamentliche Wissenschaft*
ZDMGSup	*Zeitschrift der deutschen morgenländischen Gesellschaft,* Supplements
ZThK	*Zeitschrift für Theologie und Kirche*

INTRODUCTION[1]

I. TITLE

The English title of Ecclesiastes has been handed down from the Septuagint *(ekklēsiastēs)* via the Vulgate *(Liber Ecclesiastes)*. The Greek title derives from the name of the main speaker of the book, who calls himself *ekklēsiastēs*. This Greek name is a translation of the Hebrew *qōhelet*. Qohelet is not a proper name, but rather a nickname of sorts, functioning as a type of pseudonym. The name literally means "one who assembles" or "assembler," since it is a qal feminine singular participle of the root *qhl*. The feminine participle here and elsewhere is used for occupational names (see also Ezra 2:55, 57; Neh. 3:57, 59). That Qohelet is an occupational name rather than a proper name is further indicated by its occurrence prefixed by the definite article (Eccles. 12:8).

The traditional English translations of the name/title are "the Preacher" and "the Teacher," both of which are misleading. Both translations assume that the speaker of the book is addressing a group that he has assembled. Those who believe the group is religious in orientation translate "Preacher," a rendition certainly encouraged by the Greek translation, which is related to the New Testament word for "church" *(ekklēsia)*. Others, however, rightly object that Qohelet is too untraditional to be located in a religious setting and thus believe the group he has assembled is a classroom of sorts; they thus translate "Teacher." This approach too has its fatal flaws (see the section on "Authorship").[2]

---

1. For further discussion, consult R. B. Dillard and T. Longman III, *An Introduction to the Old Testament* (Grand Rapids, MI: Zondervan, 1994), pp. 247-55.

2. P. Joüon, "Sur le nom de Qoheleth," *Biblica* 2 (1921): 53-54, argues that *Qohelet* must mean "orator of the people," not of a small elite. E. Ullendorff, "The Meaning of *qhlt*," *VT* 2 (1962): 215, however, posits a meaning "the arguer."

The following commentary, for reasons to be described below, will observe a careful distinction in reference between Qohelet and Ecclesiastes. "Qohelet" is the main speaker of the book, while "Ecclesiastes" refers to the book as a whole.

II. AUTHORSHIP

A. THE TRADITION OF SOLOMON AS AUTHOR

Traditionally, Qohelet has been taken as a nickname for Solomon, who then is argued to be the author of the book. The predominant opinion of the past is that in Ecclesiastes an old and repentant Solomon looks back over his life, particularly the period after his apostasy from the Lord, which is recorded in 1 Kings 11:1-13.[3]

A surface reading of the text appears to support this identification. The first verse, often a place for a superscription that includes authorship information,[4] reads: "The words of Qohelet, son of David, king in Jerusalem." These words seem most naturally to point to Solomon, the biological son of King David, who ruled the kingdom after his father in the tenth century B.C. In addition, in 1:12 the first-person speaker in the body of the book of Ecclesiastes identifies himself as king of Israel who ruled in Jerusalem. Furthermore, the description of this king as one who enjoyed fantastic wealth (2:4-9) and as a possessor of great wisdom (1:16) also bears resemblance to the picture of Solomon that we get in the historical books (1 Kings 3:1–10:29).

Moreover, there is likely an intentional link between Solomon and the chosen acronym Qohelet. 1 Kings 8, the story of the dedication of the temple, uses the verbal root *qhl* quite often in reference to Solomon gathering people to hear his speech, which dedicates the newly constructed temple (cf. vv. 1, 2, 14, 22, 55). Thus, the "Assembler" may be an intertextual reference to 1 Kings 8 and a subtle hint that Solomon is the referent.

It is true that the earliest recorded interpretations of the book clearly identify Qohelet with Solomon. Gregory Thaumaturgos (A.D. 213-270), a disciple of Origen, wrote an early paraphrase of the book. He rendered Eccle-

---

3. M. Luther, "Notes on Ecclesiastes," in *Luther's Works,* vol. 15, ed. and trans. J. Pelikan (St. Louis: Concordia, 1972 [1532]), p. 12, gets even more detailed and concrete by imagining Qohelet's monologue to be the reports of King Solomon's dinner conversations. Thus, Qohelet's monologue is analogous to his own Table Talk.

4. That is, Isa. 1:1; Jer. 1:1; Mic. 1:1; Nah. 1:1, but especially Prov. 1:1 and Song of Songs 1:1.

siastes 1:1, "Solomon (the son of the king and prophet David), a king more honoured and a prophet wiser than anyone else, speaks to the whole assembly of God."[5] The Jewish Targum on the book shows the same tendency. For instance, note its expansionistic tendencies in the rendering of 1:12:

> When King Solomon was sitting upon the throne of his kingdom, his heart became very proud of his riches, and he violated the word of God, by gathering many horses, chariots and riders, and amassing much gold and silver. And he married from foreign nations, whereupon the anger of the Lord was kindled against him, and he sent to him Ashmodai, king of the demons, who drove him from his kingdom's throne, and took away the ring from his hand, in order that he should roam and wander about in the world to reprove it. And he roamed about in the outlying towns and the cities of the land of Israel, weeping and lamenting, and saying, "I am Qohelet, whose name was formerly called Solomon, who was king over Israel in Jerusalem."[6]

The Targum illustrates the further tendency to use the book of Ecclesiastes to fill in gaps in the life of Solomon. The book of 1 Kings, which narrates Solomon's apostasy, never betrays a hint of any repentance before his death. However, the feeling was and, in certain quarters, still is strong that the person who wrote large parts of Proverbs and, according to 1 Kings 4:29-34, was renowned through the ancient world for his divinely given wisdom could not die in ignorance. Thus, Ecclesiastes became the witness to his return to orthodoxy at the end of his life, and his apostasy then becomes a foil to teach others of the dangers of wandering from the true God.

Even in the light of strong internal and external testimony to the contrary (see below), a small, but vocal, group of evangelical scholars still advocate this view.[7] Indeed, they argue that the text is most naturally read this way, and that to deviate from this traditional view of authorship can only be seen as a caving in to suspect views. Nonetheless, there are clear signs within the book itself that Ecclesiastes was not written by King Solomon in the tenth century B.C.

---

5. See the excellent translation and commentary on Gregory's work in J. Jarick, *Gregory Thaumaturgos' Paraphrase of Ecclesiastes,* SBLSCS 29 (Atlanta: Scholars Press, 1990).

6. From the helpful translation and commentary by E. Levine, *The Aramaic Version of Qohelet* (New York: Sepher-Hermon, 1978), p. 28.

7. For example, and most notably, W. C. Kaiser, Jr., *Ecclesiastes: Total Life,* Everyman's Bible Commentary (Chicago: Moody, 1979).

B. PROBLEMS WITH THE TRADITION

Attentive readers of the Bible have felt uneasy about the simple identification of Qohelet with Solomon for a long time. Even scholars with impeccably conservative credentials have argued against Solomonic authorship through the centuries. This list includes such luminaries as Moses Stuart,[8] Ernst W. Hengstenberg,[9] Charles H. H. Wright,[10] Edward J. Young,[11] and Derek Kidner.[12] We would certainly need to add the famous nineteenth-century Lutheran commentator, Franz Delitzsch, to this list. His comment concerning the language of Ecclesiastes has often been repeated, "if the book of Koheleth were of old Solomonic origin, then there is no history of the Hebrew language."[13]

What is the evidence that drove these and many others away from what seems the most natural reading of the text? I will consider the counterevidence to Solomonic authorship under two headings: internal and external considerations.

1. Internal Considerations

A number of subtle and even blatant hints within the book itself distance Solomon from Qohelet. The first is the use of the nickname (or more technically pseudonym) itself. One must ask what is gained or what possible reason could Solomon have had for adopting a name other than his own in this book? Is he hiding his identity from someone? If so, for what possible reason? Does the nickname add anything to the message of the book? After all, the connection to Solomon is tenuous, and no one has argued that the name contributes to the meaning of the book. It is much more likely that the nickname Qohelet was adopted by the actual writer to associate himself with Solomon, while retaining his distance from the actual person. It is a way of indicating that the

8. M. Stuart, *Commentary on Ecclesiastes* (New York: G. P. Putnam, 1851).

9. E. W. Hengstenberg, *A Commentary on Ecclesiastes* (Evansville, IN: Sovereign Grace Publishers, 1960 [1869]).

10. According to Wright, "There are, however, passages to be found in the Book of Koheleth itself in which the author lifts up his visor in such a manner as to show the intelligent reader that the character and name of Solomon were simply assumed, not for any purpose of deception, nor as 'a pious fraud,' but by a perfectly allowable literary device" (C. H. H. Wright, *The Book of Koheleth* [London: Hodder and Stoughton, 1888], p. 83).

11. E. J. Young, *An Introduction to the Old Testament* (Grand Rapids, MI: Eerdmans, 1949).

12. D. Kidner, *A Time to Mourn and a Time to Dance* (Downers Grove, IL: InterVarsity, 1976).

13. F. Delitzsch, *Proverbs, Ecclesiastes, Song of Solomon,* trans. M. G. Easton (Grand Rapids, MI: Eerdmans, 1975 [1872]), p. 190.

Solomonic persona is being adopted for literary and communicative purposes. In brief, the wise man who adopts the nickname Qohelet pretends to be Solomon while he explores avenues of meaning in the world. Solomon was known as the wisest and richest man to have ever lived. If he could not find meaning in the things of the world, who could (see 2:12)?

Second, two verses seem to be especially strong indications that Qohelet, while associated with Solomon, is not the historical personage.

Ecclesiastes 1:12:

I, Qohelet, was king over Israel in Jerusalem.

It is striking that the past tense is used here. Its use is an implicit claim that there was a time when Solomon was alive but was no longer king. Indeed, the Targum (see above) understands it that way and creates or uses an old legend that Solomon abdicated his throne in his old age. The historical books not only do not mention but also do not allow such a period in Solomon's life. According to 1 Kings 11, Solomon died while he ruled Israel.

Ecclesiastes 1:16a:

I said to myself, "I have surpassed in wisdom everyone who ruled Jerusalem before me."

This verse sounds strange on Solomon's lips. He claims more wisdom than all the rulers in Jerusalem that preceded him, but only David was ruler in Jerusalem before him, unless of course he would include Jebusite city rulers, but that would be passing strange coming from an Israelite king. After all, these were pagan, alien kings, and hostile to Israel.

Besides these two verses that distance Solomon from Qohelet, careful readers notice that the association between Qohelet and the king/Solomon only lasts for the first three chapters, after which no more is made of it. As a matter of fact, when the kingship is mentioned later in the book of Ecclesiastes, there appears to be a large gap between the speaker and the institution.

Ecclesiastes 4:1-3:

Then I turned and observed all the oppression that is done under the sun, and oh, the tears of the oppressed! There is no one to comfort them. Power is in the grasp of the oppressors. There is no one to comfort them. So I praised the dead who are already dead more than the living who are still alive. But better than both of these is the one who does not yet exist. That one has not seen the evil activity that is done under the sun.

5

How could Solomon write these verses? He was the mightiest ruler of the land. He could easily have done more than bemoan the plight of the oppressed; he could have taken steps to alleviate it. From what we know of the biblical Solomon, he did the opposite. He created a heavy burden for his people, something that continued until the end of his reign, as we know from the interesting dialogue between the people of Israel and Rehoboam, Solomon's son (1 Kings 12, especially v. 4).[14]

Ecclesiastes 5:7-8 (English 5:8-9):

If you see oppression of the poor and deprivation of justice and righteousness in the province, do not be surprised concerning the situation. For one official watches out for another, and there are officials over them. The profit of the land is taken by all; even the king benefits from the field.

As before, these verses are awkward coming from the king. It is protest literature against the king, not by him. Solomon could have reversed the policy and is not likely to have written this about himself.

Ecclesiastes 10:20:

Moreover, do not curse the king even in your thoughts;
    do not curse the rich even in your sleeping chamber,
for a bird might carry the message
    or some winged creature may tell the matter.

Such advice concerning behavior in regard to the king hardly would come from the king himself. The verse assumes that the king is a suspicious bully. Such a statement might be made about Solomon, but not by Solomon.

The internal evidence, although not conclusive, certainly provides a strong argument against the simple identification of Solomon and Qohelet. Why would the speaker who identifies himself as Qohelet want to associate himself at all with Solomon? He gives us an indication in 2:12. In the process of changing from one topic to another, Qohelet says: "I turned my attention to observe wisdom and mad folly. For what can anyone who comes after the king do but that which has already been done?"

Let me restate my contention: Qohelet is not Solomon, but he does adopt a Solomonic persona to explore avenues of meaning in the world. It is only in

---

14. See J. Bright, *A History of Israel,* 3d ed. (Philadelphia: Westminster, 1981), pp. 211-28; J. Alberto Soggin, "The Davidic-Solomonic Kingdom," in *Israelite and Judaean History,* ed. J. Hayes and J. Miller, OTL (Philadelphia: Westminster, 1977), pp. 332-80.

the first three chapters of the book that we get even a hint of association with the great king of Israel. This section describes Qohelet's search for meaning. As my study of the relevant chapters will show, Qohelet tries to find meaning in a number of different areas, including wisdom (1:16-18; 2:12-16), wealth (2:7-11), women (2:8), and building projects (2:4-6). Who knew and experienced the height of these areas more than Solomon? Solomon was the richest (1 Kings 10:14-29) and wisest (1 Kings 4:29-34) king that Israel ever knew. He also constructed more buildings (most notably the temple) and married more women than anyone (1 Kings 11:3). Nonetheless, the historical books inform us that, though Solomon reached the pinnacle, he ended his life an apostate. The person who calls himself Qohelet pretends to be Solomon in order to argue that if Solomon cannot find satisfaction and meaning in life in these areas, no one can. Solomon was the perfect literary foil for his argument. Once the search for meaning is over, the Solomonic persona is dropped, and that is when we see the distance between Qohelet and Solomon widen.

I conclude the internal evidence against Solomonic authorship by pointing out that even if one grants that Qohelet was Solomon, that would not make Solomon the author of Ecclesiastes. We must take our cue from the literary structure of the book and take seriously the change in point of view between the body of the book, on the one hand (1:12–12:7), and the prologue (1:1-11) and epilogue (12:8-14), on the other. In my view, the body of the book contains the first-person speech of Qohelet; the prologue and epilogue contain the first-person speech of an unnamed speaker who refers to Qohelet in the third person, as another person whom he knows (e.g., 12:8-12).

The traditional view interprets the change as the shift between the old Solomon and the young Solomon, but this reading is unnatural. Why would the older Solomon refer to himself as a young man using the third person? In addition, as Michael V. Fox points out, there is one occurrence in the body of the book where the speaker refers to Qohelet in the third person: " 'Observe, this I have found:' Qohelet said, 'one thing to another to find the sum of things' " (7:27).

Such a use of a third-person reference to Qohelet is intrusive and is a strong argument against identifying the so-called frame narrator with Qohelet. In Fox's words in reference to 7:27, "While one *can* speak of himself in the third-person, it is unlikely he would do so in the middle of a first-person sentence, whereas a writer quoting someone else may put a *verbum dicendi* wherever he wishes within the quotation. *'āmar haqqōhelet* are not Qohelet's words in 7:27 and therefore probably not in 1:2 and 12:8 either."[15] The use

15. M. V. Fox, "Frame-Narrative and Composition in the Book of Qohelet," *HUCA* 48 (1977): 84. This point may be confirmed by comparison with the third-person intrusions in first-person prophetic speech. The third-person references to the Lord hint at the presence of the prophetic narrator in verses like Isa. 1:11.

of the third person makes the body of the book (1:12–12:7) a virtual quotation. I will have more to say about this structural dynamic in the section "Structure" below.

2. External Evidence

As will be argued under "Genre," Qohelet's speech bears a close structural resemblance to a group of ancient Near Eastern literary texts that have been called fictional autobiographies.[16] Specifically, the body of the book (1:12–12:7) is similar in general structure to fifteen texts from Mesopotamia written in Akkadian that span a time from the Old Babylonian period (2017-1595 B.C.) down to the Seleucid period (312-ca. 150 B.C.).

As will be seen, this Akkadian genre can be divided into four subgenres, each characterized by its distinctive endings. The subgenre most like Ecclesiastes includes three texts that conclude with wisdom admonitions (the Cuthaean Legend of Naram-Sin, the Adad-guppi autobiography, and the so-called Sin of Sargon text). At this point, I will anticipate my later discussion of the genre and draw out the implications of this generic identification for the question of authorship.

First, there was a well-used genre of fictional autobiography in which a later author placed his words in the mouth of another, more famous individual. As an earlier study indicated, some of these were clearly fraudulent, with the intention of deceiving their audiences (Cruciform Monument of Maništušu), and others were not (Adad-guppi inscription).[17]

Second, it is striking that only Ecclesiastes 1:12–12:7 parallels these Mesopotamian texts. This observation highlights the fact that the prologue (1:1-11) and the epilogue (12:8-14) are a frame that is structurally distinct from the body of the book. Further, the evidence suggests that 1:12–12:7 is a separate literary unity distinct from the frame in 1:1-11 and 12:8-14. This observation combined with the change of perspective between the frame and the body of the book (see above) lends strong support to the view that a second voice is heard in the frame in addition to that of Qohelet.

3. Conclusion

In the final analysis, it is the voice in the frame, other than Qohelet, who seems most likely to be the author of the finished book. Ecclesiastes 1:12–12:7, then, is a virtual quotation.

---

16. See T. Longman III, *Fictional Akkadian Autobiography* (Winona Lake, IN: Eisenbrauns, 1991), for translations and a full discussion of these texts.
17. Longman, *Fictional Akkadian Autobiography.*

If this is true, who is the frame narrator? Unfortunately, we can say little. He (or conceivably she) is probably a wisdom teacher, one who speaks as an insider when he critiques Qohelet (12:8-12). Furthermore, he addresses his son in a manner typical of other wise teachers (12:12). I will refer to this voice, the authorial voice, as the unnamed wisdom teacher or the frame narrator.

III. EXCURSUS: WHO WAS QOHELET?

If Qohelet is not Solomon, then who is he? Once again we have little to go on. The frame narrator calls him a wise teacher (12:8); beyond that we can say little about him except to characterize his teaching, a task that will occupy the remainder of this commentary.

Before leaving this topic, however, I must reckon with Michael Fox's suggestion that Qohelet might be a literary persona, not a real person. Fox draws an analogy with the Brer Rabbit stories, in which there is a similar relationship between the main character who speaks, Uncle Remus, and the frame narrative. Fox thus suggests that Qohelet may be a literary creation and not a real person.[18] In the final analysis, I cannot decide this for certain, though it seems an unnecessary hypothesis and one without ancient parallels. For the purposes of this commentary, I will assume that Qohelet is a real person, though there is no obvious theological significance to this decision.

IV. DATE

With few exceptions, most critical scholars date the book late in the history of Israel. As we will see below, there are good arguments in favor of a late dating for Ecclesiastes.

Aarre Lauha dates Ecclesiastes to the late postexilic, but pre-Maccabean, period.[19] James Crenshaw is more precise, averring that "a date for Qohelet between 225 and 250 remains most likely."[20]

18. Fox, "Frame-Narrative," pp. 94-96.
19. A. Lauha, *Kohelet,* BKAT (Neukirchen-Vluyn: Neukirchener Verlag, 1978), p. 3. E. Bickerman, *Four Strange Books of the Bible* (New York: Schocken Books, 1967), p. 141, represents a critical position that dates the book even later to the mid-second century, the period of "Ptolemaic Judaism."
20. J. L. Crenshaw, *Ecclesiastes,* OTL (Philadelphia: Westminster, 1987), p. 50.

The main argument used by critics to promote a late date of the book is language and style (see below, "Language"). For instance, the vocabulary and syntax of Ecclesiastes are compared to late Hebrew and Aramaic, and this argument pushes scholars to date the book late. I have already quoted the conservative scholar Franz Delitzsch to this effect (see above). Daniel Fredericks,[21] however, has devoted a careful study of all the linguistic arguments used to date the book late and has concluded that they are unpersuasive.[22] Further, so little is known about the transmission of the biblical text during its earliest stages that we cannot rule out linguistic updating. The so-called late forms may not in fact have been original to the book but may reflect the updating of vocabulary and grammar by later scribes so their contemporaries could understand the book better (see further discussion under "Language").

Another approach to the question of dating demonstrates similarities between Qohelet's speech and, for instance, Hellenistic thought.[23] This method, too, is dubious since connections can be made between Qohelet and earlier thought and literary forms[24] and also with much later foreign thought.[25]

All of this is not to dispute the possibility that Ecclesiastes is non-Solomonic (see above) and late (see below), but it does question the typical arguments used to support the critical position. In the past it has also been typical for critical scholars to argue that the book contains contradictions, specifically orthodox and unorthodox statements.[26] They have reasoned that the original speaker in the book was a radically unorthodox skeptic whose

21. D. C. Fredericks, *Qoheleth's Language: Re-evaluating Its Nature and Date* (Lewiston, NY, and Queenston, Ontario: Edwin Mellen, 1988). His position will be presented more fully in the next section on "Language."

22. However, see more recently A. Schoors, *The Preacher Sought to Find Pleasing Words: A Study of the Language of Qoheleth,* part 1 (Leuven: Departement Orientalistiek/Uitgeverij Peeters, 1992), who still argues that the book's language favors a late date.

23. G. Bertram, "Hebräischer und griechischer Qohelet," *ZAW* 64 (1952): 24-69; E. H. Plumptre, *Ecclesiastes; or, the Preacher* (Cambridge, England: Cambridge University Press, 1881); and H. Ranston, *Ecclesiastes and the Early Greek Wisdom Literature* (London: Epworth, 1925).

24. For instance, M. J. Dahood, "Canaanite-Phoenician Influence in Qoheleth," *Biblica* 33 (1952): 30-52, 191-221; "The Language of Qoheleth," *CBQ* 14 (1952): 227-32; "Qoheleth and Recent Discoveries," *Biblica* 39 (1958): 302-18; "Qoheleth and Northwest Semitic Philology," *Biblica* 43 (1962): 349-65; and "The Phoenician Background of Qoheleth," *Biblica* 47 (1966): 264-82.

25. P. K. H. Lee, "Re-reading Ecclesiastes in the Light of Su Tung-P'o's Poetry," *Ching Feng* 30 (1987): 214-36.

26. For instance, compare Eccles. 8:11 and 14, which express the view that the wicked and righteous do not get what they deserve, and 8:12 and 13, which appear between them and state the opposite, namely, that the wicked will be punished (see commentary).

thought was later mitigated by one or a series of redactors.[27] The orthodox redactor was responsible, for instance, for the epilogue. A reading of the book that takes into account the two different voices of the book (see "Authorship" above and "Structure" below), however, does not have to resort to this hypothesis, since it accounts for the different perspectives by recognizing two speakers, rather than one.

V. LANGUAGE

The Hebrew of Ecclesiastes is unusual in comparison to the other books of the Hebrew Bible. No one questions this assessment. Many examples of difficult words, grammatical peculiarities,[28] and syntactical issues will be given in the commentary itself. While every scholar recognizes the language problem,[29] there is vast disagreement over the cause of it. Debate, often quite heated and personal, has risen around this topic. For reasons to be given below, however, the actual benefit of a solution for the question of dating may be quite minimal.

For some time, it appears, scholars have recognized similarities between the Hebrew of our book and the Aramaic language, and especially similarities with Mishnaic Hebrew. One of the most notable instances of this approach is the work of Franz Delitzsch. He had great confidence that the book of Ecclesiastes was influenced by Aramaic and, partly on this basis, argued that the book was late.[30] What is particularly striking about Delitzsch's position is that he was an important member of the orthodox Lutheran church in the last half of the nineteenth century, a group that might be expected to defend Solomonic origins of the book rigorously. Delitzsch's view was driven more by his understanding of the textual data than by dogmatic considerations. A more recent example of this theory may be found in the work of Charles F. Whitley. In his book *Koheleth: His Language and*

---

27. C. Siegfried, *Prediger und Hoheslied,* HKAT (Göttingen: Vandenhoeck und Ruprecht, 1898), posited nine hands contributing to the composition of Ecclesiastes. Later, G. A. Barton, *The Book of Ecclesiastes,* ICC (Edinburgh: T. and T. Clark, 1908), argued that there were three people behind the book, while E. Podechard, *L'Ecclésiaste* (Paris: Libraire Victor Lecoffre, 1912), argued that there were four.

28. For instance, A. Schoors ("The Pronouns in Qoheleth," *Hebrew Studies* 30 [1989]: 71) states: "these peculiarities, such as the exclusive use of *'ny*, the feminine demonstrative *zōh,* and the frequent occurrence of *w-,* have often been pointed out."

29. That is, ever since Grotius (*Annotationes ad Qohelet* [Paris, 1644]), who used the unusual language of the book to argue for a late date of the book.

30. See Delitzsch, *Proverbs, Ecclesiastes, Song of Solomon,* pp. 190-97.

Thought,[31] Whitley maps the connection between the Hebrew of Ecclesiastes and both Aramaic and Mishnaic Hebrew. Thus, he argues that the book's composition must be situated in the second century B.C., specifically 152-145 B.C., a date that "satisfies both the historical and linguistic considerations for the composition of the book."[32]

The view that the Hebrew of Ecclesiastes demonstrates Aramaic influence is thus an old one. More radical is the view propounded most forcefully by Frank Zimmermann,[33] though anticipated by Francis C. Burkitt,[34] that our present book of Ecclesiastes is a translation of an Aramaic original. Zimmermann was followed by two impressive experts in Semitic linguistics, Charles C. Torrey[35] and H. L. Ginsberg,[36] both of whom confirmed his thesis. Daniel Fredericks describes the three pillars that supported such a theory as "a high density of alleged Aramaisms, unexpected absence or presence of the definite article, and supposed improvements in the text obtained by restoring 'obscure' passages to the 'original' Aramaic."[37]

This view evoked a vigorous reaction from Robert Gordis.[38] Besides treating the specific passages that Zimmermann used to establish his case, he also argued that the book's Hebrew was too difficult to be a translation. He rightly noted that translation tended to smooth out syntactical and grammatical difficulties, not enhance them.[39] Gordis did not deny Aramaic influence but argued that the language of Ecclesiastes was closer to Mishnaic Hebrew than to Aramaic.

31. C. F. Whitley, *Koheleth: His Language and Thought,* BZAW 148 (Berlin: de Gruyter, 1979).

32. Whitley, *Koheleth,* p. 148.

33. F. Zimmermann, "The Aramaic Provenance of Qohelet," *JQR* 36 (1945-46): 17-45; "The Question of Hebrew in Qohelet," *JQR* 40 (1949-50): 79-102; *The Inner World of Qohelet* (New York: KTAV, 1973); and *Biblical Books Translated from the Aramaic* (New York: KTAV, 1975).

34. F. C. Burkitt, "Is Ecclesiastes a Translation?" *JTS* 23 (1921-22): 22-26.

35. C. C. Torrey, "The Question of the Original Language of Qoheleth," *JQR* 39 (1948-49): 151-60.

36. H. L. Ginsberg, *Studies in Koheleth* (New York: Jewish Theological Seminary of America, 1952).

37. Fredericks, *Qoheleth's Language,* p. 15.

38. R. Gordis, "The Original Language of Qoheleth," *JQR* 37 (1946-47): 67-84; and "The Translation Theory of Qohelet Re-examined," *JQR* 40 (1949-50): 103-16.

39. The same opinion is held by Schoors, *The Preacher Sought to Find Pleasing Words,* p. 8, who says, "This is a self-destructive theory, for why should somebody want to translate an Aramaic text into Hebrew when he neither properly understands the Aramaic original nor sufficiently masters the Hebrew language to offer a flawless translation. For a few mistranslations can betray the translational character of a text, but in the theory under consideration there are too many of them and they are too fundamental. It is also strange that a translation would have left so many downright Aramaisms."

This debate was a spirited one with occasional jabs at the opponent's competence.[40] Nonetheless, Zimmermann's view proved too radical and also fell short of demonstration; thus, none of the more recent commentaries supports his approach to the language of the book.

Attention was diverted from Zimmermann's proposal when an equally radical one was made by the noted and provocative Semitist, Mitchell J. Dahood. In 1952 Dahood argued that Ecclesiastes was written in a dialect heavily influenced by Phoenician. He asserted that the author was a Jew,[41] but a Jew who probably lived in a Phoenician city.[42] Subsequent articles sought to support his thesis.[43] While Cyrus Gordon[44] and Gary Rendsburg[45] use his evidence to argue in favor of a northern origin of Qohelet's dialect,[46] few people take Dahood's position on this matter seriously since his evidence is amenable to explanations that are in harmony with a Palestinian origin of the book without Phoenician influence.[47]

Before proceeding to a conclusion, I should briefly mention the purported presence of words that show Persian and Greek influence.[48] These words too will be discussed in context, but one may argue that the presence of Persian loanwords does not demand a late date for the book. As Fredericks rightly argues, no good reason exists to restrict the possibility of Persian's influence on Hebrew to the time when Persia was at its cultural height. Persia was in existence long before the sixth century, and there were preexilic

40. Illustrated by Zimmermann's comment ("The Question of Hebrew in Qohelet," p. 81) that Gordis, an accomplished Semitist, should "familiarize himself somewhat more with the Aramaic idiom."

41. Dahood, "The Language of Qoheleth," p. 227.

42. Dahood, "Canaanite-Phoenician Influence in Qoheleth," p. 34.

43. Compare nn. 39 and 40. Also Dahood, "Qoheleth and Recent Discoveries," pp. 302-18; and "The Phoenician Background of Qoheleth," pp. 264-82.

44. C. H. Gordon, *Ugaritic Literature* (Rome: Pontifical Biblical Institute, 1947), p. 143; compare comments by R. Gordis, "Was Koheleth a Phoenician?" *JBL* 74 (1955): 103-14.

45. Rendsburg ("The Galilean Background of Mishnaic Hebrew," in *The Galilee in Late Antiquity,* ed. L. I. Levine [New York: Jewish Theological Seminary of America, 1992], p. 238) argued that the Hebrew of Ecclesiastes is similar to both Phoenician and Mishnaic Hebrew and that this indicates its northern origin because "all three comprise what we may tentatively label the Israelian-Phoenician dialect bundle."

46. See also A. F. Rainey, "A Study of Ecclesiastes," *CTM* 35 (1964): 148-57; and more recently J. R. Davila, "Qohelet and Northern Hebrew," *MAARAV* 5-6 (1990): 69-87.

47. See critiques by R. Gordis, "Qoheleth and Qumran — A Study of Style," *Biblica* 41 (1960): 395-410; Whitley, *Koheleth,* whose book is a running critique of Dahood; and Fredericks, *Qoheleth's Language,* pp. 18-24.

48. See comments and bibliography in Fredericks, *Qoheleth's Language,* pp. 242-54.

connections between "Palestine and the East."[49] In addition, there is reason to dispute the allegation that there is a Greek influence on Qohelet's language. As Fredericks concludes, "alleged instances have adequate Biblical precedent, or natural Hebrew meanings and have no need for explanations based on Greek."[50]

Fredericks offers the most comprehensive examination of this issue.[51] He describes and evaluates all the arguments and sifts through the evidence presented by scholars who theorize that the book's language indicates a late and/or foreign origin. The present commentary will draw on the details of his work in the expository section (especially in footnotes). Through a carefully developed methodology (described in his chapter "General Methodological Concerns"), Fredericks counters the grammatical and lexical arguments used by many scholars to insist on a postexilic date for the book. He argues that his scholarly opponents have not allowed for legitimate alternative explanations (for instance, the possibility that Qohelet's language reflects the vernacular of his day). He also believes that previous studies overlooked evidence that indicates that Qohelet's language has precedents in biblical Hebrew, rendering parallels in later Hebrew irrelevant. His own conclusion is that "Qohelet's language should not be dated any later than the exilic period, and no accumulation of linguistic evidence speaks against a pre-exilic date."[52]

Fredericks's study should give rise to a healthy skepticism concerning the linguistic arguments used to date the book late. Unfortunately, some reviews[53] have accused Fredericks of allowing his evangelical theological presuppositions to unduly influence his conclusions. Antoon Schoors has recently argued that the cumulative evidence, particularly such linguistic features as "the exclusive use of 'ny, the feminine demonstrative zōh, and the frequent occurrence of w-," override Fredericks's individual treatments of these and other phenomena.[54]

This reaction to his work undermines Fredericks's own belief that "the

49. Fredericks, *Qoheleth's Language,* p. 244. Furthermore, there are only two apparent Persian loans in the book: *pardēs* (2:5) and *pitgām* (8:11).

50. Fredericks, *Qoheleth's Language,* p. 249.

51. Schoors, *The Preacher Sought to Find Pleasing Words,* arrived too late for me to make full use of it throughout the commentary; when the study is completed, it will supersede Fredericks in its coverage. He differs from Fredericks in that he concludes that the language of the book indicates a late date of the book; it "belongs to what scholars have recently called Late Biblical Hebrew" (p. 221). He allows for the possibility but not the probability that the peculiarities of the book's language are a result of dialect or vernacular (pp. 223-24).

52. Fredericks, *Qoheleth's Language,* p. 262.

53. Most fully by Schoors, *The Preacher Sought to Find Pleasing Words,* especially the general comments on pp. 14-16.

54. Schoors, *The Preacher Sought to Find Pleasing Words,* p. 14.

language [of the book] is the most important criterion for dating the book because it is less subjective than the other methods."[55] We do not know the history of the Hebrew language or the foreign languages that influenced it well enough to use Qohelet's language as a barometer of the book's origin. Are certain features late, or do they reflect vernacular or dialectical peculiarities in Hebrew? We can never be certain. My conclusion is that the language of the book is not a certain barometer of date.

VI. GENRE

A. OF THE WHOLE

The following exploration of the genre of the book of Ecclesiastes bears similarity to the modern method of form criticism, but it should not be confused with it. While the practice of form criticism has changed somewhat since Hermann Gunkel, it remains an essentially diachronic analysis of the text. Elsewhere[56] I have made the case that Gunkel formulated a form-critical method based on a neoclassical view of genre, already obsolete in his own day. The following presupposes a synchronic, descriptive approach to genre, informed by more recent literary theory.

Traditional form-critical studies of Ecclesiastes conclude that the book's genre cannot be precisely defined. Typical is Roland Murphy's conclusion that the book's overarching genre "still escapes us"[57] and James Crenshaw's comment that the book does not have one single genre.[58] In these studies, description of the book's various parts replaces a discussion of the whole.[59] While such a survey is extremely helpful (and may be found below), a more flexible approach to genre allows us to suggest literary associations for the body of the book (1:12–12:7) and invites a genre identification for the whole. Since my approach to genre differs from the typical approach found in most commentaries, I will begin with a short outline of theory and method.

55. Fredericks, *Qoheleth's Language,* p. 255.

56. T. Longman III, "Form Criticism, Recent Developments in Genre Theory, and the Evangelical," *WTJ* 44 (1985): 46-65; *Literary Approaches to Biblical Interpretation* (Grand Rapids, MI: Zondervan, 1987), pp. 76-83; and *Fictional Akkadian Autobiography,* pp. 3-21.

57. R. E. Murphy, *Wisdom Literature: Job, Proverbs, Ruth, Canticles, Ecclesiastes, and Esther,* FOTL (Grand Rapids, MI: Eerdmans, 1981), p. 129.

58. Crenshaw, *Ecclesiastes,* p. 28.

59. See, for instance, O. Kaiser, "Die Botschaft des Buches Kohelet," *ETL* 71 (1995): 49-50.

Genre identification significantly affects a reader's interpretation and application of a text. Proper identification may lead to correct interpretation, but a mistaken genre identification will certainly distort the reader's understanding.[60] For instance, to take Norman Mailer's *Ancient Evenings,* as compelling as it is as historical fiction, and treat it as a serious contribution to Egyptian historiography would be a travesty to both his novel and the pursuit of ancient history.

The Song of Songs provides a well-known biblical example of misinterpretation through faulty genre identification. For centuries the book was brutally misread by "desexing" its meaning and labelling it an "allegory." It has only been within the past century that its original message has been heard through the reestablishment of its proper genre label "love poetry."[61]

Of course, proper genre identification arises from reading the text itself and is not imposed from outside the text. Thus, genre identification derives from the give-and-take of the reading process. The text is embedded with signals of both an implicit and explicit nature to guide the reader along.

We may see this most clearly in contemporary literature with which we are familiar. Title pages customarily signal that a literary work, for instance, is "A Novel," so that no confusion will arise.

The process of genre identification becomes more difficult when the reader is separated from the literary work by culture and time. In the case of the Bible, we are separated in both regards from the text. Robert Alter makes the following statement, which has important ramifications for genre as a major literary convention:

> Every culture, even every era in a particular culture, develops distinctive and sometimes intricate codes for telling its stories, involving everything from narrative point of view, procedures of description and characterization, the management of dialogue, to the ordering of time and the organization of plot.[62]

Thus, we must proceed more gingerly and consciously to seek out those "codes" as we deal with the genre of biblical books.

The other important characteristic of genre to bear in mind is the fluidity of the very concept itself. Any single piece of literature may be described with more than one generic label. A genre is defined by similarities

---

60. See the insightful work done on genre in E. D. Hirsch, *Validity in Interpretation* (New Haven: Yale University Press, 1967); and *The Aims of Interpretation* (Chicago: University of Chicago Press, 1976).

61. J. B. White, *A Study of the Language of Love in the Song of Songs and Ancient Egyptian Poetry,* SBLDS 38 (Missoula, MT: Scholars Press, 1978).

62. R. Alter, "A Response to Critics," *JSOT* 27 (1983): 113-17.

that exist between a group of texts.[63] To group texts into genres, it is necessary to concentrate on those similarities while bracketing their differences. Thus, it is a matter of abstracting characteristics from particular texts. A piece of literature may exist in a broad genre with many members on the basis of a few shared traits as well as a narrow genre with few members on the basis of many traits. The literary critic Tsvetan Todorov pointed out that it is correct to speak of genres on a scale that ranges from one to the maximum. According to Todorov, "jedes Werk gehören zu einer 'Gattung'; alle Texte gehören zu einer 'Gattung.' "[64] This notion of genre suggests that genres are not rigid categories.

More than one genre label may apply even on the same level of abstraction. For example, Psalm 98 may be classified as literature, poem, hymn, divine warrior hymn, and then in a small genre with two members that includes Psalm 96,[65] as we move from the broadest to the narrowest classification. Genre distinctions do not fall from heaven. They are approximate ways by which we may speak of similar texts.

Thus, while there are a number of possible genre labels for the book of Ecclesiastes (wisdom literature, reflection, etc.), the present interpretation describes it as "framed wisdom autobiography." This identification draws on a genre study of the group of Mesopotamian autobiographical texts briefly introduced earlier.[66] After describing the Akkadian genre here, I will then show the analogy with the central section of the book of Ecclesiastes, the words of Qohelet (1:12–12:7).

Before I proceed, however, perhaps it will be helpful to define the central term of my proposed genre label. I define the term "autobiography" broadly as "an account of the life (or part thereof) of an individual himself or herself." Such a composition must be written in the first person and include reminiscences of the past life of the first-person narrator.[67]

It is true that a few students of the genre define autobiography in terms of modern post-Enlightenment attitudes toward the self and individuality.

---

63. Longman, *Literary Approaches to Biblical Interpretation*, pp. 76-78.

64. That is, "each [literary] work belongs to a 'genre'; the entirety of texts belong to one 'genre'." The quote comes from K. Hempfer, *Gattungstheorie* (Munich: W. Funk, 1973), p. 137. See also G. S. Morson, *The Boundaries of Genre* (Austin: University of Texas Press, 1981), p. 5.

65. See the argument in T. Longman III, "Psalm 98: A Divine Warrior Victory Song," *JETS* 27 (1984): 267-74.

66. A. Poebel, *Das appositionell bestimmte Pronomen der 1. Per. Sing. in den westsemitischen Inschriften und im Alten Testament*, AS 3 (Chicago: Oriental Institute, 1931); and Longman, *Fictional Akkadian Autobiography*.

67. Such a definition is given and defended within the history of the discussion of autobiography in Longman, *Fictional Akkadian Autobiography*, pp. 40-43.

THE BOOK OF ECCLESIASTES

However, such an approach seems myopic and prejudicial, since it highly prizes modern conceptions of the individual and excludes such masterpieces of autobiography as Augustine's *Confessions,* not to speak of other ancient Near Eastern texts such as Sinuhe, Wen-Amon, the Utnapishtim speech in the eleventh tablet of the Gilgamesh Epic, and the Sargon Birth Legend.[68]

In my study of Akkadian literary autobiography I analyzed fifteen texts written in Akkadian that shared traits in common and that I descriptively labeled "fictional autobiography."[69] The fifteen texts were united by a similar three-part structure. Not all preserved the introduction, but those that did began with a first-person identification, such as the one in the autobiography of Kurigalzu: "I am Kurigalzu, the great king, the mighty king, the king of the universe, favored of Anu and Enlil, called by the chief of the gods, a king who has no rival among all kings." For all fifteen texts, it is demonstrable that they were written years, even centuries, after the death of the first-person speaker. For this reason, they are fictional and pseudonymous. The second part of these Akkadian texts contains a personal narration, where the first-person speaker recounts his or her exceptional acts. The length of this section varies greatly among texts that make up the genre.

In all the texts there is a third section, and it is on the basis of this third part that it is possible to divide the genre of fictional autobiography into four subgenres. Some of the texts ended like nonfictional first-person royal inscriptions, with blessings and curses (Sargon Legend, Idrimi); others, like Kurigalzu, finished with a list of donations to the cult of some deity (see also the Cruciform Monument of Maništušu and Agumkakrime). Still others, of interest to biblical studies, had long sections with prophetic, near apocalyptic, endings (Uruk Prophecy; Marduk Prophecy; Šulgi Prophecy; Dynastic Prophecy, Text A). But the texts that bore the most similarity to the book of Ecclesiastes were three texts that ended with wisdom admonitions, instructions on how to behave.

68. And, further, first-person royal inscriptions. For a work that includes all these in its survey, see the magisterial volume by G. Misch, *A History of Autobiography in Antiquity* (Cambridge, MA: Harvard University Press, 1951); and U. von Wilamowitz-Moellendorff, "Die Autobiographie im Altertum," *Internationale Monatschrift für Wissenschaft, Kunst und Technik* 1 (1907): 1105-14. For modern debate on autobiography, consult R. Pascal, *Design and Truth in Autobiography* (Cambridge, MA: Harvard University Press, 1960); J. Olney, *Metaphors of Self: The Meaning of Autobiography* (Princeton: Princeton University Press, 1972); W. C. Spengemann, *The Forms of Autobiography: Episodes in the History of a Literary Genre* (New Haven: Yale University Press, 1980); S. K. Padover, *Confessions and Self-Portraits: 4600 Years of Autobiography* (Freeport, NY: Books for Libraries, 1957); K. J. Weintraub, *The Value of the Individual: Self and Circumstance in Autobiography* (Chicago: University of Chicago Press, 1978); and the especially helpful G. May, *L'autobiographie* (Paris: Universitaires de France, 1979).

69. Longman, *Fictional Akkadian Autobiography.*

18

The three texts are the Cuthaean Legend of Naram-Sin (most probably written just before the Old Babylonian period), the Sin of Sargon text (neo-Assyrian), and an Adad-guppi autobiography (neo-Babylonian). The concluding section of each of these compositions gives advice to the reader in a manner similar to other wisdom texts.[70]

The most complete of the three texts is the Cuthaean Legend.[71] At the beginning (ll. 1-4), Naram-Sin of Akkad introduces himself as the subject. The long first-person narrative (ll. 4-146) focuses on Naram-Sin's political and personal struggles with a people known as the Anubanini. These experiences lead to a series of first-person instructions that characterize this subgenre (ll. 147-75).

The parallel with Qohelet's speech in Ecclesiastes is formal and not material. That is, it shares the same three-part structure as the Cuthaean Legend, but the content of the narrative and the wisdom advice are quite different. Qohelet's speech (1:12–12:7) may be analyzed as follows:

1. Qohelet begins with a first-person introduction: "I, Qohelet, was king over Israel in Jerusalem" (1:12).
2. The second section is an extended first-person narrative (1:13–6:9), where Qohelet describes his own quest for meaning in life.[72]
3. The third section contains first-person instruction delivered by Qohelet for the benefit of those who follow after him. It is true that Qohelet offers advice in the second section of the book (e.g., 4:12; 5:2 [English 5:3]), but the final secton (7:1–12:7) contains large blocks of instructional material.

Thus, Qohelet offers the same threefold structure found in the Cuthaean Legend, and with the same effect. That is, the advice offered by Qohelet is firmly rooted in his own personal experience. His experience is the soil out of which his wisdom grows.

Qohelet's speech in the body of the book of Ecclesiastes thus employs

---

70. For instance, the Cuthaean Legend concludes its long narration of events in Naram-Sin's life with his advice: "Do not be bewildered! Do not be confused! Do not be afraid! Do not tremble! May your position be firm. Do your task in your wife's embrace. Have confidence in your walls. Fill your moats with water. Bring your chests, your grain, your silver, your goods, and your possessions into your strong city. Bind your weapons; hide them in corners. Protect your heroship and take care of yourself" (ll. 154-73). See Longman, *Fictional Akkadian Autobiography,* p. 231.

71. This composition dates from the early 2d millennium B.C. For a translation, see Longman, *Fictional Akkadian Autobiography,* pp. 228-31.

72. O. Loretz, "Zur Darbietungsform der 'Ich-Erzählung' im Buche Qohelet," *CBQ* 25 (1963): 46-59; and *Qohelet und der Alte Orient* (Freiburg: Herder, 1964).

the same pattern of autobiography as that which appears in Mesopotamian literary tradition. Such an analysis suggests a basic tripartite structure to the book as a whole, as the following outline indicates:

1:1-11	Framework — Prologue
1:12–12:7	Qohelet's Autobiographical Speech

1:12	Autobiographical Introduction
1:13–6:9	Autobiographical Narrative
6:10–12:7	Wisdom Admonitions

12:8-14	Framework — Epilogue

The division between Qohelet's speech and the frame has long been recognized on the basis of the shift in pronominal reference. The frame refers to Qohelet in the third person ("he"), while the speech is clearly autobiographical ("I"). The significance of this shift will be explored later.

B. OF THE PARTS

The genre (or form) of the various subunits may be identified as well. By far the four most commonly utilized types of writing in the book are the reflection, the proverb, the anecdote, and the wisdom instruction.[73]

In a reflection, the author states an observation or a truth, which he then ponders and evaluates. Examples include 1:5; 1:13-15; 1:16-18; 2:1-11; 2:12-17. A proverb is a pithy, highly stylized statement of a truth about life. For examples in Ecclesiastes, see 1:15; 1:18; 4:5; 7:1-12. Occasionally, it is possible to subdivide the proverbs into different types. The most studied type of proverb in the book is the so-called better than proverb, which compares and contrasts two states of affairs.[74] An anecdote is a short story told in order to illustrate a principle or truth of interest to the author (see 2:21; 4:7-8; 4:13-16; 9:13-16; 10:5-7). Lastly, an instruction is a teaching in which the author seeks to persuade his reader toward or away from a certain course of behavior or thought (4:17–5:2 [English 5:1-3]).

73. See the introductions to the subunits in the commentary proper as well as in Murphy, *Wisdom Literature*, pp. 125-49.
74. G. S. Ogden, "The 'Better'-Proverb (Ṭôb-Spruch), Rhetorical Criticism, and Qoheleth," *JBL* 96 (1977): 489-505.

VII. STRUCTURE

The book of Ecclesiastes is divided into three parts. It begins with a short prologue, introducing some of the themes of Qohelet's thought (1:1-11), continues with a long monologue by Qohelet (1:12–12:7), and concludes with a brief epilogue (12:8-14). The prologue and epilogue are differentiated from the body of the book by their third-person references to Qohelet. Together they frame Qohelet's speech. The bulk of the book is Qohelet's speech that is made up primarily of autobiographical reflections on the meaning of life.

Qohelet's "autobiography" (1:12–12:7), I have just argued, is a separate and complete literary unit. The frame (1:1-11 and 12:8-14), therefore, was composed secondarily, introducing and then guiding the reader's interpretation of the autobiography in ways to be specified in the commentary itself. In a sense, it is appropriate to say that the frame was secondary, that it was written later than the body of the book, which it is treating as a long quotation.[75] Nonetheless, the framed autobiography itself has a unity, though it is admittedly a composite unity. In this regard, I see the superscription (1:1) as an introduction to the whole book, though written as part of the frame by the unnamed wise teacher whom I consider the author of the whole book.

While the general structure of the book is clear, scholars have experienced frustration as they seek a minute analysis of the whole. Attempts to discover an underlying structure to Qohelet's musing (most notably that of Addison D. G. Wright)[76] have not been followed by many other scholars.

75. Unless, of course, the frame narrator created Qohelet out of whole cloth, which is an open possibility. If that is the case, then he could have composed the whole book at one time.

76. A. D. G. Wright ("The Riddle of the Sphinx: The Structure of the Book of Qoheleth," *CBQ* 30 [1968]: 313-34) took his key from certain repetitive formulae. He assumes that the versification goes back to the autographs and divides the book into two halves of 111 verses apiece (see also S. G. Brown, "The Structure of Ecclesiastes," *Evangelical Review of Theology* 14 [1990]: 195-208). Wright argued that the first half of Qohelet's speech (1:12–6:9) was composed of eight units, each of which ended with the "meaningless" formula. This half he entitles "Qoheleth's Investigation of Life." The second half of the book (6:10–11:6) is divided into two parts, "Qoheleth's Conclusions." The first runs (after an introduction [6:10-12]) from 7:1 to 8:17 and contains four sections, each of which ends with "not find out/who can find out." The second has six sections, all of which conclude with "do not know/no knowledge." In two later articles he added various numerical patterns to support his view ("The Riddle of the Sphinx Revisted: Numerical Patterns in the Book of Qoheleth," *CBQ* 42 [1980]: 35-52; and "Additional Numerical Patterns in Qoheleth," *CBQ* 45 [1983]: 32-43). Wright's views are rather idiosyncratic, however. His numerical patterns depend in part on the number of verses in the book, concerning which it is at least debatable whether they go back to the original composition. It also compares the number of verses with the numerical value of the word *hebel*. Further, as others have pointed out (e.g., Crenshaw, *Ecclesiastes*, pp. 40-42), the formulae do not always end a section (cf. 11:2) and not all the many repeated refrains are considered in his analysis.

Close study shows that Qohelet's thought rambles, repeats (1:12-18 and 2:11-16; 4:1-3 and 5:7-8 [English 5:8-9]; 4:4-12 and 5:9–6:9 [English 5:10–6:9]), and occasionally contradicts itself. Such a lack of order, though, far from detracting from the message of the book, actually contributes to it. As Morris Jastrow, Jr., states: "Koheleth is not afraid of the charge of inconsistency, but he would have his answer ready, 'Why not — life itself is full of inconsistencies.' "[77]

While Qohelet's thought does not follow a detailed outline, some features may be observed in its progress. His speech begins (1:12) with a formula (I, PN, king . . .) that is well known in the autobiographical tradition of the ancient Near East.[78] From 1:13 to 2:26 Qohelet recounts his search for meaning in life "under the sun," adopting the literary persona of Solomon. From 3:1–6:9 the persona is dropped but the quest for meaning continues. Ecclesiastes 6:10-12 is a transitional summary statement to the second part of Qohelet's speech. This second part is dominated by advice and instruction. The conclusion of the speech in 12:1-7 is a meditation on death, an appropriate conclusion for an autobiography.

Such an analysis yields the following general outline of Qohelet's autobiographical speech:

  I. Autobiographical Introduction (1:12)
 II. "Solomon's" Quest for the Meaning of Life (1:13–2:26)
III. The Quest Continues (3:1–6:9)
 IV. Qohelet's Wise Advice (6:10–12:7)

The outline found in the table of contents gives the structure that I follow in the commentary. Within the broad tripartite structure of the book and the fivefold outline of Qohelet's autobiographical speech, I do not find a clear and obvious structure. In the body of the commentary (particularly in the introductions to the individual units) indications will be given of the connections (or lack thereof) between preceding and following units.

---

77. M. Jastrow, Jr., *A Gentle Cynic, Being a Translation of the Book of Koheleth* (Philadelphia: Lippincott, 1919), p. 189.

78. For instance, note the first line of the Sargon Birth Legend, "I am Sargon, the king of Agade." See Longman, *Fictional Akkadian Autobiography*, p. 215. See also Poebel, *Das appositionell bestimmte Pronomen*.

VIII. LITERARY STYLE

It is difficult to describe the literary style of the book of Ecclesiastes. After all, in the words of Geoffrey N. Leech and Michael H. Short, the particular style of a writing arises from the fact that "every writer necessarily makes choices of expression, and it is in these choices, in his 'way of putting things,' that style resides. . . . Every analysis of style . . . is an attempt to find the artistic principles underlying a writer's choice of language."[79] The implication of this definition of style is that it is necessary to distinguish which features of language, grammar, and syntax are the result of the writer's conscious choice and which are the result of the language itself.

Thus, the main obstacle to describing the style of Ecclesiastes is uncertainty concerning the language of the book (see "Language"). It is hard to differentiate a product of the book's unique use of language from that of self-conscious literary artistry. A further problem of analysis arises because of the book's genre; it is otherwise unexampled in the Bible.

I may make a few comments, however. Ecclesiastes contains both poetry and prose, although recent work on the nature of poetry and prose has blurred the distinction between the two. In the past, meter and parallelism have been taken as indicative of poetry, but since the 1980s scholars have come to doubt the presence of meter in Hebrew poetry[80] and have shown that parallelism is a characteristic even in prose.[81] In Ecclesiastes there is also uncertainty. A study of different English translations shows that translators are confused over the matter. For instance, a comparison between the NRSV and the NIV shows that the translation team for the latter believed that the book contains a great deal of poetry, and thus they formatted much of the book in parallel lines.

After having completed a detailed study of the NIV text, I have come to the conclusion that the original translation team overpoeticized the text. In a number of cases they have broken prose sentences into poetic cola that show none of the classic indications of poetry (parallelism in particular). An instance of this is the NIV translation of 1:3:

> What does man gain from all his labor
>   at which he toils under the sun?

79. G. N. Leech and M. H. Short, *Style in Fiction: A Linguistic Introduction to English Fictional Prose* (London: Longman, 1981), pp. 19, 74.

80. See T. Longman III, "A Critique of Two Recent Metrical Approaches," *Biblica* 63 (1982): 230-54.

81. J. Kugel (*The Idea of Biblical Poetry: Parallelism and Its History* [New Haven: Yale University Press, 1981], pp. 76-84) discards the notion of prose and poetry and prefers the language of "high style" for heavily ornamented language.

This sentence, while rhythmical (but not metrical) like all discourse, has no parallelism between the cola.[82] It is a simple prose sentence, arbitrarily divided in half to create the semblance of parallelism.

Such an overpoetization of the book may be attributed in part to the fact that the work on the NIV preceded the recent paradigm shift in our understanding of poetical conventions.[83] While it is true that James Kugel and others define parallelism less in terms of synonymity, there still needs to be some echo of the first colon[84] in the second in order for the second line to "sharpen" the first. Also, Kugel allows for the presence of prosaic insertions in poetic contexts.

Nonetheless, there is poetry in the book of Ecclesiastes, most often in proverbial material (e.g., 1:15, 18). These issues will be treated in the commentary on individual verses.[85]

The book of Ecclesiastes presents the reader with some very sophisticated and interesting imagery as well. Perhaps the twin heights of the author's literary imagination are encountered in Ecclesiastes 3:1-8 and 12:1-7. In the first passage, he presents a highly structured poem on the different seasons of life "under the sun." In the second, he creates three metaphor clusters in order to paint a picture of senility and death.[86]

Leland Ryken[87] reminds us of the comprehensive nature of Qohelet's imagery: "There are references to the city, cultivated fields, gardens, the temple, a house, a bedchamber, courts of justice, seats of power, and battle. The preacher is concerned with all of the main areas of life — wealth, power, religion, social relationships, work and pleasure."[88]

---

82. Contra the analysis of J. G. Williams, "Proverbs and Ecclesiastes," in *The Literary Guide to the Bible,* ed. R. Alter and F. Kermode (Cambridge, MA: Harvard University Press, 1987), p. 278.

83. As presented in Kugel, *The Idea of Biblical Poetry;* and R. Alter, *The Art of Biblical Poetry* (New York: Basic Books, 1985).

84. Or, as Kugel (*The Idea of Biblical Poetry,* p. 2) puts it, "a feeling of correspondence between the two parts."

85. On the use of proverbs in Ecclesiastes, see L. Ryken, "Ecclesiastes," in *A Complete Literary Guide to the Bible,* ed. L. Ryken and T. Longman III (Grand Rapids, MI: Zondervan, 1993), pp. 276-77.

86. R. G. Moulton, *The Literary Study of the Bible,* rev. ed. (Boston: Heath, 1899), pp. 221-24.

87. L. Ryken, *The Literature of the Bible* (Grand Rapids, MI: Zondervan, 1974), p. 252.

88. For a negative assessment of Ecclesiastes' aesthetic quality, note Lowth's comment that "the language is generally low, I might almost call it mean or vulgar; it is frequently loose, unconnected, approaching to the incorrectness of conversation; and possesses very little of the poetical character, even in the composition and structure of the periods" (*De sacra poesi Hebraeorum* [London, 1753, Lecture 24], quoted from the English edition of 1835, p. 271, by Schoors, *The Preacher Sought to Find Pleasing Words,* p. 1.

IX. TEXT

The Hebrew text of Ecclesiastes is without major problems and is the basis of the following translation and commentary. The difficulties encountered in the text have to do with the unusual language, genre, and message of the book, rather than any problems with the text's transmission.

Other ancient witnesses to the text of Ecclesiastes include Greek, Syriac, Latin, and Aramaic versions. There are also fragments from Qumran, which attest to 5:14-17 (English 15-18), 6:3-6, and 7:7-9.[89] They add little to our understanding of the text, since, except for orthography, they essentially agree with the Masoretic Text. They do have some importance, however, as the earliest witness of the text's existence.

Scholars debate the nature of the Greek tradition. The Septuagint contains a translation of Ecclesiastes that is surprisingly literal, including representing the direct object marker *('et)* with the Greek preposition *syn* ("with"). It resembles the method of translation adopted by Aquila, and a number of scholars[90] thus argue that what passes for the Septuagintal Ecclesiastes is in actuality translated by Aquila, or else Aquila has edited the Septuagint of this book. Others[91] believe that the Septuagint version of Ecclesiastes differs from other books of the Greek version because it was translated later.

In the body of the commentary I will chart the course of the Septuagint's departures from the Masoretic Text. In the majority of these cases I conclude that the Septuagint mistranslates the Hebrew text (see 1:6, 17, 18; 2:12, 20, 21, 25, 26; 5:16 [English 5:17]; 7:14, 18, 19, 22, 25; 8:1, 7). Occasionally, however, it provides support for a variant, which yields a better reading in context (see 2:25; 3:18, 19, 21; 4:8, 14; 5:16 [English 5:17]; 5:19 [English 5:20]).

Jerome has translated the book into Latin twice, once in his commentary on it[92] and the other time for the Vulgate. The Peshitta follows the Masoretic Text in the main, with occasional departures that show Septuagintal influence.[93]

---

89. J. Muilenburg, "A Qohelet Scroll from Qumran," *BASOR* 135 (1954): 20-28.

90. For instance, D. Barthelémy, *Les devanciers d'Aquila,* VTSup 10 (Leiden: Brill, 1963), pp. 21-33.

91. For instance, K. Hyvarinen, *Die Übersetzung von Aquila* (Lund: Gleerup, 1977), pp. 88-99.

92. Jerome, "Commentarius in Ecclesiasten," in *Patrologiae Latine,* vol. 23, edited by J.-P. Migne (Paris: Migne, 1863), pp. 1063-1173.

93. See M. V. Fox, *Qohelet and His Contradictions,* JSOTSup 71 (Sheffield, England: Almond, 1989), p. 165; A. Schoors, "The Peshitta of Koheleth and Its Relation to the Septuagint," in *After Chalcedon: Studies in Theology and Church History,* ed. C. Laga, et al., Orientalia Lovaniensia Analecta 18 (Leuven: Peeters, 1985), pp. 347-57.

The Targum[94] is not a translation, but a paraphrase, which greatly expands the book and interprets it in keeping with a particular theological perspective. In its approach it is similar to the paraphrase of Gregory Thaumaturgos.[95] The Targum and Gregory both treat Qohelet as a consistently orthodox thinker. All of these versions and paraphrases have been consulted in preparing the following commentary.

Antoon Schoors[96] has helpfully examined all of the Ketib-Qeres in the book and has concluded that the Qere is to be preferred in all instances except 5:10 (English 5:11) and 10:20, and that these readings do not have a major impact on our understanding of the text. I follow Schoors's conclusions in the commentary.

X. CANON

The status and function of canon is much in discussion these days. Is "canonical" an achieved status or does the term describe an inherent authority that is later recognized by the people of God?[97] In other words, does the church make the canon or does the canon make the church? Herman Ridderbos provides the best defense of the latter, while disputing the former. He argues that the canonical books are self-attesting and accepted by faith, rather than provable by an external criterion such as authorship.

While I agree with Ridderbos on this issue, I will now address the issue of the external attestation to Ecclesiastes' canonical status. Interestingly, there were ancient doubts about its divine authority among the rabbis and others.

These doubts lay along three lines. The book was accused of contradictions, secularity, and even outright heresy. Indeed, all three accusations were interrelated in that Ecclesiastes was said not only to contradict itself, but also to contradict other Scriptures, which meant that its author was a heretic.

For example, Ecclesiastes was considered to be in conflict with the teaching of the Torah, which warns readers to follow the commands of God

---

94. Levine, *The Aramaic Version of Qohelet,* pp. 5-26.

95. Jarick, *Gregory Thaumaturgos' Paraphrase.*

96. A. Schoors, *"Kethibh-Qere* in Ecclesiastes," in *Studia Paulo Naster oblata II: Orientalia Antiqua,* ed. J. Quagebeur, Orientalia Lovaniensia Analecta 13 (Leuven: Peeters, 1982), pp. 215-22.

97. See H. Ridderbos, *The Authority of the New Testament Scriptures,* trans. H. De Jongste (Grand Rapids, MI: Baker, 1963), for a definition and insightful discussion of the concept of self-attestation. Though his book deals specifically with the NT canon, the principle applies to the OT as well.

and "not prostitute yourselves by going after the lusts of your own hearts and eyes" (Num. 15:39). Specifically, Ecclesiastes 11:9 states, "Be happy, young man, while you are young, and let your heart give you joy in the days of your youth. Follow the ways of your heart and whatever your eyes see."

In the first tractate of the Mishnah (*Shabbat,* ch. 3), Rabbi Tanhum of Nave is quoted as saying, "O Solomon, where is your wisdom, where is your intelligence? Not only do your words contradict the words of your father, David, they even contradict themselves."[98] The Talmud specifically cites Ecclesiastes 2:2 ("I thought, 'Laughter is madness and pleasure — what can it do?'") and 7:3 ("Anger is better than laughter, for in a troubled face the heart is made well") as contradicting 8:15 ("Then I commended pleasure, for there is nothing better").[99]

Also note Tosephta *Yadayim* 2.14, where Rabbi Simeon ben Menasia is quoted as saying, "The Song of Songs makes the hands unclean because it was spoken in the Holy Spirit.[100] Ecclesiastes does not make the hands unclean because it is [merely] Solomon's wisdom."[101] In early Jewish thought, a book makes the hands "unclean" if it is divinely inspired. In other words, it is so holy that special rituals accompany its being physically handled while it is read or carried. The important point is that a book that makes someone unclean if it is touched is a holy book, an authoritative book.[102]

I further observe that the *Pesiqta of Rab Kahana* (*Leviticus Rabbah* 28.1) states: "The sages sought to store away the Book of Ecclesiastes, because they found words in it which tended to heresy." Jerome picked up and affirmed this sentiment when he noted in the introduction to his commentary, "The Jews say that . . . this book seemed fit to be consigned to oblivion, because it asserted the creatures of God to be vain, and preferred eating, drinking, and transitory pleasures to all things; on account of this one section [i.e., Eccles. 12:13-14] [it seemed] to have deserved its authority, that it was included among the divine books."[103]

Indeed Jerome was correct that most Jewish scholars accepted the book in spite of its apparent conflicts with other Scriptures. According to *Shabbat* 30b: "The sages sought to store away the Book of Ecclesiastes. . . . And why

98. Translated from the citation given by Podechard, *L'Ecclésiaste,* p. 11.
99. R. Beckwith, *The Old Testament Canon of the New Testament Church* (London: SPCK, 1985), p. 284.
100. The Tosephta, dated perhaps to the fifth century A.D., is a collection of earlier rabbinic writings. Rabbi Simeon ben Menasia may be dated to the late second century A.D.
101. Beckwith, *The Old Testament Canon,* p. 284.
102. For more on this idea of uncleanness as it relates to canonicity, see Beckwith, *The Old Testament Canon,* pp. 278-87.
103. Both quotes are from Beckwith, *The Old Testament Canon,* p. 287.

did they not store it away? Because its beginning is words of the Law and its end is words of the Law."[104]

Once again, the rabbinic terminology needs some commentary. In this case, to "store away" a book means to get rid of it, consign it to oblivion. Certain sages made the argument to so treat the book, but apparently saner heads prevailed and treated it as one of the authoritative books. Specifically, according to *Shabbat* 30b, the beginning and end of the book show its orthodoxy, probably especially the last two verses, which encourage the fear of God and obedience to the commandments as well as warn of the coming judgment (12:13-14).

Thus, it appears that, while Ecclesiastes was questioned, its canonicity was never rejected by the mainstream Jewish community. The question, in other words, was not, "Is Ecclesiastes canonical?" but, since the book was considered authoritative, "Why is this book canonical?"

The answers, however, are not always satisfying to us in the twentieth century. Solomon's purported authorship, for instance, lent a measure of authority to the book, and thus Ecclesiastes' canonical recognition (to be distinguished from its inherent canonicity) is analogous to that of the book of Hebrews, where a common early opinion was that it was authored by Paul.

The connection with Solomon gave rise to or fed the extrabiblical legend that Solomon repented of his apostasy before the end of his life.[105] This story was embedded in the Targum to the book, as we noted earlier (see "Authorship" above). More about this Targum may be found below in "Theological Message," but we may assume that the connection with Solomon, the author of Proverbs and Song of Songs, encouraged the recognition of this book as authoritative.

Thus, we are not surprised that early Jewish and Christian sources attest its canonicity. That Ecclesiastes was among the texts found at Qumran (see "Text" above) implies that it achieved an authoritative status before the time of Christ.

Further, Roger Beckwith[106] lists and briefly comments upon a number of early Jewish witnesses to the high authority of the book of Eccesiastes: the Greek Testament of Naphtali (8:7-8), Josephus, Aquila, and the Mishnah.

Emmanuel Podechard[107] recounts a number of early rabbinic stories (4th to 6th centuries A.D.) that reflect early Jewish opinion concerning Eccle-

104. Beckwith, *The Old Testament Canon*, p. 287.

105. The Jewish legends about Solomon's departure from the throne, its occupation by the demon Ashmodai, and Solomon's eventual return have been described by in L. Ginzberg, *The Legends of the Jews*, vol. 4 (Philadelphia: Jewish Publication Society of America, 1913), pp. 168-76, with sources cited in vol. 6, pp. 299-303.

106. Beckwith, *The Old Testament Canon*, pp. 319-21.

107. Podechard, *L'Ecclésiaste*, p. 7.

siastes. The first is the Talmudic tractate *Berakot.* Here the Pharisee Simon ben Chetah cites (ca. 90-70 B.C.) Ecclesiastes 7:2 as he addresses King Janneus, introducing it with the formula "it is written." This formula is similar to that used in the NT before quotations from the OT (e.g., Matt. 4:6, 10) and indicates the absolute authority of the source that is quoted.[108]

The second story is from *Baba Batra* (4a) and comes from the period of Herod the Great (37-34 B.C.). The story recounts Herod's slaughter of the Sanhedrin. He allowed only one member, Bab ben Bouta, to survive, and Herod blinded him. Later, Herod approached ben Bouta to see whether he would curse him, but the wise sage quoted Ecclesiastes 10:20, "Do not revile the king even in your thoughts, or curse the rich in your bedroom," once again introduced by "it is written."

Third, the tractate *Shabbat* narrates an encounter between Gamaliel (first century A.D.) and one of his students. When the teacher lectured on the wonders of the messianic age, his incredulous student replied, "There is nothing new under the sun." Taking this as a serious challenge, Gamaliel then countered by showing analogies to those marvels so as not to contradict the teachings of an authoritative book.

Though there is a likely allusion to Ecclesiastes in the NT (see "From a New Testament Perspective" below) as well as in the *Shepherd of Hermas,* the first clear Christian witness to Ecclesiastes as canonical is from Melito (last half of the second century A.D.),[109] showing that the early church considered the book as authoritative. Furthermore, Clement of Alexandria also cited it in his *Stromateis* and introduced it by "it is written." No evidence exists that Ecclesiastes was ever doubted by the early church, and even Theodore of Mopsuestia, cited by many as an exception to this widespread belief, also recognized that the book was Holy Scripture.[110] Thus, the early Christian witnesses regard the book of Ecclesiastes as part of the canon with no question.

XI. THEOLOGICAL MESSAGE

So much debate surrounds the interpretation of Ecclesiastes that early Jewish scholars, as we have seen, even questioned the canonicity of the book on the grounds that it gives contradictory advice and teaches heterodox doctrine.[111] For example, the book's author, who went by the name Qohelet (see "Author-

---

108. See Beckwith, *The Old Testament Canon,* pp. 69-70.
109. Podechard, *L'Ecclésiaste,* pp. 13-14.
110. R. Murphy, *Ecclesiastes,* WBC (Dallas: Word, 1992), p. xxiii.
111. Jarick, *Gregory Thaumaturgos' Paraphrase,* pp. 1-2.

ship" above), could, on the one hand, say that he "hated life" (2:17), but, on the other hand, assert that a "live dog is better off than a dead lion" (9:4). Not infrequently, Ecclesiastes clashes with the teaching of other biblical books. For instance, while the book of Proverbs advocates a total commitment to the way of wisdom, Qohelet says, "Do not be overrighteous, neither be overwise" (7:16), and concludes that in the long run wisdom can get one no further than folly (2:12-16).

While for these reasons some Jewish interpreters rejected the canonicity of Ecclesiastes, others justified its inclusion in the canon by straining its interpretation. The Targum to the book is an instructive example.[112] It made explicit what the author skillfully and intentionally never stated, most notably the identification of Qohelet and Solomon. As all critical and many evangelical interpreters have remarked,[113] the two are not the same. Too many passages in the book could only be written by a nonroyal person (4:1-3; 5:7-8 [English 5:8-9]; 8:2-6). Nevertheless, the Targum makes the identification, and this identification in part helped the religious communities accept the book as canonical. The same Targum stretched the interpretation of individual passages beyond all reason in order to turn Qohelet = Solomon into a teacher of pure orthodoxy. Thus, when Qohelet warns about the weariness of books (12:12), the Targum turns it into an exaltation of Torah study: "And more than these, my son, take care, to make many books of wisdom without end; to study much the words of the Law, and to consider the weariness of the body."[114]

Early Christian intepretation took the same basic approach. It is noteworthy that the NT never directly quotes Ecclesiastes (but see below for a significant allusion in the book of Romans). The only mention of the book in the first couple of centuries of the church is in the *Shepherd of Hermas,* and that book alluded to only the last two verses.[115] It is in the third century that commentaries on Ecclesiastes are first attested. We have only fragments from Hippolytus of Rome and Origen, but a full text by Origen's student Gregory Thaumaturgos is available.[116] After Gregory, we have a number of early commentaries, most notably ones by Ambrose, Augustine, and Jerome, the last of which became a standard resource during the Middle Ages.

These early Christian interpreters found theological meaning in the text through allegory. For instance, Qohelet's frequent refrain advocating that his listeners seek pleasure in eating and drinking (e.g., 2:24-26; 3:12-13) is turned into an admonition to partake of the Lord's body and blood in com-

112. Levine, *The Aramaic Version of Qohelet,* p. 47.
113. See nn. 8-13 above.
114. Levine, *The Aramaic Version of Qohelet,* p. 47.
115. Jarick, *Gregory Thaumaturgos' Paraphrase,* p. 3.
116. Jarick, *Gregory Thaumaturgos' Paraphrase.*

munion.[117] Ambrose finds a reference to the Trinity in the three-strand cord of 4:12.[118]

The issue of the interpretation of Ecclesiastes continues to the present, with some commentators arguing for an orthodox teacher in the book who has a positive view of life.[119] The theological contribution of the book, according to this approach, is its affirmation of the wisdom traditions of Proverbs and its encouragement to enjoy the little pleasures of the present life in the midst of a fallen world.[120]

Such a view,[121] however, does not take into account the book's literary structure and either treats certain, more negative aspects of the book as secondary or strains at the interpretation of words and passages to make them fit a preconceived idea of the function of the book.[122]

On the contrary, the most natural reading of the book, as argued under "Authorship," takes into account the presence of two speakers — Qohelet, who refers to himself in the first person in 1:12–12:7, and a second, unnamed wise person, who describes Qohelet to his son (12:12) in the third person (1:1-11 and 12:8-14).[123] In effect, the speech of Qohelet is a quotation, which

117. See Jerome's commentary on 2:24, in "Commentarius in Ecclesiasten," p. 1070.

118. See Jarick, *Gregory Thaumaturgos' Paraphrase,* p. 316, who cites J.-P. Migne, ed., *Patrologia Latina,* vol. 16 (Paris: Migne, 1845), col. 1274; M. M. Beyenka, trans., *Saint Ambrose: Letters,* The Fathers of the Church: A New Translation, vol. 26 (Washington: Catholic University of America Press, 1954), p. 319.

119. W. C. Kaiser, *Ecclesiastes;* R. N. Whybray, *Ecclesiastes,* NCB (Grand Rapids, MI: Eerdmans, 1989); and "Qohelet, Preacher of Joy," *JSOT* 23 (1982): 87-92; G. S. Ogden, *Qoheleth* (Sheffield, England: JSOT Press, 1987); M. A. von Klopfenstein, "Kohelet und die Freude am Dasein," *Theologische Zeitschrift* 47 (1991): 97-107; G. R. Castellino, "Qohelet and His Wisdom," *CBQ* 30 (1968): 15-28.

120. See D. C. Fredericks, *Coping with Transcience: Ecclesiastes on Brevity in Life* (Sheffield, England: JSOT Press, 1993), p. 44.

121. It is not to be denied that there are ancient precedents to this view in Rashbam (A.D. 1085-1155); see S. Japhet and R. B. Salters, *Rashbam on Qohelet* (Jerusalem: Magnes; Leiden: Brill, 1985); and in M. Luther, "Notes on Ecclesiastes," pp. 7-11.

122. So W. C. Kaiser (*Ecclesiastes,* pp. 86-91) on 7:16-17 and N. Lohfink (*Kohelet,* Neue EB [Würzburg: Echter Verlag, 1980], p. 6). S. Schloesser (" 'A King is Held Captive in Her Tresses': The Liberating Deconstruction of the Search for Wisdom from Proverbs through Ecclesiastes," *Church Divinity* [1989-90]: 205-28) argues that Ecclesiastes dates from the third century and has as its purpose offsetting the secularization that was brought in by Hellenization. Thus, the effect of the book is "consolation." In Schloesser's words (see p. 219): "The common intention of the various third-century philosophers [by which he means Greek philosophers] was the construction of a philosphy of consolation (ataraxy) through a deconstruction of essentialist philosophies no longer relevant in a time of social upheaval." In the view of these scholars, Ecclesiastes is such an attempt at ataraxy (see p. 206) in an Israelite context.

123. Fox, "Frame-Narrative"; and *Qohelet and His Contradictions,* pp. 155-62; as well as T. Longman III, "Comparative Methods in Old Testament Studies: Ecclesiastes Reconsidered," *TSF Bulletin* 7, 4 (March-April 1984) 5-9; and "Structure" in the present volume.

is framed by the words of the second speaker, who is the narrator/author. Thus, in keeping with the structure of the book, we must examine its theology in two parts. First, Qohelet's theology, and then the theology of the frame narrator, which is the normative theology of the book as a whole.

XII. QOHELET'S THEOLOGY

In considering the message of Qohelet himself (1:12–12:7), we must recognize that he is a wisdom teacher who struggles with the traditions of his people, including the normative traditions of a book like Proverbs. His most frequent refrain (and there are several refrains) is "Meaningless, meaningless! All is meaningless!" He uses the term "meaningless" *(hebel)* in well over thirty passages,[124] and indeed the second wise person introduces and concludes Qohelet's teaching with the refrain (1:2 and 12:8), as if to say this is Qohelet's basic conclusion.

Qohelet is not satisfied merely to state that everything is meaningless; he specifies a number of areas and shows why they have no value. For one thing, toil *('āmāl)* is meaningless. He gives a number of reasons why toil cannot give ultimate satisfaction. Someone might work hard and succeed, but then die and have to leave it all to someone who has not worked for it (2:17-23). Furthermore, the motivation to work hard itself is evil because it springs from envy (4:4). What does Qohelet advocate in terms of toil? It is hard to say. On the one hand, he quotes a proverb to the effect that to cease work leads to destruction (4:5); on the other hand, he quickly follows this with a second proverb that encourages a tranquil lifestyle (4:6).

Qohelet also pronounces the world meaningless in light of the oppression that he sees everywhere he turns (4:1-3). The government itself is responsible for much of the suffering of the people (5:7-8 [English 5:8-9]). He is obviously moved by what he sees, but he never seeks ways to soften the suffering of the oppressed or even to become one of the comforters that they lack (4:1). He never considers action (doubly surprising if he is actually a king) and seems resigned to it all: "Observe the work of God, for who is able to straighten what he has bent?" (7:13).

Perhaps most surprising of all is his attitude toward wisdom. If there was anything that should have appealed to a wise person in Israel, it would have been the value of its wisdom (throughout the book of Proverbs, especially

---

124. See 1:12 (4 times), 14; 2:1, 11, 15, 17, 19, 21, 23, 26; 3:19; 4:4, 7, 8, 16; 5:6, 9 (English 5:7, 10); 6:2, 4, 9, 11, 12; 7:6, 15; 8:10, 14 (2 times); 9:9 (2 times); 11:8, 10; 12:8 (3 times).

Prov. 2:1-22 and 8:1-36). For Qohelet, however, wisdom has only limited, relative significance in comparison to folly. An examination of Ecclesiastes 2:12-16 illustrates his attitude. In the initial phase of his comparison between wisdom and folly, he sounds very similar to the teaching of Proverbs and concludes that "there was more profit to wisdom than folly" (v. 13). Wisdom allows a person to "get on" in the world (v. 14a). However, this advantage turns out to be short-lived as Qohelet then contemplates the long run. Both fool and wise die, rendering void the benefits of wisdom (vv. 14b-16).

Qohelet's search for meaning led him to consider many different areas of life on earth. He not only explored wisdom and toil but also considered political power (4:13-16), riches, large families, and long life (5:7–6:12 [English 5:8–6:12]). In each of these areas he encountered "meaninglessness" and expressed his frustration that life is the way it is. As we read his reflections, we are struck by two inescapable facts of human existence that are the source of his anguish: (1) death and (2) the inability to control and know the appropriate time to do anything.

In terms of the latter, it must be remembered that it was of crucial importance for a wise teacher to know the right time. The book of Proverbs does not give a list of truths that are always, everywhere appropriate, but a series of principles that are to be applied at the right time. They know the conditions under which they should answer a fool (Prov. 26:5) and when they should refrain (Prov. 26:4). As a wise man, Qohelet knew that there were right times for certain activities: "There is a time for everything, and a season for every activity under heaven" (Eccles. 3:1). He also understood, however, that he could not share God's knowledge of them. As a human being, he could never be certain that a given moment was the "right time," and this lack of knowledge, this lack of certainty, frustrated him to the point that he thought that life "under the sun" was meaningless. Humans cannot know what will happen to them in this life or the next: "No one knows what will happen. Who can tell anyone what is going to happen after him?" (10:14). "For no one knows what will happen, because who can say when it will happen?" (8:7). This leaves humans at the mercy of "time and chance" (9:11). They cannot even know when they are going to die: "Indeed, no one knows his time. Like fish that are entangled in an evil net and like birds caught in a snare, so people are ensnared in an evil time, when it suddenly falls on them" (9:12).

Yet humans do know one thing for certain. They know that they will die — "For the living know they will die" (9:5) — and this knowledge frustrated Qohelet so much that he reflected on it at great length. He concluded that death rendered every human "achievement" and status useless. After all, they will pass away and will not be remembered.

We have already seen how death nullified wisdom's advantage over folly (2:12-16). The same is true for hard work and the riches that come from work. Why bother working hard all your life when at your death the wealth gained will go to some worthless person or even a person that you do not know (2:17-23). Death rendered every status and achievement of this present life "meaningless."

Further, as far as Qohelet knew for certain, death was the end of the story.[125] He is not drawing his hearers/readers to the edge of despair just to tell them about the bliss of an afterlife. According to Qohelet, "the dead know nothing. There is no longer any reward for them, for the memory of them is forgotten" (9:5). In the long run there is no difference between humans and animals, for "both go to the same place. Both come from the dust, and both return to the dust" (3:20). Indeed, Qohelet's last words in the book are a sad and moving reflection upon death, describing a person's end using three image clusters. (1) Growing old and dying is like watching the storm clouds move in and ruin a sunny day (12:1-2). (2) It is also like an unmaintained house, slowly falling apart (12:3-5). (3) Lastly, it is like a severed rope, a broken bowl, a shattered pitcher, and a ruined wheel (12:6). Life is valuable in the short run — the rope is silver after all — but it is completely ruined at death, when the process of creation is undone and the body turns to dust and the spirit returns to God. The fundamental unity of a person as established at creation (Gen. 2:7) is thereby reversed. Qohelet has no hope that things will be "put right" after death.

What is the theological message of Qohelet's autobiography (1:12–12:7)? Life is full of trouble and then you die. Some interpreters attempt to mitigate this hard message by appealing to six passages that they interpret as offering a positive view toward life (2:24-26; 3:12-14; 3:22; 5:17-19 [English 5:18-20]; 8:15; 9:7-10).[126] One must admit, however, that Qohelet only suggested a limited type of joy in these passages. Only three areas are specified — eating, drinking, and work. In addition, Qohelet's introduction to pleasure was hardly enthusiastic. For instance, in 2:24 he merely concedes that "there is nothing better for people than. . . ." In the commentary section we will argue that here Qohelet expresses resignation rather than affirmation. Then, further, he believed that God was the only one who could allow people to experience enjoyment, a situation that brought him no ultimate satisfaction (see 2:26c where he pronounced it "meaningless"). Indeed, it is clear

125. See Crenshaw, *Ecclesiastes*, p. 26; and A. Schoors, "Koheleth: A Perspective of Life after Death?" *ETL* 61 (1985): 295-303, for a discussion of Qohelet's view of life after death. Even some scholars who interpret Ecclesiastes positively (e.g., Fredericks, *Coping with Transcience*, p. 47) realize that Qohelet did not have a strong view of the afterlife.

126. Whybray, "Qohelet, Preacher of Joy"; and A. B. Caneday, "Qohelet: Enigmatic Pessimist or Godly Sage?" *GTJ* (1986): 21-56.

throughout the book that Qohelet did not consider himself a person so blessed by God (see commentary at 5:17–6:12 [English 5:18–6:12]).

It is more in keeping with the book as a whole to understand these passages as they have been taken through much of the history of interpretation, that is, as a call to seize the day *(carpe diem)*. In the darkness of a life that has no ultimate meaning, enjoy the temporal pleasures that lighten the burden (5:18-19 [English 5:19-20]).

This raises the issue of Qohelet's view of God. As measured against other wisdom books, Qohelet certainly speaks of God fairly frequently, but what is his view of God? Does God provide any relief to Qohelet's pessimistic view of life?

If we isolate Qohelet's statements from the context of the entire book, it is possible to interpret some of them as positive. God is a giver of all good gifts (2:26), is sovereign over everything (7:13-14), is our Creator (12:1), and is the one to whom we owe our very existence (12:7). Indeed, R. R. Scott, a student of Walter C. Kaiser, Jr., has attempted to defend such a positive view of God in the book of Ecclesiastes.[127] However, reading Qohelet's statements about God in context leads one to side with those scholars who characterize Qohelet's God as distant, occasionally indifferent, and sometimes cruel.[128]

The commentary proper will present a fuller account of the intepretation of the passages mentioned here, but a brief defense of this conclusion is appropriate. I begin with the general observation that Qohelet refers to God by the generic *'ĕlōhîm*, never by God's personal, covenantal name Yahweh. This leaves the reader with a sense of distance between God and Qohelet. After all, "Yahweh" would invoke warm, covenantal feelings and memories. Furthermore, while it is true that Qohelet believes that any enjoyment that a person is fortunate enough to have comes from God, that enjoyment is superficial, temporary, and restricted to a very few, among whom Qohelet would not count himself. Indeed, that joy is simply a narcotic that numbs the recepient to the true nature of reality (5:19 [English 5:20]).

God's sovereignty is affirmed by Qohelet (3:9-18; 7:13-14; 8:16–9:1; 11:5), but this sovereignty actually calls into question God's concern for his people. He has a plan but does not reveal it to his people and those who want to know what it is (3:11; 8:16-17; 11:5). There will be a judgment in the future, but Qohelet does not expect to find justice there (3:16; 9:1). After all, there is no certainty of an afterlife for Qohelet (3:18-21). Qohelet may well believe in divine providence, but it is no source of comfort to him as he faces the unpredictable chaos of life.

---

127. R. R. Scott, "Qoheleth and Christian Interpretation: An Investigation of the View of God in Ecclesiastes" (M.A. thesis, Trinity Evangelical Divinity School, 1985).

128. See discussion and bibliography in Scott, "Qohelet and Christian Interpretation," pp. 73-81.

This raises the question of how to understand 4:17–5:6 [English 5:1-7]). As discussed in the commentary, the whole section may be interpreted one of two ways: either as reverent and thoughtful concern to be careful before a powerful God or as despair that the universe is ruled by a God that just does not seem to care much about earthly concerns ("God is in heaven and you are on earth"). I will argue that the latter understanding correctly identifies Qohelet's attitude.

Indeed, Qohelet calls on his hearers to "fear God" (5:6 [English 5:7]; 7:15-18; 8:12-13), but, as argued in the commentary, the contexts of these passages lend credence to those who believe that the fear advocated here is that of fright before a powerful and dangerous being, not respect or awe for a mighty and compassionate deity.[129]

The point is that oppression (4:1-3) and evil in the world cast doubt on a compassionate and caring deity. Qohelet sees nothing in the present or the future that gives him any confidence that God will reward the devout righteous on the one hand and punish the sinner on the other (7:15-18; 9:1-12). After all, according to Qohelet, "There are righteous people who are treated as if they did wicked deeds, and there are wicked people who are treated as if they did righteous deeds" (8:14). God is certainly powerful, however, and it is meaningless to try to change his ways in the world (6:10).

My understanding of Qohelet's thought is closest to that articulated by James Crenshaw.[130] He identified Qohelet as a prime representative of skepticism in Israel. He argued that "Israel's skeptics severed a vital nerve at two distinct junctures. They denied God's goodness if not his very existence, and they portrayed men and women as powerless to acquire essential truth."[131]

While correctly identifying the tenor of Qohelet's thinking, Crenshaw errs in identifying Qohelet's message with the message of the book, never making a distinction between the body of the book and the epilogue (for which see below). His characterization of Qohelet and his admiration for his contribution to Israel's theological development thus differs substantially from mine; I look not to Qohelet but to the frame narrator's concluding word for the normative theological contribution of the book. To that we now turn.

---

129. D. B. Macdonald, *The Hebrew Philosophical Genius* (Princeton: Princeton University Press, 1936), p. 70; see discussion in Scott, "Qohelet and Christian Interpretation," pp. 73-81.

130. See especially his "Birth of Skepticism in Ancient Israel," in *The Divine Helmsman: Studies on God's Control of Human Events,* ed. J. L. Crenshaw and S. Sandmel (New York: KTAV, 1980), pp. 1-19.

131. Crenshaw, *The Divine Helmsman,* p. 15.

XIII. THEOLOGY OF THE BOOK AS A WHOLE

Qohelet's pessimistic theology is not the concluding voice in the book. A second voice is heard at the beginning of the book (1:1-11) and at the end (12:8-15), placing a frame around Qohelet's speech and providing the perspective through which we should read his opinions. Many interpreters have acknowledged this function of the epilogue, though different explanations have been provided.[132] When the structure of the book is taken into account, then we can understand how this rather unorthodox teacher can stand in the canon.

An analogy with the book of Job further clarifies the situation. The two books are similar in structure and also evoke a similar reading strategy. The body of both books contains dubious teaching when judged in the light of the rest of the canon. For instance, the arguments of the three friends, Elihu, and even Job concerning the reasons for Job's suffering are too narrow in their understanding, and therefore all of them misunderstand God's relationship to Job's situation. Not that everything that they say is wrong, but much is out of keeping with the divine perspective revealed in the Yahweh speeches at the end of the book.

Similarly, the body of the book of Ecclesiastes, composed of the introspective autobiography of Qohelet, contains much that offends traditional OT sensibilities. The positive teaching of both books comes at the end with Yahweh's speech from the whirlwind in Job and the second wise man's warnings to his son in Ecclesiastes.

To understand the book of Ecclesiastes, then, it is important to read the epilogue closely. Even the traditional translation of a few phrases in the epilogue is suspect. Following the suggestive comments of Michael Fox,[133] I interpret 12:8 as the beginning of the frame narrator's last contribution to the book (contra the chapter divisions proposed by the NIV). The frame narrator summarizes Qohelet's thought using the latter's own refrain, "Meaningless! Meaningless! Everything is meaningless!" Next, he pays his respects to Qohelet's efforts. He acknowledges that Qohelet was a wise man who worked hard at his task. It is important, however, to note that, while true wisdom is always characterized by righteousness and godliness (Prov. 1–9), the office of wisdom teacher was occasionally occupied by some nonorthodox, even wicked, people (most notably Jonadab; cf. 2 Sam. 13:3).

---

132. For instance, 1:12–12:7 is the speech of Solomon as a young man and 12:8-14 contains his reflections late in life; see C. Bridges, *Ecclesiastes* (Carlisle, PA: Banner of Truth, 1961 [1860]), p. x.

133. Fox, "Frame-Narrative," pp. 83-106; and *Qohelet and His Contradictions,* pp. 311-21.

The next few verses are increasingly critical of Qohelet. The following translation is defended in the commentary and is dependent upon Fox:[134]

"Completely meaningless," Qohelet said. "Everything is meaningless." Furthermore, Qohelet was a wise man. He also taught the people knowledge. He heard, investigated, and put in good order many proverbs. Qohelet sought to find words of delight and to write honestly words of truth. The words of the wise are like goads, and like firmly implanted nails are the masters of collections. They are given by a shepherd.

Furthermore, of these, my son, be warned! There is no end to the making of many books, and much study wearies the body. (12:8-12)

The epilogue begins with the second wise man's summary of the teaching of Qohelet. By quoting the now familiar "meaningless" refrain, the frame narrator indicates what he considers Qohelet's ultimate conclusion: "Everything is meaningless." From this point, he proceeds with his evaluation, which begins with praise and then moves to doubt and finally to criticism.

Though faint, it is praise when the frame narrator begins by commending Qohelet's efforts as he "sought to find words of delight" and also that he "sought . . . to write honestly words of truth." This praise falls quite short of an affirmation of Qohelet's view, however, when it is recognized that the frame narrator echoes the language of 7:1-29. There Qohelet admits that he seldom succeeded in finding anything he was looking for.

The metaphors that follow (goads and implanted nails), while usually understood positively (goading the student on to learning and establishing them firmly in the truth), are better taken as negative and harmful (as argued in the commentary section). Lastly, the famous v. 12, quoted by so many students pointing out that there is "no end to the making of many books," includes, rather than excludes, Qohelet's own writings (see commentary section).

Thus, if Qohelet's lengthy speech is pessimistic and out of sorts with the rest of the OT, why is it included in the canon? Qohelet's speech is a foil, a teaching device, used by the second wise man in order to instruct his son (12:12) concerning the dangers of speculative, doubting wisdom in Israel. Just as in the book of Job, most of the book of Ecclesiastes is composed of the nonorthodox speeches[135] of the human participants of the book, speeches that are torn down and demolished in the end.

God does not speak out of the whirlwind in the book of Ecclesiastes, but a second voice appears at the end to give the normative teaching of the book in the last two verses: "The end of the matter. All has been heard. Fear

134. Fox, "Frame-Narrative," pp. 96-98.
135. That is, nonorthodox according to normative OT teaching. They would consider themselves orthodox, even fastidiously orthodox.

God and keep his commandments, for this is the whole duty of humanity. For God will bring every deed into judgment, including every hidden thing, whether good or evil" (12:13-14).

In brief compass, the second wise man, who is the implied author of the book, summarizes the message of the OT. First, he directs his son to "fear God." This phrase calls him to a right relationship with God, a relationship that understands his dependence and subordinate status with God. Second, he moves to the nature of his son's continuing relationship with God. He urges him to "keep his [God's] commandments." If the phrase "fear God" reminds the reader of the beginning of Proverbs (1:7) and the wisdom tradition, so the second imperative brings to mind the law. Finally, the frame narrator reminds his son that God "will bring every deed into judgment." He invites his son to live in the present, in the light of the future. Using modern terminology, he injects an eschatological perspective into his thinking and perhaps alludes to the prophetic material of the Bible. In a masterfully succinct manner, then, the book ends with three phrases that point away from skeptical thinking and toward a theology consonant with the rest of the OT: wisdom, law, and prophets.

XIV. FROM A NEW TESTAMENT PERSPECTIVE

Ecclesiastes is never quoted in the NT, but there is an allusion to the message of the book in Romans 8:18-21:

> I consider our present sufferings are not worth comparing with the glory that will be revealed in us. For the creation waits in eager expectation for the sons of God to be revealed. For the creation was subjected to *frustration,* not by its own choice, but by the will of the one who subjected it, in hope that the creation itself will be liberated from its bondage to decay and brought into the glorious freedom of the children of God.

The word translated "frustration" *(mataiotēs)* is the word used in the Septuagint to translate the motto word of Ecclesiastes, "meaningless" *(hebel).* While Qohelet sounds nonorthodox in the light of the rest of the canon, he presents a true assessment of the world apart from the light of God's redeeming love. His perspective on the world and life is restricted; he describes it as life "under the sun," that is, apart from heavenly realities, apart from God. In other words, his hopelessness is the result of the curse of the fall without recourse to God's redemption.[136]

136. In a recent article, D. M. Clemens ("The Law of Sin and Death: Ecclesiastes and Genesis 1–3," *Themelios* 19 [1994]: 5-8) has shown that much of Qohelet's language and thought reflects the narrative of the fall.

Qohelet sounds modern because he so vividly captures the despair of a world without God. The difference, though, is that the modern world believes that God does not exist; Qohelet believed that God existed but questioned his love and concern (4:16–5:6 [English 5:1-7]). As a result, nothing had meaning for Qohelet, not wealth, wisdom, charity. After all, death brought everything to an end. Qohelet is preoccupied with death throughout the book (2:12-16; 3:18-22; 12:1-7) because he sees nothing beyond that point.

On one level, therefore, Qohelet is exactly right. The world ("under the sun") without God is meaningless. Death ends it all, so he alternated between "hating life" (2:17) and taking what meager enjoyment God hands out (2:24-26).

As we have seen above, the message of the book is found in the simple instruction in the last few verses, not in Qohelet's speech. Nonetheless, we may still admit that Qohelet has rightly described the horror of a world under curse and apart from God. What he did not have was hope.

As we turn to the NT,[137] we see that Jesus Christ is the one who redeems us from the vanity, the meaninglessness under which Qohelet suffered. Jesus redeemed us from Qohelet's meaningless world by subjecting himself to it. Jesus is the son of God, but nonetheless he experienced the vanity of the world so he could free us from it. As he hung on the cross, his own father deserted him (Matt. 27:45-46). At this point, he experienced the frustration of the world under curse in a way that Qohelet could not even imagine. "Christ redeemed us from the curse of the law by becoming a curse for us" (Gal. 3:13; cf. earlier discussion of Rom. 8:18-21).

As a result, Christians can experience deep significance precisely in those areas where Qohelet felt most oppressed. Jesus has restored meaning to wisdom, labor, love, and life. After all, by facing death, Jesus conquered the biggest fear facing Qohelet. He showed that for believers death is not the end of all meaning, but the entrance into the very presence of God.

XV. BIBLIOGRAPHY

Aalders, G. Ch. *Het Boek de Prediker.* Commentar op het Oude Testament. Kampen: N. V. Uitgeversmaatschappij J. H. Kok, 1948.
Ackroyd, P. R. "Two Hebrew Notes." *ASTI* 5 (1967): 82-86.
Alter, R. *The Art of Biblical Narrative.* New York: Basic Books, 1981.

137. See S. Woudstra, "Koheleth's Reflections on Life" (Th.M. thesis, Westminster Theological Seminary, 1959), for a stimulating discussion of the biblical theology of the book of Ecclesiastes.

————. "A Response to Critics." *JSOT* 27 (1983): 113-17.

————. *The Art of Biblical Poetry.* New York: Basic Books, 1985.

Armstrong, J. F. "Ecclesiastes in Old Testament Theology." *Princeton Seminary Bulletin* 4 (1983): 16-25.

Baltzer, K. "Women and War in Qohelet 7:23–8:1a." *HTR* 80 (1987): 127-32.

Barthélemy, D. *Les devanciers d'Aquila.* VTSup 10. Leiden: Brill, 1963.

Barton, G. A. *The Book of Ecclesiastes.* ICC. Edinburgh: T. and T. Clark, 1908.

————. "The Text and Interpretation of Ecclesiastes 5:19." *JBL* 27 (1908): 65-66.

Barucq, A. *Ecclésiaste.* Paris: Beauchesne, 1968.

————. "Question sur le sens du travail (Qoh. 1,2; 2:21-23)." *Assemblées du Seigneur* 49 (1971): 66-71.

Baumgärtel, F. "Die Ochenstachel und die Nägel in Koh. 12." *ZAW* 81 (1969): 98.

Beckwith, R. *The Old Testament Canon of the New Testament Church.* London: SPCK, 1985.

Bergant, D. *Job, Ecclesiastes.* Wilmington, DE: Michael Glazier, 1982.

Berlin, A. *Poetics and Interpretation of Biblical Narrative.* Sheffield, England: Almond, 1983.

Bertram, G. "Hebräischer und griechischer Qohelet." *ZAW* 64 (1952): 26-49.

Bickerman, E. *Four Strange Books of the Bible.* New York: Schocken Books, 1967.

Blenkinsopp, J. "Ecclesiastes 3:1-15: Another Interpretation." *JSOT* 66 (1995): 55-64.

Bons, E. "Zur Gliederung und Kohärenz von Koh 1:12–2:11." *Biblische Notizen* 24 (1984): 73-93.

Braun, R. *Koheleth und die frühhellenistische Popularphilosophie.* BZAW 130. Berlin: de Gruyter, 1973.

Brenner, A. *Colour Terms in the Old Testament.* JSOTSup 21. Sheffield, England: JSOT Press, 1982.

Breton, S. "Qohelet: Recent Studies." *Theology Digest* 28 (1980): 147-51.

Bridges, C. *Ecclesiastes.* Carlisle, PA: Banner of Truth, 1961 (1860).

Brindle, W. A. "Righteousness and Wickedness in Ecclesiastes 7:15-18." *AUSS* 23 (1985): 243-57.

Brown, E. L. "Qoheleth's Pedagogical Structure: Cynic, Critic or Credit to His Profession?" Unpublished paper, 1983.

Brown, S. G. "The Structure of Ecclesiastes." *Evangelical Review of Theology* 14 (1990): 195-208.

Bruns, J. E. "The Imagery of Eccles 12:6a." *JBL* 84 (1965): 428-30.

Budde, K. *Der Prediger.* Tübingen: Mohr, 1923.

Burkitt, F. C. "Is Ecclesiastes a Translation?" *JTS* 23 (1921-22): 22-26.

Caneday, A. B. "Qoheleth: Enigmatic Pessimist or Godly Sage?" *GTJ* (1986): 21-56.

Carny, P. "Theodicy in the Book of Qohelet." In *Justice and Righteousness: Biblical Themes and Their Influence,* edited by H. G. Reventlow and Y. Hoffman. JSOTSup 137, pp. 71-81. Sheffield, England: JSOT Press, 1992.

Castellino, G. R. "Qohelet and His Wisdom." *CBQ* 30 (1968): 15-28.

Ceresko, A. R. "The Function of Antanaclasis (*mṣ'* 'to find'//*mṣ'* 'to reach, overtake, grasp') in Hebrew Poetry, Especially in the Book of Qoheleth." *CBQ* 44 (1982): 551-69.

Chopineau, J. "Une image de l'homme: Sur Ecclésiaste 1/2." *Etudes Théologiques et Religieuses* 53 (1978): 366-75.

———. "L'image de Qohelet dans l'exégèse contemporaine." *Revue d'Histoire et de Philosophie Religieuses* 59 (1979): 595-603.

———. "Qohelet's Modernity." *Theology Digest* 29 (1981): 117-18.

Clemens, D. M. "The Law of Sin and Death: Ecclesiastes and Genesis 1–3." *Themelios* 19 (1994): 5-8.

Corré, A. D. "A Reference to Epispasm in Koheleth." *VT* 4 (1954): 416-18.

Cotton, J. *A Brief Exposition with Practical Observations upon the Book of Ecclesiastes.* London, 1654.

Crenshaw, J. L. "The Shadow of Death in Qoheleth." In *Israelite Wisdom: Theological and Literary Essays in Honor of Samuel Terrien,* edited by J. G. Gammie, W. A. Brueggemann, W. L. Humphreys, and J. M. Ward, pp. 205-16. Missoula, MT: Scholars Press, 1978.

———. "The Eternal Gospel (Eccl. 3:11)." In *Essays in Old Testament Ethics,* edited by J. L. Crenshaw and J. T. Willis, pp. 23-55. New York: KTAV, 1974.

———. "The Birth of Skepticism in Ancient Israel." In *The Divine Helmsman: Studies on God's Control of Human Events,* edited by J. L. Crenshaw and S. Sandmel, pp. 1-19. New York: KTAV, 1980.

———. "Qoheleth in Recent Research." *HAR* 7 (1983): 41-56.

———. "The Expression *mî yôdēaʿ* in the Hebrew Bible." *VT* 36 (1986): 274-88.

———. "Youth and Old Age in Qohelet." *HAR* 10 (1986): 1-13.

———. *Ecclesiastes.* OTL. Philadelphia: Westminster, 1987.

———. "Ecclesiastes — Odd Book In." *Bible Review* 6 (1990): 28-33.

Crüsemann, F. "Hiob und Kohelet: Ein Beitrag zum Verständnis des Hiobbuches." In *Werden und Wirken des Alten Testaments,* edited by R. von Albertz, et al., pp. 373-93. Göttingen: Vandenhoeck und Ruprecht, 1980.

Dahood, M. J. "Canaanite-Phoenician Influence in Qoheleth." *Biblica* 33 (1952): 30-52, 191-221.

————. "The Language of Qoheleth." *CBQ* 14 (1952): 227-32.

————. "Qoheleth and Recent Discoveries." *Biblica* 39 (1958): 302-18.

————. "Qoheleth and Northwest Semitic Philology." *Biblica* 43 (1962): 349-65.

————. "The Phoenician Background of Qoheleth." *Biblica* 47 (1966): 264-82.

————. "Hebrew-Ugaritic Lexicography." *Biblica* 49 (1968): 355-69.

————. "Three Parallel Pairs in Ecclesiastes 10:18." *JQR* 62 (1971-72): 84-87.

Davila, J. R. "Qohelet and Northern Hebrew." *MAARAV* 5-6 (1990): 69-87.

Davis, B. C. "Ecclesiastes 12:1-8 — Death, an Impetus for Life." *BibSac* 148 (1991): 298-317.

Delitzsch, F. *Proverbs, Ecclesiastes, Song of Solomon.* Translated by M. G. Easton. Grand Rapids, MI: Eerdmans, 1975 (1872).

De Waard, J. "The Translator and Textual Criticism (with Particular Reference to Eccl 2,25)." *Biblica* 60 (1979): 509-29.

Dillard, R. B., and T. Longman III. *An Introduction to the Old Testament.* Grand Rapids, MI: Zondervan, 1994.

Driver, G. R. "Problems and Solutions." *VT* 4 (1954): 225-45.

————. "Once Again Abbreviations." *Textus* 4 (1964): 76-94.

Du Plessis, S. J. "Aspects of Morphological Peculiarities of the Language of Qoheleth." In *De Fructu Oris Sui: Essays in Honour of Adrianus Van Selms,* edited by I. H. Eybers, et al., pp. 164-80. Leiden: Brill, 1971.

Eaton, M. A. *Ecclesiastes.* Tyndale Old Testament Commentaries. Downers Grove, IL: InterVarsity, 1983.

Ellermeier, F. "Die Entmachtung der Weisheit im Denken Qohelets." *ZThK* 60 (1963): 1-20.

————. *Qohelet, Teil 1, Abschnitt 1.* Herzberg am Harz: Verlag Erwin Jungfer, 1967.

Ellul, J. *Reason for Being: A Meditation on Ecclesiastes.* Translated by J. M. Hanks. Grand Rapids, MI: Eerdmans, 1990.

Erdman, W. J. *Ecclesiastes.* Chicago: The Bible Institute Colportage Association, n.d.

Ettlinger, G. H. "The Form and Method of the Commentary on Ecclesiastes by Gregory of Agrigentum." *Studia Patristica* 18 (1985): 317-20.

Ewald, H. *Die Salomonischen Schriften.* Göttingen: Vandenhoeck und Ruprecht, 1867.

Farmer, K. A. *Who Knows What Is Good? Proverbs and Ecclesiastes.* ITC. Grand Rapids, MI: Eerdmans, 1991.

Fishbane, M. *Biblical Interpretation in Ancient Israel.* Oxford: Clarendon Press, 1985.

Forman, C. C. "The Pessimism of Ecclesiastes." *JSS* 3(1958): 336-43.

Fox, M. V. "Frame-Narrative and Composition in the Book of Qohelet." *HUCA* 48 (1977): 83-106.

—. "The Identification of Quotations in Biblical Literature." *ZAW* 92 (1980): 416-31.

—. "Qohelet's Epistemology." *HUCA* 58 (1987): 137-55.

—. "Aging and Death in Qohelet 12." *JSOT* 42 (1988): 55-77.

—. "Qohelet 1.4." *JSOT* 40 (1988): 109.

—. *Qohelet and His Contradictions.* JSOTSup 71. Sheffield, England: Almond, 1989.

Fox, M. V., and B. Porten. "Unsought Discoveries: Qohelet 7:23–8:1a." *Hebrew Studies* 19 (1978): 26-38.

Fredericks, D. C. *Qoheleth's Language: Re-evaluating Its Nature and Date.* Lewiston, NY; Queenston, Ontario: Edwin Mellen, 1988.

—. "Chiasm and Parallel Structure in Qoheleth 5:9–6:9." *JBL* 108 (1989): 17-35.

—. "Life's Storms and Structural Unity in Qoheleth 11:1–12:8." *JSOT* 52 (1991): 95-114.

—. *Coping with Transcience: Ecclesiastes on the Brevity of Life.* Sheffield, England: JSOT Press, 1993.

Frendo, A. "The 'Broken Construct Chain' in Qoh. 10:10b." *Biblica* 62 (1981): 544-45.

Galling, K. "Koheleth-Studien." *ZAW* 50 (1932): 276-99.

—. "Der Prediger." In *Die fünf Megilloth.* 2d ed. HAT 18. Tübingen: Mohr/Siebeck, 1969.

Garrett, D. A. "Qohelet on the Use and Abuse of Political Power." *Trinity Journal* 8 (1987): 159-77.

—. "Ecclesiastes 7:25-29 and the Feminist Hermeneutic." *Criswell Theological Review* 2 (1988): 309-21.

Gianto, A. "The Theme of Enjoyment in Qohelet." *Biblica* 73 (1992): 328-33.

Ginsberg, H. L. *Studies in Koheleth.* New York: Jewish Theological Seminary of America, 1952.

—. "The Structure and Contents of the Book of Koheleth." In *Wisdom in Israel and in the Ancient Near East,* edited by M. Noth and D. Winton Thomas. VTSup 3, pp. 138-48. Leiden: Brill, 1955.

—. "Ecclesiastes." In *Encyclopedia Judaica,* edited by G. Wigoder, et al., vol. 6, pp. 350-55. Jerusalem: Keter, 1971.

Ginsburg, C. D. *The Song of Songs and Coheleth,* edited by H. M. Orlinsky. New York: KTAV, 1970 (1861).

Ginzberg, L. *The Legends of the Jews,* vol. 4. Philadelphia: Jewish Publication Society, 1913.

Glasser, E. *Le procès du bonheur par Qohelet.* Paris: Cerf, 1970.

Glasson, T. F. " 'You Never Know': The Message of Ecclesiastes 11:1-6." *EQ* 55 (1983): 43-48.

Goldin, J. "The End of Ecclesiastes: Literal Exegesis and Its Transformation." In *Biblical Motifs: Origins and Transformations,* edited by A. Altmann, pp. 135-58. Cambridge, MA: Harvard University Press, 1966.

Good, E. M. "The Unfilled Sea: Style and Meaning in Ecclesiastes 1:2-11." In *Israelite Wisdom: Theological and Literary Essays in Honor of Samuel Terrien,* edited by J. G. Gammie, W. A. Brueggemann, W. L. Humphreys, and J. M. Ward, pp. 59-73. Missoula, MT: Scholars Press, 1978.

—————. *Irony in the Old Testament.* Sheffield, England: Almond, 1981 (1965).

Gordis, R. "Ecclesiastes 1:17 — Its Text and Interpretation." *JBL* 56 (1937): 323-30.

—————. "The Heptad as an Element of Biblical and Rabbinic Style." *JBL* 62 (1943): 17-26.

—————. "The Original Language of Qohelet." *JQR* 37 (1946-47): 67-84.

—————. "The Translation Theory of Qohelet Re-Examined." *JQR* 40 (1949-50): 103-16.

—————. *Koheleth — The Man and His World.* 3d ed. New York: Schocken Books, 1968.

—————. "Was Koheleth a Phoenician?" *JBL* 74 (1955): 103-14.

—————. "Qoheleth and Qumran — A Study of Style." *Biblica* 41 (1960): 395-410.

Goss, B. "Lessons from Ecclesiastes." *Reformation in Australia* 50 (1986): 4-9.

Guillaume, A. "A Note on *bl*." *JTS* 13 (1962): 320-22.

Haden, N. K. "Qohelet and the Problem of Alienation." *Christian Scholars Review* 17 (1987): 52-66.

Halperin, D. J. "The *Book of Remedies,* the Canonization of the Solomonic Writing, and the Riddle of Pseudo-Eusebius." *JQR* 72 (1982): 269-92.

Hay, A. P. "Qohelet and the Book of Creation." *JSOT* 50 (1991): 93-111.

Hays, J. D. "Verb Forms in the Expository Discourse Sections of Ecclesiastes." *Journal of Translation and Textlinguistics* 7 (1995): 9-18.

Hempfer, K. *Gattungstheorie.* Munich: W. Funk, 1973.

Hengstenberg, E. W. *A Commentary on Ecclesiastes.* Evansville, IN: Sovereign Grace Publishers, 1960 (1869).

Hertzberg, H. W. *Der Prediger.* KAT 17, 4. Gütersloh: Mohn, 1963.

Hirsch, E. D. *Validity in Interpretation.* New Haven: Yale University Press, 1967.

—————. *The Aims of Interpretation.* Chicago: University of Chicago Press, 1976.

Hirshman, M. "The Greek Fathers and the Aggada on Ecclesiastes: Formats of Exegesis in Late Antiquity." *HUCA* 59 (1988): 137-65.

Holladay, W. L. *A Concise Hebrew and Aramaic Lexicon of the Old Testament.* Grand Rapids, MI: Eerdmans; Leiden: Brill, 1988.

Hubbard, D. A. *Beyond Futility.* Grand Rapids, MI: Eerdmans, 1976.

Hyvarinen, K. *Die Übersetzung von Aquila.* Lund: Gleerup, 1977.

Irwin, W. A. "Ecclesiastes 4:13-16." *JNES* 3 (1944): 255-57.

———. "Ecclesiastes 8:2-9." *JNES* 4 (1945): 130-31.

Isaksson, B. *Studies in the Language of Qoheleth.* Studia Semitica Uppsaliensia 10. Uppsala, Sweden: Uppsala University Press, 1987.

Japhet, S., and R. B. Salters. *Rashbam on Qoheleth.* Jerusalem: Magnes; Leiden: Brill, 1985.

Jarick, J. "Gregory Thaumaturgos' Paraphrase of Ecclesiastes." *Abr-Nahrain* 17 (1989): 37-57.

———. *Gregory Thaumaturgos' Paraphrase of Ecclesiastes.* SBLSCS 29. Atlanta: Scholars Press, 1990.

———. *A Comprehensive and Bilingual Concordance of the Hebrew and Greek Texts of Ecclesiastes.* SBLSCS 36. Atlanta: Scholars Press, 1993.

Jasper, F. N. "Ecclesiastes: A Note for Our Time." *Interp* 31 (1967): 259-73.

Jastrow, Jr. M. *A Gentle Cynic, Being a Translation of the Book of Koheleth.* Philadelphia: Lippincott, 1919.

Jerome, "Commentarius in Ecclesiasten." In *Patrologiae Latine,* vol. 23, edited by J.-P. Migne, pp. 1063-1173. Paris: Migne, 1863.

Johnstone, R. K. "Confessions of a Workaholic: A Reappraisal of Qoheleth." *CBQ* 38 (1976): 14-28.

Jones, B. W. "From Gilgamesh to Qoheleth." In *The Bible in the Light of Cuneiform Literature,* edited by W. W. Hallo, B. W. Jones, and G. L. Mattingly, pp. 349-79. Lewiston, NY; Queenston, Ontario: Edwin Mellen, 1990.

Jong, S. de. "A Book on Labour: The Structuring Principles and the Main Theme of the Book of Qohelet." *JSOT* 54 (1992): 107-16.

———. "Qohelet and the Ambitious Spirit of the Ptolemaic Period." *JSOT* 61 (1994): 85-96.

Joüon, P. "Sur le nom de *Qoheleth.*" *Biblica* 2 (1921): 53-54.

Kaiser, O. "Die Botschaft der Buches Kohelet." *ETL* 71 (1995): 49-50.

Kaiser, W. C., Jr. *Ecclesiastes: Total Life.* Everyman's Bible Commentary. Chicago: Moody, 1979.

———. "Integrating Wisdom Theology into Old Testament Theology." In *A Tribute to Gleason Archer: Essays on the Old Testament,* edited by W. C. Kaiser, Jr., and R. F. Youngblood, pp. 197-209. Chicago: Moody, 1986.

Kaufmann, M. "Was Koheleth a Sceptic?" *The Expositor* 9 (1899): 389-400.

Keddie, G. *Looking for the Good Life: The Search for Fulfillment in the Light of Ecclesiastes.* Phillipsburg, NJ: Presbyterian and Reformed, 1991.

Kidner, D. *A Time to Mourn and a Time to Dance.* Downers Grove, IL: InterVarsity, 1976.

Klopfenstein, M. A. von. "Kohelet und die Freude am Dasein." *Theologische Zeitschrift* 47 (1991): 97-107.

Knobel, P. S. "Targum Qoheleth: A Linguistic and Exegetical Inquiry." Ph.D. dissertation, Yale University, 1976.

Kottsieper, I. "Die Bedeutung der Wz. *ʿṣb* und *skn* in Koh 10,9." *UF* 18 (1986): 213-22.

Kugel, J. *The Idea of Biblical Poetry: Parallelism and Its History.* New Haven: Yale University Press, 1981.

———. "Qohelet and Money." *CBQ* 51 (1989): 32-49.

Lamorte, A. *Le Livre de Qoheleth.* Paris: Libraire Fischbacher, 1932.

Lauha, A. "Die Krise des religiösen Glaubens bei Kohelet." In *Wisdom in Israel and the Ancient Near East,* edited by M. Noth and D. Winton Thomas. VTSup 3, pp. 183-91. Leiden: Brill, 1955.

———. *Kohelet.* BKAT 19. Neukirchen-Vluyn: Neukirchener Verlag, 1978.

Lee, P. K. H. "Re-reading Ecclesiastes in the Light of Su Tung-P'o's Poetry." *Ching Feng* 30 (1987): 214-36.

Leech, G. N., and M. H. Short. *Style in Fiction: A Linguistic Introduction to English Fictional Prose.* London: Longman, 1981.

Leeuwen, R. van. "Wealth and Poverty: System and Contradiction in Proverbs." *Hebrew Studies* 33 (1992): 25-36.

Leiman, H. I. *Koheleth.* Jerusalem and New York: Feldheim, 1978.

Leupold, H. C. *Exposition of Ecclesiastes.* Grand Rapids, MI: Baker, 1952.

Levine, E. *The Aramaic Version of Qohelet.* New York: Sepher-Hermon, 1978.

———. "Qohelet's Fool: A Composite Portrait." In *On Humour and the Comic in the Hebrew Bible,* edited by Y. T. Radday and A. Brenner. JSOTSup 92, pp. 277-94. Sheffield, England: JSOT Press, 1990.

Lipiński, E. "*Skn* et *sgn* dans le sémitique occidental du nord." *UF* 5 (1973): 191-207.

Loader, J. A. "Qohelet 3:2-8 — A 'Sonnet' in the Old Testament." *ZAW* 81 (1969): 239-42.

———. "Different Reactions of Job and Qohelet to the Doctrine of Retribution." *OTWSA* 15-16 (1972-73): 43-48.

———. "Relativity in Near Eastern Wisdom." *OTWSA* 15-16 (1972-73): 49-58.

———. *Polar Structures in the Book of Qohelet.* BZAW 152. Berlin: de Gruyter, 1979.

————. *Ecclesiastes*. Text and Interpretation. Grand Rapids, MI: Eerdmans, 1986.

Loewenclau, I. von. "Kohelet und Sokrates — Versuch eines Vergleiches." *ZAW* 98 (1986): 327-38.

Lohfink, N. *Kohelet*. Neue EB. Würzburg: Echter Verlag, 1980.

————. "*Melek, šallîṭ* und *môšēl* bei Kohelet und die Abfassungszeit des Buchs." *Biblica* 62 (1981): 535-43.

————. "Warum ist der Tor unfähig, böse zu handeln? (Koh 4,17)." *XXI. Deutscher Orientalistentag vom 24. bis 29. März 1980 in Berlin: Ausgewählte Vorträge,* edited by F. Steppat. ZDMGSup 5 (Wiesbaden: Steiner, 1983), pp. 113-20.

————. "Qoheleth 5:17-19 — Revelation by Joy." *CBQ* 52 (1990): 625-35.

Longman III, T. "A Critique of Two Recent Metrical Approaches." *Biblica* 63 (1982): 230-54.

————. "Comparative Methods in Old Testament Studies: Ecclesiastes Reconsidered." *TSF Bulletin* 7, 4 (March-April 1984): 5-9.

————. "Form Criticism, Recent Developments in Genre Theory, and the Evangelical." *WTJ* 44 (1985): 46-67.

————. *Literary Approaches to Biblical Interpretation*. Grand Rapids, MI: Zondervan, 1987.

————. *How to Read the Psalms*. Downers Grove, IL: InterVarsity, 1988.

————. *Fictional Akkadian Autobiography*. Winona Lake, IN: Eisenbrauns, 1991.

————. "Nahum." In *The Minor Prophets,* vol. 2, edited by T. McComiskey, pp. 765-829. Grand Rapids, MI: Baker, 1993.

Loretz, O. "Zur Darbietungsform der 'Ich-Erzählung' im Buche Qohelet." *CBQ* 25 (1963): 46-59.

————. *Qohelet und der Alte Orient*. Freiburg: Herder, 1964.

————. "Poetry and Prose in the Book of Qohelet (1:1–3:22; 7:23–8:1; 9:6-10; 12:8-14)." In *Verse in Ancient Near Eastern Prose,* edited by J. C. de Moor and W. G. E. Watson, pp. 155-89. Neukirchen-Vluyn: Neukirchener; Kevelaer, Butzon and Bercker, 1993.

Lorgunpai, S. "The Books of Ecclesiastes and Thai Buddhism." *Asia Journal of Theology* 8 (1994): 155-62.

Luther, M. "Notes on Ecclesiastes." In *Luther's Works,* vol. 15, edited and translated by J. Pelikan, pp. 3-193. St. Louis: Concordia, 1972 (1532).

Lux, R. "Ich, Kohelet, bin König . . .': Die Fiktion als Schlüssel zur Wirklichkeit in Kohelet 1,12–2,26." *Evan. Theol.* 50 (1990): 331-42.

Lys, D. *L'Ecclésiaste ou Que vaut la vie?* Paris: Letouzey et Ané, 1977.

————. "L'Être et le temps: Communication de Qohèléth." In *La sagesse de l'Ancien Testament,* edited by M. Gilbert, pp. 249-58. Leuven: Leuven University Press, 1990.

Mailer, N. *Ancient Evenings.* Boston: Little, Brown and Company, 1983.

Maltby, A. "The Book of Ecclesiastes and the After-Life." *Evangelical Quarterly* 35 (1963): 39-44.

McKenna, J. E. "The Concept of *Hebel* in the Book of Ecclesiastes." *SJT* 45 (1992): 19-28.

Min, Y.-J. "How Do the Rivers Flow? (Ecclesiastes 1.7)." *Bible Translator* 42 (1991): 226-30.

Morson, G. S. *The Boundaries of Genre.* Austin: University of Texas Press, 1981.

Moulton, R. G. *The Literary Study of the Bible.* Rev. ed. Boston: Heath, 1899.

Muilenburg, J. "A Qohelet Scroll from Qumran." *BASOR* 135 (1954): 20-28.

Mulder, J. S. M. "Qoheleth's Division and Also Its Main Point." *Von Kanaan bis Kerala: Festschrift für Prof. Mag. Dr. J. P. M. van der Ploeg O.P. zur Vollendung des siebzigsten Lebensjahres am 4. Juli 1979,* edited by W. C. Delsman, et al., pp. 149-59. Neukirchen-Vluyn: Kevelaer, Butzon and Bercker, 1982.

Müller, J. P. "Wie Sprach Qohälät von Gott?" *VT* 18 (1968): 507-21.

Murphy, R. E. *Wisdom Literature: Job, Proverbs, Ruth, Canticles, Ecclesiastes, and Esther.* FOTL. Grand Rapids, MI: Eerdmans, 1981.

———. "The Sage in Ecclesiastes and Qoheleth the Sage." In *The Sage in Israel and the Ancient Near East,* edited by J. G. Gammie and L. G. Perdue, pp. 263-71. Winona Lake, IN: Eisenbrauns, 1990.

———. "On Translating Ecclesiastes." *CBQ* 53 (1991): 571-79.

———. "Qohelet and Theology?" *BTB* 21 (1991): 30-33.

———. *Ecclesiastes.* WBC. Dallas: Word, 1992.

———. "Recent Research on Proverbs and Qohelet." *Currents in Research: Biblical Studies* 1 (1993): 119-40.

Murphy, R. E., ed. *Medieval Exegesis of Wisdom Literature: Essays by Beryl Smalley.* Atlanta: Scholars Press, 1986.

Nichols, R. W. "Samuel Beckett and Ecclesiastes on the Borders of Belief." *Encounters* 45 (1984): 11-22.

Nötscher, F. "Schicksal und Freiheit." *Biblica* 40 (1959): 446-62.

Ogden, G. S. "The 'Better'-Proverb (Ṭôb-Spruch), Rhetorical Criticism, and Qoheleth." *JBL* 96 (1977): 489-505.

———. "Historical Allusion in Qoheleth iv 13-16?" *VT* 30 (1980): 309-15.

———. "Qohelet ix 17-x 20: Variations on the Theme of Wisdom's Strength and Vulnerability." *VT* 30 (1980): 27-37.

———. "Qohelet ix 1-16." *VT* 32 (1982): 158-69.

———. "The Mathematics of Wisdom: Qoheleth." *VT* 34 (1984): 446-53.

———. "Qoheleth xi 7-xii 8: Qoheleth's Summons to Enjoyment and Reflection." *VT* 34 (1984): 27-38.

————. "The Interpretation of *dôr* in Ecclesiastes 1.4." *JSOT* 34 (1986): 91-92.

————. *Qoheleth.* Sheffield, England: JSOT Press, 1987.

————. " 'Vanity' It Certainly Is Not." *Bible Translator* 38 (1987): 301-7.

Osborn, N. D. "A Guide for Balanced Living: An Exegetical Study of Ecclesiastes 7:1-14." *Bible Translator* 21 (1970): 185-96.

Pawley, D. "Ecclesiastes: Reaching Out to the Twentieth Century." *Bible Review* 6 (1990): 34-36.

Perdue, L. G. *Wisdom and Cult.* SBLDS 30. Missoula, MT: Scholars Press, 1977.

Perry, T. A. *Dialogues with Kohelet: The Book of Ecclesiastes.* University Park, PA: Pennsylvania State University Press, 1993.

Pfeiffer, E. "Die Gottesfurcht im Buche Kohelet." In *Gottes Wort und Gottes Land,* edited by H. G. Reventlow, pp. 133-58. Göttingen: Vandenhoeck und Ruprecht, 1965.

Plath, S. *Furcht Gottes: Der Begriff* yr' *im Alten Testament.* Stuttgart: Calwer Verlag, 1962.

Plumptre, E. H. *Ecclesiastes; or, the Preacher.* Cambridge, England: Cambridge University Press, 1881.

Podechard, E. *L'Ecclésiaste.* Paris: Libraire Victor Lecoffre, 1912.

Poebel, A. *Das appositionell bestimmte Pronomen der 1. Per. Sing. in den westsemitischen Inschriften und im Alten Testament.* AS 3. Chicago: Oriental Institute, 1931.

Rainey, A. F. "A Study of Ecclesiastes." *CTM* 35 (1964): 148-57.

Ranston, H. *Ecclesiastes and the Early Greek Wisdom Literature.* London: Epworth, 1925.

Reimer, P. B. *A Time to Keep Silence — and a Time to Build: A Study of Ecclesiastes.* Toronto: Institute for Christian Studies, 1987.

Reines, C. W. "Koheleth viii,10." *JJS* 5 (1954): 86-87.

————. "Koheleth on Wisdom and Wealth." *JJS* 5 (1954): 80-84.

Rendsburg, G. A. "The Galilean Background of Mishnaic Hebrew." In *The Galilee in Late Antiquity,* edited by L. I. Levine, pp. 225-40. New York: Jewish Theological Seminary of America, 1992.

Ricker, B., and R. Pitkin. *A Time for Every Purpose.* Nashville: Nelson, 1983.

Ridderbos, H. *The Authority of the New Testament Scriptures.* Translated by H. De Jongste; Grand Rapids, MI: Baker, 1963.

Robertson, D. "Job and Ecclesiastes." *Soundings* 73 (1990): 257-72.

Roth, W. M. W. "The Numerical Sequence x/x+1 in the Old Testament." *VT* 12 (1962): 300-311.

————. *Numerical Sayings in the Old Testament: A Form-Critical Study.* VTSup 13. Leiden: Brill, 1965.

Rousseau, F. "Structure de Qohelet I 4-11 et Plan du Livre." *VT* 31 (1981): 201-17.

Rowley, H. H. "The Problems of Ecclesiastes." *JQR* 42 (1951-52): 87-90.

Ryken, L. *The Literature of the Bible.* Grand Rapids, MI: Zondervan, 1974.

———. "Ecclesiastes." In *A Complete Literary Guide to the Bible,* edited by L. Ryken and T. Longman III, pp. 268-80. Grand Rapids, MI: Zondervan, 1993.

Salters, R. B. "Text and Exegesis in Koh 10:19." *ZAW* 89 (1977): 423-26.

———. "Notes on the History of the Interpretation of Koh. 5:5." *ZAW* 90 (1978): 95-101.

———. "Notes on the Interpretation of Qoh 6:2." *ZAW* 91 (1979): 282-89.

Sawyer, J. F. A. "The Ruined House in Ecclesiastes 12: A Reconstruction of the Original Parable." *JBL* 94 (1974): 519-31.

Schaefer, G. "The Significance of Seeking God in the Purpose of the Chronicler." Ph.D. dissertation, Southern Baptist Theological Seminary, 1972.

Schloesser, S. "'A King is Held Captive in Her Tresses': The Liberating Deconstruction of the Search for Wisdom from Proverbs through Ecclesiastes." *Church Divinity* (1989-90): 205-28.

Schmidt, J. "Koheleth 4:17." *ZAW* 17 (1940-41): 279-80.

Schoors, A. "*Kethibh-Qere* in Ecclesiastes." In *Studia Paulo Naster oblata II: Orientalia Antiqua,* edited by J. Quagebeur, pp. 215-22. Orientalia Lovaniensia Analecta 13. Leuven: Peeters, 1982.

———. "Koheleth: A Perspective of Life after Death?" *ETL* 61 (1985): 295-303.

———. "The Peshitta of Koheleth and Its Relation to the Septuagint." In *After Chalcedon: Studies in Theology and Church History,* edited by C. Laga, et al., pp. 347-57. Leuven: Peeters, 1985. Orientalia Lovaniensia Analecta 18.

———. "Emphatic and Asseverative *kî* in Koheleth." In *Scripta Signa Vocis,* edited by H. Vanstiphout, et al., pp. 209-14. Groningen: Egbert Foresten, 1986.

———. "The Use of Vowel Letters in Qoheleth." *UF* 20 (1988): 277-86.

———. "The Pronouns in Qoheleth." *Hebrew Studies* 30 (1989): 71-87.

———. *The Preacher Sought to Find Pleasing Words: A Study of the Language of Qoheleth,* part 1. Leuven: Departement Orientalistiek/ Uitgeverij Peeters, 1992.

Schunck, K. D. "Drei Seleukiden im Buche Kohelet?" *VT* 9 (1959): 192-201.

Schwartz, M. "Koheleth and Camus: Two Views of Achievement." *Judaism* 35 (1986): 29-34.

Schwartzschild, R. "The Syntax of *'šr* in Biblical Hebrew with Special Reference to Qohelet." *Hebrew Studies* 31 (1990): 7-39.

Scott, R. B. Y. *Proverbs. Ecclesiastes.* AB. Garden City, NY: Doubleday, 1965.

Scott, R. R. "Qoheleth and Christian Interpretation: An Investigation of the View of God in Ecclesiastes." M.A. thesis, Trinity Evangelical Divinity School, 1985.

Serrano, J. J. "I Saw the Wicked Buried (Eccl. 8,10)." *CBQ* 16 (1954): 168-70.

Shaffer, A. "The Mesopotamian Background of Qohelet" (in Hebrew). *EI* 8 (1967): 246-50.

————. "New Information on the Origin of the 'Threefold Cord' " (in Hebrew). *EI* 9 (1969): 159-60.

Shank, H. C. "Qoheleth's World and Life View as Seen in His Recurring Phrases." *WTJ* 37 (1974): 57-73.

Sheppard, G. "The Epilogue to Qohelet as Theological Commentary." *CBQ* 39 (1977): 182-89.

Siegfried, C. *Prediger und Hoheslied.* HKAT. Göttingen: Vandenhoeck und Ruprecht, 1898.

Smith, L. L. "A Critical Evaluation of the Book of Ecclesiastes." *Journal of Bible and Religion* 21 (1953): 100-105.

Spangenberg, I. J. J. "Quotations in Ecclesiastes: An Appraisal." *Old Testament Essays* 4 (1991): 19-35.

Staerk, D. W. "Zur Exegese von Koh 10:20 und 11:1." *ZAW* 59 (1943): 216-18.

Staples, W. E. "Vanity of Vanities." *Canadian Journal of Theology* 1 (1955): 141-56.

Strange, M. "The Question of Moderation in Ecclesiastes 7:15-18." D.Sac.Th. dissertation, Catholic University of America, 1969.

Stuart, M. *Commentary on Ecclesiastes.* New York: G. P. Putnam, 1851.

Taylor, C. *The Dirge in Ecclesiastes 12.* Edinburgh: Williams and Norgate, 1874.

Templeton, D. A. "A 'Farced Epistol' to a Sinking Sun of David. *Eccesiastes* and *Finnegans Wake:* The Sinoptic View." In *Text as Pretext: Essays in Honour of Robert Davidson,* edited by R. P. Carroll. JSOTSup 138, pp. 129-39. Sheffield, England: JSOT Press, 1992.

Thomas, D. W. "A Note on *bemaddāʿakā* in Eccles. x.20." *JTS* 50 (1949): 177.

Todorov, T. *The Fantastic: A Structural Approach to a Literary Genre.* Translated by R. Howard. Ithaca, NY: Cornell University Press, 1973.

Torrey, C. C. "The Question of the Original Language of Qoheleth." *JQR* 39 (1948-49): 151-60.

————. "The Problem of Ecclesiastes iv 13-16." *VT* 2 (1952): 175-77.

Ullendorff, E. "The Meaning of *qhlt.*" *VT* 2 (1962): 215.

Verheij, A. J. C. "Paradise Retried: On Qohelet 2:4-6." *JSOT* 50 (1991): 113-15.

Wahl, O. *Der Proverbien- und Kohelet-Text der Sacra Parallela.* Würzburg: Echter Verlag, 1985.

Waldman, N. "The *dābār ra'* of Eccl 8:3." *JBL* 98 (1979): 407-8.

Waltke, B. K., and M. O'Connor. *An Introduction to Biblical Hebrew Syntax.* Winona Lake, IN: Eisenbrauns, 1990.

Watson, W. G. E. *Classical Hebrew Poetry.* JSOTSup 170. Sheffield, England: JSOT Press, 1984.

White, G. "Luther on Ecclesiastes and the Limits of Human Ability." *Neue Zeitschrift für systematische Theologie* 29 (1987): 180-94.

Whitley, C. F. *Koheleth: His Language and Thought.* BZAW 148. Berlin: de Gruyter, 1979.

Whybray, R. N. "Qoheleth the Immoralist (Qoh 7:16-17)." In *Israelite Wisdom: Theological and Literary Essays in Honor of Samuel Terrien,* edited by J. G. Gammie, W. A. Brueggemann, W. L. Humphreys, and J. M. Ward, pp. 191-204. Missoula, MT: Scholars Press, 1978.

———. "Qoheleth, Preacher of Joy." *JSOT* 23 (1982): 87-98.

———. "Ecclesiastes 1.5-7 and the Wonders of Nature." *JSOT* 41 (1988): 105-12.

———. *Ecclesiastes.* NCB. Grand Rapids, MI: Eerdmans, 1989.

———. *Ecclesiastes.* Old Testament Guides. Sheffield, England: JSOT Press, 1989.

Wildeboer, D. G. "Der Prediger." In *Die fünf Megillot.* Freiburg: Mohr, 1898.

Williams, J. G. "Proverbs and Ecclesiastes." In *The Literary Guide to the Bible,* edited by R. Alter and F. Kermode, pp. 264-82. Cambridge, MA: Harvard University Press, 1987.

Williams, R. J. *Hebrew Syntax: An Outline.* 2d ed. Toronto: University of Toronto Press, 1976.

Wilson, G. H. " 'The Words of the Wise': The Intent and Significance of Qohelet 12:9-14." *JBL* 103 (1984): 175-92.

Winston, D. *The Wisdom of Solomon.* AB 43. New York: Doubleday, 1979.

Wise, M. O. "A Calque from Aramaic in Qoheleth 6:12; 7:12; and 8:13." *JBL* 109 (1990): 249-57.

Witzenrath, H. *Süss ist das Licht.* St. Ottilien: Eos, 1979.

Woudstra, S. "Koheleth's Reflections on Life." Th.M. thesis, Westminster Theological Seminary, 1959.

Wright, A. D. G. "The Riddle of the Sphinx: The Structure of the Book of Qoheleth." *CBQ* 30 (1968): 313-34.

———. "The Riddle of the Sphinx Revisited: Numerical Patterns in the Book of Qoheleth." *CBQ* 42 (1980): 35-51.

———. "Additional Numerical Patterns in Qoheleth." *CBQ* 45 (1983): 32-43.

Wright, C. H. H. *The Book of Koheleth.* London: Hodder and Stoughton, 1888.

Wright, J. S. "Ecclesiastes." In *The Expositor's Bible Commentary,* edited by F. E. Gaebelein, vol. 5, pp. 1137-97. Grand Rapids, MI: Zondervan, 1991.

Yancey, P. "Ecclesiastes: Telling It Like It Is." *Reformed Journal* 40 (1990): 14-19.

Young, E. J. *An Introduction to the Old Testament.* Grand Rapids, MI: Eerdmans, 1949.

Young, L. *Ecclesiastes.* Philadelphia: Presbyterian Board of Publication, 1865.

Youngblood, R. F. "Qoheleth's 'Dark House' (Eccl. 12:5)." *JETS* 29 (1986): 397-410; reprinted in *A Tribute to Gleason Archer: Essays on the Old Testament,* edited by W. C. Kaiser, Jr., and R. F. Youngblood, pp. 211-28. Chicago: Moody, 1986.

Zimmerli, W. *Das Buch des Predigers Salomo.* Das Alte Testament Deutsch 16, 1. Göttingen: Vandenhoeck und Ruprecht, 1962.

———. "The Place and Limit of Wisdom in the Framework of the Old Testament Theology." *SJT* 17 (1964): 146-58.

Zimmermann, F. "The Aramaic Provenance of Qohelet." *JQR* 36 (1945-46): 17-45.

———. "The Question of Hebrew in Qohelet." *JQR* 40 (1949-50): 79-102.

———. *The Inner World of Qohelet.* New York: KTAV, 1973.

———. *Biblical Books Translated from the Aramaic.* New York: KTAV, 1975.

Zuck, R. B. "God and Man in Ecclesiastes." *BibSac* 148 (1991): 46-56.

TEXT AND
COMMENTARY

I. FRAME NARRATIVE: PROLOGUE (1:1-11)

A. SUPERSCRIPTION (1:1)

1 *The words of Qohelet, son of David, king in Jerusalem.*

Ecclesiastes opens with a superscription that introduces the speech of Qohelet in 1:12–12:7. It is the opening line of an eleven-verse section that prepares the reader for what follows by setting the mood of Qohelet's thought. This introductory section was written by a second, unnamed wisdom teacher, whom I will refer to as the frame narrator[1] (see "Authorship" and "Structure" in the introduction).

Superscriptions appear at the beginning of many other biblical books, most consistently with works of prophecy. The superscription is like the title page of a modern book, in that it provides information about the genre, author, and occasionally the subject matter and date of a book (e.g., Isa. 1:1; Jer. 1:1; Nah. 1:1). Superscriptions are found in other wisdom contexts (Prov. 1:1; Song of Songs 1:1), and the one that is closest to the opening of Ecclesiastes is found in Proverbs 1:1: "The proverbs of Solomon, son of David, king of Israel."[2] The similarity may be part of the frame narrator's strategy of near identity between Qohelet and Solomon (see "Authorship" in the introduction).

In the case of Ecclesiastes, the book's superscription provides the genre *(words)* and an authorship designation *(Qohelet, son of David, king in Jerusalem).* The date and subject matter are left unexpressed.

The most natural reading of the superscription in wisdom and prophetic literature is that it was added by a second, subsequent hand. It is not impossible that the author or speaker wrote the superscription, referring to himself in the third person, but the only reason to argue in this direction is to defend a rather mechanical view of biblical inspiration that insists only one author stands behind a single book. In my view, this superscription is the work of the frame narrator.

The frame narrator uses a general term, *words,* to describe what is to follow in 1:12–12:7. As any Hebrew dictionary will attest, *dābār* occurs over fourteen hundred times in the OT and means "word," "thing," "affair," and sometimes "event." While Qohelet narrates both events and words in the bulk of the book, it is safest to stick with the more general term "words," since it

---

1. The terminology comes from M. V. Fox, "Frame-Narrative and Composition in the Book of Qohelet," *HUCA* 48 (1977): 83-106.
2. J. L. Crenshaw (*Ecclesiastes,* OTL [Philadelphia: Westminster, 1987], p. 56) points out that Egyptian wisdom texts also have superscriptions.

introduces a speech. Though *dābār* could have the sense of oral speech, we cannot rule out the possibility that Qohelet's words were a written composition that was then used as a foil by the second wise teacher as he instructed his son (12:12) in the dangers of speculative thinking. Ecclesiastes 1:12–12:7 does carry the tone of a lecture of a teacher to his students.

For a full discussion of the name *Qohelet,* consult the introduction under "Title." See also the discussion under "Authorship."

While there is no doubt that the word *ben* in the phrase *son of David* "denotes close relationships of mind and spirit without implying actual physical kinship,"[3] here it is beyond question that the superscription intends to associate Qohelet and Solomon. The purpose for this association is given in the introduction, under "Authorship."

Both George Barton[4] and James Crenshaw[5] assert without argumentation that *king in Jerusalem* refers to Qohelet and not to David. This point is not established by grammar, since the phrase immediately follows the name David. In other words, it is difficult to tell whether the phrase is in apposition to *David* or to the entire phrase *son of David.* The issue is hardly crucial, though, since no one doubts that David ruled as king from Jerusalem, and Qohelet asserts his kingship in 1:12.

The expression *in Jerusalem* is rather strange. The Septuagint noted the problem and added "of Israel," thus "king of Israel in Jerusalem." H. L. Ginsberg[6] prefers a philological rather than a text-critical solution when he evokes a cognate from the Akkadian of Ugarit to translate "property owner in Jerusalem." I do not find these and other efforts of comparative philology persuasive. Though the normal formula was "king of Israel," there is no problem in recognizing variants, including the present *king in Jerusalem.*

B. INTRODUCTION TO QOHELET'S THOUGHT (1:2-11)

After the superscription, the frame narrator introduces the words of Qohelet with a brief, ten-verse introduction. Two textual signals make it certain that we are not hearing Qohelet's voice yet. The first is the appearance of "Qohelet said" in v. 2. This phrase, not typical of Qohelet's method of self-presentation, is found here, in 7:27 (for the significance of which see the commentary), and

3. Crenshaw, *Ecclesiastes,* p. 56.
4. G. A. Barton, *The Book of Ecclesiastes,* ICC (Edinburgh: T. and T. Clark, 1908), p. 67.
5. Crenshaw, *Ecclesiastes,* p. 56.
6. H. L. Ginsberg, "Ecclesiastes," in *Encyclopedia Judaica,* vol. 6 (Jerusalem: Keter, 1971), p. 354a.

in 12:8.[7] Second, and perhaps more importantly, 1:12 bears a likeness to the opening phrase found in the genre of Akkadian autobiography (see "Genre" in the introduction). Only after that verse may we be certain that Qohelet himself is speaking.

The function of the prologue, though, is to set the mood for what is to follow. The author/narrator of Ecclesiastes reflects the somber tone of Qohelet's ultimate conclusion by both introducing and concluding Qohelet's speech with the same refrain: "Completely meaningless, completely meaningless! Everything is meaningless!" (1:2 and 12:8).

Other commentators[8] divide vv. 2 and 3 from 4-11. Their decision is based on the belief that Qohelet starts talking in v. 4. My genre analysis (see "Genre" in the introduction), however, lends strong support to the understanding that Qohelet starts speaking in v. 12.

There is further disagreement as to whether the prologue is poetry or prose, an issue that runs throughout the book. Indeed, the larger issue of the precise distinction between poetry and prose is a vexed one.[9] While there is a little parallelism in the prologue, it is my opinion that the prologue is prose since it lacks the heightened presence of the cluster of traits that defines poetry in Hebrew: parallelism, terseness, and wordplays.[10]

2 *"Completely meaningless,"*[11] *Qohelet said, "completely meaningless!* *Everything is meaningless!"*

---

7. B. Isaksson, *Studies in the Language of Qoheleth,* Studia Semitica Uppsaliensia 10 (Uppsala, Sweden: Uppsala University Press, 1987), p. 106.

8. For instance, see Crenshaw, *Ecclesiastes,* pp. 34-49, with his detailed discussion of the history of scholarship on this question. Also consult R. E. Murphy, *Ecclesiastes,* WBC 23A (Dallas: Word, 1992), pp. 6-7.

9. The modern discussion was initiated by J. Kugel, *The Idea of Biblical Poetry: Parallelism and Its History* (New Haven: Yale University Press, 1981).

10. See T. Longman III, *How to Read the Psalms* (Downers Grove, IL: InterVarsity Press, 1988), pp. 89-122; and W. G. E. Watson, *Classical Hebrew Poetry,* JSOTSup 170 (Sheffield, England: JSOT Press, 1984), pp. 222-50.

11. The superlative here is formed by the use of the word *meaningless (hebel)* in construct relationship with its plural. A well-known parallel is found in Song of Songs 1:1 (see others listed in GKC §133i; B. K. Waltke and M. O'Connor, *An Introduction to Biblical Hebrew Syntax* [Winona Lake, IN: Eisenbrauns, 1990], §14.5).

Another issue concerns the unusual vocalization of the construct of *hebel* here. Many scholars take it as evidence of Aramaic influence (Barton, *The Book of Ecclesiastes,* p. 72; C. F. Whitley, *Koheleth: His Language and Thought,* BZAW 148 [Berlin: de Gruyter, 1979], p. 6; Crenshaw, *Ecclesiastes,* p. 57) and a linguistic argument in favor of dating the book late. Daniel Fredericks (*Qoheleth's Language: Re-evaluating Its Nature and Date* [Lewiston, NY; Queenston, Ontario: Edwin Mellen, 1988], p. 222), however, disputes this, arguing that there is more than one way for a segolate to reduce the propretonic vowel in construct in biblical Hebrew. He gives analogous examples.

59

3 *What profit is there for people[12] in all the toil that[13] they do[14] under the sun?*

4 *A generation goes, and a generation comes, but the earth remains the same forever.*

5 *The sun rises,[15] and the sun sets,[16] only to hurry around to rise again.*

6 *It blows to the south, going around to the north.[17] The wind goes around and around. The wind keeps blowing in circles.*

7 *All rivers flow to the sea, but the sea is never full. The rivers return[18] to the place from which they flow.*

8 *All things are wearisome beyond words. The eye is never satisfied with seeing, nor the ear with hearing.*

---

12. Literally, "for the man." The use of "man" in Hebrew is often, as it is here, generic. In keeping with modern sensitivities I will translate in a gender-neutral fashion when that neutrality best conveys the sense of Qohelet's message.

13. This is the first time that Qohelet uses the relative, and it is *še*, not *ʾašer*. The extensive use of *še* has generated much discussion. The fact that *še* occurs sixty-eight times in the book has led scholars (Barton, *Ecclesiastes*, p. 52; Whitley, *Koheleth*, p. 8) to argue for a late date of the book. The full picture is that *ʾašer* appears eighty-nine times. The argument is that, while *še* appears early in the history of Hebrew literature (Judg. 5:7; 6:17; 7:22; 2 Kings 6:11), it becomes dominant late (Mishnah). Ecclesiastes, in their view, represents a late situation on the way to the Mishnah. Fredericks (*Qoheleth's Language,* pp. 102-4), however, shows that Ecclesiastes is similar proportionally to Lamentations, Jonah, and the Song of Songs, implying that the situation is more like Biblical Hebrew than Mishnaic Hebrew. Consult R. Schwartzschild, "The Syntax of *ʾšr* in Biblical Hebrew with Special Reference to Qohelet," *Hebrew Studies* 31 (1990): 7-39, for the use of *ʾšr* in Ecclesiastes as evidence of its origin and use as a noun.

14. Qohelet actually uses a verb and its cognate accusative here, literally "in all their toil that they toil," illustrating his penchant toward word repetition. This repetition may be a clever literary means to support his argument that there is nothing new under the sun, that everything repeats itself.

15. The first verb in the verse is a qal perfect with prefixed *waw*. However, the conjunction *waw* seems superfluous here, and the context contains a series of participles. For these reasons, I agree with *BHS* that the *waw* and *zayin* should be transposed to produce another participial form.

16. *bāʾ* can be taken as a qal perfect or a qal participle. Since the clear verbs in the context are participles, that is the way I interpret the form of the verb in this instance.

17. The Septuagint mistranslates here. It understands only the first half of the verse to have the *sun* as its subject. Apparently, it was misled by the delayed identification of the subject.

18. For this translation of *šûb*, see Y.-J. Min, "How Do the Rivers Flow? (Ecclesiastes 1.7)," *Bible Translator* 42 (1991): 226-30.

9 *Whatever[19] is[20] will be again. What was done in the past will be done again. There is nothing new under the sun.*

10 *Here is a common expression, "Look, this is new!" But it was already here long ago. It existed before our time.*

11 *There is no remembrance[21] of the past, nor will there be any remembrance of what will be in the future. There is no remembrance of them among those who will exist in the future.*

2 The book of Ecclesiastes leaves no doubt about Qohelet's ultimate conclusion — everything is completely meaningless. The second wisdom teacher (see "Authorship" in the introduction) here introduces and later (12:8) concludes Qohelet's words with this summary statement. In doing so he utilizes a refrain that occurs repeatedly within the body of the book itself (e.g., 2:1, 15, 19; 3:19; 5:9 [English 5:10]; 6:11; 7:6; 8:10, 14; 9:9; 11:8; 12:8). Indeed, the phrase occurs over thirty-five times in the book. In addition, to make sure that the reader gets the point, the refrain is composed of a series of superlatives, making this motto an extremely strong statement.

The phrase *completely meaningless* literally reads "meaninglessness of meaninglessnesses," or more traditionally, "vanity of vanities." The latter translation, made famous by the KJV, is now problematical because the English term "vanity" is primarily used in reference to self-pride.

The superlative is formed by the use of the word twice in a construct relationship *(h^{a}bēl h^{a}bālîm)*, first in the singular and the second time in the plural. Grammatical analogies include "Song of Songs," meaning the very best song (Song of Songs 1:1), and "Holy of Holies," in reference to the most holy spot on earth (Exod. 29:37) — see other analogies in Deuteronomy 10:14 ("heaven of heavens") and Genesis 9:25 ("servant of servants").

The expression is further heightened, first, by the repetition of the superlative, and then, as if it were not already crystal clear, by the final statement that *Everything is meaningless.* According to the frame narrator, Qohelet understands that nothing is excluded from his final judgment — *meaningless (hebel).* Later, Qohelet himself qualifies the "everything" with another recurrent phrase "under the sun" (for discussion of which see the

---

19. *mah-še* is often discussed because its syntax is infrequently attested outside Ecclesiastes (within Ecclesiastes see also 3:15; 6:10; 7:24; 8:7; 10:14). *mah* usually has an interrogative force, but not here (though the Septuagint and Vulgate both mistakenly take it this way). See GKC §137c and Whitley, *Koheleth,* p. 10, for detailed discussions.

20. See Isaksson, *Studies in the Language of Qoheleth,* pp. 75-76, for a lengthy discussion of the verb's tense. Also, note my discussion at 3:15.

21. The form of the word is construct, not a late form of the absolute on analogy with *yitrôn* and *kišrôn.* In any case Fredericks (*Qoheleth's Language,* pp. 137-38) marshals evidence to deny the claim that *-ôn* forms are late.

next verse), but Qohelet himself never clearly transcends the created order to discover meaning or significance anywhere in the universe.

This phrase is of crucial importance for determining the tenor of Qohelet's thought. Even those scholars who represent the view that Qohelet is a "preacher of joy" (see "Theological Message" in the introduction) recognize this fact. R. N. Whybray, for instance, states in his commentary that 1:2 and 12:8 "form a framework for Qoheleth's sayings which is intended to leave the reader in no doubt about Qoheleth's negative attitude toward human life."[22] He goes on, however, rightly to attribute these verses to a second hand, but wrongly to argue that this later editor "misunderstood" or at least "oversimplified" Qohelet's message.

Not all interpreters in this school of thought are open to Whybray's expediency; many adopt a philological approach to the problem. It is well known that the Hebrew term *hebel* means literally "breath, breeze, vapor." Approximately half of the word's occurrences are found in the book of Ecclesiastes, but it is helpful to survey the function of the word elsewhere to see its semantic range.[23]

The word is usually used in a metaphorical way,[24] signifying either the uselessness or meaninglessness of a thing or its transitory nature (i.e., it lacks lasting substance). Herein, however, lies the debate. As Qohelet uses the term, and as the frame narrator picks it up and summarizes Qohelet's thought with it, does it signify that "everything is meaningless" or that "everything is temporary"?[25]

22. R. N. Whybray, *Ecclesiastes,* NCB (Grand Rapids, MI: Eerdmans, 1989), p. 35.

23. Against J. Chopineau ("Une image de l'homme: Sur Ecclésiaste 1/2," *Etudes Théologiques et Religieuses* 53 [1978]: 366-75), I do not believe that Qohelet is consciously or unconsciously reflecting upon the name Abel in Gen. 4, so I leave that text out of consideration. It is true that the name and the Hebrew word are related, but its appearance as a name does not aid us in deciding its meaning in Ecclesiastes.

24. Indeed, the only definite place where the usage is nonmetaphorical is Isa. 57:13, but as M. V. Fox (*Qohelet and His Contradictions,* JSOTSup 71 [Sheffield, England: Almond, 1989], p. 29) points out, a nonmetaphorical usage is also attested in Mishnaic Hebrew, Jewish Aramaic, and Syriac.

25. Other translations besides these two have been suggested, for instance "mystery" (W. E. Staples, "Vanity of Vanities," *Canadian Journal of Theology* 1 [1955]: 141-56) and "enigma" (G. S. Ogden, *Qoheleth* [Sheffield, England: JSOT Press, 1987], p. 22). But these other suggestions have not been so persuasive as to be taken seriously. Two suggestions that perhaps should be given some consideration are "irony" (E. M. Good, *Irony in the Old Testament* [Sheffield, England: Almond, 1981 (1965)]; and "The Unfilled Sea: Style and Meaning in Ecclesiastes 1:2-11," in *Israelite Wisdom: Theological and Literary Essays in Honor of Samuel Terrien,* ed. J. G. Gammie, W. A. Brueggemann, W. L. Humphreys, and J. M. Ward [Missoula, MT: Scholars Press, 1978], pp. 59-73) and "absurd" (Fox, *Qohelet and His Contradictions,* p. 31), but irony is too broad a concept

The word *hebel* occurs approximately thirty-two times outside the book of Ecclesiastes. Examining these passages and their contexts helps greatly to resolve the issue in Ecclesiastes. In thirteen passages[26] the word characterizes idols. It is absolutely certain that these passages are attributing uselessness or meaninglessness to the idols, not transitoriness. Indeed, if they were transitory, they would eventually pass away and not be the cause of such major concern. They present a crisis to Israel precisely because they are not transitory, but rather deceptive, that is, useless.

In some of these instances, there is a parallel term (e.g., "false" [*šeqer*] in Jer. 16:19 or "worthless [*šāw'*] in Zech. 10:2). These parallel terms confirm my conclusion about the meaning of *hebel* in those passages that deal with idolatry.

A survey of the remaining passages indicates that there are a number of other passages where only "meaningless" is possible.[27] The occasional parallel terms once again support this contextual decision ("in vain" [*rîq*] in Isa. 30:7; "lie" [*kāzāb*] in Ps. 62:10 (English 62:9); "false" [*šeqer*] in Prov. 31:30).

There are admittedly some passages where the meaning "temporary" or "fleeting" is a contextual possibility (see, e.g., Ps. 39:5-6 [English 39:4-5]):

> Show me, O LORD, my life's end
> and the number of my days;
> let me know how fleeting is my life.
> You have made my days a mere handbreadth;
> the span of my years is as nothing before you.
> Each man's life is but a *breath*.

Thus, the immediately preceding context concentrates on the temporality of human life. Even here, however, the meaning "meaningless" is a strong possibility. In other words, the preceding cola could be leading up to the climax in the last colon that states the implication of the transience of human life, that it is meaningless. The next verse goes on to make that point:

---

and absurdity, which is narrower, is too modern. Fox (*Qohelet and His Contradictions*, p. 31) defines "absurd" as "a disparity between two phenomena that are supposed to be joined by a link of harmony or causality but are actually disjunct or even conflicting." "Meaningless" carries this connotation adequately and does not carry the same modern connotations.

26. Deut. 32:21; 2 Kings 17:15 (in its first occurrence in the verse); Ps. 31:7 (English 31:6); 57:13; Jer. 2:5; 8:19; 10:8, 15; 14:22; 16:19; 51:18; Jon. 2:8; Zech. 10:2.

27. For example, 2 Kings 17:15 (in its second occurrence in the verse); Job 9:29; 21:34; 27:12; 35:16; Ps. 31:7; 39:7 (English 39:6); 62:10 (English 62:9); 78:33; 94:11; Prov. 13:11; Isa. 30:7; Lam. 4:17.

Man is a mere phantom as he goes to and fro:
He bustles about, but only in vain;
he heaps up wealth, not knowing who will get it.

The point is not to insist that *hebel* must mean "meaninglessness" in Psalm 39 but to point out that there are only a handful of passages where it may mean "temporary" (Ps. 39:12 [English 39:11]; Job 7:16; Prov. 31:30; Ps. 144:4). Furthermore, since the translation "temporary" is not certain for these latter passages, there must be more than a philological argument behind the recent efforts to suggest "temporary" as the normative translation of the word in Ecclesiastes.[28]

The most important versions understood *hebel* as "meaningless" in the book of Ecclesiastes. While some early Greek translations (Aquila, Theodotion, and Symmachus) simply translated the word according to its concrete meaning "breath" *(atmos),* the Septuagint used the word "emptiness, frustration" *(mataiotēs),* and the Vulgate used *vanitas,* which of course shaped the traditional English rendering. The NT is likely alluding to this word in Romans 8:18, where Paul uses the term *mataiotēs* (see "From a New Testament Perspective" in the introduction).

In the final analysis, the meaning of the word in Ecclesiastes must be decided on the basis of the immediate context. Though the usage of the word outside the book strongly predisposes us toward a translation of "vanity," we should remain open as we approach each context. Indeed, it is possible that *hebel* is used differently in different contexts, and we will have to keep this in mind.

The problem with considering the context of the refrain is that it depends on the meaning of the whole book. We are thus involved in a form of the hermeneutical spiral in which the meaning of a word depends on the meaning of the book as a whole, and the meaning of the book contributes to our understanding of the word. In the section "Theological Message" in the introduction, we noted that not only philology and text criticism but also the best assessment of the book's overall message support "meaningless" as the meaning of *hebel* in Ecclesiastes.[29]

---

28. Most notably that of D. C. Fredericks, *Coping with Transience: Ecclesiastes on the Brevity of Life* (Sheffield, England: JSOT Press, 1993). Fredericks desires to resurrect an orthodox Qohelet in order to legitimate the normative theological teaching of the entire book.

29. J. E. McKenna's "The Concept of *Hebel* in the Book of Ecclesiastes," *SJT* 45 (1992): 19-28, came out too late for me to integrate his thoughts into the body of the commentary. His approach is more theological than philological, but he makes an impassioned plea not to "reduce the concept of *hebel* in Qohelet down to be entailed by causalities or particulars found only within the reciprocities intrinsic to created reality." McKenna

Everything is meaningless. Qohelet leaves nothing out. He cannot find meaning in anybody or anything. The frame narrator has placed the refrain in this introductory position to prepare us for what is to come. Qohelet will prove his point in his monologue, especially in the first part, where he is searching for meaning in things and people "under the sun" (see 1:3). Then the frame narrator will drive the point home by repeating 1:2 in 12:8.

3 Immediately following the motto (or *Leitwort*), the frame narrator picks up another key expression of Qohelet. It is in the form of the rhetorical question, *What profit is there?*[30] The question is asked merely for effect. No answer is expected, and none is needed because the answer is obvious. By using a rhetorical question, the frame narrator makes Qohelet's point emphatically. Both men appeal to common knowledge and common experience. In other words, they assume that everyone knows the answer to the question. There is no profit! If there is no meaning (v. 2), how could there be profit to labor?

The rhetorical question serves one other related function: it involves the reader. Though the answer is obvious, the reader must nonetheless supply it.

Profit (yitrôn) is a key word in Ecclesiastes, appearing nine times (1:3; 2:11,13; 3:9; 5:8, 15 [English 5:9, 16]; 7:12; 10:10,11). Strikingly, it occurs nowhere else in the OT. The term derives from the common verb *ytr* "to be left over," "to remain."[31]

The frame narrator points out that Qohelet is making a universal statement *(in all)*. He leaves nothing out of view here. In the phrase *the toil that they do* the noun and verb derive from the same root, *'ml*. While the word can mean simply "work" or "labor," it more often carries a negative connotation, "hard work," "drudgery," or even "misery" (Num. 23:21; Isa. 59:4; Jer. 20:18; Ps. 7:15 [English 7:14]). Because that connotation certainly is appropriate for its use in Ecclesiastes, I have chosen to translate it as *toil*.

---

believes that *hebel* is not to be understood in light of supposed similarities to existentialism but rather in the light of Karl Barth's ideas about the created status of nothingness. Also, in the forthcoming *New International Dictionary of Old Testament Theology and Exegesis,* ed. W. VanGemeren (Grand Rapids, MI: Zondervan), G. Johnston demonstrates that the most common meaning of *hebel* by far is "empty" or "meaningless." Indeed, in his survey of ancient Near Eastern cognates he lists no attested occurrence of the sense "transience" or its synonyms.

30. The question is repeated in Eccles. 3:9 and 5:15 (English 5:16). Variants of the phrase (containing the word *profit [yitrôn])* are found in Eccles. 2:11, 13, and 10:11.

31. M. J. Dahood ("Canaanite-Phoenician Influence in Qoheleth," *Biblica* 33 [1952]: 221) argued that it is a technical commercial term, "profit," that is, what is left over after expenses are met. Dahood bases his argument on a Phonenician parallel (see "Language" in the introduction), but his conclusion does not depend on an acceptance of his linguistic hypothesis. Whitley (*Koheleth,* p. 37) leans in this direction but correctly states that we cannot be absolutely certain that the term carries this technical sense here.

Perhaps only the *hebel* refrain is more widely known than Qohelet's phrase *under the sun,* which is a common expression in the book of Ecclesiastes (twenty-nine times)[32] and one that appears nowhere else in the OT. It is, however, conceptually similar to the expressions "under heaven" (Exod. 17:14; Deut. 7:24; 9:14; Eccles. 2:3; 3:1) and "on earth" (Eccles. 5:1 [English 5:2]; 7:20; 8:14, 16; 11:2). Qohelet thus restricts his remarks to terrestrial human activity and work. The question is, however, Does Qohelet ever clearly transcend the terrestrial realm? He talks about God, but does God ever bring him the calm and peace that one would expect to be due a wise man of Yahweh? Does he believe that God has any relevance for the human realm? Herbert Leupold answered this question affirmatively.[33] He paraphrased Qohelet's statement in this way: "Let us for the sake of argument momentarily rule out the higher things." I, however, deny that Qohelet is merely playing such a philosophical game and argue that he truly feels the pain and anxiety that he expresses so strongly.

While the phrase *under the sun* occurs nowhere else in the Hebrew canon, it is attested in extrabiblical literature. Harry Ranston used its occurrence in Greek literature to support his claim for a late composition of the book under Hellenistic influence.[34] Others counteract this now dated approach by citing earlier Semitic parallels, particularly its appearance in an Elamite inscription of the twelfth century B.C., the Phoenician inscriptions of Tabnit (sixth century B.C.) and Eshmunazar (fifth century B.C.), as well as the Gilgamesh Epic (Akkadian version from the neo-Assyrian period): "Only the gods [live] forever under the sun. As for mankind, numbered are their days, whatever they achieve is but the wind."[35]

In brief, Qohelet's frequent use of the phrase *under the sun* highlights the restricted scope of his inquiry. His worldview does not allow him to take a transcendent yet immanent God into consideration in his quest for meaning. In the Bible this viewpoint is unique to Qohelet. The choice of the metaphorical phrase *under the sun* rather than the more prosaic "on earth" intends to appeal to the imagination of the reader in a memorable way. Perhaps the phrase also communicates the discomfort of Qohelet's perspective by invoking an image of sweltering heat.

4 Qohelet now hints at the reason why human beings see no profit to their exertions. Nothing ever changes except perhaps the time. In the midst of apparent activity, the earth remains the same.

32. Eccles. 1:3, 9; 2:11, 17, 18, 19, 20, 22; 3:16; 4:1, 3, 7, 15; 5:13, 18 (English 5:14, 19); 6:1, 12; 7:11; 8:9, 15 (twice), 17; 9:3, 6, 9 (twice), 11, 13; 10:5.

33. H. C. Leupold, *Exposition of Ecclesiastes* (Grand Rapids, MI: Baker, 1952), pp. 42-43.

34. H. Ranston, *Ecclesiastes and the Early Greek Wisdom Literature* (London: Epworth, 1925).

35. *ANET,* p. 79, cited by Crenshaw, *Ecclesiastes,* p. 60.

In recent years there has been a reassessment of the meaning of the word *generation*. The noun is related to a verb *(dwr)* that denotes circular movement.[36] The noun has traditionally been understood to mean *generation*. If so, Qohelet contrasts the impermanence of humans over against the permanence of the inanimate world.[37] Jerome stated the irony of the verse: "What is more vain than this vanity: that the earth, which was made for humans, stays — but humans themselves, the lords of the earth, suddenly dissolve into the dust?"[38]

In 1986, however, Graham Ogden published a short article arguing that the word *dôr* did not relate to human generations at least here in Ecclesiastes, but to the cycles of nature.[39] He sees a contrast "between a cyclic movement within nature which contrasts with the earth's permanence."[40] He then notes that vv. 5-7 develop the idea of the changes in nature and that the rest of the prologue shows the permanence of the earth.[41]

Michael Fox[42] agreed with Ogden's interpretation of *dôr* but disagreed with his understanding of *hāʾāreṣ*. In Fox's estimation *hāʾāreṣ* meant not the physical world, but humanity. He thus understood the verse to have a negative cast: "the poem shows that the persistent, toilsome, movements of natural phenomena, of which mankind, taken as a whole, is one, do not really affect anything. All this is meant to show that, by analogy, human toil cannot be expected to do so."[43]

It is difficult, if not impossible, to adjudicate these issues. The arguments can cut more than one way, as we can observe by looking at the two verbs, *goes* and *comes*. They are both qal participles, modifying the twice repeated *dôr*. The participle is used throughout this section, according to Isaksson,[44] to give a "nuance of repetition, continuation." The two verbs are extremely common verbs of motion. The first is from *hālak* and means "goes," in the sense of "go away," while the second is from *bôʾ* and means "comes

---

36. Hebrew has a noun, *dwôr,* meaning "circle" or "ball" (cf. Isa. 22:18). See BDB, p. 189, for comments on the basic meaning of the verbal root.

37. D. Kidner, *A Time to Mourn and a Time to Dance* (Downers Grove, IL: InterVarsity, 1976), p. 25.

38. Quoted by Crenshaw, *Ecclesiastes,* p. 63.

39. G. S. Ogden, "The Interpretation of *dôr* in Ecclesiastes 1.4," *JSOT* 34 (1986): 91-92, though he does not provide an alternative translation.

40. Ogden, "The Interpretation of *dôr,*" p. 91.

41. This view is supported by R. N. Whybray, "Ecclesiastes 1.5-7 and the Wonders of Nature," *JSOT* 41 (1988): 105-12.

42. M. V. Fox, "Qohelet 1.4," *JSOT* 40 (1988): 109.

43. Fox, "Qohelet 1.4," p. 109.

44. Isaksson, *Studies in the Language of Qoheleth,* p. 66. See also Waltke and O'Connor, *Biblical Hebrew Syntax,* §37.6e.

toward." They are opposites of one another and therefore constitute a merism (i.e., all motion).

The sequence of the verbs ("go" and "come") has also been the subject of discussion, since one might expect the sequence to be reversed if human generations were meant ("come" and "go"). Fox believes that the sequence is inappropriate for human generations and thus supports Ogden's contention.[45] Hans Hertzberg, however, earlier pointed out that the verbs may not have this sense here, since *bô'* in reference to the sun's setting in the next verse clearly means "to go away." Hertzberg does not mention the fact that *hālak* occurs four times in the next few verses in the sense of "to go."[46]

I have chosen to translate the verbs in accordance with their usual meanings and do not feel the force of Fox's argument. The sequence does not negate the possibility that human generations are meant; the point is the cyclicality of the phenomenon, which can be expressed by either verb sequence. The sequence "a generation comes, and a generation goes" may sound right to us only because that has been the traditional rendering of this verse into English and has become a stock expression. Furthermore, perhaps here Qohelet uses *hālak* first in reference to death in keeping with the pessimistic tone of his message.

James Crenshaw is probably correct in saying that *dôr* has both human and natural cycles in mind.[47] It is impossible to be dogmatic one way or the other.

but the earth remains the same forever. The initial conjunction is the simple *waw,* but the contrast between the two parts of the verse leads one on semantic grounds to translate it as disjunctive *(but).* There has been much debate over the chronological scope of *ʿôlām,* here translated *forever,* and it is unclear whether the ancient Hebrews had a concept of eternity similar to our own. It is my position, however, that here *forever* refers to the future as far as the mind can conceive.

5 Verse 4 enunciated the principle that the earth remains the same despite the constant cycle of humans and nature. Creation is characterized by apparent change that disguises actual sameness. The rest of the prologue (vv. 5-11) will now illustrate that principle.

The first specific illustration is the sun. In the continued rising and setting of the sun, Qohelet sees the sameness of the earth within cyclic change. After all, the sun seems to be constantly moving around the earth, but the pattern is the same each and every day. Even if one observes changes in the sun's course over a year, it always stays within the same limits.

45. Fox, "Qohelet 1.4," p. 109; and Ogden, "The Interpretation of *dôr,*" pp. 91-92.
46. H. W. Hertzberg, *Der Prediger,* KAT 17, 4 (Gütersloh: Mohn, 1963), p. 70.
47. Crenshaw, *Ecclesiastes,* p. 62.

The sun rises, and the sun sets. It is likely that the first verb is a participle after emendation (see n. 15), and the second is to be understood as such. Thus, the idea of continuous, repetitive action appears in this verse. The repetition of the subject *sun (šemeš),* like "generation" *(dôr)* in the previous verse, also highlights repetitive monotony.

only to hurry around is an idiomatic translation of what may literally be rendered "and to its place it pants." "Place" *(māqôm)* probably refers to the idea that the sun entered a subterranean room after crossing the sky and then set out again the next morning. This would be similar to the idea in Psalm 19:6, 7 (English 19:5, 6), which describes the sun as "a bridegroom coming forth from his pavilion, like a champion rejoicing to run his course."[48]

The word *hurry (šā'ap)* is literally "pant." Commentators have rightly pointed out that the OT uses it in a positive as well as a negative sense. Positively, the word means to pant with eagerness or desire (for God's commands in Ps. 119:131), negatively, to pant with exhaustion (like a woman in childbirth in Isa. 42:14). Depending on which nuance is adopted in Ecclesiastes, either the sun joyously rushes back to its starting point so that it can once again begin its glorious march across the sky, or the sun toils across the sky, only to reach its destination and achieve no rest, no closure, but needing to rush back and do the whole meaningless task over again.[49] Context and the overall message of the book will determine one's understanding (see "Theological Message" in the introduction). In my opinion, the negative meaning is supported and was so understood by the Septuagint "drags" *(helkei)* and Targum "crawls" *(štyp).*[50]

6 The second illustration from nature is the wind. Once again, the idea of sameness within apparent change is illustrated: the wind gives the appearance of great commotion, but, when analyzed closely, is just going in circles. Nothing is changing at all. It is just more of the same.

Qohelet uses delayed identification to build suspense in the verse. There are five verbs before the subject "wind" *(rûaḥ)* occurs in the sentence. All five verbs (and perhaps the one that follows as well) are participles (see comment on v. 5 for the function of participles).

The movement of the wind in circles evokes the idea of much action with little consequence. James Crenshaw correctly notes that the use of repetitive participles, *hôlēk* ("going," two times) and *sôbēb* ("going around,"

---

48. Hertzberg, *Der Prediger,* p. 70.

49. Whybray ("Ecclesiastes 1.5-7," pp. 105-12; and *Ecclesiastes,* NCB, p. 41) disagrees with Crenshaw (*Ecclesiastes,* pp. 63-64), the latter taking the negative and the former taking the positive view of the sun's heavy breathing.

50. See Whitley, *Koheleth,* p. 9. In its textual notes, *BHS* recommends omitting the third colon *(zôreaḥ hû' šām)* as an addition, but this, along with its suggestion to divide *šā'ap* into *šāb 'ap,* is unnecessary and without support.

three times), gives a "sense of being caught in a rut."[51] R. N. Whybray, however, manages to eke out a positive message here. He argues, rather unpersuasively, that the wind here is reliable and not arbitrary, found in its proper "circuits."[52]

Two directions, *north . . . south,* are mentioned to complement the east-west implied by the previous verse. The argument that this description of the pattern of the wind militates against an Egyptian setting of the book[53] presses this figurative language too far.[54]

7 We come now to the last illustration of the principle of ceaseless, but futile, change. Like the winds of the previous verse, the apparently changing waters of the earth are really circling back to their point of origin, changing nothing. Once again, we have an illustration of illusive change; things appear to be changing but are really staying the same.

Ibn Ezra noted that vv. 4-7 cite the four fundamental elements of earth, fire, wind, and water.[55] This interesting observation may be invalidated by the fact that the first, earth in v. 4, is actually the setting in which the other three (sun, wind, river/sea) operate. Beginning with v. 5, the order is sun, wind, and river. Perhaps this sequence is driven from highest (sun) to nearest (river) with the wind in between.

The verse observes that rivers, while constantly flowing into a sea, do not affect the water level, which remains constant. As Graham Ogden notes, the verse entails an action that "does not move toward completion; it knows only constant and cyclic motion."[56]

the sea. James Crenshaw suggests that the Dead Sea in particular was in the mind of the writer. The Jordan River continually empties into the Dead Sea from the north, but it is never filled, though no river flows out of it.[57] Certainly it illustrates the point, though dogmatic assertion is impossible here.

There is a debate whether the meaning of *the rivers return* is that they continue pumping water into the sea with no lasting effect (NRSV, NASB, NAB, JB) or whether the water continues to return to the source of the river to flow once again (NIV, NKJV).[58] Either meaning does not change the

---

51. Crenshaw, *Ecclesiastes,* p. 64.

52. Whybray, *Ecclesiastes,* NCB, pp. 41-42.

53. As argued by Whybray (*Ecclesiastes,* NCB, p. 42) and A. Lauha (*Kohelet,* BKAT 19 [Neukirchen-Vluyn: Neukirchener Verlag, 1978], p. 35), who point to the fact that Egyptian wind patterns are predictable.

54. So Crenshaw, *Ecclesiastes,* p. 65, who rightly points out that poetic language cannot be pressed in such a literal manner.

55. Cited by Hertzberg, *Der Prediger,* p. 71.

56. Ogden, *Qoheleth,* p. 31.

57. Crenshaw, *Ecclesiastes,* p. 65.

58. Min, "How Do the Rivers Flow?," p. 226.

principle that is clearly taught here: all this activity does nothing significant. We should avoid, however, any unnecessary speculation about the mechanics of the return of the water to its origins — for instance, vaporization[59] or underground rivers. The unfilled sea is a metaphor that brings to the surface a theme that will now become explicit in the next verse, that is, that human experience is characterized by insatiable desire.

Many of the words of this verse echo throughout the section, for example, "flow" (hōlᵉkîm, vv. 4, 6), the "place" (māqôm), and "return" (šābîm, vs. 6). The effect of this repetition supports the message of the section — sameness in the midst of illusory change.

8 This verse is pivotal in establishing the pessimistic tone of this section of the text. The immediately preceding verses observed that the earth may be characterized by illusive change. In actuality everything is the same. Nothing ever really changes. As a result, human experience is dull and unsatisfying.

All things. As is well known, Hebrew *dābār* may be translated in a number of ways, most notably by "things" or "words." Recent commentators have rightly seen that this verse flows from the previous verses, and therefore the "things" would refer to the forces of nature mentioned there. Indeed, as R. N. Whybray has said,[60] the *dābār* in v. 10 is a specific instance of the *haddᵉbārîm* in v. 8, and the former can be nothing other than "thing."

Despite Graham Ogden's valiant efforts,[61] *wearisome (yᵉgēʿîm)* has negative connotations. Indeed, to suggest, as he does, that the closely related word in 12:12 is really a positive statement is extremely doubtful. The two most closely related uses of the term confirm a negative connotation (Deut. 25:18; 2 Sam. 17:2, both of which use the word to mean "weary" or "tired"), as does the rendering of the Septuagint, "feeble" *(egkopos).*

Literally, *beyond words* is "a man is not able to say." The sense of the statement is that the weariness of all things is so mind-boggling that it exceeds human ability to describe it. *BHS* suggests an emendation, which Whybray[62] attributes to Kurt Galling, that *yûkal* be changed to *yᵉkalleh* to yield the translation "perfect [his speaking]." That is, no one is able to speak effectively. While making the clause fit in more smoothly with the following two lines, the change is unnecessary and certainly unwarranted since, as is, the MT is capable of a sensible translation.

It is true, however, that this clause has a syntactical structure roughly similar to the next two: they all begin with the negative particle *(lōʾ),* followed

---

59. So Ibn Ezra, cited by Whybray, *Ecclesiastes,* NCB, p. 42.
60. Whybray, *Ecclesiastes,* NCB, p. 44.
61. Ogden, *Qoheleth,* pp. 31-32.
62. Whybray, *Ecclesiastes,* NCB, p. 44.

by the verb in the imperfect (the first is masculine, the next two feminine), followed by the subject, and finally a verbal phrase formed with the infinitive construct. The last two clauses give further explanation why things are so wearisome. It is beyond humans to have a sense of complete satisfaction that leads to closure. Eyes may see much and ears hear constantly, but it is never enough — there is more to hear and more to see.

9 The frame narrator continues to set the stage for Qohelet's autobiography by turning now to history. He notes its futility. History is going nowhere. History, like the earth, appears to change, but in actuality it stays the same. Nothing new ever happens.

It is true that Hebrew historiography as expressed in the historical and prophetical books had a strong cyclical character to it, but it also involved progression. Earlier events like the exodus anticipate and are used to describe later events (like the return from exile, e.g., Hos. 2:14-15), but the exile is a new act on God's part. In other words, normative Hebrew historiography may be described as a progressive spiral, not a meaningless cycle. Further, as David Hubbard points out,[63] Qohelet's attitude cuts against the message of redemptive history, particularly that of the prophets whose ultimate vision is of a "new heaven and a new earth" (Isa. 43:19). In addition, Hans Hertzberg[64] reminds us of Numbers 16:30 ("But if the LORD brings about something totally new . . ."), which also represents the typical OT view that God does indeed introduce new things into history.

Over against the normative biblical view stands the thought of Qohelet, as represented here by the frame narrator, that the past will perpetually repeat itself in the future (see "Theological Message" in the introduction). Indeed, Qohelet's thought may be compared to the skeptics of the NT period as recorded by 2 Pet. 3:3-5: "First of all, you must understand that in the last days scoffers will come, scoffing and following their own evil desires. They will say, 'Where is this "coming" he promised? Ever since our fathers died, everything goes on as it has since the beginning of creation.' But they deliberately forget."

Verse 9 is rhythmic, almost poetic in its effect. There is a double repetition of *mah-še (whatever . . . what)* as well as *hû' še,* in addition to the recurrent use of the verbs *hāyâ* ("to be") and *'āśâ* ("to do"). These word and phrase repetitions heighten the idea of the cyclic repetition of human experience.

What was done in the past will be done again. In the context of what Qohelet later says, this is not a happy thought. The past, the present, and the future are filled with oppression, hard work, and loneliness (4:1-12). There is nothing to look forward to.

63. D. A. Hubbard, *Beyond Futility* (Grand Rapids, MI: Eerdmans, 1976), pp. 20-21.

64. Hertzberg, *Der Prediger,* p. 72.

Commentators who wish to preserve Qohelet's orthodoxy make great efforts to limit the scope of the statement, *There is nothing new.*[65] Others try to fit his thought with the prevailing ideas of their own day. John Cotton in his mid-seventeenth-century commentary mentions Origen's citation of Plato's belief that the world experienced 49,000-year cycles. He also cites Cardinal Cajetan's more general belief that this verse is connected with cycles of natural bodies, along with Jerome's opinion that the verse has in mind the fact that all things that happen on earth first exist in the mind of God.[66]

It is certainly true that Qohelet, as here represented by the frame narrator, limits his observation to the earthly realm, but this observation does not preserve his orthodoxy, since, as just mentioned, the rest of the OT stresses that God acts in new ways even on the earth. This Qohelet never admits. For *under the sun,* see v. 3.

10   In this verse, the frame narrator deals with a likely objection to the principle enunciated in the previous verse. How can it be that there is nothing new under the sun when people are constantly making the claim to have created or discovered something for the first time? As a matter of fact, this objection takes on an even stronger force in the twentieth century, where apparent rapid change is the rule. Yet a number of commentators rebut the objection by noting that inventions and innovations are not new but simply rediscoveries of what had been forgotten in the past.[67] Those who acknowledge that some things are new (e.g., space travel, nuclear power) point out that, although the technological advances are new, the people who wield them are not. Human beings of today are the same sinful human beings of the past, and thus there are no new developments or progress in the human race. This is the sentiment expressed by Ernst Hengstenberg:

> Many an undertaking gives promise at its commencement of passing beyond the limits fixed by the old curse-laden world. The world exultingly shouts them welcome. But very soon it becomes evident that in them also a worm is concealed, and they sink down to a level with that which our poor earth has produced in former ages.[68]

---

65. For instance, Leupold, *Exposition of Ecclesiastes,* p. 48, where he cites analogues to the use of *kol* in this verse (Judg. 13:14 and Ps. 143:2).

66. J. Cotton, *A Brief Exposition with Practical Observations upon the Book of Ecclesiastes* (London, 1654), p. 76.

67. A view represented by W. C. Kaiser, Jr., *Ecclesiastes: Total Life,* Everyman's Bible Commentary (Chicago: Moody, 1979), pp. 50-51.

68. E. W. Hengstenberg, *A Commentary on Ecclesiastes* (Evansville, IN: Sovereign Grace Publishers, 1960 [1869]), pp. 57-58. For a similar view, see J. Ellul, *Reason for Being: A Meditation on Ecclesiastes,* trans. J. M. Hanks (Grand Rapids, MI: Eerdmans, 1990).

The Hebrew syntax of *Here is a common expression* is difficult, and every translation must make concessions that are not totally justified by the normal rules of Hebrew lexicography and grammar. The sentence is deceptively simple on a superficial reading, made up of the not infrequent (especially in Ecclesiastes) existential particle *'ên* ("there is/are not"), followed by the common noun *dābār* ("word, thing") plus the relative pronoun with the verb *'āmar* ("to say") in the third masculine singular imperfect. A wooden rendition of the sentence is: "There is a word that it/he says."

There have been several different approaches to this clause. The Septuagint reads "The one who speaks even says" *(hos lalēsei kai erei),* but according to Robert Gordis,[69] the Greek translators probably had a misvocalized Hebrew text in front of them (i.e., *dōbēr* ["they are speaking"] versus MT *dābār*). Gordis argues that *yēš* introduces the protasis of a conditional sentence, but this is far from certain.[70] R. Norman Whybray, in contrast, asserts that this is an unmarked question,[71] an interpretation that stands behind the NIV, "Is there anything of which one can say . . . ?" This hypothesis is, of course, possible, but it is drawn from necessity and rests on questionable grammar. The above translation reads the sentence literally and takes "word" as the subject of the verb in the relative clause: "There is a word that says. . . ." Further, as with most interpreters, I understand *dābār* to refer to the quoted sentence that follows, thus *expression*. Context leads to the idiomatic translation offered.

The word *already (kᵉbār)* has generated much discussion because it appears nowhere outside Ecclesiastes in the Hebrew Bible but is frequent in the Mishnah. Thus, it is used to argue in favor of a late date for the book. Even Daniel Fredericks[72] admits that the word is a "Mishnaism," though, he believes, this does not lead us to date the book late.

ᶜôlām (long ago) looks either to the indefinitely distant future or to the indefinitely distant past. In this case, the word's association with *kᵉbār (already)* makes it clear that the distant past is meant.[73] *millᵉpānēnû, before our time,* is a variant, often considered late,[74] of *lᵉpānēnû,* with the same meaning.

---

69. R. Gordis, *Koheleth — The Man and His World* (New York: Schocken Books, 1951), p. 207.

70. Gordis, *Koheleth,* p. 207; followed by Hertzberg, *Der Prediger,* pp. 68, 74-75; and Isaksson, *Studies in the Language of Qoheleth,* p. 108.

71. Whybray, *Ecclesiastes,* NCB, p. 45.

72. Fredericks, *Qoheleth's Language,* pp. 184, 228; cf. pp. 171-75, 260. A "Mishnaism" is a Hebrew word or grammatical feature that bears similarity in form and/or meaning to one that occurs in postbiblical Hebrew.

73. Crenshaw (*Ecclesiastes,* p. 68) and Whitley (*Koheleth,* p. 11) cite analogues to the plural *lᵉᶜōlāmîm* governed by a singular verb.

74. Whybray, *Ecclesiastes,* NCB, p. 46.

Thus, the verse rebuts the objection that new things take place on the earth by asserting that what appears new to people has happened before. They just forget about it. In any case, even if it is granted that new discoveries are made, people remain the same.

11 This verse explains why what appears novel to us is really not new but a repeat of something old. Old things seem new to us because we have forgotten or are ignorant of them. Writing a commentary on a biblical book is a good example. During research the scholar might grow excited at a new discovery only to find the same thought expressed by previous writers on the subject.

But the verse does more than depress us with our ignorance of the past in the present. It reminds us that we should not expect anything different in the future. Those generations that follow us will be ignorant of who we are and what we are doing just as we are ignorant of the past and of those who preceded us. Thus, significance is not located in the past or the future, or even the present. The prologue concludes here on this depressing note.

Disagreements exist over the exact referent for *of the past . . . in the future*. There is no doubt that *rî˒šōnîm* (literally, "the first") points to the past and *˒aḥᵃrōnîm* (literally, "the last") indicates the future. Some, however, look at the masculine endings and claim that "people" are meant. James Crenshaw,[75] for example, believes that the referent must be personal because an impersonal referent would be indicated by the feminine plural. This contention, however, is disputed by the use of the masculine plural ending elsewhere to indicate nonpersonal referents (Exod. 34:1; Num. 6:12). Actually, the form could indicate either things or people. The fact that the previous verse had denied the possibility of a "new thing" makes the former more likely.

II. QOHELET'S AUTOBIOGRAPHICAL SPEECH (1:12–12:7)

A new narrative voice is heard in 1:12. Qohelet himself speaks for the first time. This section continues until there is a shift from the first person to the third person in 12:8. Qohelet's reflections on life and his wisdom admonitions, therefore, constitute the body of the book.

75. Crenshaw, *Ecclesiastes,* p. 68.

A. AUTOBIOGRAPHICAL INTRODUCTION (1:12)

12 *I,*[76] *Qohelet, have been king over Israel in Jerusalem.*

12 This verse follows the pattern of autobiographical introductions in Egypt, Syria, and especially Mesopotamia.[77]

Much weight has been placed on the perfective aspect of *hāyâ (have been),* and commentators have been quick to point to this as unusual.[78] One more readily expects an imperfect (or perhaps an imperfect or nominal sentence), indicating English present tense, for a king who was still living. The appearance of the verb in the perfect has led to a number of different hypotheses. First, one of the oldest explanations is that given in the rabbinic tradition, as exemplified by the Targum.[79] The Aramaic translation (see quote on p. 3) fills in the narrative gaps by stating that the demon Ashmodai seduced King Solomon from the throne. Thus, for a period, it was appropriate for the living Solomon to say that he "was" king. This view is virtually impossible to maintain from the historical books. Second, another school of thought argues that the perfect aspect of the verb is a textual signal for royal fiction that the author here adopts (see "Authorship" in the introduction).[80] Third, more recently, scholars have recognized that the verb in the perfect can have the force "have been and still is."[81] Nonetheless, normally the verb describes a completed action in the past and is well rendered by the English perfect *(have been).*

The phrase *king over Israel in Jerusalem* is similar to the formula in 1:1 (see comments there). Here, however, *over Israel* is new. This addition assures the reader that the speaker meant to indicate Solomon. Besides David,

---

76. *I* (*ʾanî*) occurs twenty-nine times in Ecclesiastes, as opposed to "I" (*ʾānōkî*), which never appears. The exclusive use of *ʾanî* has been taken as an indication that the book is late (D. Lys, *L'Ecclésiaste ou Que vaut la vie?* [Paris: Letouzey et Ané, 1977], p. 143). Fredericks (*Qoheleth's Language,* pp. 141-46) disputes Lys's attempt to date the book on the basis of what he considers to be a simple stylistic variation that has no bearing on when the book was written.

77. See T. Longman III, *Fictional Akkadian Autobiography* (Winona Lake, IN: Eisenbrauns, 1991). See also the discussion in the introduction under "Structure" and "Genre."

78. See discussions by Crenshaw, *Ecclesiastes,* p. 71; Murphy, *Ecclesiastes,* p. 13; Leupold, *Exposition of Ecclesiastes,* pp. 51-52.

79. E. Levine, *The Aramaic Version of Qohelet* (New York: Sepher-Hermon, 1978), pp. 28, 49.

80. O. Loretz, "Zur Darbietungsform der 'Ich-Erzählung' im Buche Qohelet," *CBQ* 25 (1963): 46-59; and *Qohelet und der Alte Orient* (Freiburg: Herder, 1964).

81. So Isaksson, *Studies in the Language of Qoheleth,* pp. 50-51.

whose son Qohelet is, only Solomon ruled over Israel from Jerusalem, because the divided kingdom began with his successor, Rehoboam.

B. "SOLOMON'S" QUEST FOR THE MEANING OF LIFE (1:13–2:26)

The first major section of Qohelet's autobiography recounts his vain search for meaning in life. After brief reflection on his search, he narrates how he looked for meaning in pleasure, wisdom, and folly, as well as in his work. Nonetheless, the spectre of death hangs over his head, making empty his achievements and successes. At the end, he concludes that if this life offers anything at all, it is in the occasional moments of joy in the simple pleasures of life.

1. Introductory Reflections (1:13-18)

13 *I devoted myself to search and to explore wisely*[82] *all that is done under heaven. It is an evil task that God has given to the human race to keep them occupied.*

14 *I observed all that is done*[83] *under the sun. And really,*[84] *it is all meaningless and a chasing of the wind.*

15 *What is bent cannot be straightened;*
   what is missing cannot be counted.

16 *I said to myself, "I have surpassed in wisdom everyone who ruled Jerusalem before me. I have observed all forms of wisdom and knowledge."*

17 *I devoted myself*[85] *to understand wisdom and knowledge, madness and folly. I understood that this is also a chasing of the wind.*

---

82. See Waltke and O'Connor, *Biblical Hebrew Syntax*, pp. 196-97, §11.2.5d, who describe the preposition as a *beth comitantiae-mental* that may be rendered as an adverb.

83. See Isaksson, *Studies in the Language of Qoheleth*, pp. 69-74, for an extended discussion of the translation of the niphal of *'āśâ*.

84. So translating *hinnēh*, which often functions as an attention getter. This and other functions of *hinnēh* are described in A. Berlin, *Poetics and Interpretation of Biblical Narrative* (Sheffield, England: Almond, 1983), pp. 91-95.

85. Here the same idiom recurs from 1:13 except that the verb is an imperfective with a prefixed *wā*, as opposed to the perfective form. Isaksson (*Studies in the Language of Qoheleth*, pp. 58-63) has a lengthy but extremely helpful discussion of the sequence of verbal aspect and determines that the imperfective form is used here due to the influence of the direct speech in the previous verse.

18 *For with much wisdom comes much frustration;*[86]
he who adds to knowledge adds to pain.

After introducing himself in v. 12, Qohelet describes his search and anticipates his depressing conclusion. This section may be subdivided into two parts: vv. 13-15 and vv. 16-18. In vv. 13-15 Qohelet describes his wisdom task, concluding with the expression "trying to catch the wind" followed by a proverbial saying. The same pattern holds true for vv. 16-18. Roland Murphy[87] provides the following helpful outline:

I. First Reflection	vv. 13-15
A. Statement of the vanity of pursuing wisdom	vv. 13-14
B. A proverb quoted in support	v. 15
II. Second Reflection	vv. 16-18
A. Statement of the vanity of pursuing wisdom	vv. 16-17
B. A proverb quoted in support	v. 18

13 Qohelet informs the reader of his task as well as his negative feelings toward it. The scope of his enterprise is incredibly extensive — everything done on earth. In this way, he implies that his conclusions admit no exceptions or possibility of reversal once further facts come to light. He will carry through this program in the first few chapters, in particular, as he examines different meanings for existence. He anticipates his negative conclusions by calling his work an *evil task* that God has imposed not only on him but also on the entire human race. The task is evil because no solution is found after much hard work. The search leads to frustration rather than resolution.

The idiom *I devoted myself* occurs in 1:17; 8:9, 16. It is formed from the verb *nātan* with *lēb* "heart" as the direct object.[88] *Nātan* is a frequently occurring verb with the basic meaning of "to give," but in the present idiom it means "to set" or "to determine." As is well known, *lēb* refers not to the emotions, as in English, but to the mind and will, or even the core of one's personality (e.g., Ps. 131:1).[89] Qohelet thus uses the idiom to indicate his focused, deeply personal, disciplined pursuit of the object of his study.

86. The Septuagint misreads as "knowledge" *(gnōseōs)*, but it was corrected by the later Greek translations of Aquila, Symmachus, and Theodotion; see J. Jarick, *Gregory Thaumaturgos' Paraphrase,* SBLSCS 29 (Atlanta: Scholars Press, 1990), p. 26.

87. R. E. Murphy, *Wisdom Literature: Job, Proverbs, Ruth, Canticles, Ecclesiastes, and Esther,* FOTL (Grand Rapids, MI: Eerdmans, 1981), p. 134.

88. *BHS* suggests emending 7:25 (see commentary) to include a form of *nātan* before *libbî,* which would add a fifth occurrence.

89. Cf. BDB, p. 525.

Qohelet uses two infinite constructs, *to search and to explore,* to describe the method of his study. The first *(lidrôš)* is by far the more common. It has a well-known cultic connection in other contexts where God is the object of searching ("to seek the Lord").[90] Here, however, the object of his study is *all that is done under heaven.*

The second verb, *to explore (tûr),* is less common and has a narrower semantic range than the first. Its most distinctive usage occurs in the story of the spies sent into the promised land in the early stage of the wilderness wanderings (Num. 13:2, 16, 17, 21, 25, 32; 14:6, 7, 34, 36, 38). These chapters color most commentators' understanding of the use of the verb in Ecclesiastes (note its use also in Eccles. 2:3; 7:25), including the present one. For instance, Ernst Hengstenberg believes that in some passages (i.e., Num. 10:33; Deut. 1:33; Ezek. 20:6) the verb has a broader meaning than "to search out" or "to explore" and suggests a meaning "to try thoroughly" or "to test."[91] These three passages, however, have God as their subject, and so Hengstenberg may have felt it inappropriate to conceive of God as a spy searching out an area as if he did not know it already. The best understanding of these passages, though, is that they are anthropomorphisms (i.e., they speak of God as if he were an ordinary human). God is at the head of the tribes preparing the way for them, discovering campsites and preceding them into the promised land.

These two verbs, *to search* and *to explore,* are thus near synonyms, and to differentiate the two, while possible, is somewhat tenuous. Nevertheless, some commentators attempt to do so. George Barton, for instance, claims that " 'search' means to investigate the roots of a matter, and 'explore' to investigate a subject on all sides."[92] Robert Gordis[93] says that the first verb means "to penetrate to the root of the matter," and the second, "to investigate it from all sides." Also, Hengstenberg differentiates the two verbs on the basis of the deepness *(drš)* and wideness *(tûr)* of the search.[94] Again, I regard such fine distinctions as tenuous and lacking semantic defense.

Since *wisely* is actually a prepositional phrase *(be* plus the noun *ḥokmâ),* it could alternatively be rendered "by" or "through wisdom." Wisdom is an important theme in the book (see "Theological Message" in the introduction). The frame narrator later refers to Qohelet as a wise man *(ḥākām)* in the epilogue (12:9). Here Qohelet says that his study was characterized and guided by wisdom. In this way, he shows his continuity with the wisdom tradition of Israel as it is

90. G. Schaeffer, "The Significance of Seeking God in the Purpose of the Chronicler" (Ph.D. dissertation, Southern Baptist Theological Seminary, 1972).

91. Hengstenberg, *A Commentary on Ecclesiastes,* p. 61.

92. So Barton, *The Book of Ecclesiastes,* p. 78.

93. Gordis, *Koheleth,* p. 209.

94. Hengstenberg, *A Commentary on Ecclesiastes,* pp. 61-63.

exemplified particularly in a book like Proverbs. He immediately demonstrates radical discontinuity with the wisdom teachers of Proverbs, however, when he calls his task *evil* in this verse and later when he questions the traditional claim that wisdom brings life (cf. Prov. 8:35). He apparently rejects that view, believing rather that in the light of death wisdom is meaningless (2:13-16).

The object of his study is comprehensive — *all that is done under heaven,* that is, all activity on earth. We must remember, however, that he believes that there is nothing new on earth. The present and the future bring nothing new, so if the present is meaningless, the future will bring nothing to change that unhappy prospect.

The phrase *under heaven* is a rough synonym for "under the sun," for it is similarly used in the book of Ecclesiastes (cf. 1:3). Some Hebrew manuscripts and a number of versions replace "under heaven" with the more common "under the sun," but this is probably an overcorrection caused by the more common occurrence of the latter phrase in the book.

Lively discussion continues about the phrase *evil task . . . to keep them occupied,* which has great importance in determining Qohelet's frame of mind as he reflects on his study. The first issue concerns the four possible roots from which we are to derive the noun *'inyān.* Most Hebrew dictionaries list four verbs with the root consonants *'nh* (the most obvious verbal root for the noun *'inyān*): (1) "to answer" (qal); (2) "to humble, subdue" (piel); (3) "to be busy, to be concerned about"; and (4) "to sing."[95] Options (1) and (4) do not fit the context, but either (2) or (3) is possible both for the noun and for the verb that follows. The noun occurs in the OT only in Ecclesiastes (see also 3:10), but it occurs a number of times in later rabbinic materials in the sense of "task, situation, occupation, affair."[96] Thus, it seems safest to go with this meaning, rather than something like "affliction."[97]

The adjective *rā'* casts a negative nuance over the task God has given humanity. The Hebrew word, however, can mean everything from "bad" to "evil." As representing the former pole, the NIV translates the phrase "a heavy burden," and the NRSV, "an unhappy business." In my opinion, these translations ill fit the acerbic attitude of Qohelet (see "Theological Message" in the introduction).[98] *evil* is a translation more in keeping with Qohelet's subtle criticism of God throughout the book (cf. commentary on 4:17–5:6 [English 5:1-7]).

95. BDB, pp. 772-76; see Crenshaw, *Ecclesiastes,* p. 72.

96. Cf. M. Jastrow, Jr.. *Dictionary of the Targumim Babli Yerushalmi and Midrashic Literature* (New York: Shalom, 1967), p. 1095.

97. With Murphy, *Ecclesiastes,* p. 11; Crenshaw, *Ecclesiastes,* pp. 72-73.

98. Though it does not decide the issue, it is interesting to note that the word has moral overtones more frequently than not in the Hebrew Bible. See G. H. Livingston, *"ra',"* in *TWOT,* vol. 2 (Chicago: Moody, 1980), pp. 855-56.

14 Qohelet proceeds to inform the reader why the task God has given the human race, and in particular himself, is evil. In this verse he tells us that even after he has examined everything under the sun he could find no meaning.

By the use of *I observed* Qohelet signals to us that he bases his conclusions on personal experience in the world.[99] He does not appeal to revelation or any kind of special insight into God or the world, even though the task that he has undertaken is divinely mandated (1:13). See 1:13 for *all that is done*.

under the sun. The synonymous phrase was used in the previous verse. This is the first occasion that Qohelet himself (as opposed to the unnamed frame narrator) uses the phrase. For its meaning, see 1:3. The literary effect is to link the two writers, as if to underscore their common understanding of the arena in which Qohelet operates. For *meaningless,* see 1:2.

The precise translation of the frequent refrain *chasing the wind* (see also 2:11, 17, 26; 4:4, 6; 6:9) is elusive, but its interpretation is not. At issue is the meaning and underlying root of the key word *reʿût* (*raʿyôn* in 1:17; 2:22; 4:16). Hebrew has four different roots with the consonants *rʿh*: (1) "to feed," "to shepherd," "to tend," "to herd"; (2) "to associate with"; (3) "to strive": and (4) "to desire."[100] The last is connected to an Aramaic root *(reʿût)* found in Ezra 5:17 and 7:18. It is also possible to derive *reʿût* from the Hebrew root *rʿʿ* "to break," and understand the abstract nominal form in the metaphorical sense as "vexation" and the *rûaḥ* as "spirit," with the resulting translation "vexation of the spirit." A survey of other commentaries shows a general consensus that these are the options, as well as an appropriate tentativeness in choosing one of the possibilities over the others.[101]

Hosea 12:2 (English 12:1) may help solve the problem. The same idiom occurs in this passage and in parallel with "chases *(rādap)* the east wind." This parallel has led some, including the present translation, to understand the verb *rāʾâ* as close in meaning to *rādap*. We cannot have the same level of certainty as past interpreters, however, because recent studies of parallelism have shown that there is always progression between the first and the second cola of a poetic line.[102] Thus, the NIV translates Hosea 12:2a (English 12:1a), "Ephraim feeds on the wind."

Though I translate "chases," the meaning of the line is clear whichever

---

99. That this is a major emphasis in Qohelet's thought may be seen by the fact that he uses the first-person qal perfect of *rʿh* in eighteen other texts (Eccles. 2:13, 24; 3:10, 16, 22; 4:1, 4, 15; 5:12, 17 [English 5:13, 18]; 6:1; 7:15; 8:9, 10, 17; 9:13; 10:5, 7).

100. BDB, pp. 944-46.

101. See, for instance, Crenshaw (*Ecclesiastes,* p. 68), who translates "shepherding the wind" but notes other options as possible; and Murphy (*Ecclesiastes,* pp. 11-12), who chooses the rendition "chasing the wind," with similar hesitation.

102. As Kugel argues in *The Idea of Biblical Poetry.*

option is chosen. Whether it is "chasing," "striving after," "feeding," or "herding" the wind (or for that matter "vexation of spirit"), the point is that life on earth is futile and frustrating. In this way, the phrase reinforces the conclusion that life is *hebel, meaningless.*

15 Two characteristics identify this verse as a proverbial saying. The first is its parallel structure, formally differentiating it from its literary context. The syntactical order of each parallel line is nearly identical, beginning with the subject, followed by the same negated verb *(lō' yûkal),* and ending with an infinitive construct with a prefixed preposition *lamed.* The second trait is its slightly enigmatic character. The saying is both pithy and thought provoking, features typical of proverbs.

In summary, the thrust of the verse is that there is something fundamentally wrong with life on earth, and, since the world as it is has come about as a result of God's will (v. 13), there is absolutely nothing that humans can do about it.

Verse 14 informed us that the scope of Qohelet's observations encompasses the whole world, so, in the context, *what is bent* and *what is missing* must refer to everything on earth. *bent* is the translation of a pual participle from *'wt* ("to make crooked"). The word can have a moral meaning: "crooked" in the sense of wicked or perverted. Indeed, Graham Ogden[103] points to Proverbs 12:8 and Job 33:27 to argue for such a meaning, but the context, which is describing what is done on the earth, and the verse's closest parallel in 7:13, which explicitly makes God the agent of the "bending," militates against such a view.[104] This is the reason why I avoid the translation "crooked," which might easily be misunderstood to carry a moral connotation.

be straightened is a qal infinitive construct of *tqn* ("to become straight"). The verb occurs in the OT only in Ecclesiastes (1:15; 7:13; 12:9); the last two occurrences are in the piel. In Mishnaic Hebrew it occurs only in the piel and hiphil. The fact that our present verse demands a passive meaning has led many to emend it to a niphal infinitive construct (see *BHS*) or possibly a pual.[105] Hans Hertzberg rejects any emendation and stays with what he considers the most difficult reading.[106] After all, there are analogies of qal verbs that carry a passive sense.[107] In any case, the sense of the verse suggests that the verb has a passive sense.

what is missing is an abstract noun form, usually taken as a late form

103. Ogden, *Qoheleth,* pp. 35-36.
104. Note that Ogden (*Qoheleth,* p. 35) states that the root of the verb is *'wh,* not *'wt* (with the lexicons).
105. G. R. Driver, "Problems and Solutions," *VT* 4 (1954): 225.
106. Hertzberg, *Der Prediger,* p. 78.
107. Whitley, *Koheleth,* pp. 13-14.

found elsewhere only in the Mishnah, but this is disputed by Daniel Fredericks, who shows that it comes from a common biblical root *(ḥsr).*[108]

As James Crenshaw points out,[109] the second colon expresses a "truism," since it is obvious that if something is missing it cannot *be counted.* The essentially flawed nature of the world is something self-evident and cannot be disputed.

16 This verse introduces the second introductory reflection. Here Qohelet presents his credentials. He sounds rather presumptuous in his claims of unsurpassed wisdom, but that is not the point. The point is, if *he* cannot find meaning in or through wisdom, then who can? It is here that we see the importance of the Solomonic fiction as well as its transparency. Solomon was the paradigmatic wise king in Israel. As such, he was wealthy and wise. If Solomon could not find happiness in his wisdom (and the historical books reckon his reign as ultimately unsuccessful, planting seeds of division in the kingdom), then no one else can. The transparency of the connection with Solomon may be seen in the elusive manner by which Qohelet associates himself with that king. He never comes out and states he is Solomon, always saying it vaguely enough to signal distance between himself and that king.

I said to myself is literally, "I spoke with my mind (heart)" *(dibbartî ᵃnî ᶜim-libbî).* There is a similar expression of interior dialogue found in Ecclesiastes 2:1; 3:17, 18. The noun *dābār* (related to the verb *dbr* "spoke") with the expression *ᶜim-libbî* ("with/in my mind") is found in Deuteronomy 15:9, Joshua 14:7, and Psalm 77:7 and refers to one's thought life.

The first-person pronoun is pleonastic here, but its function is not clear. Most pleonastic occurrences of the pronoun are thought to be emphatic, and perhaps that is the force of its use in the present verse.[110]

There are really two Hebrew verbs behind *I have surpassed.* They are near synonyms brought together as a hendiadys (the hiphils of *gdl* and *ysp,* literally, "I have made myself great and have enhanced"), thus illustrating Qohelet's love of using two nearly synonymous terms, perhaps again, like the use of repetition in general, lending literary support to the message that life is essentially repetitive and boring.

everyone who ruled Jerusalem before me is literally "over everyone who was before me over Jerusalem." This enigmatic expression has led to different interpretations. The first takes its key from the preposition before

---

108. Fredericks, *Qoheleth's Language,* pp. 181-82.

109. Crenshaw, *Ecclesiastes,* p. 74.

110. Indeed, Waltke and O'Connor (*Biblical Hebrew Syntax,* p. 296) cite T. Muraoka (*Emphatic Words and Structures in Biblical Hebrew* [Leiden: Brill; Jerusalem: Magnes, 1985], p. 58), when they discuss pronouns that occur after verbs and involve "psychological focus" or impart a sense of "profound meditation."

Jerusalem, translated *over* (*'al*). It indicates more than existence or citizenship in Jerusalem; it is the preposition used in formulas indicating rulership (see 1:12). The problem, however, is that the only Israelite king to rule over Jerusalem before Solomon was David, thus making his claim somewhat silly. Perhaps, however, this places too much weight on the preposition, and Qohelet thus only claims that his wisdom surpasses any previous inhabitant of Jerusalem. Second, the Septuagint suggests such an approach by translating "in Jerusalem." Retroversion would suggest a different Hebrew preposition than the one represented in *BHS,* and indeed there are some Hebrew manuscripts that show *beth* ("in") rather than *'al.* It is more likely, however, that the Greek translators and later copyists were simply struggling with the same issues that the preposition *'al* poses for us today. They were pressing the language too hard, not realizing that this is a loose association with Solomon, not a strict identification, and, therefore, we need not worry about his lack of many royal predecessors.[111]

Ancient readers would have recognized the literary device. The author alludes here and elsewhere to Solomon to further his argument, but the fiction is presented in an intentionally obvious way.

The verb *I have observed* (from *rā'â* "to see") shows the empirical nature of Qohelet's method of investigation (see 1:14). It would be foolhardy to try to press too fine a distinction between the nouns *wisdom* and *knowledge.* They are both used frequently in the wisdom tradition, as Proverbs attests. Qohelet again uses two nearly synonymous words together in order to make his point emphatically. It serves as a hendiadys, meaning "full knowledge."

17 Qohelet now relates the first of his searches for meaning. He tells us that he studied both wisdom and folly without saying why he studied both. Perhaps he looked for meaning or pleasure in one or the other. Perhaps he studied both in order to differentiate wisdom from folly and follow the former. Or perhaps he is attempting to be truly objective, or to get the full picture since wisdom and folly are two sides of the same coin. In any case, his search, by his own admission, was a failure.

Translators of Ecclesiastes disagree on the proper rendition of the phrase here translated *to understand wisdom and knowledge, madness and folly.* The present translation follows the Septuagint and the Targum, which take the second *da'at* as a noun (similar to REB, NAB, and NJB). The MT verse division understands it to be a second infinitive construct with the prefixed preposition on the first serving double duty (so NRSV, "And I applied my mind to know wisdom and to know madness and folly").

Though the versions understand the division of words correctly, they

111. See discussion in Hertzberg, *Der Prediger,* p. 84.

nevertheless misunderstand the meaning of some of the words. The Septuagint, for instance, has "parables" for "madness." As Gordis[112] explains, this is an inner-Septuagintal error on the part of a copyist, who probably heard the word wrongly, since the correct translation was *paraphoras,* which means "errors," rather than *parabolas.*

The Greek translators also misunderstood the word "folly" because of its unique spelling. Here it is spelled with an initial *ś,* rather than its usual *s,* as in 2:3, 13; 7:25; 10:1, 13. Thus, the translators incorrectly took it from the verbal root *śkl* "to be wise," rather than seeing it as a by-form of *siklût (folly).*

18 The second reflection, like the first, concludes with a proverbial saying, easily identified by its pithy parallelism. With the exception of the introductory particle *(kî, for),* every word occurs either twice or with a close synonym.

This verse does not summarize Qohelet's attitude before his search, the point from which he presses on,[113] but rather reflects negatively on the process and the conclusions of his search for meaning. Beginning with the next verse, Qohelet goes back and describes the search in more detail.

Proverbs emphasizes that wisdom brings joy and life. Qohelet begs to differ, complaining that it brings *frustration* and *pain.* R. N. Whybray[114] hypothesizes that the origin of this proverb may be discovered by comparison with Egyptian wisdom, which describes the physical pain a student endures at the hand of his teacher. It is, however, impossible to determine whether the proverb is created or quoted by Qohelet. It is most likely that the suffering Qohelet envisions as the result of an increase in knowledge is mental anguish, not corporal punishment.

SUMMARY OF CHAPTER 1

The first chapter of Ecclesiastes has two major sections. Verses 1-11, which I call the prologue, come from the unnamed frame narrator, who first intro-duces the main speaker of the book by means of a superscription (v. 1). He continues by anticipating Qohelet's mood and conclusions (vv. 2-11). We see here for the first time refrains, which are common throughout the book (e.g., "meaningless," "under the sun," "what profit?") and other phrases that are among the most memorable in the book (e.g., "there is nothing new under the sun"). In context, these phrases highlight the somber mood of Qohelet.

112. Gordis, *Koheleth,* p. 212.
113. Contra Ogden, *Qoheleth,* p. 37.
114. Whybray, *Ecclesiastes,* NCB, p. 51.

One of the main themes of these verses is the monotonous sameness of the world in spite of the illusion of change.

The second part of the first chapter (vv. 12-18) begins the speech of the main speaker of the book, Qohelet. After a traditional autobiographical introduction (v. 12), Qohelet reports in retrospect on his search for meaning. He anticipates its negative conclusion at the very beginning (v. 14). He then recounts different areas in which he sought meaning in life, beginning with wisdom and folly (v. 17), and through the artful use of two proverbs (vv. 15 and 18), he reports that he was unable to find ultimate meaning in either.

In this chapter, Qohelet reveals his disappointment with God. God has given humanity in general and Qohelet in particular "an evil task" (v. 13). His initial comments about meaning "under the sun" are negative and show his frustration. In the next chapter, he will continue his search for meaning in life.

2. The Pursuit of Meaning in Pleasure (2:1-11)

Qohelet turns from his consideration of wisdom and folly to pleasure. He hoped to find meaning in pleasure and sets out to test its possibilities. Even before narrating the exact contours of his quest, he tells us his conclusion: it is meaningless.

Nonetheless, he continues to explain both the search and his conclusion is some detail. The pleasure that Qohelet explores is self-oriented. He tried to find joy in drinking and sex. He also used his great wealth to build for himself a great house and grounds. He had many servants. In spite of all of his efforts to find meaning in such self-seeking pleasures, he failed.

Roland Murphy rightly identified this section as a reflection.[1] Qohelet here looks back on his actions as he sought to find meaning in pleasure and carefully considers their significance.

> 1 *I said to myself,[2] "Come on, I will now test you with pleasure and experience the good life." But this too proved meaningless.*
> 2 *I thought, "Laughter is madness[3] and pleasure — what can it[4] do?"*

1. Murphy, *Wisdom Literature*, pp. 134-35. On p. 181 Murphy defines the reflection as a genre that "states a thesis or goal which the writer considers and evaluates in a very personal way."

2. See the comments on the near parallel phrase in 1:16.

3. This word derives from the same root as the word in 1:17. This is an instance of a poal participle.

4. *zōh* is a feminine singular demonstrative pronoun. The issue is that here and elsewhere in Ecclesiastes *zōh* stands for *z'ōt*. This is often taken as a Mishnaism, but for counterarguments, see Fredericks, *Qoheleth's Language*, p. 100.

3 *Still guided by wisdom, I mentally explored by cheering myself with wine and embracing folly until I could see what[5] was good for people to do under heaven during the few days of their life.*

4 *I did great works. I built for myself houses and planted for myself vineyards.*

5 *I made for myself gardens and parks. I planted every kind of fruit tree in them.*

6 *I made for myself pools to water the flourishing forest of trees.*

7 *I acquired male and female servants, and I had house-born servants as well. I also acquired herds and flocks. I had more than anyone before me in Jerusalem.[6]*

8 *I also amassed for myself silver and gold, the treasure of kings and provinces.[7] I gathered[8] for myself male and female singers and many concubines — the pleasure of humankind.*

9 *I surpassed[9] all who lived before me in Jerusalem, and all the while, my wisdom stayed with me.*

10 *I did not refuse myself anything that my eyes desired. I did not hold myself back from any pleasure that made me feel happy in all my toil. This was my reward from all my toil.*

11 *But then I turned my attention to[10] all the acts that my hands performed*

---

5. The context helps us translate this phrase. It is not a typical use of the expression *'ē-zeh*. See Waltke and O'Connor, *Biblical Hebrew Syntax,* p. 327; and Crenshaw, *Ecclesiastes,* p. 78.

6. This verse has a number of minor textual variations. For instance, some manuscripts add *lî* ("to me") after the initial verb. This is an unnecessary addition motivated by the frequent occurrence of *lî* in this section of Ecclesiastes. Also note that the first occurrence of *hāyâ (had)* in this verse is a singular in the MT but plural in some Hebrew manuscripts, the Septuagint, and the Syriac version, but this is an unnecessary emendation (cf. GKC §145u). Lastly, the second occurrence of *hāyâ (had)* is unnecessarily emended from plural to singular on the basis of a number of manuscripts and versions.

7. There is an anomaly in the use of the article here. The article does not appear prefixed to *kings,* but it is prefixed to *provinces.* For different emendations and suggestions that have been proposed, see Whitley, *Koheleth,* p. 21. Gordis ("The Original Language of Qohelet," *JQR* 37 [1946-47]: 81-83; and *Koheleth,* p. 218) indicates that the article is used unusually in Ecclesiastes.

8. This translates the common Hebrew verb *'āśâ* according to its context. The difficulty is that in English we do not speak of someone "making" a choir.

9. The verse is similar to 1:16 with the exception that the first verb in this verse is in the qal, not the hiphil. Note Lys (*L'Ecclésiaste,* p. 217): "La juxtaposition des deux verbes de même sens constitue une sorte de superlatif." ("The juxtaposition of two verbs with the same sense constitutes a type of superlative.")

10. For *pānâ* in this meaning and followed unusually by the preposition *beth,* see Job 6:28.

and to the toil that I toiled hard to do. Indeed, they were all meaningless and like trying to catch the wind. There was no profit under the sun.

1 The section begins with Qohelet's announcement that he will explore the real value of pleasure. He will narrate what he means specifically in the following verses, but for now he simply states his intention and anticipates his ultimate conclusion. There is no lasting meaning in the pursuit of pleasure.

The verse appropriately introduces a reflection on life. It is a conversation between Qohelet and his "personified mind."[11] He speaks to himself and urges himself into action with the command to "come on" *(lᵉkâ nā').*

The verbal root of *I will test you* is *nāsâ,* not *nāsak* as it is taken in the Vulgate *(affluam).* The ending is a full spelling of the second-person pronominal ending and refers to Qohelet's mind or inner voice.

It is true that the word *pleasure (śimḥâ)* can denote joy arising from indisputably moral behavior, for instance, the joy in God and worshipping him,[12] but the examples that follow indicate that Qohelet is speaking of a more sensual, material joy.

The good life is a rather modern rendition of the Hebrew phrase, which is simply the common word "good" *(ṭôb).* The word occurs frequently in Ecclesiastes, and the precise nuance must be gleaned from the context.

2 Qohelet here continues his thought about the significance of pleasure. He pronounces judgment using two separate words, *laughter* and *pleasure,* which he used in v. 1. James Crenshaw[13] is likely right in regarding the first as indicating superficial joy, and the second as indicating a more profound joy, though the latter is used of both throughout the Bible. In any case, whether they are used synonymously or with different nuances, the force of the verse is to deny the possibility of meaning through pleasure.

Proverbs noted that *laughter* and *pleasure* often hide grief and sorrow (14:13). Indeed, Proverbs frequently pictures fools laughing on the road to destruction (10:23; 26:19; 29:9). Nonetheless, the wise, and even Lady Wisdom herself, laugh (1:26; 8:30, 31; 31:25). The difference between the fool and the wise person in Proverbs is the timing of their laughter and its object. While Qohelet recognizes that there is an appropriate time for laughter (Eccles. 3:4), he also notes that the wise person cannot discern the times (see 8:8; 9:11, 12; 10:14). So here in 2:2, as well as 7:3, 6, and 10:19, Qohelet denigrates laughter.

3 Qohelet now specifies his exploration of pleasure as a source of meaning or profit in life, beginning with the most sensual one, alcohol. He is

11. Crenshaw, *Ecclesiastes,* p. 176.
12. So Lys, *L'Ecclésiaste,* pp. 180-81.
13. Crenshaw, *Ecclesiastes,* p. 77.

looking for something worthwhile, something meaningful in the short years that human beings have on this earth.

The verse is very difficult to translate smoothly, but its general sense is quite clear. He began by *cheering himself with wine.* The verb here translated *cheering* has been widely discussed. The basic meaning of the root *mšk* is "to pull" or "to drag." Some argue that the meaning here is like that found in the Talmud, "to refresh," but Daniel Fredericks debates this.[14] Still others contend that the word is the result of metathesis and should be read from the root *śmk* (see *BHS*). The difficulty in this reconstruction is that the initial sibilant is wrong, so proponents must also posit a by-form. A third approach is that of Godfrey Driver,[15] who cites Aramaic and Arabic cognates with the meaning "to sustain," but R. Norman Whybray correctly criticizes this view.[16] Whybray takes his key from the context and admits that the precise sense and etymology of the verb leave the interpreter with questions.[17]

Most, especially conservative, interpreters are careful to preserve Qohelet's dignity in this experiment with wine. For instance, Leupold[18] emphasizes that Qohelet explored wine "not as a debauchee, but as a connoisseur." His textual clue is the phrase *still guided by wisdom.* Leupold thus finds it hard to believe that Qohelet ever drank so much as to be intoxicated. While we cannot be sure one way or the other, the phrase indicates only that Qohelet is carefully weighing the significance of the act as it relates to his overall search for meaning, not that he always retained his rational abilities. As with *cheering,* some have argued that the primary biblical Hebrew meaning of *nāhag* (here translated as *guided*) does not appear to be operative. Charles Whitley,[19] for instance, says that the verb normally means "to drive" or "to lead," while here it seems to have the sense of "to behave," which was its meaning in later Hebrew. Fredericks[20] once again takes issue with the argument that this verb is an indication of a late date of composition. In any case, the meaning *guide* is appropriate to the context and is listed in the dictionaries as a well-attested meaning in the qal.

Qohelet does indeed describe his experiment by saying *he mentally explored* the experience of at least heightened awareness, if not downright intoxication. Literally, this expression is rendered "I explored in my heart,"

---

14. Fredericks, *Qoheleth's Language,* p. 187.

15. G. R. Driver, "Problems and Solutions," pp. 225-26.

16. Whybray, *Ecclesiastes,* NCB, p. 53.

17. Even though we are left with difficulties, this is no reason to submit to the drastic emendation and rereadings offered by A. D. Corré, "A Reference to Epispasm in Koheleth," *VT* 4 (1954): 416-18.

18. Leupold, *Exposition of Ecclesiastes,* p. 60.

19. Whitley, *Koheleth,* pp. 19-20.

20. Fredericks, *Qoheleth's Language,* p. 188.

but "heart" is taken here in its typical idiomatic sense of "the center of one's mental activities."[21] For *explored,* consult the comments to 1:13.

It may be possible to establish that Qohelet is more than a connoisseur of fine wines by appeal to the phrase *embracing folly.* Michael Fox argues, along with *BHS,* that there is a textual error here, specifically, that the preposition *lamed* should be emended to the negative *lō'.* This is conjectural and not necessary. For *folly,* see the comments to its semantic equivalent, though phonological variant, in 1:17.

Qohelet specifies that the days of the human race are *few* on earth, and this comment fits in with his overall theme that death renders all human endeavor fruitless.

4 We now shift from the purely sensual and self-centered pleasure of alcohol to the more grandiose achievements of constructing large works. Qohelet built houses and planted vineyards. The language of this and the following verses (particularly the repeated *for myself*) makes it quite clear that Qohelet's efforts are still self-centered.

I did great works introduces the next few verses, which describe a number of Qohelet's building projects. Here we see the usefulness of the fictional association with Solomon. Who built more than he? His great building projects are clearly enumerated in the historical books (1 Kings 7:1-12; 9:15; 2 Chron. 8:1-6), and Song of Songs 8:1 (cf. 1 Chron. 27:27) associates Solomon with vineyards. If Solomon could find no significance or profit in his building activity, what hope was there for anyone else?

Adrian Verheij goes beyond this theory and posits that Qohelet here not only associates himself with Solomon by allusion but also with God. He notes that the language in this verse and the next two correspond closely to God's creation of the garden of Eden. He suggestively argues that "the passage can be read as referring to a failed attempt on the part of 'Qohelet' at creating something like Paradise."[22]

Note that at this point Qohelet is not talking about philanthropy or public building. The ethical dative *myself (lî)* occurs twice in this verse and a number of times in the verses that fill out this section. As Robert Gordis states, this building was for "the end of his own pleasure."[23]

5-6 These verses continue Qohelet's description of his viticultural endeavors begun in the previous verse. He built gardens and parks with every kind of fruit tree. He also constructed irrigation pools to provide the necessary water for their cultivation and growth.

21. See BDB, pp. 524-25.

22. A. J. C. Verheij, "Paradise Retried: On Qohelet 2:4-6," *JSOT* 50 (1991): 113-15.

23. Gordis, *Koheleth,* p. 217.

The language, particularly the plurals, emphasizes the magnificence of his works. The continued use of the ethical dative, *for myself (lî)*, further indicates Qohelet's self-orientation. His purpose is self-pleasure, not philanthropy.

In both verses, he uses the rather bland word *made*. Indeed, the language in these verses is rather uninteresting, with the exception of *parks*. The Hebrew word *pardēsîm* is apparently a loanword related to Persian *pair:daēza*. The word means "enclosure" and is also found in Nehemiah 2:8 and Song of Songs 4:13. Aarre Lauha[24] and George Barton[25] cite this word as evidence of a late date for the language in Ecclesiastes, but Daniel Fredericks argues otherwise.[26]

every kind of fruit tree in them reminds the attentive reader of the description of Eden found in Genesis 1:11, 29; 2:9, and once again heightens the magnificence of Qohelet's garden paradise.

7   Qohelet's large property holdings required many servants, and in this verse he tells us that he owned both male and female servants, whom he purchased, as well as their offspring, born while their parents were working for him; as a result, they also belonged to him. Genesis 15:3 and 17:12, 27 appear aware of such a distinction. Exodus 21:2-11 comments that, though a Hebrew slave only must serve for seven years, any children that he has during this time belong to his master. Furthermore, this verse mentions Qohelet's wealth of herds and flocks, concluding with a general statement of his unprecedented wealth.

Solomon, of course, had many slaves (1 Kings 10:5) as well as *herds and flocks*. The *herds* refer to large farm animals like cattle, while *flocks* indicate smaller livestock such as sheep and goats. The point is that Qohelet was very rich. Some scholars[27] take the lack of mention of horses as an indication that this is Solomonic fiction, since that king had a penchant for horses. This attempts to draw too much from the verse, though the conclusion is nonetheless correct.

anyone before me in Jerusalem. See 1:16.

8   Qohelet rounds off his description of sensual pleasures by reverting to three more items, returning to the level of sensuality noted in verse 3. First, he possesses great amounts of precious gold and silver, the money of his day. Second, he constructs a choir to regale himself. Third, he describes his sexual explorations.

First, he describes his royal *treasure (sᵉgullat)*. The term is often used

24. Lauha, *Kohelet*, p. 7.
25. Barton, *The Book of Ecclesiastes*, p. 52.
26. Fredericks, *Qoheleth's Language*, pp. 242-45.
27. For instance, Lauha, *Kohelet*, p. 50.

of Israel as God's treasured possession (Exod. 19:5; Deut. 7:6; 14:2; 26:18), but is also found elsewhere in the sense of precious goods (1 Chron. 29:3). The treasure is the product of foreign tribute *(the treasure of kings)* and of taxation *(and provinces)*. The latter has been debated because the Hebrew term seems to be late (for the irregular use of the article, see n. 7 in the translation). While many regard the word as a postexilic Aramaism, Fredericks gives evidence that it is preexilic.[28] In this case, it is probably best to regard it as a reference to Solomon's new administrative districts that he created in order to cut across traditional tribal boundaries. These districts were responsible for the monthly upkeep of the central state structure (1 Kings 4:7-19). Solomon's silver and gold reserves are mentioned in the historical books (1 Kings 10:14-25; 2 Chron. 9:27).

Qohelet also enjoyed music by creating a choir of mixed gender. It is possible that the fact that his choir was made up of men and women differentiates it from the cultic choirs, which would have been composed of levitical men only.

The final arena of sensual pleasure mentioned by Qohelet as part of his experimentation is sex. The allusion is somewhat indirect, but nonetheless clear. It is also fitting for Qohelet, who continues his Solomonic fiction. After all, Solomon was a well-known lover (1 Kings 11:1-3) whose sexual exploits contributed to his downfall. It would have been surprising in the extreme if this aspect of his life went unmentioned.

Nonetheless, the wording here is difficult. *many concubines* is a hapax legomenon and was treated in a variety of ways by the ancient versions. The Septuagint started things off on the wrong track by taking the word from an Aramaic root *(sdy,* "to pour out"), thus rendering the line "male and female wine stewards." In this it was followed by the Peshitta. The Vulgate, the Targum, and Aquila were close to the Septuagint in translating "goblet." The etymology of the word is unclear, but the context is not. The reference to women is supported by the following phrase, *the pleasure of humankind.* Possible etymologies, though, include *šdd* "to seize," supposing a reference to women seized in battle, or, much more likely, *šd* "breast," and thus a crude reference to women who are used for sexual pleasure only. The analogy that has often been drawn since the time of Ibn Ezra is to Judges 5:30 (see *BHS*), where the NIV translation of a "girl or two" hides the reference to the girls as "wombs," or perhaps, to speak frankly in modern obscenity, "cunts." In Ecclesiastes 2:8 we have the singular followed by the plural, which is likely a form of the plural (but see comments by Michael Fox.[29])

These *concubines* are called *the pleasure of humankind.* The term

28. Fredericks, *Qoheleth's Language,* p. 230.
29. Fox, *Qohelet and His Contradictions,* p. 181.

pleasure here refers to erotic pleasure as in Song of Songs 7:7, though it may also carry the broader reference to "luxury" as in Proverbs 19:10 and Micah 1:16; 2:9.

9 Verses 9-11 provide a kind of summary statement to this section on sensual pleasures. Verse 9 boasts that Qohelet lived better and celebrated life harder than anyone else. He did it while retaining his wisdom; that is, he kept his mind alert to evaluate possible benefits during the sensual experience.

The verse echoes the sentiment also expressed in 1:16 and 2:7. In 1:16 Qohelet asserts his superiority over all previous kings in the area of wisdom; 2:7, 9 do not restrict the claim of superiority explicitly to kings but extend it to everyone who lived in Jerusalem before him. Also, instead of wisdom, in 2:7 and 9 Qohelet claims that he *surpasses* others in the realm of material pleasures.

Once again, as in 2:3, Qohelet maintains that he remained wise even as he indulged in his pleasure. Edward Plumptre offers an analogy with Goethe in that he, like Qohelet, "analyzed his voluptuousness, and studied his own faculties of enjoyment."[30] For the translation of *'āmad lî* as "to stay with," compare its use in Ecclesiastes 8:3, Psalm 102:27, and Jeremiah 48:11.

10 Qohelet makes it clear in v. 10 that he exercised no restraint, no self-denial in his pursuit for meaning in sensual pleasure. In light of the preceding verses we may not limit his exploration to the "higher" pleasures. He explored fully the delights of wine, women, and song, as well as architecture and gardening. What is new in this verse is that Qohelet believed pleasure was a consequence of his efforts (see comment below on *reward*).

James Crenshaw[31] is correct in pointing out that his experiment is at odds with Numbers 15:39: "You will have these tassels to look at and so you will remember all the commands of the LORD, that you may obey them and not prostitute yourselves by going after the lusts of your own heart and eyes." The sentiment is also far from the statement of humility expressed by the psalmist in Psalm 131:1.

anything that my eyes desired is literally rendered "anything that my eyes requested." Whatever he wanted he got for himself, a sentiment that he repeats in the next sentence.

in all my toil. The preposition here is *min* and not the usual *bᵉ*. This led some ancient copyists to emend the text accordingly (see the note in *BHS*). There are analogies, however, elsewhere in the biblical text (Prov. 5:18; 2 Chron. 20:27).[32]

---

30. E. H. Plumptre, *Ecclesiastes; or, the I   er* (Cambridge, England: Cambridge University Press, 1881), p. 117.

31. Crenshaw, *Ecclesiastes,* p. 81.

32. Cf. Barton, *The Book of Ecclesiastes,* p. 92; and Crenshaw, *Ecclesiastes,* p. 81.

The term *reward* occurs here for the first time but will surface again elsewhere (2:21; 3:22; 5:17-18 [English 5:18-19]; 9:6, 9; 11:2). It literally signifies a "share" or a "portion." Franz Delitzsch[33] and Hans Hertzberg[34] compare it to the word *yitrôn* "profit," to which it is related.

One of Qohelet's favorite words is *toil* (see the discussion in 1:3). The issue here is whether *toil* indicates all the labor that Qohelet performs under the sun or simply refers to his efforts to discover meaning in material pleasure. In either case the negative connotations of the word need to be taken into account.

11 Though Qohelet discovered that there was a "reward" for his efforts, the ultimate objects of his search, "profit" and "meaning," were lacking. This verse states this conclusion in no uncertain terms. He worked hard, but there were no lasting results from his labors.

acts and *toil* may here either designate the efforts involved in the search or have a broader connotation. Indeed Charles Whitley,[35] James Crenshaw,[36] and others argue that *toil* is perhaps better translated "gain" or "wealth" in this context. See the discussion of the word in 1:3.

Qohelet ends the section by citing three of his most common phrases — *meaningless, there was no profit,* and *under the sun.* They are discussed in 1:2 and 3. Each imparts a note of pessimism, and together they are a very negative conclusion.

3. Death Renders Both Wisdom and Folly Meaningless (2:12-17)

This section is pivotal toward understanding how Qohelet's thinking is affected by his fear of death. He considers wisdom (a subject he has already taken up in 1:12-18) — he is, after all, a wise man (12:9). If meaning is found anywhere, we expect Qohelet to find it here. That such an issue was even raised seems inconceivable, however, in the light of the exaltation of wisdom in Proverbs. Yet Qohelet is no ordinary wise man. He sees the relative value of wisdom in comparison to folly in much the same way that he admits the "reward" of material pleasure. Further thought, however, leads him to contemplate the benefits of wisdom in the light of his impending death. Death renders all things, including wisdom, meaningless. Thus, it is the inescapable fact of death that leads Qohelet to deny any substantial or long-lasting significance to wisdom.

---

33. F. Delitzsch, *Proverbs, Ecclesiastes, Song of Solomon,* trans. M. G. Easton (Grand Rapids, MI: Eerdmans, 1975 [1872]), p. 243.
34. Hertzberg, *Der Prediger,* p. 89.
35. Whitley, *Koheleth,* p. 23.
36. Crenshaw, *Ecclesiastes,* p. 83.

Formally, this section is a reflection,[37] similar to the immediately preceding one (2:1-11). Here Qohelet looks back at his life as a wise man, and he carefully considers its significance.

12 *I turned my attention[38] to observe wisdom and mad folly.[39] For what can anyone who comes after the king do but that which has already been done?*

13 *I observed that there was more profit to wisdom than folly, like the profit[40] of light over darkness.*

14 *The wise have eyes in their head, while fools walk around in darkness. But I also[41] understand that the same fate awaits both of them.*

15 *I said to myself,[42] "Even I will meet the same fate as the fool,[43] why then have I become so wise?" So I said to myself,[44] "This too is meaningless."*

16 *For the memory of neither the wise nor the fool endures forever. The days arrive only too soon when both will be forgotten. How will the wise person die? Like the fool!*

17 *So I hated life, for the work that is done[45] under the sun is evil to me. Indeed, all is meaningless and a chasing of the wind.*

12 With a characteristic phrase *(I turned my attention)* Qohelet changes the subject. He turns from the topic of pleasure again to the topic of wisdom and folly (see 1:12-18). He then claims that his, the king's, efforts cannot be

---

37. So Murphy, *Wisdom Literature*, p. 135.

38. This is the same expression as began 2:11, but note that in the present verse we find the preposition *le* instead of the preposition *be*. There is no apparent difference in meaning.

39. Literally, "madness and folly." I translate the expression as a hendiadys.

40. Note the unusual vocalization of this word *(kîtrôn* as opposed to *keyitrôn)*. *BHS* indicates that many Hebrew manuscripts differ from Leningradensis by offering a normal vocalization (see GKC §24e for an alternative explanation).

41. There is considerable discussion over the force of the particle *gam* here. The two main alternatives, due to semantic range and context, are emphatic and adversative. Barton *(The Book of Ecclesiastes,* p. 93) argues that if it were adversative, the particle would appear at the beginning of the sentence. The *waw* rather provides the adversative sense, while the *gam* is taken adverbially.

42. See 1:16; 2:1.

43. Literally, "Like the fate of the fool will encounter even me."

44. This phrase is similar to the one that opens the verse except that an alternative verb is used *(dbr* for *'mr)*.

45. For the issue of the English tense of this expression, see Isaksson, *Studies in the Language of Qoheleth,* pp. 64-74. I render it present with Isaksson because Qohelet still experiences it in the present.

superseded by anyone who follows him, the implication being that if he cannot find meaning or significance here, then no one can.

The initial verb *(pānâ)* is the same as that of v. 11 and provides a kind of verbal link between the two units. This time it is followed by a verb in the infinitive construct, *observe,* literally "to see." Qohelet uses this word more than any other to introduce the observations that he has made in the process of his search (see 1:14).

Qohelet states the new object of his study. This time he deals with the polar opposites of *wisdom* and *mad folly.* He quickly dispenses with *mad folly,* which is seen as useless in comparison with wisdom, but even the latter will not stand up under close scrutiny. For the two Hebrew words that make up the expression *mad folly (hôlēlôt wᵉsiklût),* see 1:17 (cf. 2:2, 3).

It is the second half of the verse that has troubled interpreters. Michael Fox goes so far as to say, "Qoh 2:12b makes no sense as it stands."[46] His statement may be extreme, but there are difficulties that may not be ignored, and the translation offered above may be accused of glossing over some of the problems in the attempt to provide a smooth rendering.

A woodenly literal translation of v. 12b is: "What is the person who comes after the king? That he has already done." A host of observations and emendations have been offered during the history of interpretation, and we should note that this verse was not understood clearly even in the early versions. The Septuagint went off the mark in at least two points. First, it misunderstood the opening interrogative and translated it as the equivalent of *mî* ("who?") rather than *māh* ("what?"). Second, it took the root *mlk* as equivalent to Aramaic "to counsel, to plan," thus rendering it *boulē* ("counsel"). The resulting translation is: "Who is the person who follows after counsel, in that he does it." The Targum, Peshitta, Aquila, and Theodotion take the word *mlk* as "king," as it is in the Masoretic tradition.

Some of the most frequent suggestions toward interpretation are: (1) to insert the verb *yaʿᵃśeh* ("he acts") after the interrogative *māh*. This emendation has been justified on two grounds. Either there was a homoioteleuton (that is, an omission of text) as the scribe's eyes skipped from the *h* at the end of the *māh* to the *h* at the end of the verb, or, less likely but still possible, there was an aposiopes (a rhetorical trope that involves the suppression of the verb).[47] (2) A second possibility is to emend *ʿāśûhû* to a singular form (along with evidence from Hebrew manuscripts and the Septuagint) or take it as an impersonal passive ("is done"). Qohelet in this way asserts the universal applicability of his experiment. He sets himself up as the king and concludes that, if the king cannot find meaning, then no one else will be able to do so.

46. Fox, *Qohelet and His Contradictions,* p. 183.
47. Hertzberg, *Der Prediger,* p. 80.

This verse is the last time that Qohelet explicitly adopts the royal personage. Indeed, later he will distance himself from the king (see "Authorship" in the introduction).

13 Qohelet's initial impression is not surprising for a Hebrew wisdom teacher, though it certainly strikes the reader as understated: Wisdom is better than folly, as light is better than darkness. This seems obvious, but Qohelet is setting his reader up for the surprising reversal that takes place in the verses that follow.

observed links this verse with the preceding one. Qohelet's investigation revealed to him that there was indeed an advantage (another possible translation of *profit* [*yitrôn;* see 1:3]) to wisdom in comparison to its opposite, folly. It is an obvious advantage to him, as obvious as the difference between *light* and *darkness.* Symbolic value need not be read into the use of *light* and *darkness* in this and the next verse. He is simply evoking everyday common sense to make his point. Both *wisdom* and *folly* (1:17; 2:3; 2:12), as well as *light* and *darkness,* are related to one another by means of the comparative *min.*[48]

Robert Gordis[49] argues that this verse begins a quotation that ends in v. 14a. The argument in favor of 14a is stronger than that for 13. R. N. Whybray[50] presents a persuasive case against this verse as part of a quotation. He notes the use of vocabulary characteristic of Qohelet and the awkward prose.[51]

14 The first half of the verse continues the rather bland affirmation of the benefit of wisdom over folly. It also extends the light and darkness analogy but integrates the two very effectively. Wise people walk around with a clear head in a (supposedly) well-lit room. Fools walk around as if blind. The analogy is to life. Wise people can "get on" with the world, but the fool keeps stumbling over obstacles.

The second half of the verse introduces the surprising reversal. So far Qohelet has said nothing really startling, but in v. 14b he introduces the idea of a common fate. That fate is death, and it comes to wise and fool alike, rendering wisdom meaningless in the long run.

It is impossible to be as dogmatic as Whybray in identifying the first half of this verse as a proverb. It definitely has a "proverbial ring" to it, but we cannot be certain. In either case, it represents Qohelet's own thinking about the matter, so whether Qohelet has inserted it from another source is relatively

48. See GKC §113b.
49. Gordis, *Koheleth,* pp. 221-22.
50. Whybray, *Ecclesiastes,* NCB, pp. 57-58.
51. See also M. V. Fox, "The Identification of Quotations in Biblical Literature," *ZAW* 92 (1980): 416-31.

insignificant.[52] It furthers his point in v. 13 that wisdom far excels folly. One who has wisdom sees clearly, as opposed to the fool who walks about as if in a dark room. The image evoked here contrasts the wise, those who are able to get on in the world, with fools, who cannot navigate the obstacles of life. It is a very practical contrast that Qohelet draws. Wisdom's profit is that it allows the person to succeed in life right now.

The last sentence of the verse takes into account the long-term future and thus is a negative assessment of wisdom. The subject, *fate,* and the verb, *awaits,* derive from the same root, *qrh. Fate,* as used elsewhere in the OT, does not carry a negative connotation (e.g., Ruth 2:3), but Crenshaw rightly believes that this is not true in Ecclesiastes.[53] After all, it is frequently linked with death, the one certain fact of life that shakes Qohelet to his very core (see 2:15; 3:19 [3 times]; 9:2, 3). It is true, however, that fate is not an evil power even in Qohelet's mind. It rather refers to those things that happen to an individual over which there is no control. The fate that both the wise and the fool will surely encounter is death.

15 Here the verse quotes Qohelet's inner dialogue as he acknowledges the hard reality of the similarity of his fate to the fate of the fool. He perceptively and brutally applies the principle stated in v. 14 to himself and thus throws into doubt the whole wisdom enterprise.[54]

The realization that he will suffer the *same fate* (= death) as the fool leads Qohelet to question his lifetime search for wisdom. The point is that he is not just a wise man — he is one of the best in his field. Interpreters have differed over the force of *'āz (then)* and *yôtēr (so).* The latter may be either a noun or an adverb.[55] Those who take *yôtēr* as a noun often emend *'āz* to an interrogative (usually *'ēy*).[56] It is true that some Greek manuscripts and the Syriac, Vulgate, and Coptic versions omit *'āz* from consideration, and the Septuagint moves it into the next clause. Nonetheless, if the verb is understood as "becomes wise" as it often is, if *yôtēr* is taken as an adverb, and if *'āz* is translated in a temporal rather than logical sense,[57] then the MT is perfectly understandable.

Qohelet concludes with the judgment that *This (zeh)* is *meaningless (hebel,* for which see 1:2). There is ambiguity as to the antecedent of *This.* Is

---

52. Fox, "The Identification of Quotations in Biblical Literature," pp. 416-31.

53. Crenshaw, *Ecclesiastes,* p. 85.

54. The pleonastic *gam-ʾᵃnî,* translated *even I,* strongly emphasizes the first-person suffix on the verb, fixing attention on Qohelet himself.

55. A verb is unlikely because *ytr* never elsewhere occurs in the qal, only in the niphal and hiphil.

56. See Whitley, *Koheleth,* pp. 24-25, who translates "And why am I wise, where is the advantage?"

57. See Crenshaw, *Ecclesiastes,* p. 85.

wisdom itself meaningless? Or is it the conclusion that wisdom and folly are both the same in the final analysis? Most likely the latter is true, because Qohelet states a relative superiority of wisdom over folly. In either case, Qohelet leaves us in no doubt concerning the reason for the *meaningless* verdict — death, a subject to which he will return often.

16 Now we learn that it is not only death that frustrates Qohelet. He knows that sooner or later not only he as an individual wise man but even his very memory will be eradicated from the earth. He will be forgotten, and this fact also renders the pursuit of wisdom insignificant to him.

Qohelet's assessment of the short-lived reputation of the wise person cuts against traditional wisdom teaching:

> The memory of the righteous will be a blessing,
>   but the name of the wicked will rot. (Proverbs 10:7)

Indeed, it appears that the author of Wisdom of Solomon 2:4 intended to correct Qohelet as he described the godless as those who said to themselves:

> Our name will be forgotten with the passage of time,
> and none will recall our deeds;
> our life will be gone like the traces of a cloud
> and dispersed as mist,
> pursued by the sun's rays
> and overborne by its heat.[58]

To Qohelet, however, death rendered everything, including precious wisdom, null and void. Psalm 49:11-21 (English 10-20) expresses the same sentiment, but the contrast with Qohelet comes in v. 15:

> But God will redeem my life from the grave;
>   he will surely take me to himself.

Qohelet neither here nor elsewhere expresses such a hope.

only too soon is an attempt to translate the Hebrew compound *bᵉšek-kᵉbār*, which is composed of a preposition *(bᵉ)*, the relative pronoun *(še)*, and the temporal particle *(kᵉbār*, for which see the comment on 1:10). Most scholars correctly take the combination of the preposition and particle in the same sense as the classical *ba'ᵃšer*, "for" or "because." The meaning of the temporal particle is "already," which is difficult with the phrase "the coming days" but is here taken to mean "in the near future."

---

58. Translation from D. Winston, *The Wisdom of Solomon*, AB 43 (Garden City, NY: Doubleday, 1979), p. 111.

Much discussion attends the particle *'êk,* here rendered *how.* Some emend to the emphatic *'ak,* but this ignores the fact that *'êk* may also have emphatic force. In any case, the interrogative works here as Qohelet both poses the question to himself and answers it.

17 Qohelet draws a tragic conclusion from the observations he has made in this section. Work was evil, with the result that life was hateful to him. The final conclusion of the section is a repeat of his common refrains that everything lacked meaning and was like trying to chase the wind.

I hated life is a personal statement, but, since he does not particularize it to himself by saying "my life," it has the force of suggestion to his readers as well.[59] That is, everybody's life is worth hating.

As R. N. Whybray argues,[60] Qohelet is not the first wise person to express such despair in the OT (see Job 3 and 2 Sam. 17:23, where Ahithophel commits suicide). But what Whybray neglects to mention is that these too are examples of unorthodox wisdom. Indeed, Proverbs embraces life with a passion.[61] Whybray further cites Ecclesiastes 9:4-6 as an example of a more optimistic view of life. It should be noted, however, that this section simply says that life is better than death, and all are agreed that Qohelet never goes so far as to advocate suicide. The only positive feature of life in 9:4-6 is that the person who possesses it knows that death is coming, hardly the attitude of the sage in Proverbs. The *carpe diem* passages that Whybray also cites will be dealt with individually.

The phrase *evil to me* is difficult, because *ra'* is used so often in the OT. It often has a strongly moral tone, and that is the way it is translated here, in keeping with my understanding of the context. I believe Qohelet here subtly accuses God of moral evil. The word can carry a less negative overtone with a translation like "distressing," "grievous," or the like, and this approach is witnessed as early as the Jewish Targum and the paraphrase by Gregory Thaumaturgos. The Septuagint has *ponēron* ("distressed") and the Vulgate, *malum* ("bad"), both perfectly compatible with the translation "evil."

See 1:2 for the concluding statement, which echoes the dominant theme of the book.

4. Death Renders Toil Meaningless (2:18-23)

The introduction of a new topic, toil, signals a new section. Finding no ultimate meaning in wisdom, Qohelet now explores the possibility that

---

59. Several Hebrew manuscripts, the Peshitta, and the Targum add the first common singular suffix to "life."

60. Whybray, *Ecclesiastes,* NCB, pp. 60-61.

61. Crenshaw, *Ecclesiastes,* p. 86, cites Prov. 8:35 and 3:16 as examples.

toil (*'āmāl*) can provide the kind of satisfaction that he so earnestly desires. But right from the start he leaves the reader in no doubt as to his conclusion. Though never explicitly mentioned, the nemesis of death is carried over from the previous section: as it did with wisdom, death renders toil ultimately without meaning.

Roland Murphy is correct when he describes the formal nature of this section as a "reflection," similar to the two that have just preceded it (2:1-11; 2:12-17).[62]

18 *Then I hated all my toil that I do[63] under the sun, because I have to leave it to whomever comes after me.*

19 *Who knows whether that person will be wise or foolish? But he will control[64] all the toil for which I so wisely toiled[65] under the sun. This too is meaningless.*

20 *So I began to despair[66] of all the toil that I did under the sun.*

21 *For[67] there was a person who toiled with wisdom and with knowledge and with success, but he had to leave[68] his reward[69] to an individual[70] who did not work for it. This too is meaningless and a great evil.*

22 *For what do people get for all their toil and anxiety that they experience under the sun?*

23 *For all their days their task is filled with pain and frustration. Even at night their minds do not rest. This also is meaningless.*

62. See Murphy, *Wisdom Literature*, pp. 134-36.

63. According to Whitley (*Koheleth*, p. 26), this is a stative participle. Isaksson (*Studies in the Language of Qoheleth*, p. 29) argues that it should be translated in the present.

64. This word, according to Whitley (*Koheleth*, p. 29), occurs normally in late texts, but Fredericks (*Qoheleth's Language*, p. 239) argues that it is a preexilic Aramaism.

65. I am here treating two verbs ("to toil" [*'ml*] and "to be wise" [*ḥkm*]) as a hendiadys. See Waltke and O'Connor, *Biblical Hebrew Syntax*, p. 365, for the understanding that these verbs are fientive in force.

66. See GKC §64c for the pointing of this verb. Also consult Fredericks, *Qoheleth's Language*, pp. 182-83, for arguments against using this word to support a late dating of the book. After all, it occurs in passages like 1 Sam. 27:1.

67. Taking the *kî* in its causal sense, though it could conceivably be emphatic.

68. This verb probably "expresses the future with a nuance of compulsion," so Isaksson, *Studies in the Language of Qoheleth*, pp. 119-20.

69. For this difficult grammatical construction (particularly the presence of the suffix on the verb), consult GKC §131m and Delitzsch, *Proverbs, Ecclesiastes, Song of Solomon*, p. 250.

70. This is the same word as "person" earlier in the verse (*'ādām*), literally "human."

18 The conjunction (a simple *waw*, but taken as a causal link with the preceding [*Then*]) connects this new section with the previous one. The content of the verse makes it clear that it is the anticipation of death that throws its shadow across the new topic of consideration, namely toil.

Qohelet begins by expressing his negative conclusion concerning the next area that he explores for meaning, his work. He works hard, then he dies. What happens to his wealth after his death? He has no control over it. It will go to someone, but to whom? The recognition of his powerlessness in this regard frustrates him.

The verse has strong verbal links with 1:3 (the repetition of the root *'ml*) and 2:17 (the root *šn*). In the latter Qohelet stated his hatred for life in general. Here he expresses his dislike of work in particular (for a discussion of *'āmāl,* see 1:3).

In this verse, Qohelet states his hatred for his work and then gives the first reason. His thoughts run cold at the idea that upon his death his *'āmāl* will go to someone who comes after him. Here we see how *'āmāl* entails not only the toil itself but also the results of that toil.

He gives his reasons in a clause that begins with *because*. This word translates the relative pronoun *še*.[71] *have to leave it* is a form of the hiphil imperfect of the verbal root *nwḥ* with a third masculine singular suffix. The suffix refers to the *toil*.

The one who receives the fruits of his work is referred to indefinitely, *to whomever.* Although the MT is not as indefinite as it could be (literally, "to the man"), the Targum made the recipient more indefinite by repointing the word to omit the definite article (so literally, "to a man"). It is likely that Qohelet meant it as referring to all people. This approach differs from the early Jewish interpretation of the verse, which takes the word as a subtle reference to Solomon and Rehoboam.[72]

19 This verse continues and completes the thought of v. 18b. Death renders even wisdom foolish. Qohelet sees this happening even in inheritance. He may work diligently and wisely through his whole life, but, when he dies, a fool may take over and benefit from his labor. Contemplating this possibility leads Qohelet once again to conclude that life is *meaningless*.

The verse begins with what will become a characteristic expression of Qohelet (see also 3:21; 6:12; 8:1), *Who knows.* It occurs in other contexts in the OT and with different force (2 Sam. 12:12; Joel 2:14; Jonah 3:9; Ps. 90:11;

---

71. Crenshaw (*Ecclesiastes,* p. 87) and others give a list of other occurrences both in Ecclesiastes (4:9; 8:15) and outside it (Song of Songs 1:6; Gen. 30:18; 31:49) where the relative pronoun (in these cases *'ašer)* has a causal force.

72. C. D. Ginsburg, *The Song of Songs and Coheleth,* ed. H. M. Orlinsky (New York: KTAV, 1970 [1861]), p. 295.

Esth. 4:14; Prov. 24:33), but as James Crenshaw points out, Qohelet uses this phrase to "express utter skepticism."[73] He uses this rhetorical device to reveal that no one, especially himself, knows the answer to the question, and this frustrates him greatly.[74]

This is ambiguous in the context. It certainly refers to the discussion of the past verses — that is, the possibility that work, projects, and the results of work might pass on to a fool — but the nonspecific nature of the reference, both here and elsewhere, gives the impression that "the whole mess is meaningless."

20   In this and the following verses, Qohelet offers a second argument for the meaninglessness of toil. He begins his argument in his characteristic manner of first presenting his negative conclusion and then providing the reasons for his pessimism. The previous verse concluded with a *hebel (meaningless)* phrase that often concludes a section, but not here. Qohelet continues the argument into the next verse.

His first argument induced him to despair. The word here translated *began* is literally "I turned" or "I turned around." "Turned to despair" is an awkward idiom in English, and the idea is that he turned from feeling no despair to feeling despair, so *began* is appropriate. Though translated differently because of context, this rendering is not an argument in favor of those who draw a semantic distinction between this verb and the use of *pānâ* earlier (2:11, 12).[75]

Everyone agrees with the meaning of *despair (ya'ēš)* in general, though there are attempts at a more specific nuance. The verb occurs in five other places in the Bible (1 Sam. 27:1; Isa. 57:10; Jer. 2:25; 18:12; Job 6:26) with this meaning, but always in the niphal, whereas the piel infinitive occurs here. Another possibility for the meaning of the piel is given by Charles Whitley and Michael Fox.[76] They suggest that Qohelet has become disillusioned with his toil and its reward. R. N. Whybray, however, thinks that the verb indicates that Qohelet has resigned himself to an unchangeable fact of life.[77] According to all these interpretations, it is clear that Qohelet cannot find meaning and satisfaction in his work.

The early history of interpretation took an interesting detour with this

73. Crenshaw, *Ecclesiastes*, p. 87.

74. For an extensive treatment of the phrase, see J. L. Crenshaw, "The Expression *mî yôdēa'* in the Hebrew Bible," *VT* 36 (1986): 274-88.

75. Contra Delitzsch (*Proverbs, Ecclesiastes, Song of Solomon*, p. 249), who states, "The distinction lies in this, that *pnh* signifies a clear turning round; *sbb*, a turning away from one thing to another, a turning in the direction of something new that presents itself." See also Gordis, *Koheleth*, p. 223.

76. Whitley, *Koheleth*, p. 27; and Fox, *Qohelet and His Contradictions*, p. 187.

77. Whybray, *Ecclesiastes*, NCB, p. 61.

passage. The Septuagint rendered *despair* with "to renounce" *(apotaxasthai),* and so too the Vulgate *(renunciavit).* The Septuagint thus opened the way for the faulty view that the repentant Solomon speaks here and renounces his former way of life (see the thought of Gregory Thaumaturgos).[78]

21 Qohelet now illustrates his point with an anecdote, a characteristic of his style. In this brief and rather general anecdote, Qohelet describes a person who works industriously and with skill, achieving success. This is the type of person that many envy, but Qohelet goes on to inform his reader that this fortunate person left his fortune to someone who did not work for it, implying that the recipient did not deserve the fortune. Qohelet draws the moral in his typical way, calling it a meaningless and even evil situation.

As usual with Qohelet this brief anecdote is introduced by the existential particle *yēš (there is),*[79] but there are longer stories as well (e.g., 9:13-16). These stories serve to concretize his concepts, but they lack vividness because they are nonspecific, having a generic *person* (literally, "man") as their subject. It is wrongheaded to try to identify anyone with this person, including Qohelet himself, though he could probably see such a thing happening to him.

In this anecdote Qohelet envisions an individual who accrued some material gain *(reward)* through hard work. There is no suspicion surrounding the gain since it was achieved *with wisdom and with knowledge and with success.* Discussion has centered on the last of these words, *success (kišrôn).* The Septuagint got off on the wrong track by translating "in a manly way" or "with fortitude" *(en andreia).* The noun, which occurs only in Ecclesiastes (see also 4:4; 5:10 [English 5:11]), should be connected with the rare but more frequent verb "to succeed, to prosper" *(kšr),* which is a common Semitic root (note the use of the cognate root in the name of the Ugaritic god, Koṭar-wa-Ḥasis).[80]

The fruits of this hard work, though, go to an *individual* who did nothing to work for it. It is doubtful that this verse alludes to the normal process of inheritance, since the one who benefits is designated by *individual* rather than "son." Qohelet imagines a situation where a stranger somehow comes to enjoy the results of his labor.[81]

Qohelet concludes with a punch by calling the situation described in this verse *a great evil.* It is true that the Hebrew root *rʿh* is amenable to a less intense translation (see the NIV's "a great misfortune"), but I believe that the

---

78. See the thought of Gregory Thaumaturgos (Jarick, *Gregory Thaumaturgos' Paraphrase,* pp. 46-47).

79. See also Ecclesiastes 4:8; 5:12 (English 5:13); 6:1-3; 7:15; 8:14; 10:5-7.

80. Fredericks (*Qoheleth's Language,* p. 229) shows that the word and its root occur in preexilic Hebrew as well as in many Semitic languages, thus refuting the idea that it is an Aramaism and evidence for late dating.

81. See Ginsburg, *The Song of Songs and Coheleth,* pp. 297-98, and compare 6:2.

context fits better with a stronger translation that brings out Qohelet's moral outrage over the unfairness of life.

22 Qohelet reinforces his conclusion in the previous verse by asking and implicitly answering a question. This answer will be given a rationale in the next verse. As a rhetorical question, we understand its negative force. The question concerns the gain or profit of work. What is the bottom line? After all, work involves tremendous physical and mental activity. For Qohelet, the bottom line is that one's toil simply is not worth the effort. The question in this verse is very similar to those verses that use the word "profit" (*yitrôn*, e.g., 1:3), though this one does not.

what do people get is literally "what is to a man?" The verb is a qal participle of the relatively rare root *hwh*. While some have argued that this form is a late Mishnaic word due to its occurrence in Nehemiah 6:6 and the Mishnah,[82] other and more recent writers[83] have recognized that it also occurs in early biblical texts (Gen. 27:29 and perhaps Job 37:6).[84] The fact that it only occurs as a participle in Nehemiah and Ecclesiastes has more to do with function than with date. James Crenshaw[85] also notes its early occurrence in the Aramaic inscription of Zinjirli (ca. eighth century B.C.).

anxiety is a rather dynamic translation of the Hebrew idiom "strivings of his heart." The word "strivings" is from the root *r'h* and occurs in Ecclesiastes in two nominal forms ending in *-ût* and *-ôn*, as here. See the discussion of the root in connection with 1:14.

23 Verse 22 posed and implicitly answered a rhetorical question. Now we have the rationale for the answer.[86] Two points are made. First, people who work hard have days filled with heavy physical and mental exertion. Second, at night, when they might have the opportunity to replenish their resources, they are still exerting mental effort. Work has no meaning, even though it never stops.

Qohelet divides the rationale in two parts and along temporal lines. The sentences characterize the life of hard-working people during the day and then also describe how those people spend their nights. Qohelet uses the term *task* to describe their activity during the day. He had the option of selecting the term "toil" (*'āmāl*) but used instead the term that he already employed in 1:13 (*'inyān*), where he called it "evil." Here he associates it with two equally negative words, *pain* and *frustration*. This pair also appears in 1:18, though

---

82. Cf. Whitley, *Koheleth*, p. 28.
83. Gordis, *Koheleth*, pp. 224-25; cf. Lys (*L'Ecclésiaste*, p. 274), who calls it a "forme ancienne de *hyh*."
84. Though some dictionaries list the latter as a homonym.
85. Crenshaw, *Ecclesiastes*, p. 89.
86. The rationale is typically introduced, as here, with the particle *kî, for*.

in reverse order (see the commentary there). People could work hard during the day if they knew that the night would bring respite. But Qohelet understands that *rest* does not come even at night.

minds do not rest is an idiomatic translation for "their hearts do not lie down (in bed)." The contemporary proverb "No rest for the weary" would be good news to Qohelet, who knows that there is "No rest for the hard worker."

The gist of the previous section is simply stated. Hard work brings no rewards for the present, nor can the worker look forward to a future reward since there is no escape from the daily grind and, as he implies elsewhere (3:18-22; 12:1-7), there is doubt if not denial of the afterlife. Indeed, there is frustration now, and this is accompanied by the strong possibility that someone else will benefit from the work, and not a person chosen by the one who has earned the reward. Qohelet's final statement in the section should surprise no one — *meaningless;* see 1:2.

Qohelet's frustration arises out of his expectation that hard work should bring lasting reward. After all, that was what one major strand of wisdom teaching seemed to promise. Those who work hard will thrive, while the lazy will languish (e.g., 6:6-11). In the tradition of the three friends of Job, Qohelet represents a mechanical reading of the Bible's retribution theology, which would include Deuteronomy as well as Proverbs. But even these books sound a minor chord in recognizing that the world does not operate in such a clear-cut manner.[87]

5. Carpe Diem! — *God Allows Some to Enjoy Life (2:24-26)*

This section is the first of a number of passages (3:12-14; 3:22; 5:17-19 [English 5:18-20]; 8:15; 9:7-10) that allow for the possibility that life may be enjoyed in the present. Here Qohelet advocates, though resignedly, pursuing what appears to be the simple pleasures of life. If there is no ultimate meaning in wisdom or one's work, then one must look to enjoy life as the opportunities present themselves. Such an attitude toward life has been given a motto long after Qohelet lived and wrote: *carpe diem,* a Latin phrase that means "seize the day!" Don't wait for tomorrow, get all the enjoyment out of life that is possible in the present. In the darkness of a life that has no ultimate meaning, seize upon the temporal pleasures that lighten the burden.

A close reading of this section reveals that Qohelet believes that these simple pleasures come from the hand of God, a situation that brings him no ultimate satisfaction (2:26c). Indeed, it is clear throughout the book that,

87. R. van Leeuwen, "Wealth and Poverty: System and Contradiction in Proverbs," *Hebrew Studies* 33 (1992): 25-36.

though God grants enjoyment to some, Qohelet does not identify himself among the privileged few (6:2).[88]

24 *There is nothing better for people than*[89] *to eat and drink and enjoy their toil. This too, I see, is from the hand of God.*

25 *For who will eat and who will worry apart from him?*

26 *For he gives wisdom, knowledge, and pleasure to the one who pleases him, but he gives to the one who is offensive the task of gathering wealth*[90] *to be given to the one who pleases God.*[91] *This too is meaningless and chasing the wind.*

24 With this verse Qohelet begins the first major summary of his thinking in 1:13–2:23. He gives his practical advice in the light of his conclusion that meaning may not be found in either wisdom or hard work, two areas highly prized by the traditional wisdom teachers of Israel.

The lifestyle he advocates is the pursuit of the basic necessities of life: food, drink, and enjoyment in work. One wonders how Qohelet ever expected anyone to enjoy their work after reading the previous section, but perhaps that was not his real intention. Certainly, he understands, as we can see from the second half of the verse, that no one is able to enjoy even these simple pleasures unless God allows it.

The opening phrase of the verse indicates that Qohelet did not communicate his advice with much fervor. *There is nothing better ('ēn-ṭôb bā-)* is a formula that Qohelet uses in three other places (3:12, 22; 8:15) as well as in the present verse. He purposely avoids an unqualified positive statement such as "This is good." Instead, he couches his language in a way that communicates his reluctance and his lack of enthusiasm.[92] What follows is Qohelet's advice for those who live in a fallen world.

Qohelet then encourages the reader to *eat* and to *drink.* There is no

---

88. My understanding of the *carpe diem* passages stands in stark contrast to the so-called Qohelet, preacher of joy interpretation advocated by R. N. Whybray, "Qoheleth, Preacher of Joy?" *JSOT* 23 (1982): 87-98; and W. Kaiser, *Ecclesiastes*, pp. 43-46.

89. My translation assumes a haplography (omitted because of the final *mem* on *'ādām*), thus prefixing a *mem* before the relative pronoun, standing for the preposition *min* functioning as a comparative. Compare the Syriac and Targum and note the analogy of 3:22. Most manuscripts of the Septuagint and the Vulgate do not assume a haplography and thus end up with the exact opposite of what Qohelet is trying to say. For the particulars, see Delitzsch, *Proverbs, Ecclesiastes, Song of Solomon*, p. 251.

90. A hendiadys, literally "to gather and to amass."

91. R. Braun, *Koheleth und die frühhellenistische Popularphilosophie*, BZAW 130 (Berlin: de Gruyter, 1973), pp. 51-52.

92. Crenshaw, *Ecclesiastes*, p. 88.

good reason to take this in any other than its most natural sense, that is, as referring to physical enjoyment. Nonetheless, Qohelet here probably does not advocate total license. After all, he has already informed us that ultimate meaning is not found in pleasure (2:1-11).

A third area of enjoyment is somewhat surprising in that it is the *toil* that Qohelet had just warned provides no meaning to life (2:17-23). Qohelet is not inconsistent here, however. He is arguing for limited enjoyment, not ultimate satisfaction, and as the next sentence makes clear, he does not believe that everyone has this rather restricted possibility for enjoyment.

To *enjoy* is literally to "look upon the good." The context makes it obvious that the moral sense of "good" is not intended.

In reality, however, even this limited enjoyment is beyond human achievement. It is in God's control *(the hand of God),* and he will mete it out to whomever he wants. Read from a Christian perspective this phrase sounds positive. The modern Christian reader imagines that the benevolent God he knows is in control, and breathes a sigh of relief. Qohelet, however, is not so sure of God (ch. 5). He admits the possibility that God gives enjoyment to some, but his own writings reveal that he does not consider himself among the "blessed."

25 Qohelet appeals now to God's sovereign distribution of food and drink as a further explanation that any enjoyment, and indeed any worry, comes from God's hand. By means of a rhetorical question, Qohelet reminds his readers of something that he expects they already know — enjoyment and worry in life come from God himself. He sends both the good and the bad of life to people.

Qohelet has a penchant for asking rhetorical questions, questions that are introduced by the interogative *who (mî;* cf. 2:19; 3:21, 22; 5:9 [English 5:10]; 6:12; 7:13, 24; 8:1, 4; 9:4; 10:14). Bo Isaksson points out that the questions are almost always followed by the imperfect "due to the common use of the generalized PC [prefix conjugation] with a future nuance."[93]

The first verb *eat* is clear and connects with the previous verse, but much controversy surrounds the etymology and meaning of the second verb *(yāḥûš).* Differences arise as early as the first Greek translation. Many early Greek manuscripts, including Theodotion, and the Peshitta take the verb *ḥûš* as "to drink" (Greek *pinō*), while other Greek manuscripts, including Symmachus and Aquila, translate it "to refrain" *(pheidomai).* These early Greek renditions are paralleled by the two main interpretive options at present. These are "to enjoy" or "to worry." The difficulty is that the Hebrew word occurs only here in Ecclesiastes, and its normal sense elsewhere, "to hasten," seems

---

93. Isaksson, *Studies in the Language of Qoheleth,* p. 133.

inappropriate. The first option probably arises from the sense that v. 25 follows
v. 24. Since *eat* begins that verse as well, many feel that context determines
a meaning "to drink," or more generally "to enjoy oneself." This appears to
be the motivation behind the translation *pinō* in certain Greek texts.[94] Friedrich
Ellermeier,[95] however, connects it with Akkadian *ḫâšu* and argues for the
sense of "to worry." Daniel Fredericks, in a concise discussion of the word's
etymology,[96] also mentions the possibility that the word is a semantic development from "to hasten," "to worry," or "to be agitated." There is also the
possibility suggested by the critical apparatus of *BHS* and others that the verbal
root is *ḥûś* and not *ḥûš.* If so, then perhaps it could be a by-form of *ḥûś,* "to
be troubled."

Further textual difficulties come at the end of the verse. First there is
a hapax grammatical form where the noun *ḥûṣ* "street" or "outside" is
followed by the preposition *min.* This phrase should clearly be translated *apart
from* or the like, but it is also true that it is a frequent late form, one that even
Fredericks admits as evidence of at least the late exilic period.[97]

While I have repointed and translated *from him,* the MT says "from
me." Nonetheless, as Michael Fox rightly points out, for Qohelet to say
"that no one will eat or drink except for me" is "neither relevant nor
true."[98] We thus emend with the Septuagint, Syriac, and some Hebrew
manuscripts.[99]

26   The last verse of the section gives Qohelet's understanding of how
God deals with people. It is a difficult text to interpret and can be read in one
of two ways, but in the final analysis context must determine its meaning.
The verse speaks of two classes of people, here translated (1) *the one who
pleases him/God* and (2) *the one who is offensive.* It is possible, and it is the
opinion of a number of commentators,[100] to understand both phrases in a
moral sense and to translate the second phrase according to its admittedly
more common meaning, "sinner." According to this line of thinking, Qohelet
admits that God gives good things to good people and bad things to bad
people.

---

94. Whybray, *Ecclesiastes,* NCB, p. 64.

95. F. Ellermeier, "Die Entmachtung der Weisheit im Denken Qohelets," *ZThK*
60 (1963): 1-20.

96. Fredericks, *Qoheleth's Language,* p. 225.

97. Fredericks, *Qoheleth's Language,* p. 263.

98. Fox, *Qohelet and His Contradictions,* p. 188.

99. For a full discussion of all possibilities, see J. De Waard, "The Translator and
Textual Criticism (with Particular Reference to Eccl 2,25)," *Biblica* 60 (1979): 509-29,
though I do not agree with each of his conclusions.

100. See most recently Whybray, *Ecclesiastes,* NCB, pp. 64-65; and Ogden,
Qoheleth, p. 49.

Context, however, forbids this otherwise acceptable interpretation. In the first place, 2:21 contradicts this approach. There we learned that the rewards for hard work went to someone who did nothing and thus was not deserving of them. R. N. Whybray admits that the contradiction exists but lamely argues that both sides needed to be stated in order to encompass the whole truth.[101] The truth supposedly could be expressed only through two opposing statements with no attempt at harmonization. I find this very difficult to accept. In this I follow Hans Hertzberg,[102] Michael Fox, who offers an impressive list of nonmoral uses of *hāṭā'*,[103] and James Crenshaw.[104]

Furthermore, the last statement of the verse, which is also the last statement of the section, is that *This . . . is meaningless.* The typically ambiguous *This* likely refers to more than v. 26, but it certainly includes it. One is thus left to ask, Why would Qohelet think it meaningless if good things happened to good people and bad things to bad? After all, throughout the book it is precisely the lack of connection between ethical behavior and reward that causes Qohelet so much frustration.

SUMMARY OF CHAPTER 2

Chapter 2 continues Qohelet's search for meaning. He begins the chapter by reflecting on his experiment with pleasure (2:1-11). He tried wine, building magnificent buildings, women, and wealth, all to no avail. None could satisfy him. He then reverts to wisdom, a subject he dealt with at the end of the previous chapter, and once again it falls short (2:12-17). Though wisdom is better than folly, death eradicates any lasting significance it might have. It cannot spare him from the same fate as the fool. Lastly, he turns to work, but it too is ultimately useless to him. The chapter then concludes with an exhortation to enjoy the lesser pleasures of life. After all, God does allow a privileged few to enjoy life. But that is no comfort to Qohelet, who regards even that divine concession as meaningless.

101. Whybray, *Ecclesiastes,* NCB, p. 65.
102. Hertzberg, *Der Prediger,* pp. 94-95.
103. Fox, *Qohelet and His Contradictions,* pp. 188-90.
104. Crenshaw, *Ecclesiastes,* pp. 90-91; see also the detailed analysis by M. Strange, "The Question of Moderation in Ecclesiastes 7:15-18" (D. Sac.Th. dissertation, Catholic University of America, 1969), pp. 40-42.

C. THE QUEST CONTINUES (3:1–6:9)

1. The Burden of the "Proper Time" (3:1-15)

Qohelet now raises a subject characteristic of ancient Near Eastern wisdom literature — the proper time.[1] After all, it is the wise person who knows the right time to say or to do the right thing (Prov. 15:23). Two contradictory actions may indeed each be appropriate when applied to the correct time (Prov. 26:4, 5). The first part of this unit (vv. 1-8) is a poem that beautifully expresses the theme that a set, or appointed, time exists for everything. The poem ensnares the reader with its lilting rhythm, with its near constant use of the infinitive construct form (see below for exceptions), and with the repetition of the first word, "time" (ʿēt, the repetition technically labeled anaphora). The poetic lines pit one action or state against its opposite.[2] The beauty of the poem, however, obscures its bleak message. The poem must be read in its immediate context, which includes vv. 9-15 and gives the implications of the state of affairs described in the poem. Verse 9 follows immediately upon the heels of the poem by rudely repeating the thought of 1:3, "What profit is there?" In the final analysis Qohelet powerfully expresses that everything is frustratingly out of the control of human beings.

In the light of these truths about life and experience, Qohelet once again advocates the simple pleasures of life. However, he adds, not everyone can enjoy even drink, food, and work. The ability to do so depends on God's gift.

1 *For everything there is a season,*
   and a time for every activity under heaven.
2 *A time to be born and a time to die;*
   a time to plant and a time to uproot what has been planted.
3 *A time to kill and a time to heal;*
   a time to tear down and a time to build.

1. Mention should be made of the recent article by J. Blenkinsopp, "Ecclesiastes 3:1-15: Another Interpretation," *JSOT* 66 (1995): 55-64, where he argues that the poem is not Qohelet's but a quotation from a "stoicizing Jewish sage" (p. 64). His argument depends on a strict grammatical interpretation of *lāledet* in 3:2a as "to bring a child into the world" rather than "to be born." This in turn leads him to take *lāmût* as "to take one's life," though it is more naturally taken as "to die." Blenkinsopp goes on to say that this attitude toward suicide is thoroughly Stoic. To me, this seems too large an implication to draw from a rather minor grammatical observation.
2. For a detailed analysis, see J. A. Loader, "Qohelet 3:2-8 — A 'Sonnet' in the Old Testament," *ZAW* 81 (1969): 239-42; and *Polar Structures in the Book of Qohelet,* BZAW 152 (Berlin: de Gruyter, 1979), pp. 29-33.

4 A time to cry and a time to laugh;
   a time of mourning and a time of dancing.

5 A time to cast stones and a time to gather stones;[3]
   a time to embrace and a time to refrain from embracing.

6 A time to seek and a time to give up as lost;[4]
   a time to keep and a time to throw away.

7 A time to tear and a time to sew;
   a time to be silent and a time to speak.

8 A time to love and a time to hate;
   a time of war and a time of peace.

9 What profit do people have from their toils?

10 I observed the task that God has given to the human race to keep them
   occupied.

11 He makes[5] everything appropriate[6] in its time. He also places eternity
   in their hearts. But still, no one[7] can discover what God is doing from
   beginning to end.[8]

12 I know[9] that there is nothing better for them[10] than to be happy and
   enjoy themselves during their lives.

3. Note the unusual lack of the preposition *lamed* here with the infinitive construct.

4. Gordis (*Koheleth*, p. 230) called this "a declarative use of the Piel," and Fredericks (*Qoheleth's Language*, pp. 176-77) argues against the position that this use of the verb is an indication of lateness.

5. Following Whybray (*Ecclesiastes*, NCB, p. 72), who states that "most commentators see a reference to the creation of the world and in particular to Gen. 1. However, it is more probable that the perfect tense is used here in the Hebrew to express a general truth and should be rendered by the present tense in English."

6. The word *yāpeh* means beautiful when referring to something physical, like human appearance (Gen. 39:6), but when referring to actions and states like those listed in vv. 1-8 the English term *appropriate* conveys the sense more clearly (see Fox, *Qohelet and His Contradictions*, p. 193, who cites it as a common usage in Mishnaic Hebrew).

7. GKC §152y cites this construction as an example of a double negative *(min* plus *b^elî).*

8. Hertzberg (*Der Prediger*, p. 28) argues that this word is late, but Fredericks (*Qoheleth's Language*, pp. 204, 233) has pointed to early use (Amos 3:15) of a cognate verbal form to counteract this position.

9. This phrase *(yāda'tî kî)* is typical of Qohelet's autobiographical style. See 1:17, 2:14, 3:14, and note also 8:12 (a participial form of *yāda').*

10. There is a lack of concord between the plural suffix here *(bām)* and the singular suffix on "lives" *(b^eḥayyāw,* here translated plural to achieve gender inclusiveness). Indeed, *BHS* suggests an emendation of *bām* to *bā'ādām* ("nothing better for someone than"), based on the parallel in 2:24 plus the evidence of two Hebrew manuscripts and the Targum (see also Whitley, *Koheleth*, pp. 33-34). One, however, can equally argue that the singular suffix on "lives" is a collective (so Crenshaw, *Ecclesiastes*, p. 98).

13 *Also everyone who eats, drinks, and enjoys their toil — that[11] is a gift of God.*

14 *I know[12] that everything God does lasts forever. Nothing can[13] be added to it or taken from it. God has acted,[14] so that[15] they might fear him.*

15 *Whatever is, already has been. What will be[16] has already been. God makes the same things happen over and over again.*

1 Qohelet begins this, his most memorable poem, with the statement that everything and every activity on earth has its time. The following seven verses will particularize this opening statement.

Qohelet intends to cover *everything,* leaving no exceptions. The second colon[17] is more specific in that it refers to *every activity.*[18] The Hebrew word for *activity (ḥēpeṣ)* has an interesting etymology. In certain contexts it means "pleasure," and that meaning actually occurs elsewhere in Ecclesiastes (5:3 [English 5:4]; 12:10), but in other contexts it clearly means "activity" (here and in 3:17; 5:7 [English 5:8]; 8:6). We know little about the exact relationship between these two meanings of the same root. There may be a semantic development from one meaning to the next, or perhaps they are homonyms. In either case, it is dubious to marshal such etymological information to posit that this passage is "upbeat,"[19] in the sense that the activity is pleasurable.

It is difficult, if not impossible, to draw a distinction between the two "time" words in this verse. *season (zᵉmān)* occurs in late Hebrew and Aramaic

11. The third feminine singular independent pronoun here "is used to denote the whole following case" (Isaksson, *Studies in the Language of Qoheleth,* p. 99).

12. See n. 9.

13. For this kind of modal clause, see Waltke and O'Connor, *Biblical Hebrew Syntax,* p. 609.

14. There is no direct object in Hebrew. Some translations (NIV) feel a need to add one, but this is unnecessary.

15. Here *še* is used to introduce a purpose clause, as *ᵃšer* occasionally does (Deut. 4:10, 40); cf. Whitley, *Koheleth,* p. 34.

16. Note Waltke and O'Connor, *Biblical Hebrew Syntax,* p. 610, where *hāyâ* with *lamed* is described as "periphrasis of the imperfect"; see GKC §114a, i.

17. Scholars differ in their use of terms that describe the parts of a poetic line. "Colon" is a technical term referring to a phrase, clause, or sentence that functions as one of the building blocks of a parallel line. In this case we have a bicolon, a parallelism composed of two cola. For more on the terms that describe Hebrew poetry, cf. Watson, *Classical Hebrew Poetry,* pp. 11-15.

18. Indeed, Kugel (*The Idea of Biblical Poetry,* pp. 11-12, 51-54, 56-57, 95-100) believes that the second colon of a parallel pair always in some way specifies the thought of the first colon.

19. Ogden, *Qoheleth,* p. 52.

passages in the Bible.[20] Franz Delitzsch[21] and Daniel Fredericks[22] remind us that the word has an ancient Akkadian cognate, indicating that it is an older word than one might at first believe.

The more common Hebrew term for *time ('ēt)* occurs uncharacteristically in the second colon of the line, where we usually find the rarer term. We cannot be sure why the poet chose to reverse the normal order, but it is probably due to the fact that *time ('ēt)* is the term that is repeated throughout the whole poem. Both words, according to most commentators, "indicate specific points in time rather than continuity."[23]

What follows is a list of activities that are not prescriptive, but rather descriptive, of what actually happens *under heaven* (Qohelet's alternative phrase to the more common "under the sun," for which see 1:3). After all, it would be hard to say that there is a good time to be born, to die, or to lose something.

2 Verses 2-8 contain fourteen pairs of contrasting opposites. The citing of opposites in this way is a common figure of speech (merism)[24] in Hebrew poetry, and it denotes completeness.

The first two pairs encompass the entire life cycle, first of a human *(be born . . . die)* and then of a plant *(plant . . . uproot).*[25] No person or plant controls the start or finish of its existence, so the descriptive (rather than prescriptive) nature of the list is established right from the start.

The four verbs of the verse are qal infinitive constructs, prefixed with a *lamed.* The qal form is unusual only for the last verb of the verse *(to uproot; la'ăqôr),* which normally occurs in the niphal (Zeph. 2:4) or piel (2 Sam. 8:4). Though some scholars make the case for a positive rendering of this root ("to harvest"),[26] this is unlikely in light of the close parallel with "to die" in the first part of the verse.[27] It is also true that in all other cases the verb has a negative meaning in its literal and metaphorical senses (Zeph. 2:4; Gen. 49:30; 2 Sam. 8:4).

20. Cf. Neh. 2:6l; Esth. 9:27, 31; Ezra 5:3; Dan. 2:16, 21; 3:7, 8; 4:33; 6:11, 14; 7:12, 22, 25.

21. Delitzsch, *Proverbs, Ecclesiastes, Song of Songs,* p. 255.

22. Fredericks, *Qoheleth's Language,* pp. 197-98 and 223-24.

23. Crenshaw, *Ecclesiastes,* p. 92.

24. See Watson, *Classical Hebrew Poetry,* pp. 321-24, for more on merism.

25. Of course, it is looking at the life cycle of a plant from the perspective of human activity. If it were about the plant itself, the verb would be passive. Nonetheless, the effect of the line is to circumscribe the life cycle of the plant.

26. See Ogden, *Qoheleth,* p. 52.

27. While it is true that parallelism is a complex phenomenon and it is never the case that parallel words are exact synonyms, close reading of the poem indicates that the poet gives his pairs in pairs. That is, the first contrasting pair is semantically related to the second pair. The breakup of the poem into verses captures this by separating the pairs of pairs into individual verses.

3 The poem continues with two additional pairs of contrasting opposites. This time, however, there is a notable twist. Whereas in v. 2 the positive/desirable/constructive actions precede the undesirable, in this verse the reverse occurs. On the negative side the verse speaks of killing and tearing down, while on the positive it acknowledges that there are occasions when healing and building take place.

The first pair describes the sphere of the animate, most likely specifically human *(to kill . . . to heal). kill* and *heal* are not exact semantic opposites, but the former is an intentional act to end a life, and the latter refers to efforts to preserve a life. There is certainly no need to follow *BHS* when it emends the verb *hrg (to kill)* to *hrs* "to destroy" or *hdp* "to drive out." The poet, once again, is describing what occurs under the sun; he is not making moral pronouncements. The killing here may refer to the legitimate ending of life (at least according to the worldview of the OT), such as capital punishment or the waging of holy war.

The second pair *(to tear down . . . to build)* connects at least loosely with the first. Indeed, the four pairs in vv. 2 and 3 are associated in that they cite beginnings and endings. *tear down* and *build* normally belong to the semantic domain of construction. It is also conceivable that the broader context is warfare here. An attacking army tears down buildings, but after hostilities cease, they are built once again. This case cannot be pressed too strongly since the words are widely used outside battle contexts.[28]

4 We move next to the realm of emotions. This verse presents two closely related pairs of contrasting emotions. First, on the negative side the verse states that there are occasions that elicit unpleasant emotions, crying and mourning. On the other, positive side stand laughter and dancing.

The first colon contrasts crying with laughter. The second colon focuses the contrast, making it more specific and, one might say, more concrete as it contrasts mourning with dancing. We also move from the personal to the public expression of these emotions as we move from the first to the second colon. That is, the second pair may evoke the image of a public ritual, whereas the first pair does not.

The one grammatical peculiarity of this verse is the omission of the preposition *lamed* before the second pair. The two verbs that make up the second pair are nonetheless infinitives construct and in this case have "gerundial meaning."[29] This results in a shift from a noun plus purpose clause to a construct chain (see v. 8b as a further example).

Franz Delitzsch[30] remarks that there is consonance between *libnôt,*

---

28. For *prṣ,* see Gen. 38:29 and 2 Sam. 6:8. For *bnh,* see Gen. 33:17; 41:7.
29. Whitley, *Koheleth,* p. 31; see also GKC §114b.
30. Delitzsch, *Proverbs, Ecclesiastes, Song of Solomon,* p. 257.

which appears at the end of v. 3, and *libkôt,* which begins v. 4, and that the assonance between *sᵉpôd* and *rᵉqôd* may suggest the choice of the latter, a relatively rare term. Assonance might also explain the omission of the *lamed* since the sound *lis-* (ending in a sibilant) of *lispôd* does not match *lir-* of *lirqôd* (a harder sound).[31]

5 The fourth pair of contrasting opposites are harder to categorize because they do not seem related at first, unlike the other pairs of contrasting opposites that precede and follow it. The first speaks of throwing and then gathering stones, the second of embracing and not embracing.

Indeed, this fourth pair of contrasting opposites stands out in more than one way. First, both pairs are lengthier than the others, and no textual evidence supports a change.[32] Second, the meaning of the first pair (v. 5a) is obscure and debated, whereas all the others are simple and clear. Among the many suggestions, two have been taken more seriously. Based on a reading of the *Midrash Rabbah,* some commentators see a sexual reference in the idiom. The Midrash, as quoted by Robert Gordis,[33] who follows it, reads: "A time to cast stones — when your wife is clean (menstrually), and a time to gather stones in — when your wife is unclean." However, there is little evidence besides the *Midrash Rabbah* that supports the interpretation that "to cast stones" means to make love. R. N. Whybray suggests a more literal and commonsense approach to the phrase, which is the one adopted here. He sees the contrast as "the need to clear away stones from a field in order to make it suitable for agricultural use (cf. Isa. 5:2) and, by contrast, to the deliberate ruining of an enemy's field by throwing stones into it (2 Kg. 3:19, 25)."[34]

An unusual feature of the second pair is that, instead of using antonyms to express opposites, the contrast is stated by using the verb *ḥbq (embrace)* positively in the first half and then by negating it in the second colon through the introduction of the infinitive phrase *rḥq min (to refrain from).* The verb *ḥbq (embrace)* refers to a gesture or action that denotes affection for another. It can be used to refer to sexual intercourse (Prov. 5:20), but it can also be used to refer to other levels and types of affection, especially in the context of greetings or welcomes, particularly for the first time or after separation (Gen. 29:13; 2 Kings 4:16). The latter seems to be the case here.

---

31. This suggestion comes from a personal communication with Robert Hubbard.

32. For instance, omission of the direct object "stones," which would make the verse fit in better with its context. But on the principle of "the most difficult reading," this observation becomes an argument in favor of no textual emendation. Furthermore, such an emendation would make the first pair significantly shorter than the second, which would be unlikely.

33. Gordis, *Koheleth,* p. 230; J. A. Loader (*Ecclesiastes,* Text and Interpretation [Grand Rapids, MI: Eerdmans, 1986], pp. 36-37) also supports this line of interpretation.

34. Whybray, *Ecclesiastes,* NCB, p. 71.

6   The fifth pair of contrasting opposites has to do with possession. On the one hand, there are occasions when we need to look for something or keep something, but on the other hand, there are occasions when we give up the search or throw something away.

There is a time to look for something and a time to give up according to Qohelet. Nonetheless, just as it is impossible for people to know the day of their death, control their weeping and laughing or their mourning and rejoicing, so it is hard, sometimes impossible, to know when something is irrevocably lost. So, frustratingly, time will continue to be wasted looking for it.

Note the ambiguous reference to the object of the search in the first pair and the reference of the verbs in the second. In this way, Qohelet keeps his statement general rather than particular.

7   Up to this point the two pairs of contrasting opposites in each verse have been closely related to one another. The relationship between the two pairs in this verse is not so obvious. First, Qohelet contrasts tearing and sewing. Then, in the second colon he moves to the arena of speech and contrasts silence and speech.

Gordis, however, names "mourning" as the cultural context of the verse, and perhaps he is correct.[35] It is true, after all, that tearing clothes was an important ancient biblical mourning ritual (Gen. 37:29; 2 Sam. 13:31) and that the clothes would be repaired at the close of the mourning period. For this reason, the mourning background to v. 7a makes sense. However, the connection of v. 7b with the expression of grief is questionable. It is true that silence is occasionally described as a reaction to tragedy (perhaps Lev. 10:3 and certainly Job 2:13, where there is a connection with the rending of clothes). Nonetheless, we cannot be dogmatic about this connection because it is not established by the text itself. Further, the focus of v. 7b on the time of speaking and silence may be connected with the very important wisdom theme of knowing the proper time to speak and to refrain from speaking (see Prov. 10:19; 13:3; 16:24; 17:27; 21:23; 25:11, and especially 15:23).[36]

8   This last verse of the poem presents two contrasting pairs with a definite connection. The first pair *(love . . . hate)* cite strong personal emotions of attraction and repulsion. These emotions on a corporate and public level manifest themselves as the states of *peace* and *war,* the contrasting pair of the second colon. Qohelet expresses the latter pair in nominal form, perhaps simply to effect a sense of closure,[37] and in this regard he also arranges the verse is the form of a chiasm:

---

35. See Gordis, *Koheleth,* pp. 230-31.
36. See Whybray, *Ecclesiastes,* NCB, pp. 71-72.
37. Ginsburg, *The Song of Songs and Coheleth,* p. 307.

Once again, it is imporant to emphasize that the poem does not advocate these emotions/states/actions, but simply describes them as parts of the full spectrum of human experience.

9 The poem has now ended, and Qohelet continues by drawing out its implications, providing a prose reflection on the preceding verses. The main point of the poem is that God has established periods, moments, or times for a wide diversity of emotions and activities. The following verses describe Qohelet's reaction to these observations. Is the world a wonderfully ordered and varied place of joy?

Qohelet's initial reaction reveals that he would answer that question in the negative. Once again he asks the rhetorical question concerning the profit of toil in the world. Without detailed explanation, Qohelet casts doubt over the benefit of a world where everything has its proper season or opportune moment. As we read on in the section, we will discover why. By means of this opening rhetorical question,[38] Qohelet states that there is no purpose to doing anything[39] in this fallen world. The rationale for this judgment follows in the next verses.

10 Verse 10 develops and continues the thought of v. 9. Qohelet follows his question with the statement that he has kept watch on the task that God has assigned to human beings and that keeps them active and busy. He will give the depressing results of his observation in the next verse.

This verse closely repeats a previous thought. While this line has the introductory phrase of 1:14 (see discussion there), the rest of the verse is nearly identical to 1:13 (see discussion of vocabulary there). The main difference is that the *task* there is explicitly designated as *evil*. The context here, however, makes it plain that the negative connotation is still present.

11 This verse is widely thought to be one of the hardest in the book to interpret, but its difficulty is not a function of the vocabulary. Taken individually, the words are fairly common; the question centers on their precise meaning in the present context. Indeed, the first part of the verse strikes the reader as one of the most beautiful and inspiring of the Bible. Apparently

---

38. For detailed exegetical description of this phrase, see 1:3, where it occurs for the first time (note also the latter repetition in 5:15 [English 5:16]). Also note the use of the noun *profit (yitrôn)* outside the formula in 2:11, 13; 5:8 (English 5:9); 7:12; 10:10, 11.

39. *ʿāśâ*, according to the dictionaries, has a broader meaning than simply performing an occupation.

flowing from the poem in vv. 1-8, this verse comments that God has made *everything appropriate in its time*. Indeed, if this statement occurred immediately after the poem, it would give us a very positive perspective on those first eight verses.

The following sentence also sounds positive when first read. Qohelet notes that God has *placed eternity in* [the human] *heart*. Since eternity is a divine attribute and since its counterpart, mortality, is something dreaded and feared, one would think that Qohelet was pleased by this truth. However, the context makes it clear that he was not happy as a result of these observations about God's workings in the world and in the human heart — the verse is yet another cry of frustration on Qohelet's part. He goes on in the last part of the verse to complain that God has kept his human creatures from knowing what is going on in his creation. It is as if God is baiting or toying with his human creatures, giving them a desire for something that is well beyond their reach.

From v. 10 we see that *he* in this verse refers to God. The all-inclusive nature of the direct object, *everything,* once again will not permit the reader to exclude anything from Qohelet's conclusion. Indeed, the subtle allusions to creation by the use of carefully chosen vocabulary takes us back to the beginning of time, though it does not exclude what God has done since that time.

It is interesting to note the rather significant allusions to Genesis 1 in this verse.[40] Even the vocabulary is reminscent, though not identical, with that used in Genesis 1. For instance, in Genesis 1 God pronounces each step of his creation "good" *(ṭôb)*.[41] Qohelet's word "beautiful" *(yāpeh)* may also be a reflex of this divine pronouncement. Further, the placing of *ʿōlām, eternity,* in human beings might be analogous to God endowing his human creatures with his image (Gen. 1:26-27). Also, of course, Qohelet uses a verb that is common in Genesis 1, the verb "to make" *(ʿāśâ)*. The other choice is *bārāʾ,* which is used sparingly in the creation account and with special reference to the creation of humanity.

It is difficult to assess the significance of these allusions. Perhaps the use of *yāpeh* rather than *ṭôb* and *ʿāśâ* rather than *bārāʾ* reflects Qohelet's lack of enthusiasm about God's creation, which the context indicates is present.[42] We do not feel confident enough, however, to be dogmatic about our observation.

In the broader context the expression *in its time* is a significant qualification of what precedes. The phrase takes us back to 3:1, where the only

40. As noted by Isaksson, *Studies in the Language of Qoheleth,* p. 79.
41. See Gen. 1:4, 10, 12, 18, 21, 31.
42. In this case, it is perhaps telling that Qohelet uses the common and bland verb *ʿāśâ* rather than the other word for making or creating that is found in Gen. 1, *bārāʾ.*

difference is that our present verse tells us that God is involved with the connection between an activity or thing and its proper time. After surveying the list in vv. 1-8, one may ask whether it is correct to say that everything in that list is *appropriate*. The reader might understand that such negative emotions as sadness and mourning are appropriate, but what of hate and warfare? The question, however, would arise only in a modern context. The righteous hatred of the imprecatory psalms and the holy wars of Israel demonstrate that Qohelet understood that even these would have their appropriate times. Nevertheless, as we will see at the end of the verse, Qohelet is not satisfied with the idea that there are appropriate times for all activities.

In the second sentence of the verse we learn something additional (signaled by *also, gam*). God has done something else that sounds marvelous on the surface but, in the final analysis, is the source of much human frustration. He has *placed eternity in their hearts*. Reading the verse in context makes it plain that the hearts in question are human hearts. God has put *ʿōlām* in the heart, which is the base of human personality, "the center of existence."[43] What is this *ʿōlām?* Debate has raged, and modern commentators are tentative in their conclusion because a decisive argument for any position seems beyond reach. James Crenshaw[44] has helpfully summarized the four competing positions: "(1) eternity, (2) world, (3) course of the world, and (4) knowledge or ignorance."[45] Each of these has its ancient and modern advocates, but the two that have attracted the most agreement in the modern world of scholarship are (1) and (4), and my comments will accordingly concentrate on these.

The translation "ignorance" may have ancient roots,[46] but it has gained followers in recent days,[47] propelled at least in part by analogy with the Ugaritic stem *ǵlm,* "to be dark."[48] Though the root *ʿlm* has this meaning in Ecclesiastes 12:14, the predominant use of *ʿōlām* in the book is clearly, according to context, the expected "eternity" (1:4, 10; 2:16; 3:14; 9:6). These other occurrences are a strong presumptive argument in favor of "eternity"

---

43. The phrase is from N. K. Haden, "Qohelet and the Problem of Alienation," *Christian Scholars Review* 17 (1987): 61.

44. Crenshaw, "The Eternal Gospel (Eccl. 3:11)," in *Essays in Old Testament Ethics,* ed. J. L. Crenshaw and J. T. Willis (New York: KTAV, 1974), p. 40.

45. There is a fifth option as well, namely, to emend. The most common emendation, notably found in *BHK* and Fox (*Qohelet and His Contradictions,* p. 194), is to emend to *ʿāmāl* "toil" (a metathesis of *ʿlm*).

46. Ginsburg, *The Song of Songs and Coheleth,* p. 311, cites Coverdale as someone who gives serious consideration to this view, though it is probably related to an even earlier suggestion by the scholar Ibn Ezra.

47. As noted by Whitley, *Koheleth,* pp. 52-53; and Whybray, *Ecclesiastes,* NCB, pp. 73-74.

48. Since Hebrew does not have the *ǵ* phoneme, the Ugaritic consonants *ǵ* and *ʿ* are both equivalent to Hebrew *ʿ*.

in this verse. The difficulty most people have with the meaning "eternity" is that it sounds so uncharacteristically positive for Qohelet. Once again, this is only so if the phrase is isolated from the last part of v. 11 and everything that precedes it. This placement of eternity in the heart of humans leads to frustration. In recent literature no one has captured the sense of this phrase better than John Jarick, as he comments on both the Hebrew and Septuagintal text:

> In 7:27, 28 Koheleth recorded that he had wanted to discover the sum of things, but could not; and in 8:17 he noted that people seek to find out "all the work of God . . . that is done under the sun," but cannot. 3:11 makes excellent sense as a kind of parallel to these two verses. The human being has *aiōn*, "eternity," in his heart — his Creator has made him a thinking being, and he wants to pass beyond his fragmentary knowledge and discern the fuller meaning of the whole pattern — but the Creator will not let the creature be his equal. As surely as God has put *aiōn* in the human heart (a consciousness that there is more than the immediate *kairos* of this or that [vv. 2-8] in which the creature finds itself), he has also put a veil upon the human heart, so that the finite human mind is unable to reach beyond the *kairos* into the *aiōn* to see as God does.[49]

Thus, Walter Kaiser, Jr.,[50] is correct to say that 3:11 talks of "a deep-seated desire, a compulsive drive . . . to know the character, composition, and meaning of the world . . . and to discern its purpose and destiny." But Kaiser goes on to argue that Qohelet believes people can rest in God. In this he is wrong. Qohelet's compulsive "drive to know" leads to frustration and exasperation, not to rest. This is made clear by the final phrase in the verse. There may indeed be appropriate times for everything, and God does know these times, but, speaking of humans, *no one can discover what God is doing.* This expression does not arise from a flippant "leave it to God" attitude, but from an agony of desire to know what is going on. But such knowledge is inscrutable. There is nothing *(from beginning to end)* that human beings can truly fathom.

12   This verse introduces the conclusion, which flows from the previous verses. If the bigger picture of life is inscrutable to human beings, then they are reduced to lesser goals. Once the search for ultimate meaning in life is thwarted, the best course is to seek the little, sensual pleasure of life. Qohelet communicates his conclusion by means of a variant of the *carpe diem* formula (see the commentary at 2:24). The context and the language of the verse indicate that this conclusion is a statement of resignation, not enthusiasm. The best that life can offer is happiness and enjoyment, the contents of which will

49. Jarick, *Gregory Thaumaturgos' Paraphrase,* p. 65.
50. W. Kaiser, *Ecclesiastes,* p. 66.

be described in the next verse. In brief, Qohelet advises his hearers to give up trying to fathom God's way in the world. Rather, enjoy the present.

Qohelet's statement has an objective tone to it. By his use of third-person narration, he presents himself as an impartial observer. It is clear, though, from his expressions of pain throughout the book, that Qohelet understood that he too was subject to the same realities and conclusions. He was not just an observer; he was both observer and participant.

The phrase *there is nothing better* may also be found in 2:24, as well as 3:22 and 8:15. These are all variants of the *carpe diem* formula, which expresses a resigned awareness that life's enjoyment will come from small sensual pleasures, rather than an understanding of the grander scheme of things. Again, it is significant to point out that the expression admits that what follows is not the highest, best imaginable good but life in a fallen world, which is the best humans can do under the circumstances.

I have rendered the expression *la‘ašôt ṭôb* (literally "to do good") in a nonmoral sense *(enjoy themselves).* Daniel Fredericks disagrees, arguing for a moral force to the expression,[51] but the immediate context of 3:13, which uses *ṭôb* with the verb *rā‘â* "to experience," leads me to adopt a nonmoral sense.[52]

13 Verse 13[53] is linked with the previous verse by *also (wᵉgam),* which signals that the content of this verse is associated with what precedes it. In v. 12, Qohelet concludes that the best humans can do is to enjoy life as well as they can in the present. Verse 13 specifies this enjoyment in the same manner as 2:24: eating, drinking, and enjoying work (see that verse for comments). Yet the final thought of the verse is new. Qohelet points out that no one can take even these small, temporal enjoyments for granted. God must permit the opportunity and the attitude that is predisposed toward it. As James Crenshaw rightly states it, "even the power to follow his advice is a divine gift."[54]

51. Fredericks, *Qoheleth's Language,* p. 247. Most occurrences of the phrase *(‘āśâ ṭôb)* are outside the book of Ecclesiastes (Num. 24:14; Ps. 37:3, 27; 119:65). Also note the indisputably moral use of the phrase in Eccles. 7:20. This supports the moral reading of the phrase in Eccles. 3:12.

52. Some scholars (cf. Whitley, *Koheleth,* p. 34) wrongly suggest that a nonmoral meaning implies a Hellenistic date for the book. See Fredericks, *Qoheleth's Language,* p. 247, for references to early nonmoral uses of the phrase (e.g., 2 Sam. 12:18, in this instance with *rā‘â*).

53. Though the meaning of the verse is relatively clear, its syntax immediately strikes the reader as abrupt. Whybray (*Ecclesiastes,* NCB, p. 74) calls it "very loose," and this observation leads Lauha (*Kohelet,* p. 69) to conclude that it is an addition *(Zusatz),* always the easy way out of a textual jam. The difficulty is that the first part of the verse is not a complete sentence. It is interrupted in the middle, and then the verse continues with a brief, but complete, independent sentence.

54. Crenshaw, *Ecclesiastes,* p. 99.

It is true, as John Jarick pointed out,[55] that Qohelet consistently links God with the possibility of enjoyment in the present (2:24-26; 3:13, 22; 8:15). It is fair to deduce, however, that from his frequent expressions of pain and frustration Qohelet did not himself feel that God granted him this *gift,* which serves as anesthesia toward the problems of the present fallen world (see 5:18, 19 [English 5:19, 20], where again we encounter the *gift of God*). This insight points to Qohelet's underlying problem: he feels unfairly treated.

14 Qohelet reaches yet another (see v. 12) conclusion based on his observation in vv. 1-8, and he begins it again with *I know.* In essence, Qohelet comments that whatever God does endures, and no one can change God's plan. No matter how frustrating God's world is, people must learn to put up with it. Furthermore, he asserts that God's purpose behind his actions is to strike fear in the hearts of his creatures (see below).

Qohelet speaks vaguely and generally when he refers to *everything God does* (the verb is from *'āśâ*). By this expression he certainly refers to "making" (*'āśâ,* v. 11) everything appropriate for its time, and thus he refers back to vv. 1-8. It likely also includes God's placing "eternity" in human hearts. The point of the present verse is: try as they might, whether they like it or not, humans cannot change their situation. The syntax and semantics of the sentence, *Nothing can be added to it or taken from it,* indicate that it is a proverbial statement. As a proverb, we are not surprised to find similar statements with nearly identical vocabulary elsewhere (Deut. 4:12; 13:1 [English 12:32]; and in part in Prov. 30:6). Furthermore, Ben Sira uses the expression in a way reminiscent of Qohelet when he states, "One cannot take away and one cannot add, and one should not investigate God's wonders" (Sir. 18:6).[56]

The final clause gives the reason why God acts in the way that he does. Here we should hear Qohelet's conclusion, but he expressed his feelings in such a way that it has been impossible for commentators to reach agreement his meaning. After all, the expression to *fear* God is perhaps one of the most pious statements in the Bible (see Prov. 1:7 and Ps. 111). Nonetheless, commentators who read this sentence as an expression of a right attitude with God[57] do not take into account the overwhelmingly negative context that surrounds the phrase,[58] both here and in its other occurrences in the book of Ecclesiastes (5:6 [English 5:7]; 7:18; 8:12, 13 [see discussion]; 12:13[59] is a separate case; see discussion there). A fuller treatment of this phrase in the

---

55. Jarick, *Gregory Thaumaturgos' Paraphrase,* p. 68.

56. Quoted by Fox, *Qohelet and His Contradictions,* p. 195.

57. Whybray, *Ecclesiastes,* NCB, p. 75.

58. See, for instance, Crenshaw, *Ecclesiastes,* pp. 99-100.

59. "The end of the matter. All has been heard. Fear God, and keep his commandments, for this is the whole duty of humanity" (12:13).

context of the whole book may be found in "Theological Message" in the introduction. In brief, though, Qohelet believes that God acts the way that he does to frighten people into submission, not to arouse a sense of respectful awe of his power and might.

15 This verse, which concludes the section that began the chapter, emphasizes the thought of the previous verse — what God does lasts forever and nothing can alter it. It performs this function by repeating the language of 1:9, which will become important as we attempt to interpret the enigmatic second half of the verse. In brief, the verse states that nothing new ever happens or will ever happen. God just repeats himself through time, and humans cannot make things better.

Differences exist in regard to the correct English tense to use in order to rightly render the first verb. I have translated it as a present, *is,* and note Bo Isaksson's perceptive comment that "the whole emphasis in the book lies on the actual life under the sun, and what is spoken of in the preceding verses as well as in the following is what is going on just now, in the present life."[60] Graham Ogden takes the view that the verb should be translated by an English past tense, but he does not argue for it.[61] In any case, Qohelet's point in this verse is that — past, present, future — there is nothing new under the sun.

Qohelet sees God behind this monotonous situation. The present translation, *God makes the same things happen over and over again,* is a rather idiomatic treatment of what may more literally be taken as "God seeks what is sought/pursued." The finite verb of the sentence *(yᵉbaqqēš)* and the niphal participle that serves as the direct object *(nirdāp)* derive from roots that are near synonyms (see their use in Ps. 34:15 [English 34:14]). The likely meaning of the phrase is, as Jarick puts it,[62] "God keeps on seeking what he has sought before." The next question to ask is, What is God seeking? James Crenshaw conveniently lists four options: (1) the persecuted, (2) the events of the past, (3) the same, (4) what God sought previously.[63] He points out that most of the versions, with the exception of the Vulgate, opted for the first possibility: God seeks the persecuted, the poor, the downtrodden. This approach, which understands the niphal participle as a reference to those who are sought by their enemies, is not convincing. The Vulgate, however, represents an approach that not only is sensitive to the immediate context but also, equally importantly, follows the similar thought of 1:9. It translates the clause *et Deus instaurat quod abiit* ("and God repeats

60. Isaksson, *Studies in the Language of Qoheleth,* p. 29.
61. Ogden, *Qoheleth,* p. 57.
62. Jarick, *Gregory Thaumaturgos' Paraphrase,* p. 71.
63. Crenshaw, *Ecclesiastes,* p. 100.

what has passed away").[64] In other words of Qohelet, there is "nothing new under the sun" (1:9), thanks to God and the way he runs the world.

In vv. 1-15 Qohelet acknowledges the order of God's universe. There are proper times and seasons. Nonetheless, since human beings cannot know these times, the result is frustration. In the light of humanity's inability to discover the larger picture or significance of God's creation, Qohelet advocates settling for the lesser pleasures of life. However, not everyone can avail themselves of these diversions, only those whom God so blesses. The implication is that other people, including Qohelet himself, must struggle with depressing reality.

2. Is There Any Justice? (3:16-22)

Verse 16 begins a new topic (introduced by the telltale *Furthermore I observed*) as Qohelet now shifts his attention to the issue of justice. He clearly states the problem in v. 16 — there is no place of justice on earth. This observation leads him to assert God's future judgment in v. 17, a verse that provides linkage with the previous section in its repetition of the phrase "a time for every activity," found also in 3:1. The thought of divine judgment, however, provides him only brief solace because he then shifts to his ultimate nemesis, death. Death raises a question mark over the possibility of even divine judgment since at best there is only a glimmer of hope, according to Qohelet, that our fate is any different from an animal's (v. 21). Thus, he is led once again to assert the relative benefit of the pleasures of the present. The future is, after all, completely uncertain (v. 22c).

16 *Furthermore I observed under the sun:*
    The place of judgment — injustice was there!
    The place of righteousness — injustice was there!
17 *I said to myself,[65] "God will judge the righteous and the unjust, for there is a time for every activity and for every deed too.[66]*

---

64. Fox, *Qohelet and His Contradictions,* p. 197.

65. See 2:11 for the identical expression. For a slight variant and comment, see 1:16.

66. For the difficulties and options for the adverb *šām,* here translated *too,* see Whitley, *Koheleth,* pp. 34-36. The translation offered here follows Whitley in tentatively treating it as an asseverative. Isaksson (*Studies in the Language of Qoheleth,* p. 176) is in agreement. Perhaps the most common alternative rendering is to emend the word to a form of the verb *śîm* in the sense of "to appoint" (so R. B. Y. Scott, *Proverbs. Ecclesiastes,* AB [Garden City, NY: Doubleday, 1965], p. 265; and the RSV). For a refutation of this approach, see Whybray, *Ecclesiastes,* NCB, p. 78.

18 *I said to myself[67] concerning[68] the human race, "God tests them so that they may see they are like animals."*

19 *For the fate of[69] human beings and the fate of animals are the same fate.[70] One dies like the other. There is one breath for all. Human beings have no advantage over the animals, for everything is meaningless.*

20 *All go to the same place. All come from the dust, and all return to the dust.*

21 *Who[71] knows whether the breath of humans goes up above and the breath of animals goes down to the depths of the earth?*

22 *So I observed[72] that there is nothing better than for people to rejoice in their work, for that is their reward.[73] For who can bring them to see what will happen after them?*

16 Qohelet introduces his new topic in a typical manner by using the first-person singular perfect form of *rāʾâ, I observed* (for other occurrences and comment, see 1:14), signaling yet another reflection. The connecting word *Furthermore (weʿôd)* provides a link with what precedes.[74] Here is yet another observation that supports his thesis that the present world is without profit and meaning. In this verse, Qohelet reports that he sees injustice in the place where you most expect justice — the law court. The implication of the verse is that guilt and innocence are confused in the law court — the innocent are judged guilty and the guilty judged innocent. Thus, Qohelet questions whether a person can expect to receive what he or she really deserves.

After the prose introduction (v. 16a), we have what appears to be a parallel line composed of two cola. Thus, I have followed *BHS* and rendered them in a poetic format. The parallelism is so strong, indeed, that there is just the variation of a single word between the two. The near identity of the two cola imparts a strong note of emphasis to the statement; the variation of the word sharpens the expression of moral outrage. *The place of judgment* is

---

67. See Eccles. 2:1.

68. Many scholars (see, e.g., Whitley, *Koheleth*, p. 36) believe that this expresion is a sign of lateness. However, see Fredericks, *Qoheleth's Language*, pp. 204-6.

69. Here and in the next occurrence of *fate (miqreh)*, the versions and context support the emendation to *miqrēh*, the construct form of the same noun.

70. I emend the verse by removing the *waw* before *miqreh*, with the support of the versions.

71. The Septuagint and the Syriac, as well as some Hebrew manuscripts, prefix a *waw* "and" to the verse.

72. See comment at 1:14.

73. See comment at 2:10.

74. For the expression *under the sun*, see 1:3.

certainly a reference to the place where law was to be adjudicated, the law court. *The place of righteousness* is the same place, but here the expression heightens the belief that the law courts were a place where righteous judgments would be made. The innocent should be declared innocent and the guilty declared guilty. On the contrary, Qohelet asserts, the courts are the place of *injustice.*[75]

The syntax of these two sentences is abrupt in the Hebrew, though most English translations attempt to smooth it out. I have retained the abruptness, though, because it communicates the outrage Qohelet feels at the situation. It is as if the outrage outpaces his ability to articulate words.

The reader can see that Qohelet abandons the Solomonic persona in this verse. Political and legal justice were the ultimate responsibility of the king in ancient Israel. That Qohelet observes it and expresses his distaste for it, and in no way owns responsibility for it, is one of the many signs that Qohelet is not actually Solomon or any of the kings of Israel or Judah.

17 The verse begins with the expression *I said to myself ('āmartî 'anî b*e*libbî),* which is a typical phrase in Qohelet's reflections (1:16; 2:11).

Verse 16 addressed the injustice found in human law courts. Apparently, the innocent were declared guilty and the guilty innocent. Qohelet ponders this observation from a theological point of view. He reminds himself of what he was surely taught growing up in Israel, namely that, though human justice is a rare and fleeting quality, God will set things right. The lack of human justice evokes a statement about divine justice: God would set things right. The innocent and guilty would get what they actually deserve from the hand of God.

However, in the verses to follow, Qohelet will raise issues that cast doubt on the validity of this assertion. In v. 17 he states that there is a *time for every activity and for every deed.* This phrase alludes to 3:1 and is here applied to the time of fair judgment. However, we have already seen that, although God has such times carefully planned out, his creatures cannot know them and thus they become frustrated.

Qohelet implies that the time of fair judgment and proper retribution is not in the present. Yet in the following verses Qohelet also does not express a concept of eternal life and a judgment day, when all things will be set aright.[76]

Thus, we have a tension, if not a simple contradiction, in Qohelet's thinking. Qohelet asserts his belief in divine retribution but does not allow a

---

75. As mentioned, the repetitions in this poetic line are for emphasis and negate the need to emend, following the Septuagint and the Targum, the second *injustice (hārāša')* to "revolt" *(happāša')*; cf. *BHS*.

76. Contra A. Maltby, "The Book of Ecclesiastes and the After-Life," *EQ* 35 (1963): 39-44.

time for it, and he goes on in the next few verses to cast doubt on the concept of divine retribution itself. As described in the introduction, Qohelet is a doubting wisdom teacher who struggles with the religious traditions of Israel, specifically, with how their teachings square with human experience.

18 In the previous verse Qohelet stated a simple theological truth: God will judge the righteous and the unjust. However, this observation does not settle once and for all the issue of injustice in the place of judgment (v. 16). His internal dialogue continues, signaled by the introductory *I said to myself.* This phrase is repeated from v. 17 and may indicate an internal dialogue or struggle between two opposing ideas within the mind of Qohelet.[77]

In this verse his mind reflects on death. If there is no justice in the present (v. 16), perhaps the afterlife will provide redress. This verse introduces Qohelet's discussion, which extends through v. 22, of the similarity between humans and animals. He is not making a blanket comparison; he specifies one area of commonality — death. Both animals and humans die. We here see that Qohelet believes that the deaths of both humans and animals are identical in consequence. Death signals the end; nothing comes after.

In short, this section is one of a number that indicate to us that Qohelet did not have a conception of the afterlife. Without such, he realizes that there is no place for divine retribution outside the present evil world. In other words, his observation extends beyond "under the sun" to what takes place in the afterlife, but he concludes that there is nothing there.

Though the general sense of this verse is understandable, the particular words and their syntax are difficult. The first difficulty is the form here translated as *tests them.* With this rendering, I follow the traditional route of explanation, taking the form as derived from *brr* ("to separate").[78] The problem, however, is that this is not a definitely attested meaning of the word. It is true that it means "to separate, choose, select, purify" in a number of passages (Neh. 5:18; Ezek. 20:38; Dan. 11:35). From these meanings I derive the translation "test" based on the present context. This meaning is supported by some of the ancient versions (Targum, Vulgate), but the verb's morphology is still in question. Most scholars take the form (*lᵉbārām*) as an infinitive construct with a *lamed* prefix, but that leaves the sentence without a finite verb, an odd situation in Hebrew grammar. Perhaps it is best to understand the form as a qal perfect of the same root, *brr*, with an asseverative *lamed*, but this would involve emendation of the vowel pointing. Fortunately, the sense of the verse is not affected by this decision, and I would translate it the same way in either case.

77. This gives the impression of a change of mind between vv. 17 and 18, "First I thought. . . . Then I thought. . . ."

78. See Crenshaw, *Ecclesiastes,* p. 103.

The Septuagint apparently read what is pointed in the MT as a qal infinitive construct of *rā'â* ("to see") as a hiphil, *lar'ōt* ("to show")." It appears that from ancient times it was felt that the sentence with the qal had to mean something like "God tests them to see," as if God did not know that they were like animals. That, however, throws doubt on God's omniscience. R. N. Whybray suggests that the qal infinitive in this case can imply that humans, not God, are the ones who see that they are like animals.[79] He thus avoids the theological conundrum while preserving the MT. I adopt his suggestion here.

19 Here we get the evidence for the assertion made in v. 18 that humans and animals are alike. How are they alike? They are similar in that both die. Once again we are back to Qohelet's central concern and the worry that leads him to assert the meaninglessness of life — death. We are reminded of 2:16, where the fates of the wise and the fool are compared.

Qohelet's observation of the world proves his point. He has seen the death of animals and the death of humans. Every breathing creature dies (Ps. 49:12, 13; 104:29). Their fate, in the sense of what must happen to them (see Eccles. 2:14 for a discussion of *miqreh*), is that they will die. This inescapable fact reveals to him that humans have no *advantage* over the animals. The word *môtar* occurs only here in Ecclesiastes, though see Proverbs 14:23 and 21:5. However, it derives from the same root as the frequent word *yitrôn*, "profit" (first occurrence is in 1:3), and that helps give us its meaning.

Thus, Qohelet questions the concept of afterlife in this and the following verses. It is difficult to know what the common theological belief about the afterlife was at the time of his writing. Little in the OT bears on it, and we do not know when to date Ecclesiastes relative to other texts that assume or allude to an afterlife (Ps. 49:15; Isa. 26:19; Dan. 12:1-4). Whether belief in the afterlife was common or not, his questioning of it does not allow him to resolve the real issue of the passage — retribution. When will God set things right?

20 This verse specifies the thought of the previous verses and confirms their argument. There is no difference in fate between humans and animals. Both share the same origin and the same final destiny. Animals and humans are both part and parcel of creation. This observation throws into doubt the human assumption of superiority over the animals and questions God's teaching that humans should rule over the animals (Ps. 8:6-8).

Whybray is only partially correct when he states that "the thought of the whole verse is again completely in accordance with traditional Israelite beliefs."[80] There is no doubt that orthodox tradition knew that humans were

---

79. Whybray, *Ecclesiastes,* NCB, p. 78.
80. Whybray, *Ecclesiastes,* NCB, p. 80.

THE BOOK OF ECCLESIASTES

composed of the same stuff as the rest of creation. After all, this is the teaching of Genesis 2:7 (which mentions that Adam was created out of the dust of the ground, symbolically associating humanity with the rest of creation), which is supported by Genesis 3:19, Psalm 90:3, 104:29, Job 10:9, and 34:15. But when Genesis 2 teaches about the creation of humanity, it does so in a context that shows not only human kinship with creation (i.e., "human" [*'ādām*] and "ground" [*'adāmâ*]), but also its special and distinct relationship with God. After all, it is only humans who are created in the image of God, and it is only humans about whom we hear that God "breathed into his nostrils the breath of life" (Gen. 2:7).

Thus, while it is true that Qohelet is right that humans were created from the dust of the earth and that they will return to that dust, it is not true that this is the whole teaching of the OT about the creation of human beings. Contra Whybray, Qohelet at least implicitly departs in this section from normative OT teaching, which affirms a special kinship to God and human rulership over the animals.

21 In the light of the above, Qohelet now asks us to consider whether there is any difference between animals and humans in terms of their destiny after death. Does the spirit of one go to God and the other not? Qohelet probably has in mind some concept of the afterlife here.[81] To make sense of this question, it is likely that some people or schools of thought believed that such a distinction was indeed the case and that life after death was a reality. However, in the light of our uncertainty concerning the date of the book, this would be difficult to establish with confidence. At the very least, then, Qohelet is frustrated with the unknowability of the afterlife, if not its existence.

The rhetorical question does not necessarily deny the possibility of the afterlife, but it does deny a certainty about it. Christian Ginsburg,[82] basing his argument on Rashbam (Samuel ben Meir, Jewish theologian from the twelfth century A.D.), points out the connection with v. 19 and comments that, while it is obvious to everyone that the fate of the human body is identical to that of the animals, it is not certain about their *breath (rûaḥ)*. Certainty on the issue is beyond the pale of human possibility.

The translation *breath* is used here for Hebrew *rûaḥ* in order to be consistent with v. 19, where "spirit" would be inappropriate. It should be pointed out, however, that "spirit" would work in v. 21 since *breath* there represents life and perhaps what we understand as "spirit" (so the NRSV).[83]

The present translation depends in part on a very simple textual emendation that has ample support from the versions. The two participles, here

81. For the similar language at 12:7, see the commentary there.
82. Ginsburg, *The Song of Songs and Coheleth*, p. 319.
83. See Lys, *L'Ecclésiaste*, p. 395.

translated *goes up* and *goes down,* have prefixed *h*'s (*hā'ōlâ* and *hayyōredet,* respectively). The Masoretes pointed the prefixes as definite article markers, which had the effect of turning the verse into a statement: "the breath (or spirit) of humans goes up above and the breath (or spirit) of animals goes down." Perhaps the Masoretes wanted to turn Qohelet into a more traditional theologian who believed in the distinction between humans and animals, but the result of their pointing is out of keeping with the context and ignores the force of the introductory *Who knows (mî yôdēa').* The interrogative character of the verse is firmly established by the introductory *Who,* contra Walter Kaiser, Jr.,[84] who argues that *mî* should be taken in a noninterrogative sense.[85] Kaiser's argument is a desperate attempt to defend his thesis that Qohelet is consistently orthodox (see "Theological Message" in the introduction).

22 Since Qohelet is uncertain about the afterlife, he cannot be sure that the righteous and wicked get what they actually deserve. The realization that death renders justice uncertain leads Qohelet to assert again the relative value of enjoying the present. He does so using language reminiscent of 2:24-26 and 3:12-14 and anticipatory of 5:17-19 (English 5:18-20), 8:15, and 9:7-10. All of these, including the present verse, are the so-called *carpe diem* ("seize the day") passages. In other words, if justice cannot be found in the present (v. 16) or the future (vv. 18-21), then humans should take advantage of every opportunity for pleasure presented to them now.[86] Once again, though, it is clear that these "pleasures" in the present life are simply the best that we can do under the circumstances. The last sentence of the verse, again a rhetorical question (see 3:21) expecting a negative answer,[87] shows clearly that Qohelet's advice is motivated by our limitations.

The phrase *after them* is a circuitous manner of saying "after their death." As above, Qohelet here is uncertain whether (and probably doubts that) life continues after death. No one knows for certain. Robert Gordis[88] argues that the suffix is "petrified" (that is, frozen in form) and the term simply means "afterwards" or the like. Such a rendering would have Qohelet pondering his earthly future, an interpretation that is possible but not likely, since the context indicates that it would be more likely that Qohelet is thinking, though in a confused way, about the afterlife.

---

84. W. Kaiser, *Ecclesiastes,* pp. 70-71.

85. But see the comment to Eccles. 2:19 and also the article by Crenshaw, "The Expression *mî yôdēa'* in the Hebrew Bible," where he persuasively argues that the phrase signals Qohelet's complete skepticism.

86. See "Theological Message" in the introduction for the overall impact of all the *carpe diem* passages.

87. Contra W. Kaiser, *Ecclesiastes,* pp. 71-72.

88. Gordis, *Koheleth,* p. 238.

SUMMARY OF CHAPTER 3

The chapter is divided into two major sections. In the first, Qohelet poetically expresses the truth that the universe is ordered and well made. There is a time for everything, and God knows the times. However, this poem, which sounds so uplifting on the surface, is actually quite depressing. While God knows the times, he keeps that knowledge to himself; human beings are not privy to it. As a result, the wisdom enterprise is undermined, and human experience becomes hugely frustrating. Accordingly, Qohelet resignedly invites people to enjoy the small pleasures of life, provided God allows them to do so (vv. 12-13). God's purpose is to frighten people. In Qohelet's estimation, he is a cosmic bully (vv. 14-15).

In the second part of the chapter (3:16-22), the question of justice is raised. Injustice appeared to reign even in the place where one might expect righteousness — the court of law. Qohelet briefly entertains the possibility that everything will be put right in the future, but then he pulls the carpet out from his own argument by saying that death may very well be the end of it all for human beings, as for animals. Once again, in the light of these depressing facts, Qohelet advocates the simple pleasures of life. After all, what else is there for human beings?

3. Better Off Dead (4:1-3)

The opening section of chapter 4 raises the issue of oppression in the world, particularly the exploitation of the powerless by the powerful. Qohelet's observation on oppression leads to his, by this time not surprising, conclusion that, though we may lament the existence of oppression, we cannot do anything about it.

Connections may be found with the units before (the general theme of injustice; cf. 3:16-22) and after (cf. 5:8-9 [English 5:9-10]).[1] Nonetheless, the theme of oppression is significantly different, focusing on the absence of any consolation or hope for the oppressed, and justifies treating this passage separately.

Of course, such a perspective on the topic of oppression seems awkward when attributed to the mind of Solomon. Not only could Solomon

---

1. For a suggested structural link between this unit and the two following units of the chapter (vv. 4-6 and 7-9), see Ogden, *Qoheleth,* pp. 65-66. He argues that the first two verses of each unit are an observation given a "better . . . than" conclusion. His analysis is not precise, though. As I look at the first unit, the observation appears in the first verse, not the first two. Also v. 9, the third "better-than" proverb, introduces the section of vv. 9-12 rather than concludes the one in vv. 7-8.

have done something about oppression, but he, according to the historical books, contributed heavily to it in the last days of his life (1 Kings 11). This passage is a subtle signal, which, along with many other indications, demonstrates that the relationship between Solomon and Qohelet in the earlier part of the book is a literary and rhetorical one.

1 *Then I turned[2] and observed all the oppression[3] that is[4] done under the sun, and oh,[5] the tears of the oppressed! There is no one to comfort them. Power is in the grasp of the oppressors. There is no one to comfort them.*

2 *So I praised[6] the dead who are already dead more than the living who are still[7] alive.[8]*

3 *But better than both of these is the one who does not yet exist. That one has not seen the evil activity that is done under the sun.*

1 Qohelet begins his discussion of oppression in the same detached, clinical manner that he approached other topics: *I observed,* which signals yet another reflection.[9] The subject of oppression, though, overwhelms him at least momentarily: *oh, the tears of the oppressed.* Nonetheless, he does not personally engage the subject or enjoin others to resist the oppressors. He simply resigns himself to the situation that the oppressors have the power, and those

2. I do not interpret the force of the verb *šûb* here by translating "again" ("I again observed . . . all the oppression") as many other translations (NRSV, REB, NAB, NJB) do, since Qohelet does not earlier deal with oppression as such. The use of *šûb* likely signals the start of a new topic; that is, he redirects his eyes to examine a new area. See the identical expression in 4:7 and a similar one in 9:11.

3. The Hebrew noun is plural here (*hāʿašuqîm,* literally, "oppressions"), but I treat it as a collective.

4. For the tense of this expression *(naʿašîm)* both here and in v. 3, see Isaksson, *Studies in the Language of Qoheleth,* pp. 69-74.

5. So translating *hinnēh;* see Crenshaw, *Ecclesiastes,* p. 101.

6. This form *(wešabbēh)* is the infinitives absolute, and it stands in the place of a finite verb. With such a function it is not unprecedented that it is followed by an explicit subject, especially considering that the subject is first person. See GK §113gg. Waltke and O'Connor (*Biblical Hebrew Syntax,* p. 596, n. 60) call this a "systematic exception" to the rule that infinitives absolute do not express an explicit subject and name it a *qātali anāku* construction. See also Isaksson, *Studies in the Language of Qoheleth,* pp. 63-65; and A. Schoors, *The Preacher Sought to Find Pleasing Words: A Study of the Language of Qoheleth,* part 1 (Leuven: Departement Orientalistiek/Uitgeverij Peeters, 1992), p. 178.

7. See Waltke and O'Connor, *Biblical Hebrew Syntax,* p. 658, n. 45; Fredericks, *Qoheleth's Language,* p. 189; and Whitley, *Koheleth,* p. 41, for the view that this word *(ʿadenâ)* is the result of a contraction between *ʿad* and *hinnēh.*

8. For the dating of *ʿaden (ʿadenâ),* see Fredericks, *Qoheleth's Language,* p. 189.

9. Murphy, *Wisdom Literature,* pp. 136-37.

who do not are at their mercy. Qohelet neither acts to alleviate their suffering nor asks others to do so. Michael Fox points out that this is true of all the passages in which he treats oppression (3:16; 8:9, 10): "He is just sorry that we must see these things."[10]

Note the twofold repetition of the phrase *There is no one to comfort them*. In the past scholars were quick to emend the second occurrence (see the *BHS* textual note). More recently, this type of repetition is recognized as a stylistic trait of Qohelet (see 3:16).[11] The repetition expresses Qohelet's passion and despair about the subject.

2 Qohelet expresses his dismay concerning the oppression of the weak by the strong. It is better off to be dead than to live in such a world.

In this verse Qohelet uses the first of a number of so-called better-than proverbs.[12] The function of the form is simple: it takes one thing or a relationship between two things and compares it favorably with another thing or another relationship. In this case, Qohelet reacts to the pervasive oppression that he observed on earth by favoring death over life. Those who are alive, it is implied in this verse and made explicit in the next, must continue to be aware of oppression and witness it, while the dead are totally oblivious. Later, Qohelet will appear to contradict himself by saying that he praised, in the sense of commended, not death but pleasure (8:15). This thought is not surprising, however, since he affirms both death and pleasure as an anesthesia against the hard realities of life (5:19 [English 5:20]). This usage of the verbal root behind *praised (šbḥ)* is surprising, in that the psalmist uses it elsewhere to express his admiration for God and his attributes (Ps. 63:4).

Walter Kaiser, Jr., attempts to put a positive spin on Qohelet's failure of nerve in the face of oppression by citing two other biblical characters who react with a death wish in the light of oppressive enemies, Jonah (Jon. 4:3) and Elijah (1 Kings 19:4).[13] He fails to mention, though, that in both cases God rebukes them for their attitude (Jon. 4:10-11 and 1 Kings 19:5-9).

3 This verse carries forward and intensifies the thought of v. 2. In v. 2 Qohelet said it was better to be dead than alive. Here he goes beyond that sentiment by asserting that it was better never to have lived than to have lived and died. Thus, Qohelet emphasizes his abhorrence of oppression, by claiming that those who have never been born are better off even than the dead. The dead, after all, had to experience the world of oppression. Those

---

10. Fox, *Qohelet and His Contradictions,* p. 201.

11. Whybray, *Ecclesiastes,* NCB, p. 81.

12. G. S. Odgen, "The 'Better'-Proverb (Tôb-Spruch), Rhetorical Criticism, and Qoheleth," *JBL* 96 (1977): 489-505.

13. W. Kaiser, Jr., *Ecclesiastes,* p. 72.

who have not yet been born are spared that. The sentiment is similar to that expressed by Job in his lament:

> May the day of my birth perish,
>   and the night it was said, "A boy is born!"
> That day — may it turn to darkness;
>   may God above not care about it;
>   may no light shine upon it.
> May darkness and deep shadow claim it once more;
>   may a cloud settle over it;
>   may blackness overwhelm its light. (Job 3:3-5)

See also Jeremiah:

> Why did I ever come out of the womb
>   to see trouble and sorrow
>   and to end my days in shame? (20:18)

Indeed, John Jarick points out that even "the schools of Hillel and Shammai, which could not agree on whether the words of Koheleth should be included in the biblical collection, did agree that it is better not to be born than to be born!"[14]

The key phrase *does not yet exist (ʿaden lōʾ hāyâ)* is somewhat problematical. The word *yet (ʿaden)* appears to be a form composed of *ʿad* and *hin* (see the comments on the related *ʿadenâ* in 4:2). What is intriguing is that Qohelet specifies those who have not yet been born rather than those aborted before birth, those stillborn, or those who never were and never will be born.

The syntax of the verse has also bothered interpreters, particularly the function of *ʾēt ʾašer,* which occurs in only a few places in the Bible.[15] While some want to read the *ʾēt* as the marker of the accusative[16] and as the distant object either of the verb *praise* in v. 2 or of an unexpressed verb (see the Vulgate, which supplies a verb [*judicavi*]), others take the phrase as marking the nominative.[17] As R. N. Whybray remarks in conclusion to his discussion of the problem, "The general sense is not affected."[18] It is better not to have lived at all than to live and witness awful oppression.

---

14. Jarick, *Gregory Thaumaturgos' Paraphrase,* p. 85.

15. For instance, 1 Kings 8:31 (but this may be a scribal error for *ʾim;* see 2 Chron. 6:22); Jer. 38:16 (but the Qere provides a different reading); and Jer. 6:18 (where it is the accusative of an imperative).

16. Whybray, *Ecclesiastes,* NCB, p. 83.

17. GKC §117m; Lys, *L'Ecclésiaste,* p. 416.

18. Whybray, *Ecclesiastes,* NCB, p. 83.

4. Once Again — The Meaninglessness of Work (4:4-6)

The frustration of work was a major theme in 1:12–2:26, and Qohelet turns to it again in this short section. In the earlier discussion Qohelet emphasized the meaninglessness of working hard and not being able to enjoy the success. Here he grants the success, but now turns to the motivating cause of that success — jealousy. This observation leads him to quote two proverbs, the first promoting work and the second promoting rest. By not advocating hard work in an unqualified way, he "stands clearly against the wisdom of the older wisdom teachers."[19]

4 *Then I observed that all toil and all success[20] in work results from jealousy of one's neighbors. This too is meaningless and chasing the wind.*

5 *Fools fold[21] their hands
and consume their own flesh.*

6 *Better one handful with rest[22]
than two fistfuls[23] with toil —
and chasing the wind.*

4 Qohelet opens yet another reflection with a statement of the object of his observation. He contemplates *toil* and *success in work.* He shares his insight that both result from *jealousy.* That is, as people look at their neighbors, they work hard in order to keep ahead of them. His conclusion is that the cycle of jealousy leading to hard work and success is meaningless.

jealousy (qin'â, here in construct) has positive and negative connota-

---

19. I. J. J. Spannenberg, "Quotations in Ecclesiastes: An Appraisal," *Old Testament Essays* 4 (1991): 25.

20. A number of contemporary commentators prefer "skill" as a translation of *kišrôn;* note in particular Fox, *Qohelet and His Contradictions,* p. 202. This approach is legitimate, since the Ugaritic cognate *(ktr)* clearly has this meaning. The word's use, though, in 5:10 (English 5:11), where it must mean "success" or "profit" rather than "skill," persuades me to translate it in this way here as well (see also 2:21). By the way, Fox himself translates the word "success" in 5:10 (English 5:11). His argument that the context in ch. 4 demands "skill" is unpersuasive.

21. Isaksson (*Studies in the Language of Qoheleth,* pp. 136-37) argues that these participles should be understood as "gnomic presents."

22. Whybray (*Ecclesiastes,* NCB, p. 85) cites GKC §131p, r to support reading both *rest (nāḥat)* and *toil ('āmāl)* as adverbial accusatives. The alternative is to consider them in construct relationship with *kap* and *hopnayim.* To take the latter route, however, requires an emendation, understanding the final *mem* not as a marker of the absolute dual but as an enclitic *mem* (so Whitley, *Koheleth,* p. 42).

23. See Fox, *Qohelet and His Contradictions,* p. 203.

tions in the Bible. The Targum and perhaps the Septuagint play on the ambivalence of the word, the former when it "adds a lengthy note to this verse to the effect that if a person's *qn'h* prompts him to do good, that is good in Heaven's judgment, but if his *qn'h* prompts him to do evil, that is bad in Heaven's judgment."[24] Some modern commentators pick up on the word's positive connotation and turn Qohelet's statement into a positive one. Graham Ogden, for instance, states that the word should be translated "rivalry," and it "provides the incentive for the effort expended in work and in the sharpening of proficiency."[25] James Crenshaw adds a quotation from *Baba Batra* 21a: "the rivalry of scholars increases wisdom."[26] In effect, these commentators turn Qohelet into an advocate of capitalism.

A study of the word throughout the OT, however, will not support such an interpretation. There is no doubt about a positive side to jealousy, but only in terms of two relationships: the divine-human relationship (Isa. 11:13; 26:11; Ps. 69:10 [English 9]; Nah. 1:2) and the marriage relationship (Num. 5:14, 30; Prov. 6:34). These are the only two relationships that allow, indeed require, exclusivity. Jealousy is to be eschewed in all other relationships as a damaging attitude:

> A heart at peace gives life to the body,
>   but envy *(qin'â)* rots the bones. (Prov. 14:30)

Indeed, it is precisely in the area about which Qohelet is talking that jealousy is a most heinous attitude, since most jealousy or rivalry of neighbors is due to covetousness and thus results in the breaking of the tenth commandment (Exod. 20:17; Deut. 5:21).

The attempts to turn this negative observation into a positive one are ill-founded. Taking a look into the human heart, Qohelet sees only a selfish motive, getting ahead of one's neighbors, behind work. This motive can never be satisfied, so it leads to ceaseless work and despair. Thus, Qohelet looks at the motivations of the heart, and it turns him sour.

The words *results from* do not reflect any Hebrew words. They are added to make what is fairly awkward Hebrew syntax smoother.

5   The terse, pithy form, the sarcastic image, and the parallels to the book of Proverbs (Prov. 6:9-11; 10:4; 12:24; 19:15; 20:13; 24:30-34) signal that Qohelet here quotes a proverb. The intention of the proverb is to ridicule the lazy fool. People who refuse to work (*fold their hands;* see the specific parallels in Prov. 6:10 and 24:33) end up with nothing but their own flesh to

---

24. Jarick, *Gregory Thaumaturgos' Paraphrase,* p. 87.
25. Ogden, *Qoheleth,* p. 67.
26. Crenshaw, *Ecclesiastes,* p. 108.

eat. They in essence must become cannibals of themselves. The implication is that they will kill themselves by starvation. Of course, he is being sarcastic and using hyperbole. He mocks the lazy. Since they do not raise anything, they must eat their own flesh.

Christian Ginsburg[27] gives a helpful history of this interpretation from the earliest times, but then rashly counters it with a positive interpretation. That is, he believes that Qohelet is advocating this lifestyle. These people do not work but still can live off their own resources. Such an interpretation is immediately countered by the fact that they are called *fools,* a word that always carries negative connotations.

6 The same characteristics that led me to identify v. 5 as a proverb bring me to the same conclusion here. Specifically, I note the characteristic features of a "better-than" proverb, a typical form of advice that Qohelet uses to bring a section to conclusion (see 4:3). While "meter" may not be the best explanation,[28] there is a poetic imbalance created by the concluding phrase, *chasing wind.* This phrase, also characteristic of Qohelet, was likely added by him to an already existing proverb, giving it his own distinctive stamp.

The proverb commends *rest* over *toil,* a view that does not surprise us in the light of what Qohelet has already said about *toil.* However, it appears at first reading to be in tension with v. 5, which described the destructive results of inactivity. These two proverbs are not contradictory, however. It must be remembered that proverbs do not make unconditional claims. The first could be right in certain situations and the second in other situations (the most notorious example is found in Prov. 26:4, 5). Nonetheless, we must pay close attention to the movement of the three verses that make up this small section. In the first verse, Qohelet gave his opinion that toil and success were the result of jealousy between neighbors and labeled it "meaningless." Verse 5, though, says total inactivity leads to starvation. This concluding verse commends *rest* over *toil.* It is likely that Qohelet prefers, as the best possibility in a bad situation, "a small morsel with peace to an elaborate meal accompanied by strife (Prov. 15:15; 16:8; 17:1)."[29]

5. Another Reflection on Meaninglessness: The Lonely Miser (4:7-8)

Qohelet continues to explore life and presents the reader with examples of meaninglessness. Here we have a brief example of the anecdotes that will

27. Ginsburg, *The Song of Songs and Coheleth,* pp. 324-25.
28. T. Longman III, "A Critique of Two Recent Metrical Approaches," *Biblica* 63 (1982): 230-54.
29. Crenshaw, *Ecclesiastes,* p. 109.

increasingly characterize his style. There are no names given in the story, just a description. By keeping the story general in this fashion, it becomes easier for readers to think of their own acquaintances and say, in effect, "I know somebody like that."

The character described in this particular story embodies traits both of the previous section (4:4-6: meaningless toil) and the following section (4:9-12: loneliness). The picture of a lonely individual working hard, without companionship and without satisfaction with the income, no matter how high, is that of a miser.[30]

> 7 *Then I turned and observed[31] an example of meaninglessness under the sun.*
>
> 8 *There was a person, who was all alone.[32] He also had no son or brother. He toiled endlessly and was never satisfied[33] with his wealth.[34] "And for whom do I toil, depriving myself of good?" Also, this is meaningless and an evil task.[35]*

7 This verse announces Qohelet's intention to present an example of meaninglessness to the reader. *Then I turned and observed* signals a new topic, but also provides continuity with the preceding sections. The direct object *meaninglessness* appears abruptly in the sentence — Qohelet has, after all, been observing meaninglessness in different places all throughout this first part of the book. Since this verse's function is to introduce the story of a particular example of meaninglessness in the next verse, with justification then most translations add a word or a phrase before their translation of *hebel* (e.g., the NIV: "something meaningless"). Similarly, I render the word *an example of meaninglessness*.

8 Once again Qohelet makes his point by telling an anecdote,

---

30. Ginsburg, *The Song of Songs and Coheleth*, p. 326.

31. See 4:1 for another example of Qohelet's idiomatic use of the verbs *šûb* and *rā'â*.

32. The Hebrew is literally rendered, "There was one, but not a second." The above translation attempts to reflect the meaning of the sentence in context.

33. This rendition is a dynamic-equivalent translation of the literal "his eye was not satisfied," reading the Qere (singular "eye") along with the versions and most Hebrew manuscripts. For the combination of "eye" with the verb "to satisfy," see also 1:8.

34. The possessive pronoun is added because of context. The word *wealth* (*'ōšer*) does not carry a pronominal suffix.

35. See 1:13 for the fullest discussion of *evil task* (*'inyan* [the Leningrad manuscript has the variant *'inyān*] *rā'*. *'inyān* also occurs in 2:23, 26; 3:10; 5:2, 13 (English 5:3, 14); and 8:16.

introduced here as elsewhere by the particle *yēš* (discussed in 2:21). It is the sad story of a man who has absolutely no human relationships of any type. The Hebrew phrase, *who was all alone (ʾeḥād weʾēn šēnî)*, is a general one indicating that the man had no friend, no business partner, no wife (contra all those commentators who have tried to specify one of these relationships).[36] Furthermore, he had neither *son (bēn)* nor *brother (ʾāḥ)*, the two closest male relations across two generations and also the two relatives who might benefit from his toil through inheritance. Qohelet further pictures this individual as spending all of his time working hard to amass money and never deriving any pleasure from the wealth that is the result of his efforts.

for whom do I toil (ûlmî ʾanî ʿāmēl) introduces an abrupt transition into the verse. Up to this point, Qohelet referred to this lonely miser in the third person. Here he interjects the first person. Either he discloses the autobiographical nature of his remarks or, as most commentators think, he identifies himself so closely with the plight of the main character of the story that he has the individual speak in the first person. In either case, the effect of the question is to throw all of the efforts of this individual into doubt, and thus Qohelet appropriately concludes the verse with a *hebel* saying, compounded in this instance with another, less frequent, refrain that labels the *toil* of the miser as *an evil task*.

6. The Advantages of Companionship (4:9-12)

Thinking about the lonely miser leads Qohelet to consider the advantages of companionship. Companionship is a help when there is work to be done or when one falls down and needs help getting up. Further, a companion can keep a friend warm on a cold night and can help fight off enemies.

Robert Gordis, while arguing against certain scholars who want to excise this section, interprets it as sarcasm directed against family life. He feels that Qohelet damns companionship by giving it faint praise.[37] While it is true that neither enduring nor monumental significance is ascribed to companionship, it nonetheless carries real significance, and Qohelet is positively disposed to it, showing its advantages by a number of illustrative situations and concluding his discussion with a proverb. If Qohelet's association with the lonely miser is as close as the first-person language indicates, then his comments here may be read with at least a tinge of pathetic longing.

36. See the survey provided by Ginsburg, *The Song of Songs and Coheleth,* pp. 326-27.
37. Gordis, *Koheleth,* p. 242.

9 *Two are better than one,*[38] *for*[39] *they can get a good return for their toil.*

10 *For if one of them*[40] *falls down, the other can help his friend up. But pity*[41] *the person who falls when there is not another to help.*

11 *Also, if two people lie down*[42] *together, they keep warm,*[43] *but how can one person keep warm?*

12 *And though someone can overpower*[44] *one person,*[45] *two can resist the attacker.*[46]

"A three-stranded[47] *cord does not quickly snap."*

38. Ogden ("The 'Better'-Proverb," p. 49) points out that the "two is better than one" pattern of this verse is an inversion of the traditional order "to insist that there are advantages to accrue at times from 'more' rather than 'less,' the appended *kî*-clause justifying the thesis."

39. Causal function of *ᵃšer,* described by Waltke and O'Connor, *Biblical Hebrew Syntax,* p. 38, §4a.3.

40. Translated according to GKC §124o, which calls it an "indefinite singular." Gordis (*Koheleth,* p. 242) has argued along the same lines, taking the plural as "partitive" and translating "if either of them falls." See Gen. 11:3 and Judg. 6:29 for other examples.

41. See Fredericks, *Qoheleth's Language,* pp. 177-78, concerning the question of the date of this unusual form (*'î* instead of *'ôy).* He argues that it is not necessarily a sign of late language. Some interpreters as early as the Targum have taken this as a form of Aramaic *'illû,* "if, whereas." See Jarick, *Gregory Thaumaturgos' Paraphrase,* p. 96, for this information and also the indication that the Masoretic accentuation clearly takes the form as "woe to one," here translated as *pity the one.* The forms *'î* and related *'ôy* are exclamations (see Waltke and O'Connor, *Biblical Hebrew Syntax,* p. 652). See also Eccles. 10:16.

42. In this context the verb *škb* "to lie down" has been legitimately translated "sleep."

43. According to Isaksson, *Studies in the Language of Qoheleth,* p. 93, this form is clearly a *waw* plus perfect and not an adjective, arguing that the adjective would be pointed *wᵉham.*

44. *tqp* is attested only in late Hebrew as even Fredericks (*Qoheleth's Language,* pp. 194, 206, 240-41, 251, 260, 261, 263) admits, though he argues that its appearance does not support a postexilic date for the book.

45. Taking *hā'eḥād* as the direct object, the pronominal suffix on the verb anticipating it (see 2:21 and Whitley, *Koheleth,* p. 44). Fox (*Qohelet and His Contradictions,* p. 204) mentions that neither the Septuagint, Vulgate, nor Syriac reflects the pronominal suffix.

46. *the attacker* is a contextual translation of the third-person pronominal suffix on the verb. The translation attempts to avoid a gender-specific reference.

47. This is a pual participle that, according to Waltke and O'Connor, *Biblical Hebrew Syntax,* p. 423, means "to do three times." The translation "threefold" is their suggestion.

9 This verse states the principle of the following sections and gives the first illustration of it. The principle is that companionship is better than isolation, and it follows from the negative example of the lonely miser given in the previous section. The principle is easily stated in the form of a "better-than proverb" that *two are better than one.* There is nothing in this verse or section to restrict its application to marriage as some, like Gordis,[48] would have us believe. Indeed, Qohelet's conflicting, but sometimes less than enamored (7:28), comments about the opposite sex work against seeing this principle as exclusively or primarily referring to marriage.

The language of the first example found in this verse is economic *(return . . . toil),* and leads one to think that Qohelet has a business partner in mind here, even though it must be admitted that what Qohelet means by *return* here is ambiguous. While it could mean that they get larger profits, it could also, in the words of Franz Delitzsch, refer to "the pleasant conscious-ness of doing good to the other by his labour, and especially of being helpful to him." According to Delitzsch, this is the "idea of the reward of faithful fellowship."[49]

10 Qohelet provides another example of the benefits of companion-ship over against loneliness. This is the first of three verses that seem the-matically connected to a journey. It is a simple point: A companion is able to rescue a traveler from a fall. While I believe we are to assume that this fall is a serious one (i.e., into a pit or off a cliff), nonetheless it is an example of simple wisdom, what today we might call "homespun." This does not preclude the possibility that Michael Fox is correct to see this as an image that points to more profound situations than falling on a trip.[50] That is, it may also teach that companionship is important when one encounters any difficulty in life.

11 Qohelet's second example of the benefits of friendship may also derive from a journey. He contrasts the image of two people traveling together who at night share body heat to keep each other warm with the pathetic image of the lonely traveler who at night vainly tries to keep himself warm. While as early as the Targum the argument has been made that this refers to a married couple, it is far more likely, and the predominant opinion today, that the two are companions (a view that goes back at least as far as the eighth chapter of *Aboth de-Rabbi Nathan* [second century A.D.]).[51]

12 The last example also finds its most natural setting during a journey. The roads in the ancient Near East were often hazardous as one traveled beyond the effective control of towns and cities. A lone traveler,

48. Gordis, *Koheleth,* p. 242.
49. Delitzsch, *Proverbs, Ecclesiastes, Song of Songs,* p. 277.
50. Fox, *Qohelet and His Contradictions,* p. 204.
51. Delitzsch. *Proverbs, Ecclesiastes, and Song of Songs,* p. 277.

according to Qohelet, was easy prey of robbers, while two could provide resistance and aid to one another.

The whole section concludes with a proverb, and one that has generated a significant discussion due to the unexpected occurrence of the number three, its possible ancient Near Eastern background, and the Christological speculation that grew up around it in early church history.

It is true that throughout this section it has been the number two that has been the positive opposite to one. The lonely miser stands over against the benefits of the friendship of two people. It is really not all that surprising, though, that in the final statement *three* would be used to generate a climactic conclusion, and this in the manner of a typical numerical parallelism.[52] If one is bad, and two is good, how much better is three! In this regard note the Targum's interpretation, "if two righteous people in a generation are useful, how much more useful are three righteous people in a generation!"[53]

In terms of Near Eastern background, Aaron Shaffer identified an ancient analogue.[54] In an earlier article Shaffer showed a connection with an episode in the Sumerian text *Gilgamesh and Huwawa*. Enkidu is about to give up a mission, and Gilgamesh tells him (in Shaffer's translation): "Stop, Enkidu! The second man will not die. The boat-in-tow will not sink. No man will cut the three-ply cord." He further showed connections between this Sumerian text and the entirety of Ecclesiastes 4:9-12. In a second article, he showed a connection with the Akkadian version of *Gilgamesh*. Schaffer's work shows that Qohelet is likely alluding to a well-known ancient Near Eastern proverb concerning the benefits of friendship.

Then, lastly, from the earliest times this proverb has been subjected to various, rather forced, Christological interpretations. According to John Jarick, "Ambrose saw Christ as the one who lifts up his companion (v. 10) and warms him (v. 11), and the one who went from the house of bondsman to be king (v. 13). Jerome had also seen the Trinity in Koheleth's saying concerning the threefold cord."[55] Another common interpretation in early Christianity was to identify the three cords as faith, hope, and love. These interesting yet fanciful interpretations were refuted by Edward Plumptre, who simply states that these ideas "lie altogether outside the range of the thoughts of the Debater."[56] The point of the

52. Watson, *Classical Hebrew Poetry,* p. 282.

53. Jarick, *Gregory Thaumaturgos' Paraphrase,* p. 100.

54. A. Shaffer, "The Mesopotamian Background of Qoh 4:9-12" (in Hebrew), *EI* 8 (1967): 246-50; and "New Information on the Origin of the 'Threefold Cord'" (in Hebrew), *EI* 9 (1969): 159-60.

55. Jarick, *Gregory Thaumaturgos' Paraphrase,* pp. 359-60, n. 49; see his references to the primary sources.

56. Plumptre, *Ecclesiastes; or, the Preacher* p. 143.

image of the three-strand cord is rather that strength can be gained through human relationships.

7. Political Power Is Meaningless: An Anecdote (4:13-16)

This section has only a loose connection with the rest of the chapter. Roland Murphy states that it is connected, but he gives little or no explanation.[57] Christian Ginsburg argues that it is the fourth illustration in the chapter of the principle that being sociable is to one's advantage, but his conclusion ignores the leading characteristics of the main characters in the stories.[58] As we will see, it is primarily wisdom and folly that again are contrasted, and this anecdote (for other anecdotes see 4:8-9 and 9:13-16) illustrates the point that we already came across in 2:12-17: While wisdom is superior to folly in the short run, in the long run the advantages of wisdom are nonexistent.

The anecdote is surprisingly ambiguous in its second part (vv. 15-16). William Irwin goes so far as to say that this section "is characteristic of Hebrew usage at its worst."[59] As a matter of fact, it is even difficult to decide whether there are two or three characters involved. Two are clearly presented in v. 13; the issue is whether "the next youth" is the same as the "poor, wise" youth of v. 13. I will argue below that there are in actuality three characters in this brief anecdote.

Close readers have seen a connection between the "poor, wise" youth and Joseph.[60] Indeed, Joseph also emerged from prison to become a leader (though not a king [melek]; see Gen. 37:41-57). This and other attempts to identify a historical background to the anecdote are unpersuasive, because even if Qohelet uses some elements of historical tradition, he is simply telling a fictional story to make a didactic point.

> 13 A poor but[61] wise youth is better than an old and foolish king who no longer pays attention to advice,[62]

57. Murphy, Wisdom Literature, pp. 137-38.
58. Ginsburg, The Song of Songs and Coheleth, p. 330.
59. W. A. Irwin, "Ecclesiastes 4:13-16," JNES 3 (1944): 255.
60. See Crenshaw, Ecclesiastes, p. 112; G. S. Ogden, "Historical Allusion in Qoheleth iv 13-16?" VT 30 (1980): 309-15.
61. This is the simple waw-conjunction, but the surprising connection between poverty and wisdom necessitates the translation but. After all, wisdom was supposed to stave off poverty.
62. The literal "who does not know to be advised still" (ʾašer lōʾ-yādaʿ lᵉhizzāhēr ʿôd) is too awkward in English to be so rendered. The literal translation, though, shows the Hebrew syntax to be a qal perfect third-person singular of ydʿ ("know") followed by a niphal infinitive construct of zhr ("advise").

14 *though he came from a prison*[63] *to become king, even though he was born poor*[64] *in his kingdom.*

15 *I observed all who lived, those who walked under the sun, with the next youth, who replaced him.*

16 *There was no end to all the people, to all those whom he led. Yet people who lived later did not like him. This too is meaningless and chasing wind.*

13 The first verse of the unit introduces two of the characters and does so by way of contrast. Indeed, the contrast could not be more complete since it occurs on three levels. First, they are opposites in terms of social status, *poor*[65] *. . . king.* Second, they are opposite in age, *youth*[66] *. . . old.* Third, they are opposite in knowledge, the most important distinction between the pair: *wise . . . foolish.* This contrast is the determinative one for the story. The other two contrasts are there in order to reverse expectations. In the ancient Near East, and in the OT, the normal situation would be that the *old king* would be *wise* and the *poor youth* would be *foolish.* But here the story is that youth, poverty, and, we will see, even imprisonment are overcome by wisdom.

The king's foolishness is explained in the last clause of the verse. His problem is that he does not *pay attention to advice,* a sure sign of foolishness, especially in a king, as the following references show:[67]

> For a lack of guidance a nation falls,
>   but many advisers make victory sure. (Prov. 11:14)

63. Assuming that *hāsûrîm* stands for *hāʾǎsûrîm* ("prisoners," so some Hebrew manuscripts as well as the Septuagint, Syriac, and Vulgate; see *BHS* note). GKC §35d states that this is a case of an apocopated *aleph* following the articles. Whitley (*Koheleth,* pp. 45-46), however, uncharacteristically (and unwisely) follows M. Dahood ("Qoheleth and Northwest Semitic Philology," *Biblica* 43 [1962]: 356-57), when he cites Ugaritic *msrr ʾṣr,* late Hebrew *sûrîm,* and others (with the wrong sibilant) as cognate. Whitley translates "for from the womb even a king goes forth."

64. Contra K. D. Schunck, "Drei Seleukiden im Buche Kohelet?" *VT* 9 (1959): 195-96, who argues that *rāš* needs to be emended to *rōʾš* ("head"), on the basis of the fact that another word for "poor" was used in the previous verse. He thus shapes his argument that the anecdote has a Seleucid background.

65. E. Podechard (*L'Ecclésiaste* [Paris: Libraire Victor Lecoffre, 1912], p. 167) believed *miškēn* to be a late Aramaic term, but both Whitley (*Koheleth,* p. 44) and Fredericks (*Qoheleth's Language,* p. 232) show connections with Akkadian *muškēnu,* which occurs much earlier.

66. The term *yeled* derives from a verbal root "to be born," and thus many have felt it means a child. Its use in connection with Joseph in Gen. 37:30 and 42:20, as well as in reference to Rehoboam's friends (1 Kings 12:8, referring to men who were probably over forty years old), indicates that it is a relative term in that it designates a wide span of ages.

67. I owe these references to Lauha, *Kohelet,* p. 92.

Plans fail for lack of counsel,
  but with many advisers they succeed. (Prov. 15:22)

Make plans by seeking advice;
  if you wage war, obtain guidance. (Prov. 20:18)

For waging war you need guidance,
  and for victory many advisers. (Prov. 24:6)

One important point of these references is that failure to seek and follow advice dooms royal ventures to failure. That is why ignoring advice is a mark of a fool.

14 Due to syntactical difficulties, it is impossible to be dogmatic about the antecedent of the subject of the subordinate clause *(though he came from . . .)*. Is it the old king or the youth whose origins are poverty and jail? In favor of the old king is the fact that he is the nearest antecedent. One might argue that the phrase *his kingdom* points to the old king, but this is not persuasive. In favor of the latter antecedent, the lad who becomes king, is the low state of the individual, particularly that he is *poor.* Though a different Hebrew word *(rāš)* is used for *poor* than the one in v. 13 *(miškēn),* it still provides a continuity of theme. The humble origins of the youth are relevant to the story. This youth did supplant the old king, *though* he came from prison and *even though* he was born poor in the old king's kingdom. Among recent commentators, Graham Ogden[68] is an exception to the rule when he takes this verse as a reference to the old king. For the debate over the identification of the old king and the youth, see the introduction to this section.

15 Verses 13 and 14 describe two individuals. An old, foolish king is replaced by a poor but wise youth, who rose to the highest office in the land from jail. Verse 15 introduces a third individual, who replaces the poor youth, thus illustrating the temporal glory and ultimate meaninglessness of this world (see v. 16).

Qohelet transports himself to the scene with his characteristic phrase *I observed* (see 1:14). He then uses two phrases that refer to all of teeming humanity, *all who lived* and *those who walked under the sun.* The latter phrase, which centers around a form of the verb "to walk" *(hlk)* contrasts with the *youth,* who "stands" (literal rendition of the verb *'md, replaced).*[69] The *youth* is enigmatically modified by the Hebrew word *haššēnî,* most often translated "second," if not ignored altogether (so NRSV).

The main issue surrounding the interpretation of v. 15 is the identity

68. Ogden, "Historical Allusion in Qoheleth iv 13-16?" pp. 309-15; and *Qoheleth,* pp. 71-72.
69. Ogden, *Qoheleth,* p. 73.

of the *youth*. Numerous arguments have been put forward to identify this youth in relation to the one encountered in v. 13. Some have taken "second" as a reference to "second in command," while Christian Ginsburg offers the novel suggestion that it comes from a verb "to form a second" and translates it "sociable youth."[70] Still others feel that the verse is out of order and belongs with 4:7-12, where "two" is favorably contrasted with the solitary individual.[71] But R. N. Whybray, James Crenshaw, and Michael Fox are correct in their opinion that a second youth is in mind here in addition to the one mentioned in v. 13.[72] The point of the verse is that, though the wisdom of the first young man brought him to the throne of the foolish old man, his own rule was short-lived; the story demonstrates the limited life of wisdom. I have followed Fox in rendering *haššēnî* as *next* rather than "second," because the latter translation assumes that the youth has already been introduced. In short, wisdom may bring a king temporary success, but it cannot guarantee him his greatest wish — a long reign and a hereditary successor.

16 Once again ambiguity attends the antecedent of the pronouns of this verse. Since we ended the last verse focused on the second youth, the third character of the anecdote, we must assume that he is the object of the opening of this verse. That is, the first and the second clauses *(There was no end . . . whom he led)* refer to the popularity of the "next youth." This conclusion is clouded, however, by grammatical and text-critical issues. For instance, an alternative rendering of the second clause, which is in apposition to the first, is, "to all those who are before them" as opposed to "all those before whom he was."[73] I agree with Fox that it is absurd to think of this phrase as referring to the generations that preceded the old king and the first young wise man, since such a reference makes no sense in the context.

The sense of the verse, in my opinion, leads to the following interpretation. Countless people followed the "next youth" of v. 15, who replaced the wise young man of vv. 13 and 14, who came to the throne from humble origins to replace the old, foolish king of v. 13. Yet not even the final king mentioned, the popular one, continued to enjoy the people's favor. In the end, people did not like even him.

Though we cannot grasp the precise interpretation of this section, the moral lesson is obvious. Political power is *meaningless and like chasing wind,*[74] even political power attended by old age, wisdom, and popularity.

70. Ginsburg, *The Song of Songs and Coheleth*, p. 333.

71. Whitley, *Koheleth*, p. 46.

72. Whybray, *Ecclesiastes*, NCB, pp. 89-90; Crenshaw, *Ecclesiastes*, pp. 113-14; Fox, *Qohelet and His Contradictions*, pp. 207-8.

73. Whybray, *Ecclesiastes*, NCB, pp. 90-91; Crenshaw, *Ecclesiastes*, pp. 113-14; Fox, *Qohelet and His Contradictions*, p. 208.

74. For the interpretation of these motto phrases of Qohelet, see 1:2 and 1:14.

SUMMARY OF CHAPTER 4

Chapter 4 continues to look for solace in a world devoid of meaning. The chapter opens with a depressing glance at the way in which the strong take advantage of the weak (vv. 1-3). The situation is so bad that Qohelet judges the dead happier than the living, a remarkable statement given the immediately preceding section (3:18-22), which registered uncertainty about one's fate after death. Perhaps for that reason Qohelet pronounces the one never born the happiest of all.

Qohelet then proceeds to revisit the topic of work and again finds it inadequate to satisfy his craving for meaning (vv. 4-6). It is jealousy that propels one to work hard, but in the final analysis nothing is gained by it. This leads Qohelet to tell a short anecdote of the lonely miser (vv. 7-8), a man who works hard but has no one with whom to enjoy the fruits of his labor. This sad picture leads Qohelet to comment on the advantages of companionship (vv. 9-12). Companionship seems to be a solace in an uncertain and unsatisfying world. However, this temporary exercise in hopeful thinking comes crashing down in the next section as Qohelet tells another anecdote of a young, wise man whose gifts earn him some notoriety and popularity, but who in the end finds himself pushed into obscurity — one more illustration that there is no lasting meaning to life in this world.

8. God Is in Heaven (4:17–5:6 [English 5:1-7])

The English versification corrected what was surely a slight error in the Hebrew breakup of the chapters, since 4:17 clearly begins a new topic that focuses on issues surrounding the formal religious institutions (or cult) of Israel. While the cult is not a major theme of wisdom literature, neither is it totally absent.[1] It is thus not surprising that Qohelet deals with the theme.

The section is made up of admonitions[2] along with motive clauses. As Aarre Lauha points out, this section deals with three topics: (1) sacrifice (4:17 [English 5:1], (2) prayers (5:1-2 [English 5:2-3]), and (3) vows (5:3-6 [English 5:4-7]).[3]

Qohelet's tone in this section is hard to determine. It is clear that he does not wholeheartedly affirm or encourage the cult, but he does not abandon

---

1. L. G. Perdue, *Wisdom and Cult,* SBLDS 30 (Missoula, MT: Scholars Press, 1977).

2. Or prohibitions, although the distinction is hard to maintain; see Murphy, *Wisdom Literature,* pp. 172 and 181.

3. Lauha, *Kohelet,* p. 97.

it either. How is one to understand his statement "God is in heaven and you are on earth" (5:1 [English 5:2])? Is this piety or an expression of God's disinterest? The context of the entire book will have to be kept in mind as we answer these questions in the following commentary.

4:17 (5:1) *Watch your step[4] when you go to the house of God. Draw near[5] to listen rather than[6] offer the sacrifice of fools.[7] For they do not know that they are doing evil.*

5:1 (2) *Do not be quick[8] with your mouth, and do not let your heart rush to utter a word[9] before God. For God is in heaven and you are on earth. Therefore, let your words be few.*

2 (3) *For dreams[10] come with[11] much work, and the voice of the fool with many words.*

3 (4) *When you make a vow to God, do not delay to fulfill it, for there is no pleasure in fools. You, however,[12] fulfill what you have vowed.*

4 (5) *It is better that you do not make a vow[13] than that you make a vow and not fulfill it.*

4. Literally (according to the Ketib [*ragleykā*]) "steps," but the comparable English idiom is singular, and indeed, the Qere is singular *(ragl^ekā)*.

5. Treating the infinitive absolute as an imperative (GKC §113aa, bb). It is also possible to treat the infinitive absolute as the subject here (GKC §113b; see Lauha, *Kohelet*, p. 96).

6. GKC §133e explains this as an example of a "pregnant use of the *min*" in which "the attributive idea . . . must . . . be supplied from the context." Other examples are given there.

7. This translation involves the transposition of the two words. In the Hebrew the word *fools* precedes *sacrifice*.

8. Whitley (*Koheleth,* p. 48) argues that this meaning of *bhl* (piel) is characteristic of late Hebrew (appearing only here and in 7:9; 8:3; 2 Chron. 35:21; and Esth. 2:9). He asserts that the only preexilic meaning is "to terrify." Fredericks (*Qoheleth's Language,* p. 218) provides the counterarguments. He shows a similar semantic development from "frighten" to "hasten" in the biblical Hebrew verb *tpz,* and he also notes that *bhl* has the meaning "to hasten" in texts like Prov. 28:22 and Zeph. 1:18.

9. Alternatively, this could be translated "bring a matter before God." In either case, prayer is clearly meant.

10. Literally, "the dream." The use of the article "is generic" (Crenshaw, *Ecclesiastes,* p. 116).

11. In the sense of "accompanied by" — both here and in the second half of the verse (Fox, *Qohelet and His Contradictions,* p. 211).

12. Reading *'āt* ("you") for *'ēt* (direct object marker) with some Greek manuscripts, Syriac, and the Targum (so Lauha, *Kohelet,* p. 96). This heightens the contrast between the second-person subject and the fool; thus, I have added the word *however.*

13. The *'ašer* clause here serves as the subject of the main clause.

5 (6) *Do not let[14] your mouth cause your flesh to commit sin.[15] And do not say to the messenger that it was a mistake. Why[16] should God be angry with your words[17] and destroy the work of your hands?*

6 (7) *For when dreams multiply, so do meaningless words.[18] Instead, fear God.*

4:17 (5:1) The expression *watch your step* is Qohelet's warning to his readers/hearers[19] to be cautious in their behavior as they approach God. Jesus eradicated the distinction between holy and profane places, but in the OT specially designated places appear. The distinction between holy and common space is abolished only with the death and resurrection of Christ, and this is symbolized in the Gospels by the ripping of the temple veil (Matt. 27:51). During Qohelet's time, God's presence was manifest only in certain locales, and paramount among these was the *house of God,* the temple. Of course, as is likely, the book of Qohelet may be postexilic. If so, then *house of God* is a reference to any local worship site.

In the second part of the verse, Qohelet admonishes people to *listen* when they approach God. This verb *(šmʿ)* has connotations of obedience.[20] Qohelet continues with the warning not to offer the *sacrifice of fools.* One of the difficulties of this verse is the meaning of this phrase. Since he is encouraging listening and not an alternative to sacrifice, does this mean that all sacrifices are those of fools? Or is there a certain type of sacrifice that is foolish? If one thinks of Qohelet as an orthodox wise man here, a position that I have argued against in this commentary, then one will have a specific notion of what a *sacrifice of fools* entails. It would be one offered in form only, the type of sacrifice inveighed against by the psalmist (e.g., Ps. 40:7-9 [English 6-8]) and prophets (Mic. 6:6-8). If he is less than fully orthodox, he would regard religious formalism as reprehensible.

Most commentators feel that there is something wrong with the third colon. A literal translation is "for they do not know to do evil." Godfrey Driver[21]

---

14. For this meaning of *ntn,* see Whitley, *Koheleth,* p. 48.

15. The prefixed *h* that is characteristic of the hiphil infinitive construct is here elided (Whitley, *Koheleth,* p. 48; and GKC §53q).

16. Waltke and O'Connor (*Biblical Hebrew Syntax,* p. 324) suggests that this use of *lāmmâ* is "quasi-rhetorical" and could be translated "otherwise." Whitley (*Koheleth,* p. 49) suggests the meaning "lest."

17. Literally, "against your voice."

18. Literally, "many *[harbēh]* meaningless words."

19. Actually the singular here. Perhaps Qohelet is instructing a particular pupil. I have pluralized the reference, however, to convey that he addresses both males and females.

20. Perdue, *Wisdom and Cult,* p. 182.

21. G. R. Driver, "Once Again Abbreviations," *Textus* 4 (1964): 79.

believed that the problem arose because the text was abbreviated in such a way that, when it was written out again, the *mem* that prefixed the infinitive dropped out. The resulting form would be *ml'śwt,* and the sentence would be translated "knowing not otherwise than to do evil."[22] Charles Whitley[23] pointed out that another, more elegant, route to the same conclusion is to assume a textual corruption, namely, a haplography of the *mem.* Those who choose not to emend the text seem to think that the only way to fill out the sentence is to attribute an inability to do evil on the part of those who are foolish, "They do not know *how* to do evil." Along with Graham Ogden,[24] I believe that the sentence without emendation may be understood as it is translated here. With such a translation, the meaning is that they are so foolish that they are not even aware that their sacrifices are evil, an offense to God.

5:1 (2)   This verse is composed of three parts: a command, a motive clause, and then a second command that is implied by the motive. The command is to be reticent before God. The motive is the vast distance between God and human beings, and the second command reemphasizes the need to be quiet before God.

The topic of this verse and the next is clearly prayer, but the tone of the verse is once again ambiguous, and the verse could conceivably be read two ways.[25] On the one hand, a pious Qohelet could be warning his readers not to badger God with superfluous talk. After all, God is *in heaven,* that is, he is in control. This approach considers Qohelet's warning as an anticipation of Matthew 6:7-8: "And when you pray, do not keep on babbling words. Do not be like them, for your Father knows what you need before you ask him." Qohelet, however, has been anything but pious up to this point. His damper on prayer stands over against the torrent of the psalmist's heartfelt words in that Qohelet advises people to approach God in prayer only rarely, and then only briefly, as if the danger is taking too much of God's precious time. Qohelet warns his readers to be cautious in approaching God with words because *God is in heaven and you are on earth.*[26] We take this statement not as an assertion of divine power, but of divine distance, perhaps even of indifference.

2 (3)   Qohelet bolsters his commands of the previous verse with an analogy. As argued below, we cannot be certain about the exact nature of the

22. Note that J. Schmidt ("Koheleth 4:17," *ZAW* 17 [1940-41]: 279-80) wants to emend further and change *rā'* to *rēa'* with the resulting translation, "for they do not know how to do anything else" *(Denn sie wissen nicht Anderes zu tun).*

23. Whitley, *Koheleth,* p. 47.

24. Ogden, *Qoheleth,* p. 76, though I disagree with him abut the nonmoral use of *rā'* here.

25. Jarick, *Gregory Thaumaturgos' Paraphrase,* p. 110.

26. The form of this motive clause is that of an antithetical proverb.

comparison. Work leads to many dreams; foolishness leads to many words. Perhaps, though, the idea is that hard work so tires a person that one starts losing touch with reality. The analogy may suggest that those who are so foolish as to think their many words have any appreciable effect on God are also living in a fantasy world.

The conjunction *For (kî)* links this verse to the previous one and signals that what follows serves as the motive for reticence in prayer before God. The pithy poetic form of the verse, as well as its content, announces that Qohelet here quotes a proverb. It is more likely that he is quoting rather than creating a proverb, especially since it does not fit perfectly with the point he is making.

For example, the exact relationship between the two halves of the proverb is uncertain. Though a comparative particle is not used in this verse, I deem it likely that an analogy is set up between the first and the second cola of the proverb. The NIV makes this explicit by adopting an "As . . . so" format for its translation.[27] This translation is a good dynamic equivalent for the Hebrew, but the Hebrew simply puts the two cola side by side and expects the reader to make the comparison explicit (the NRSV more closely reflects the Hebrew).

On the surface, the content of the two cola is not obviously related. The first colon makes the observation that dreams often accompany the pre-occupation of overwork. Some scholars[28] make a connection with the second part of the verse and the context by citing the supposed function of the cult prophet (or Levitical singer in the postexilic period), who upon getting a request from a worshipper would then expect to receive a dream revelation from God. According to these interpreters, Qohelet objects to this practice because he does not believe that such divine communications are possible. While these practices are well known in other parts of the ancient Near East (witness the beginning of the Ugaritic tale Aqht), they are not clearly attested as a normal part of Israelite worship, though God does occasionally speak through dreams during the time of the OT (Gen. 37:5-7; 40:8-23; Job 4:12-21; 33:14-22).

If there is a close connection between the first colon and the second colon, it escapes the modern reader.[29] Above, I have speculated that the point is: as hard work causes one to lose touch with reality, so the words produced by fools are also a mere fantasy. But this is nothing more than a guess. In any case, the second part of the verse is the punch line that has an obvious connection with the context. The first colon serves its purpose by citing an

27. Ginsburg (*The Song of Songs and Coheleth*, p. 338) provides a list of inter-preters who go this route.

28. See Perdue, *Wisdom and Cult*, p. 184.

29. Whybray, *Ecclesiastes*, NCB, p. 94; Gordis, *Koheleth*, p. 248.

analogy that has unpleasant associations. To paraphrase, as one can expect dreams (an uneasy sleep) during the preoccupation that accompanies heavy work, so one can expect to find a fool behind a loquacious speaker.

Thus, while the exact impact of the proverb escapes us (and may never have been present in the first instance), the point is clearly drawn: only a fool prays a lot (see also 10:12-14 for the connection between wordiness and foolishness).

3 (4)   Qohelet now addresses the issue of vows. Like sacrifice and prayer, a vow was a cultic tribute to God. When taking a vow, worshippers committed themselves to undertake some kind of action, often a sacrifice, if God would answer a specific request (Gen. 28:20-22; Judg. 11:30-31, 39; 1 Sam. 1:11) or simply to curry God's favor (Ps. 132:2-5).

Qohelet warns his hearers to fulfill the vows that they have taken upon themselves. His caution about vows is almost identical to deuteronomic law on vows (Deut. 23:22a [English 23:21a]).[30] Indeed, Qohelet's views on vows are virtually the same as the rest of the canon. Proverbs 20:25 is especially noteworthy:

> It is a trap for a man to dedicate something rashly
>   and only later to consider his vows.

And outside the canon, but still within the sphere of wisdom literature, we may also cite Ben Sira 18:22:

> Let nothing prevent you from paying a vow promptly, and so do not wait until death to be released from it.[31]

The motive clause of our verse in Ecclesiastes is introduced by *for (kî),* and, though most translations (see NIV, NRSV) treat God as the subject, it is actually an impersonal construction. While Michael Fox[32] is likely correct in saying that this may indicate a hesitation to speak of divine emotions, it may alternatively encompass a broader circle of disapproval. No one, divine or human, likes to see a person default on a religious obligation.

4 (5)   Qohelet does more than warn his hearers to fulfill vows they have already made. He also encourages them not to make vows in the first place.

Qohelet expresses himself here with a characteristic "better-than" proverb (see 4:2). Quite simply, those who do not fulfill their vows are in a

---

30. The linguistic differences may be understood as the different preferences of wisdom over against deuteronomic literature.

31. So quoted by Crenshaw, *Ecclesiastes,* p. 117.

32. Fox, *Qohelet and His Contradictions,* p. 211.

worse situation than those who never make them in the first place. After all, vows are optional; they are not commanded. Thus, he warns his hearers not to play religious games — to make vows and then try to get out of them. Jesus later also threatens those who try to manipulate the law to avoid repaying a vow (Matt. 23:16-22).

5 (6)   The most likely interpretation understands this verse to continue Qohelet's caution about vows. People's mouths can drag them into sin if they make a vow they are unable to keep. When the temple messenger makes his rounds to their house to get them to fulfill their vow, then they will be reduced to lame excuses. This tactic, Qohelet asserts, will anger God, who will then find some way to harm the recalcitrant vow taker.

As Graham Ogden points out,[33] the vocabulary reflects that of Deuteronomy 23:22-24 (see above). The force of the first part of the verse, then, is that one's *mouth* would lead to *sin* by speaking a vow that the person *(flesh)* never fulfills. R. N. Whybray does not believe that this sentence has to do with vows, doubting that "Qohelet would have rather pointlessly repeated what he had already said."[34] This seems a rather weak argument, however, since the clear antecedent to a sin committed by a person's mouth is a vow that is not honored.

The most perplexing aspect of this verse, though, is the difficult reference to the *mal'āk,* here translated *messenger.*[35] This seems the simplest rendering, but its precise reference is unclear. Apparently, during Qohelet's time there were people whose duty it was to check up on those who had not fulfilled their public vows, a kind of religious bill collector. We do not, however, have any other biblical reference to this office, and it is unclear whether these people were priests.[36] The lack of information about the office led to alternatives as early as the Septuagint (followed by the Peshitta), which translated *mal'āk* as "God." Aquila, Theodotion, and Symmachus all corrected the Septuagint tradition, but they rendered the phrase "angel," which is another philologically correct rendering of *mal'āk.* Christian Ginsburg[37] has a long excursus on angels, arguing for this translation, but it seems unnecessary to assume a supernatural messenger is meant.

33. Ogden, *Qoheleth,* p. 79.

34. Whybray, *Ecclesiastes,* NCB, p. 95; see also Ginsburg, *Song of Songs and Coheleth,* p. 339; and Perdue, *Wisdom and Cult,* pp. 185-86, for rival interpretations.

35. Consult Fredericks, *Qoheleth's Language,* p. 200, for a list of the interpretive options.

36. For those who argue that they are priests, see the Targum and R. B. Salters, "Notes on the History of the Interpretation of Koh. 5:5," *ZAW* 90 (1978): 95-101. For those who deny the connection, see the Midrash *Koheleth Rabbah* and Gordis, *Koheleth,* p. 249.

37. H. L. Ginsberg, *Studies in Koheleth* (New York: Jewish Theological Seminary of America, 1952), pp. 340-44.

Qohelet warns his hearers/readers not to tell the messenger that their vow was a *mistake*. The word *šᵉgāgâ* must be understood in the light of Leviticus 4:2-35 and Numbers 15:22-31, which contrast a sin committed in ignorance with an intentional sin. Our word is associated with the former, and Qohelet's point is that the *mal'āk* will see through the ruse and consider the excuse weak. Since the sin will be judged an intentional one, it will bring on God's wrath and result in the destruction of the person's *work*. It must be remembered that it is in an area of *work* that Qohelet has hope of joy in the present life. Its destruction is therefore disastrous.[38]

6 (7)   This verse is difficult to translate and understand. Once again (see 5:2 [English 5:3]), we have the association of dreams and many words. Perhaps the point of comparison is fantasy. Dreams are out of touch with reality, and so, argues Qohelet, are many words in a cultic setting. Qohelet encourages his hearers away from a familiarity with God and toward a relationship characterized by fear.

Though all the words of the verse are well attested, the syntax renders it impossible to translate the verse with certainty. Many opt to emend the text. Michael Fox[39] removes the *waw* before *dᵉbārîm* and changes *brb* to *krb* to yield the translation "for a lot of talk is [like] a lot of dreams and absurdities. Rather, fear God!" Aarre Lauha presents a different proposal by transposing *dbrm* and *hblm*, giving the translation:

Indeed: "With an abundance of words
comes dreams and vanity in abundance
— you, however, heed God![40]

No textual suggestion can be more than a guess since the Septuagint and Peshitta basically reproduce the MT and its attendant difficulties. The Vulgate, while it makes sense, is clearly a free rendition. If there was textual corruption, it happened very early.

Perhaps, then, the solution lies in the realm of philology rather than that of text criticism. Nonetheless, such proposals must be considered tentative since the prepositions and conjunctions of the verse are amenable to more than one interpretation. Any Hebrew grammar will show multiple uses of the conjunctions *kî* and *waw* as well as the preposition *beth*. The *kî* could be causal, temporal, conditional, adversative, concessive, asseverative, resulta-

---

38. See J. Kugel, "Qohelet and Money," *CBQ* 51 (1989): 34-35, for the view that we should read the qal of *ḥbl* and understand its meaning to be "to take possession of a pledge."

39. Fox, *Qohelet and His Contradictions,* p. 212.

40. "Fürwahr: 'bei der Fülle "der Worte" sind Träume und Eitelkeit in Menge, du 'aber — hege du Achtung vor Gott!" Lauha, *Kohelet,* p. 96 (my translation).

tive, nominalizing, or recitative.[41] The *waw* can serve a coordinative, disjunctive, adversative, alternative, explicative, pleonastic, accompaniment, comparative, emphatic, sarcastic, resumptive, adjunctive, or distributive function.[42] The preposition *beth* "expresses rest or movement in place or time"[43] and thus has locative, temporal, adversative, instrumental, transitive, agental, causal, and several other meanings.[44] Context often makes the specific instance clear, but such is not the case in our verse. I find that as I argue for a translation that makes sense in the context, I am choosing meanings that are not highly attested. Thus, as with other translations, mine can only be tentatively offered.

The verse opens with *kî*, which I here take in a causal sense, identifying the first part of the verse as a motive clause. It gives a final reason for caution in cultic observance. The preposition *beth* is taken in a temporal sense,[45] and the first *waw* is treated as the *waw* apodosis *(when dreams multiply)*.[46] I treat the second *waw* as a simple coordinate linking two nouns, but then understand the phrase as a hendiadys *(meaningless words)*.

The precise nature of the translation of the first sentence in the verse may be questioned in its detail, and in the final analysis the present state of the text may be the result of a textual corruption, but the clear meaning of the nouns associates "words" with "dreams" and "meaningless," thus making the same point as earlier (especially 5:2 [English 5:3]): only a fool would speak a lot in the cult.

The last phrase is clearly stated. Qohelet insists that *instead* (the *kî* is adversative) his hearer/reader should *fear God*. This is the first of a number of times that Qohelet makes this point, and it plays a pivotal role in his overall message (see "Theological Message" in the introduction).

9. The Network of Oppression (5:7-8 [English 5:8-9])

This brief section once again (see 3:16; 4:1-3) treats the topic of political oppression. Government officials all the way up to the king use their position for their own advantage, with the result that the people suffer.

Like the preceding unit (4:17–5:6 [English 5:1-7]), it is an instruction[47] concerning behavior before an authority. But, while the previous passage

---

41. R. J. Williams, *Hebrew Syntax: An Outline,* 2d ed. (Toronto: University of Toronto Press, 1976), pp. 444-52.
42. Williams, *Hebrew Syntax,* §§ 430-42.
43. Williams, *Hebrew Syntax,* § 239.
44. Williams, *Hebrew Syntax,* §§ 240-52.
45. Perdue, *Wisdom and Cult,* pp. 187, 248.
46. GKC §143d; and Perdue, *Wisdom and Cult,* pp. 187, 248.
47. Murphy, *Wisdom Literature,* pp. 138-39.

simply urged caution before divine authority, the present one urges resignation before human authority.

Both verses have their philological and grammatical difficulties, and these have given rise to slightly different interpretive approaches (see below under v. 7 [English v. 8]). In spite of the differences, all commentators recognize that Qohelet decries oppression on the political level (though Graham Ogden[48] sees a silver lining in that the political oppression pushes one toward the fear of God).

> 7 (8) *If you see oppression of the poor and deprivation[49] of justice and righteousness in the province,[50] do not be surprised concerning the situation.[51] For one official[52] watches out for another, and there are officials over them.*
>
> 8 (9) *The profit of the land is taken by all; even the king benefits from the field.*

7 (8)   All approaches to this verse recognize that Qohelet describes difficulties with the political system. Some argue that the verse declaims the inequities of an excessive bureaucracy in what might be called the "red tape" interpretation.[53] Others, like Franz Delitzsch,[54] believe that the problem arises as higher officials fleece those lower than they are until the poor, who have no one below them to oppress, are reached. Delitzsch argues for this position in the light of a third approach, that of Ferdinand Hitzig, that the officials are protecting each other against the rights of the people they govern. As Hitzig colorfully expresses it: "they mutually protect each other's advantage; one crow does not peck out the eyes of another."[55]

48. Odgen, *Qoheleth*, pp. 79-80.

49. The word *gēzel* (in construct) is literally "robbery," but *deprivation* is a good modern equivalent in this context.

50. Since the word is singular and preceded by the article, this may be a specific reference to Judah during the Persian period. Some, however, believe that the word *province* (*meḏînâ*) refers to a courtroom based on the verbal root *dîn* (e.g., Ogden, *Qoheleth*, p. 80). See 2:8 for a fuller discussion of this word in a context where it would very unlikely have the latter sense.

51. For a discussion of *situation* (*ḥēpeṣ*), see 3:1 (cf. 3:17 and 8:6).

52. The word *gāḇōah* is normally an adjective meaning "high," but here it has a substantive force with the meaning "high official." The word may carry negative connotations because it also can mean "haughty" (1 Sam. 2:3; Ps. 10:4).

53. For instance, Kidner, *A Time to Mourn and a Time to Dance*, p. 54, who states that Qohelet's description of the officials "suggests possibilities of Kafka-esque evasiveness."

54. Delitzsch, *Proverbs, Ecclesiastes, Song of Solomon*, p. 293.

55. Quoted by Delitzsch, *Proverbs, Ecclesiastes, Song of Songs*, p. 293. The viewpoint advocated by Hitzig is also found in Ellul, *Reason for Being*, pp. 80-81.

157

The key to the differences has to do with the nuance of *šōmēr*, here tentatively translated *watches out*. In what sense should this verb be taken? Do officials guard one another's interest? Perhaps they are looking for an opportunity to take advantage of one another. Or is there one official in charge of the activities of another ad infinitum, so that nothing gets accomplished? While we may not be able to resolve this issue precisely, there is no doubt that the situation results in *oppression* and the *deprivation of justice and righteousness.* The preoccupation with other things means that no one is watching out for justice. Justice and righteousness were at the center of government's responsibility, not just in the OT, but in the ancient Near East as well (these words may well correspond to the Akkadian words *mīšaru* and *andurāru,* which reflect the legal rights of a people that the king was to protect).

Graham Ogden[56] suggests a positive interpretation of this verse, and does so by following the Targum. They agree that Qohelet describes human oppression, but they believe that *šōmēr* indicates that there are checks and balances over the officials, with the one at the very top (either the king or God himself) as the ultimate assurance of justice. This view reads too much into the passage.

8 (9) In the context, I understand this verse to continue the thought of the previous one, which described governmental oppression and exploitation of the poor. Verse 8 (English 9) says that this line of corruption goes to the very top; *even the king* himself takes advantage of his politically powerful position to get the *profit of the land.*

It must be admitted that this verse is an extreme example of a problem that plagues commentators throughout the book. The syntax and meaning of words render the verse an "insuperable crux,"[57] and possible interpretations include positive and negative construals. Once again, one's understanding of the context, message, and structure of the book plays a pivotal role.

There is no text-critical solution to the problem of this verse.[58] The Septuagint simply follows the Hebrew in the main and has its own syntactical difficulties. The Vulgate runs roughshod over the difficulties, perhaps the only recourse for those who have to provide a translation.

As representative of a positive reading of the verse, we examine the interpretation of Michael Eaton.[59] After discussing the problems with the verse and giving his philological arguments, Eaton translates the verse, "But an advantage to a land for everyone is: a king over cultivated land." He then

---

56. Ogden, *Qoheleth,* pp. 80-81.

57. Gordis, *Koheleth,* p. 250.

58. An interesting, though not very essential, text-critical point is the Ketib (feminine *hî'*)-Qere (masculine *hû'*) associated with the third-person independent pronoun (see GKC §321).

59. Gordis, *Koheleth,* p. 250.

goes on to say that Qohelet believes that the king can check the oppression described in the previous verse.[60]

The justification for the negative translation adopted above is as follows. First, it must be admitted that the preceding verse, with all of its problems, leaves little room for hope. Second, in the other contexts in which political leaders, and especially kings, are mentioned, they are not viewed as the great saviors of the land. In 8:2-6, for instance, Qohelet teaches how to avoid the wrath of the king, whose word, though wrong or oppressive, cannot be gainsaid. Qohelet has already stated that there are two classes of individuals, the oppressed and the oppressors, and there is no one to rescue the former from the latter (4:1-3). For *profit*, see 1:3. The *land* is the land that is ruled by the king. In sum, the book's negative view of leadership elsewhere strongly suggests that the same view prevails here.

It is with the next phrase that we run into serious difficulties, leading some to convenient, though unsupported, emendations.[61] I take *bakkōl hû'* (note the remarks about the Ketib-Qere above) as a nominative sentence with the independent pronoun referring back to *profit*. Literally, then, it is rendered, "The profit of the land, it is in all (this)," referring to the profit that is gained by the officials mentioned in v. 7 (English 8). The major difficulty of the second clause is the meaning of the verb, a niphal from *'ābad,* which in its other attested occurrences (Deut. 21:4 and Ezek. 36:9, 34) refers to a cultivated field. Here, however, Charles Whitley[62] is likely right that the verb has a middle sense of "cultivates for himself," "is served by" or "benefits."[63]

When all is said and done, problems persist. Ogden is probably right to say, "this is one of those verses whose interpretation we may never ascertain,"[64] and R. N. Whybray's reluctance to enter into the discussion has much to commend it.[65]

10. The Meaninglessness of Wealth (5:9–6:9 [English 5:10–6:9])

Differences arise concerning the exact ending of this next section. R. N. Whybray,[66] for instance, wants to conclude the section with the chapter's end

60. M. A. Eaton, *Ecclesiastes,* Tyndale Old Testament Commentaries (Downers Grove, IL: InterVarsity, 1983), pp. 101-2.

61. Fox, *Qohelet and His Contradictions,* p. 213.

62. Whitley, *Koheleth,* pp. 50-51.

63. So Crenshaw, *Ecclesiastes,* p. 119.

64. Ogden, *Qoheleth,* p. 81.

65. Though he significantly admits that "it seems unlikely that Qohelet entertained some mitigating scrap of hope that the king might intervene to put it right" (see Whybray, *Ecclesiastes,* NCB, p. 98).

66. Whybray, *Ecclesiastes,* NCB, p. 98.

on the grounds that the *carpe diem* section (5:17-19 [English 5:18-20]) provides closure. However, he also recognizes a thematic connection with the first unit in chapter 6. Structure is a problem throughout the book (see "Structure" in the introduction), but fortunately it rarely makes a significant impact on interpretation.

The theme that unites the section is wealth, and this thematic unity provides an argument for treating the section from 5:9 (English 5:10) to 6:9 as one large unit. This division is adopted here.[67] Throughout this unit, Qohelet questions whether meaning or enjoyment is possible through the acquisition and use of wealth. Not surprisingly, given the pattern of his thought thus far, his answer is that it too is "meaningless" (*hebel;* see 5:9 [English 5:10] and 6:9). Through a series of reflective statements, proverbs, and stories,[68] Qohelet drives home his conclusion that wealth is meaningless.

5:9 (10)   *Those who love money never have enough money;*
      those who love riches[69] never have enough[70] gain.[71]
      This is also meaningless.

10 (11)   *When prosperity increases, those who consume it increase. So what success[72] is there for its owner,[73] except to admire it?[74]*

11 (12)   *Sweet is the sleep of laborers, whether they eat much or little. But the abundance of the wealthy does not allow them to sleep.[75]*

---

67. Following many modern commentators, including Crenshaw (*Ecclesiastes,* pp. 119-30) and Murphy (*Ecclesiastes,* pp. 44-59).

68. So Murphy, *Wisdom Literature,* pp. 138-39.

69. The *beth* prefix on *hāmôn* may be the result of dittography *(BHS),* since *'āhab* is nowhere else attested with the preposition *beth.*

70. In Hebrew the verb is elided from the second colon, though I provide it in English for smoothness of translation. Otherwise, we are left with the peculiar expression "those who love riches, no gain." This kind of elision is common in Hebrew poetry (Watson, *Classical Hebrew Poetry,* pp. 303-6), thus rendering text-critical emendation of the type described and proposed by Whitley (*Koheleth,* p. 51) unnecessary. But it is true that the Peshitta offers evidence for an alternative when it revocalizes *tebû'â* as *t͏ᵉbô'ēhû* "it will not come to him" (so Gordis, *Koheleth,* p. 251).

71. Alternate, but closely related, translations of *t͏ᵉbû'â* include "income" or "profit."

72. Some persist in calling *kišrôn* "late" (e.g., Ogden, *Qoheleth,* p. 82), but see Fredericks (*Qoheleth's Language,* pp. 229, 252).

73. For the plural having a singular force with some nouns, including *ba'al,* see GKC §124i.

74. The Ketib *(r͏ᵉ'ît* or *r͏ᵉ'îyat)* and the Qere *(r͏ᵉ'ôt)* are nominal forms, each a hapax legomenon. That is why some (e.g., Whybray, *Ecclesiastes,* NCB, p. 99) opt to emend to the infinitive construct, *r͏ᵉ'ôt,* a reading that has the support of a small number of Hebrew manuscripts.

75. For this form of the infinitive, see GKC §69n.

12 (13) *There is a sickening evil*[76] *I have observed*[77] *under the sun:*[78] *wealth hoarded to the harm of its owner.*[79]

13 (14) *And that wealth was lost in an evil situation. Though a son was born, there is nothing to leave him.*[80]

14 (15) *As he left his mother's womb, so he will return,*[81] *going as he came — naked. And he will take nothing from his toil*[82] *that he is able to bring*[83] *into his possession.*[84]

15 (16) *And this*[85] *indeed*[86] *is a sickening evil: Just as*[87] *they come so they go, so what profit is there for those who toil for the wind?*

76. The Septuagint has only "sickness" for *rā'â ḥôlâ (sickening evil)*.

77. For the force of the verb *rā'â* in the book, see 1:14.

78. For the phrase *under the sun*, see 1:3.

79. Literally, "hoarded by its owner to his harm" (so Crenshaw, *Ecclesiastes*, p. 122; against Gordis, *Koheleth*, p. 252).

80. Literally, "there is nothing in his hand," taking *him* as the *son*.

81. Or "he will again go as he came" (Gordis, *Koheleth*, p. 252; Lauha, *Kohelet*, p. 106), but the sense is awkward. It sounds as if he is *going* a second time, though it is the thought of commentators that the repetition focuses on the *nakedness*. The Hebrew, however, does not read that way.

82. See Whitley, *Koheleth*, p. 52, for a full discussion of the preposition *beth* in this context. While some take it as an instrumental *beth*, Whitley is correct that it often carries the force of *from*.

83. Reading hiphil *(šeyyōlēk)* with MT, not qal *(hina poreuthai = šeyyēlēk)* with the Septuagint. Lauha (*Kohelet*, p. 107) hypothesizes that the Septuagint reading is due to the *scripto defectiva* in the MT.

84. Literally, "in his hand" *(b^eyādô)*.

85. For this form of the demonstrative, see n. 4 to 2:2.

86. The Qumran text does not read a *waw* before the *gam*. Most interpreters understand the *gam* to have the commonly attested sense of "also" (see Williams, *Hebrew Syntax*, §378). Against this reading it must be said that v. 15 does not add a new *sickening evil* but emphasizes by repetition the evil of the previous verse.

87. There is much discussion of the unique phrase *kol-'ummat še*). Since it is otherwise unattested, it becomes the proving ground of scholars' pet theories. Ginsburg (*The Song of Songs and Coheleth*, p. 195) and S. J. Du Plessis ("Aspects of Morphological Peculiarities of the Language of Qoheleth," in *De Fructu Oris Sui: Essays in Honour of Adrianus Van Selms*, ed. I. H. Eybers, et al. [Leiden: Brill, 1971], pp. 164-80) understand it to be an Aramaism (see also Ogden, *Qoheleth*, p. 85). Dahood sees parallels with Phoenician ("The Language of Qoheleth," *CBQ* 14 [1952]: 229). Isaksson (*Studies in the Language of Qoheleth*, p. 195), on the contrary, takes it as a sign of vernacular speech.

It is true that the vocalization may have occurred under the influence of Aramaic during the history of transmission (see Fredericks, *Qoheleth's Language*, pp. 228-29), on analogy with the phrase *kol-q^ebal* (GKC §161b). But it was Ibn-Giat, known from Qimchi, quoted by Delitzsch (*Proverbs, Ecclesiastes, Song of Solomon*, p. 300), who noted that the original form should have been vocalized *kil'ummat* and understood as the comparative *k^e* plus the common compound preposition *l^e'ummat* ("like, as").

161

16 (17) *Indeed, they eat*[88] *in darkness*[89] *all their days with great resent-ment,*[90] *illness,*[91] *and frustration.*

17 (18) *Indeed, this is what I have observed to be good:*[92] *that it is appro-priate to eat, to drink, and to enjoy all the toil that one does under the sun the few days God has given to that person, for that is his reward.*

18 (19) *Furthermore, everyone to whom God gives wealth and possessions*[93] *and allows*[94] *them to eat of it and to accept their reward and to take pleasure in their toil — this is God's gift.*

88. The Septuagint mistakenly read $w^{a'}\bar{e}bel$ for $y\bar{o}'kal$. This may be translated, "And all his days (he spends) in darkness and mourning and much anger and illness and rage." This misreading compounds the difficulty of the verse in that now there is no explicit verb for either part of the verse. Ogden (*Qoheleth*, p. 85; see also Delitzsch, *Proverbs, Ecclesiastes, Song of Solomon*, p. 300) surprisingly and with no explanation follows the Septuagint.

89. Kugel ("Qohelet and Money," p. 39) emends $h\check{s}k$ to $h\acute{s}k$ and translates "Yea, all his days he eats in spare fashion."

90. The MT points the word as a verb ($k\bar{a}'as$ "to be irritated, to be angry"), but with the versions and with the sense of the context I repoint as a noun ($ka'as$ "resentment").

91. The pronominal suffix ($w^e\d{h}\bar{a}l^ey\hat{o}$) is a textual error. See the Septuagint and its daughter translations for support to read simply $w\bar{a}\d{h}^ol\hat{i}$.

92. The relationship between *ṭôb* and *yāpeh*, separated by *'ašer*, is quite difficult. I here follow Fox (*Qohelet and His Contradictions*, p. 218), who argues that the relative pronoun in this context is best "represented as a colon." N. Lohfink ("Qoheleth 5:17-19 — Revelation by Joy," *CBQ 52* [1990]: 625) translates this phrase "the supreme good." I am here ignoring the Masoretic accentuation. 5:17 (English 5:18) is also a rare example of a long verse without an *athnach* indicating its middle. For the fullest discussion of the accentuation of this verse, see Delitzsch (*Proverbs, Ecclesiastes, Song of Songs*, p. 300). Ginsburg (*Song of Songs and Coheleth*, p. 355) is an example of a scholar who follows the Masoretic scheme.

Some scholars have argued for Greek influence here (e.g., D. G. Wildeboer, "Der Prediger," in *Die fünf Megillot* [Freiburg: Mohr, 1898], p. 435; and N. Lohfink, *Kohelet*, Neue EB [Würzburg: Echter Verlag, 1980], p. 45). But Fredericks (*Qoheleth's Language*, p. 246) disputes this. Also note Lauha (*Kohelet*, p. 112), who says, "Die Konstruktion mit 'šr bei Kohelet ist aber von ganz anderer Art als der koordinierte Wortbau des griechischen Idioms. Vor allem liegt der Unterschied darin, dass der griechische Ausdruck zur ästhetisch-ethischen Charakterisierung von Personen verwendet wurde, Kohelet dagegen von kon-kreten Dingen spricht" ("The construction with 'šr by Qohelet is totally different than the cognate construction of the Greek idiom. Above all, the difference lies in the fact that the Greek expression is used in order to give an aesthetic-ethical characterization of people; Qohelet, however, speaks of concrete things").

93. The appearance of $n^ek\bar{a}s\hat{i}m$ in Josh. 22:8 belies the attempt to argue that it is a late Aramaism. Fredericks (*Qoheleth's Language*, pp. 232-33) also points to an earlier Akkadian cognate (*nikkassu*), which itself is related to a Sumerian word.

94. The hiphil form of the verb (*hišlîṭô*) also occurs in Eccles. 6:2, the qal in 8:9. There are also two nominal forms in Ecclesiastes (see 8:4, 8 for *šilṭôn* and 7:19, 8:8, and 10:5 for *šallîṭ*). Fredericks (*Qoheleth's Language*, p. 239) once again successfully counters arguments that insist the use of the word is late.

19 (20) *Indeed, they do not remember much about the days of their lives*
for God keeps them[95] *so busy*[96] *with the pleasure of their heart.*

6:1 *There is an evil*[97] *I have observed under the sun,*[98] *and it is frequent*
among humans.

2 *There are those to whom God gives wealth, possessions, and*
honor;[99] *they lack nothing that they desire. But God does not allow*
them to eat of it, but a stranger[100] *will eat of it. This is meaningless,*
and it is a sickening evil.

3 *A person may*[101] *have one hundred children and live many years.*
However[102] *many are the days of his life, if he is not satisfied with*
the good things he has, and does not even get a proper burial, then
better, I say, to be a stillborn baby.

95. Reading a pronominal suffix *(maʿᵃnēhû* for MT *maʿᵃneh)* along with the
Septuagint, Peshitta, and the Targum. It is possible that the versions had the same Hebrew
text we have but simply understood that the verbal root implied a pronominal suffix
(Lohfink, "Qohelet 5:17-19," p. 626).

96. Taking *maʿᵃnēhû* as the hiphil participle of *ʿnh* III ("to keep someone
busy"). We have seen the qal already in 1:13 and 3:10 (cf. comments there). Gordis
(Koheleth, pp. 255-57) and Delitzsch *(Proverbs, Ecclesiastes, Song of Solomon,* p. 303)
are exceptions in deriving the meaning of the word from *ʿnh* I "to answer." Lohfink
("Qohelet 5:17-19") does as well and believes that this verse, which speaks of God's
revelation of joy, is a key text for interpreting the entire book. The Septuagint reads
"distracted" (from *perspaō)* and the Vulgate "keeps occupied" *(occupet),* supporting
my reading.

97. A number of manuscripts add "sickening" *(ḥôlâ),* but this addition is probably
on analogy with 5:11 (English 5:12) and is the result of smoothing out the text.

98. For an explanation of the phrase *(taḥat haššāmeš),* see 1:3.

99. The exact meaning of *kābôd* in this context is not certain. It can be another
term for riches, but here I understand it to refer to high social standing or esteem. R. B.
Salters ("Notes on the Interpretation of Qoh 6:2," *ZAW* 91 [1979]: 282-89) argues that
such a meaning is incompatible with the verb "to eat," even if that verb is taken
metaphorically to mean "to enjoy." He asks whether it is possible for someone to
"enjoy" the "honor" given to him. The answer, contra Salters, is yes, once it is
understood that "honor" usually comes with certain privileges and preferential treatment.

100. Or possibly even simply "someone else." Though this word *(nokrî)* often
means "foreigner," here the point is that someone other than the owner enjoys the wealth
(so Gordis, *Koheleth,* p. 257; and see espcially the extended discussion by Salters, "Notes
on the Interpretation of Qoh 6:2," pp. 286-89).

101. To reflect the conditional *ʾim,* which begins the clause. An alternative rendering would begin a translation with "if."

102. So Gordis, *Koheleth,* p. 258, who takes the clause *(wᵉrab šeyyihyû yᵉmê-*
šānāw) as concessive, though the "syntax is strange" (Whybray, *Ecclesiastes,* NCB,
p. 105). Ogden *(Qoheleth,* p. 91) lamely takes it as repetition (with the previous clause)
for emphasis.

4 *For without meaning it comes,*[103] *and in darkness it goes, and in darkness its name is shrouded.*

5 *Morever,*[104] *it never saw the sun and did not know the sun.*[105] *There is more rest*[106] *for this one than for that one.*

6 *Even if*[107] *someone should live one thousand years two times over but does not experience good times — do not all*[108] *go to the same place?*[109]

7 *All toil of humans is for their mouths,*[110] *but the appetite is never filled.*

8 *For what advantage does a wise person have over a fool? What do the poor have by knowing how to act in front of the living?*

9 *Better the sight of the eyes than wandering desire. This is also meaningless and chasing the wind.*

103. According to Isaksson (*Studies in the Language of Qohelet*, p. 131), *bāʾ* is the perfect aspect of the verb, the other two verbs of the verse being imperfect. He believes that the perfect precedes the imperfects in this verse "since the coming is viewed as an established fact, whereas the departing (and shrouding) is expressed as being in the course of fulfillment." It should be noted, however, that the Qumran manuscript of Ecclesiastes (J. Muilenburg, "A Qohelet Scroll from Qumran," *BASOR* 135 [1954]: 20-28) has *hlk* (perfect) rather than *ylk* (imperfect; see *BHS*).

104. Taking *gam* in an augmentative sense. It could be argued, though, that it has an emphatic ("indeed") or perhaps concessive ("though") sense (Crenshaw [*Ecclesiastes*, p. 120] seems to translate it both ways: "Indeed, although . . .").

105. The Hebrew (*gam-šemeš lôʾ-rāʾâ wᵉlôʾ yādāʿ*) is awkward. "The sun" occurs only one time in the Hebrew, but I believe that it is meant to be the direct object of the first two verbs in the verse.

106. Gordis (*Koheleth*, p. 259) argues that this word must mean "satisfaction," not "rest" here and accordingly should be considered a Mishnaism. Fredericks (*Qoheleth's Language*, p. 188) has pointed out that the typical biblical Hebrew meaning "rest" is perfectly appropriate here.

107. The word *ʾillû* occurs in only one other place in the Hebrew Bible (Esth. 7:4), but also is found in Mishnaic Hebrew (Whitley, *Koheleth*, p. 58) and bears similarities with Aramaic. Thus, scholars have used the word to support their view of Qohelet's language. Fredericks (*Qoheleth's Language*, pp. 178, 196-97, 217, 241) has pointed out that the word is a contraction (from *ʾim lû;* see Qumran text, which has *wʾim lw*) and may accordingly originate from the vernacular.

108. Taking the preceding subject as an impersonal rather than a specific reference to the rich person and the stillborn. If we adopt the latter route, then we can translate *hakkōl* as "both" instead of "all."

109. Sheol, for which see P. R. Ackroyd, "Two Hebrew Notes," *ASTI* 5 (1967): 84; and my comment on 6:7.

110. Luther (originally ca. 1532) argued that this expression meant "according to his measure" (on the basis of Exod. 12:4 and Gen. 47:12), but as C. H. H. Wright observed (*The Book of Koheleth* [London: Hodder and Stoughton, 1888], p. 375), it is really "equivalent to for his enjoyment."

9 (10)   The section begins with a proverb expressing the insatiability of wealth.[111] No matter how much money a person has, there is always the possibility of and the desire for more. The implication is that those who set the acquisition of money as their highest goal in life have a never-ending task. They will never reach their goal, and, therefore, their life is "meaningless."

Qohelet does not wait until the very end (but see also 6:9) to give us his conclusion concerning the love of money. It is *meaningless* (see 1:2). This conclusion is in tension with the predominant attitude of Proverbs toward wealth. There wealth is something that can result from wise behavior, is a gift of God (Prov. 3:9-10, 16; 8:18; 13:21; 14:24; 15:6; 19:4; 21:21; 24:3-4), and is worthy of pursuit. While Proverbs also recognizes that one can get rich and be wicked, or be wise and poor, it is fair to say that Qohelet does not share that book's optimism about riches.

10 (11)   The first half of the verse offers yet another proverb about the problems of wealth and perhaps gives a reason why no one finds satisfaction in their wealth.[112] As one's means increase, so do "bills." Whether *those who consume it* are creditors or hangers-on makes no difference to the point of the verse; the one who has the wealth seldom has the opportunity to really enjoy its fruits.

The second colon draws out the implication of the first. The wealthy person really has no pleasure in his riches except to see them pass through his hands *(admire it)*. There is some debate over the precise meaning of *success,* for which see 2:11 and 4:4.

11 (12)   We now read a third reason in as many verses why wealth is more of a problem than a blessing. The rich cannot sleep well. It is not important to Qohelet's point whether the insomnia is the result of worry or indigestion.[113] Perhaps we should look to v. 9 (English v. 10) to provide the answer: the rich are so driven to multiply their wealth that they cannot sleep. Or perhaps to v. 12 (English v. 13): the rich cannot sleep because they worry about losing their wealth. In either case, the irony is that laborers sleep soundly, though they do not enjoy the same level of prosperity. Qohelet knows that the wealthy work hard for their riches, but it is a different kind of work. The

---

111. The proverbial form of this verse may be seen in the semantic parallelism, the repetition of *money (kesep),* and the ellipsis of the verb.

112. The proverbial form of v. 10a is inferred from its short, pithy statement, its parallelism, and its artful use of nearly identical verbs in the first (the infinitive construct of *rābâ*) and second (qal perfect of *rābab*) cola.

113. The Septuagint made the former approach explicit with its translation, *ho emplēstheis tou ploutēsai,* translated by Jarick (*Gregory Thaumaturgos' Paraphrase,* p. 125) as "the one who is satiated with becoming wealthy." Jarick also points to Gregory Thaumaturgos,, who "does not speak of the person *per se* but of the phenomenon: *ploutou epithymia,* 'the desire for wealth.'"

laborers' physical exertion means that they can sleep regardless of the condition of their stomach. The Septuagint, Symmachus, and Theodotion understand the *laborer* as a "slave" (repointing the Hebrew to *hāʿebed* and translating *tou doulou*), but this is unnecessary and unlikely.

12 (13)   Qohelet here introduces a *sickening evil* that he will describe in the next few verses (vv. 12-16 [English vv. 13-17]). Qohelet has previously used the existential particle *there is (yēš)* to introduce an example story (2:21 [see discussion] and 4:8). Nonetheless, it is unclear whether the next few verses provide one or two *evil* situations. Bo Isaksson[114] discusses two such possibilities: (1) that vv. 12 and 13 (English vv. 13 and 14) provide a single case of one person whom Qohelet has observed, or (2) that v. 13 (English v. 14) "explicates" or describes the *sickening evil* of v. 12 (English v. 13). I would suggest a more likely third possibility that takes into account the repetition of *sickening evil* in v. 15 (English v. 16). That is, Qohelet gives two different scenarios, both of which are *evil* and which are united by the futility of wealth. The first is in v. 12 (English v. 13), which is the tragedy of the wealthy person who hoards all of his money *(to the harm of its owner)*. As Robert Gordis indicates,[115] "The guarding of wealth entails anxiety and care." The money, since it is never used, does not bring joy or pleasure in any way. Qohelet does not provide a specific explanation, but perhaps the rich person is too worried that it might be stolen by robbers, or else he is concerned about using it wisely. The second scenario will be described in the comment on v. 13 (English v. 14).

13 (14)   Here the problem entails riches that are *lost* through some unspecified misfortune. The *situation* is unspecified in order to give the readers' imaginations freedom to connect it to potential misfortunes in their own lives. One's mind, though, wanders to Job, whose wealth was devastated through a series of different misfortunes. The *situation* is *evil* in that it harms the wealthy person; the word does not impute evil actions to the person as the cause of the loss (see the comment on the phrase at Eccles. 1:13).

The inability to pass any wealth on to the *son* is the most negative aspect of the situation. Once again, wealth proves no advantage to the person who, at least temporarily, has it.

14 (15)   While there is room for debate,[116] the antecedent to the subject of the verbs here is the father, not the son, of the previous verse. After all, it is the father's loss of wealth that was the subject there. He was the one who labored so hard in vain to amass wealth. Now death spoils it. Qohelet here introduces death, the topic that preoccupies him throughout the book, in

114. Isaksson, *Studies in the Language of Qoheleth,* pp. 95-96.
115. Gordis, *Koheleth,* p. 252.
116. See the opposing view of Gordis, *Koheleth,* p. 253.

words reminiscent of Job 1:21. Individuals as babies arrive in this world naked and with nothing to call their own, and they leave in the same state, even if they grow up and earn enormous wealth. "You can't take it with you" is the sentiment of this line. It is unimportant whether Qohelet is consciously evoking Job here.[117] It is clearly the case that the Job passage is pithier and more poetic. Qohelet gives a prose restatement of the thought.

15 (16)   For the main part, this verse repeats with emphasis the thought of the previous one. Human beings depart life as they enter it — naked and helpless. Once again (see v. 12 [English v. 13]) Qohelet calls this a *sickening evil*. As he has already done a number of times earlier (beginning with 1:3), he asks a rhetorical question, expecting a negative answer: There is no *profit* (see 1:3) for those who *toil* (see 1:3) *for wind*. The last phrase evokes the earlier expression "chasing the wind" (see 1:14). Since holding onto wealth is problematical during life and impossible at death, the laborer really toils for something of little or no substance — *the wind*. In the long run such toil is a waste of time.

16 (17)   This verse concludes the anecdote that began in v. 12 (English v. 13) (which itself is part of the topic of wealth's meaninglessness that began in v. 9 [English v. 10]). Specifically, it continues and explicates the end of v. 15 (English v. 16) that people who strive for meaning in wealth are reaching for a hopeless goal.

Qohelet first introduces the depressing metaphor of these people eating *in darkness*. We must remember that Qohelet allows that some may enjoy the simple pleasures of life, which include eating (e.g., 2:24 and, more immediately, 5:17 [English 5:18]). But people who work for the unattainable goal of wealth cannot enjoy even this. They are pictured as alone and blind in their eating. To do away with the metaphor of eating, which may at first seem strange (so the Septuagint [see my translation] and Dahood),[118] eliminates a powerful image and replaces it with a bland prosaic reading, "they spend their days in darkness."[119]

The syntax of the second colon seems awkward, since it lacks a verb, but this verse can be an example of "noun-clauses shortened in an unusual manner" because of the strong emotion behind the expression.[120] The preposition *in* does not occur in the second colon, but its occurrence in the first governs the nouns in the second (it may be understood as an ellipsis).

---

117. Ogden (*Qoheleth*, p. 84) believes so, but Gordis (*Koheleth*, p. 253) denies the connection with Job.

118. M. J. Dahood, "The Phoenician Background of Qoheleth," *Biblica* 47 (1966): 272.

119. See Whitley, *Koheleth*, pp. 54-55, for a rebuttal of Dahood's position.

120. See GKC §147e.

17 (18) The next three verses turn away from that which provides no meaning, wealth, to that which at least dulls the pain. Verses 17-19 (English 18-20) express a similar sentiment to what we have already encountered in 2:24-26, 3:12-14, and 3:22, and what we will find in 8:15 and 9:7-10. As there, we do not have a statement of "almost boundless optimism,"[121] but of resignation to the limited best that life can offer (*carpe diem* — see "Qohelet's Theology" in the introduction). That is, in the light of the absence of a meaningful life, Qohelet advocates a life pursuing the small pleasures afforded by food, drink, and work.

Qohelet offers his conclusion, signaled by the characteristic *I observed* (see 1:14), which, along with the third-person statement of the conclusion, gives an objective twist to his pronouncement in this verse. His conclusion is that the best humans can expect in life is *to eat, to drink, and to enjoy their toil* (for a discussion of this language, see 2:24). It is true that Qohelet is more assertive here than earlier, where he utilized the reluctant "there is nothing better than" formula. Nonetheless, his depressing tone may be heard in the last words of the verse, *the few days God has given that person, for that is his reward.* For *reward,* see 2:10.

18 (19) Here the limited enjoyment of v. 17 (English v. 18) is further restricted. Not everyone who has wealth can enjoy it. As Christian Ginsburg stated, "Not only is there nothing left for man but present enjoyment, but even for this he is dependent upon God."[122] Not everyone can enjoy their *reward* in life. Only those *to whom God gives wealth* and those he *allows to eat . . . to accept . . . and to take pleasure* may really find satisfaction in this life, even in this very limited way. Does God grant his *gift* to many? Qohelet does not directly answer this question here, but from his tone the answer is no (and see 6:2). It is certainly the case that Qohelet does not believe himself to be a recipient of this anesthetizing pleasure (see next verse).

19 (20) One can almost feel Qohelet's envy as he describes those to whom God has given riches and the ability to enjoy them. They are the ones, unlike himself as his speech continually testifies, who are able to take his advice and enjoy life now. He is suffering, but they have an anesthetic to life's harsh realities. As Michael Fox noted, according to Qohelet, "Pleasure is an anodyne to the pain of consciousness."[123] Indeed, it is difficult to put everything that Qohelet says about *pleasure (śimḥâ)* together. One strand of his teaching commends it (3:12, 22; 8:15; 9:7; 11:9, etc.), while another strand of teaching may be represented by:

---

121. So Ogden, *Qoheleth,* p. 86.
122. Ginsburg, *The Song of Songs and Coheleth,* p. 365.
123. Fox, *Qohelet and His Contradictions,* p. 73.

The heart of the wise is in a house of mourning,
and the heart of fools in a house of pleasure.

                    (7:4; see also 2:1, 2, 10, etc.)

A survey of all the passages in which Qohelet speaks of *pleasure* reveals that, while Qohelet commends it during life for those who are able to find it, he knows that it has no ultimate meaning, no profit *(yitrôn),* and so it is ultimately meaningless *(hebel).* Pleasure is all there is during one's earthly existence, advises Qohelet, so enjoy it now, if you can.

6:1   Qohelet, with his characteristic use of *there is* (the particle *yēš;* see list and discussion at 2:21), introduces yet another anecdote. In this instance, he once again supports his case that there is no ultimate meaning in wealth. As a matter of fact, in 6:1-6 he claims that many well-off people cannot experience the enjoyment described in 5:17-19 (English 5:18-20), not because they lack resources, but because God will not let them enjoy life. Indeed, Qohelet says that this situation is *frequent,* indicating that it is more common than having the ability to enjoy whatever "good gifts" God has seen fit to bestow upon a person.

He labels the situation to follow *evil,* a strongly moral word. As usual, he presents his conclusions, at least at first, formally and with an air of detachment (*I observed,* 1:14). Before naming the *evil,* Qohelet states that it occurs frequently *among humans.* The word *frequent* is derived from the root *rbb,* which often refers to quantity (my view; so also the Vulgate [*frequens*], Rashi, Luther, and Graham Ogden),[124] but can also denote qualitative greatness (so Rashbam, Ibn Ezra, NIV, NRSV), something like "weighs heavily upon humanity."

2   The anecdote introduced in the first verse is now presented. There are people who have it all — money, material blessings, power — who cannot enjoy it. God does not allow them to enjoy their wealth, but others do not even know how to enjoy it. This situation frustrates Qohelet. After all, most people do not even have wealth and power, and they live on the fantasy that having it would result in satisfaction. Qohelet bitterly denies that these things produce meaning.

There is no question concerning Qohelet's attitude toward this situation, since he describes it as "evil" in v. 1 and as a *sickening evil* here. Qohelet gives the reverse situation to what he said in 5:18 (English 5:19), using nearly similar syntax and vocabulary.[125] In 5:18 (English 5:19) God gives some people "wealth and possessions" and "allows them to eat of it." In this verse Qohelet has in mind those to whom God has given these same gifts, even

---

124. Ogden, *Qoheleth,* p. 90.
125. Isaksson, *Studies in the Language of Qoheleth,* pp. 120-22.

adding *honor* (thus paralleling the list in 2 Chron. 1:11), but here *God does not allow them to eat of it.* The striking thing about Qohelet's comment is that he directly and solely attributes this negative state of affairs to God. It is God who does not permit the enjoyment of these gifts, thus frustrating the recipients and also Qohelet. The attempts to mitigate divine responsibility here have been numerous and may be illustrated by the Targum, which adds the foreign idea of the rich person's sins: "But the Lord has not given him power, on account of his sins, to enjoy it."[126]

God not only prohibits the owner to enjoy the wealth but also adds further insult because a *stranger will eat of it.* This statement reflects the similar statement of 3:17-23 that someone who works hard must leave the fruits of his labor to another. Thus, Qohelet pronounces this predicament *meaningless* (see 1:2).

3 Verses 3-5 expand upon the theme of the person who has the resources to enjoy life but cannot do so because God does not allow him. In this verse, however, it is not the abundance of riches that are highlighted but the other chief joys of life: children and long life. Other biblical passages rejoice in large numbers of children. For instance, Psalm 127 likens sons to arrows and exclaims, "Blessed is the man whose quiver is full of them" (v. 4). As for long life, we turn to the book of Proverbs, where the parent encourages the child to follow his teaching, "for they will prolong your life many years" (3:2).

Qohelet, though, here takes exception to this common biblical teaching. He finds it more than conceivable that a person may be blessed with abundant offspring and a long life but still be absolutely miserable. So miserable, indeed, that *a stillborn baby* has had a better life, for reasons that will be made explicit in the next two verses.

The difficulty with the present verse is the phrase here translated *and does not even get a proper burial.* To many its appearance is awkward in its present context. This problem has been treated in the past by emendation[127] or by transposing verses.[128] Perhaps the most intriguing and tempting alternative is to take the clause as a reference to the stillborn child who does not get a burial,[129] but this requires taking the pronominal suffix on the preposition *lamed* as anticipatory of the stillborn, which is possible but not at all likely. I thus stay close to the MT and understand the meaning to be that, though someone may have the external trappings of a happy life, he may be miserable, and his dead body may be treated in a horrid fashion

---

126. Levine, *The Aramaic Version of Qohelet,* p. 36.
127. So Gordis (*Koheleth,* pp. 258-59) emends *not (lô')* to "if" *(lû').*
128. R. B. Y. Scott, *Proverbs, Ecclesiastes,* pp. 231-32.
129. So Crenshaw, *Ecclesiastes,* pp. 126-27.

(Deut. 28:26; 2 Kings 9:10; Jer. 14:16). The idea expressed in this verse is also found in Ecclesiastes 4:2.

4 The verse clearly builds upon the previous one by expanding the description of the stillborn. The stillborn exists momentarily but has no identity. Michael Fox,[130] on the contrary, takes the verse as a description of the toiler, on the weak grounds that the stillborn has no name to be shrouded.[131] Yet the very next verse says of the same subject that it did not see the sun, a description applicable only to the stillborn.

The hard-hitting imprecation of Psalm 58 climaxes with "like a stillborn child, may they not see the sun" (v. 9 [English v. 8]). The psalmist could not think of a more horrid fate to wish upon his enemies. But, according to Qohelet, the stillborn's fate is much preferred to the life of one to whom God has given riches, long life, and many children, but not the ability to enjoy it all.

The line has a rhythmic, if not poetic, feeling to it, partly evoked by the word pair *comes* and *goes* (also in 5:15 [English 5:16]; see also 1:4), as well as the similarity in sound between *without meaning (bahebel)* and *darkness (baḥōšek,* two times).

According to Qohelet, both the stillborn's fate and that of those who are not permitted to enjoy life are horrid. The advantage, however, goes to the stillborn because it lacks consciousness. Qohelet has already granted this same advantage to the one who has not yet been born (4:3).

5 Qohelet continues his description of the advantages of the stillborn over the miserable rich. The verse augments *(Moreover)* the previous verse with its emphasis on darkness. The darkness results from the fact that the stillborn never *saw the sun.* What this means is further clarified by *did not know.* We expect a direct object after *know,* but as other commentators have pointed out, the verb occurs elsewhere with the meaning "have knowledge" (Isa. 44:9; 45:20).[132] Thus, Qohelet points out the obvious, that the stillborn never reaches consciousness, with the implication that the stillborn never experiences the hardships and misery of the present life. In this way, the stillborn has *rest,* unlike the rich, who struggle continuously. The first *this one* refers to the stillborn, the second, to the rich person.

This verse is in tension with Ecclesiastes 11:7, "Truly, sweet is the light, and it is pleasant for the eyes to see the sun," and it is such tensions that lead me to characterize Qohelet as a confused, skeptical wise man (see "Authorship" in the introduction).

130. Fox, *Qohelet and His Contradictions,* p. 220.
131. M. Luther, "Notes on Ecclesiastes," in *Luther's Works,* vol. 15, ed. and trans. J. Pelikan (St. Louis: Concordia, 1972 [1532]), p. 96.
132. See Whybray, *Ecclesiastes,* NCB, p. 106.

While the Septuagint correctly understood the phrase *more . . . for this one than for that one* as referring to the stillborn and the rich person, respectively, the Targum and the Vulgate moralize the clause so that it indicates a failure of morality. Thus, the Vulgate, *non vidit solem neque cognovit distantiam boni et male* ("it does not see the sun nor know the difference between good and bad"), and the Targum "And even the light of the sun he saw not, and did not know good from evil, to discern between this world and the world to come."[133] In his commentary, interestingly enough, Jerome (1112b) reverts to the Hebrew and translates *Et quidem solem non vidit, nec cognovit, requies huic magis quam illi* ("And it did not see even the sun, nor know [it], that one has more rest than the other one").

6 Qohelet earlier (6:3) had used hyperbole in reference to the blessing of children. He also there alluded to long life. Here he gets more specific, hypothesizing about someone who lives two thousand years. Though someone lives to this incredibly old age (more than twice the age of Methuselah!), those years are still meaningless if he is unable to enjoy them. And in any case, though two thousand years is a long time, even that life comes to a close. Death again spoils the enjoyment of life, however long.

Once again, Qohelet's attitude contrasts with the predominant voice in the book of Proverbs, which extols a long and enjoyable life as the reward of the one who seeks wisdom (Prov. 3:16, 18; 4:10; 28:16).

7 Most commentators agree that 6:7-9 has at least a loose connection with 5:6–6:6 (English 5:7–6:6) in that it concerns seeking meaning and satisfaction through material wealth. Verse 7 presents another reason to discourage the attempt. In a proverb, Qohelet instructs his reader that the only reason why humans work is to satisfy their sensual desires, but also that such a goal is impossible to reach because the *appetite* or desire is never *filled,* in the sense of satisfied. Thus, the search for contentment is never ending, and so is the speaker's frustration.

This verse, therefore, stands in tension with the so-called *carpe diem* passages (see the list with comment on 3:22). Qohelet there recommends the pleasures associated with toil, eating, and drinking. These enjoyments are the best that life has to offer. At the very least, we see here that he does not believe that these pleasures lead to contentment. Human life is characterized by continual striving.

Peter Ackroyd[134] and Mitchell Dahood[135] have offered a suggestive alternative interpretation of the suffix on the word *mouth.* Ackroyd argued first that the suffix refers to the "one place" of 6:6, thus Sheol. While it is

---

133. Thus Levine, *The Aramiac Version of Qohelet,* p. 37.
134. Ackroyd, "Two Hebrew Notes," pp. 84-86.
135. M. J. Dahood, "Hebrew-Ugaritic Lexicography," *Biblica* 49 (1968): 368.

true that Sheol is at times personified as an open mouth in both Hebrew and Ugaritic poetic texts, it is much more natural to take *humans* as the near antecedent. It makes perfectly good sense in the context, and the book of Proverbs provides analogies:

> The laborer's appetite works for him;
>   his hunger drives him on. (Prov. 16:26)

The sentiment expressed in this verse was seen earlier in part in 6:3 and also 1:8. That sentiment is well paraphrased by Christian Ginsburg when he writes that Qohelet perceived "his life to be a protracted scene of toil, turmoil, and dissatisfaction, ever labouring to satisfy his soul, which cannot be satisfied."[136]

8   Qohelet now raises the question of the advantage of the wise person over the fool. As we will see, the connection of this verse with the context is a bit tenuous, but we must remember that it was commonly thought in ancient Israel that wisdom issued in wealth. But if wealth is no real benefit, then wisdom itself is in doubt.

Two large issues face the interpreter in this verse: (1) the first sentence is clear but at least initially does not appear to fit the context, and (2) the second sentence has a more obvious link with the context, but its meaning is not clear.

I start with (2). The second sentence connects with the section's topic of wealth through the economic term *poor*. It is true that many commentators have difficulty with how the term functions in this verse,[137] but the term is appropriate for the broader context, is supported by all the versions, and, as we will see, is understandable in the narrow context of the verse as well. The translation I have offered does gloss over some of the difficulties. More literally, the sentence reads, "What for the poor knowing to walk before the living (or life)." My translation takes into account the ellipsis of *advantage* from the first sentence, understands the participle to be "an attributive participle characterizing the poor man,"[138] and takes the verb *walk* as a metaphor for "to behave," "to conduct oneself," or *to act*. But what does it mean? For that we turn to the first sentence.

My translation of the first sentence is straightforward and in need of no special comment. The difficulty is that it raises the issue of the *advantage* of the wise over the fool, which is not an issue in either vv. 7, 9, or the broader context of 5:9–6:9 (English 5:10–6:9). Indeed, the thought expressed here is most like that in 2:12-17. Resorting to emendation or transposition or treating the verse as

---

136. Ginsburg, *The Song of Songs and Coheleth,* p. 374.

137. For a variety of textual emendations and philological suggestions, see Whitley, *Koheleth,* p. 59.

138. Isaksson, *Studies in the Language of Qoheleth,* p. 137.

a gloss is hardly credible. Since the verse appears in the early versions, it is an ad hoc argument to solve the problem in this way. A solution presents itself when we remember that one of the functions of wisdom, according to normative wisdom teaching, was to show the way to material riches. The wise would be blessed. Qohelet, however, questions this teaching. The wise have no advantage in quenching the desire for material good. And this leads to the teaching of the second sentence as I have understood it above. The *poor*, therefore, have no advantage in utilizing wisdom, which would teach them how to behave in order to get ahead in the world, to find satisfaction in wealth. Perhaps wisdom could make them rich, but it cannot satisfy their desires.

I note the tendency to give an eschatological twist to the last phrase, *in front of the living*.[139] For instance, the Targum renders: "And what is this poor man to do except to study the Law of the Lord, so he will know how he will have to walk in the presence of the righteous in paradise," and the Vulgate reads: "and he will go where life is" (*pergat illuc ubi est vita,* but see Jerome in his commentary: "What advantage has the poor man, unless he knows how to walk before the living?" [*quid pauperi, nisi scire, ut vadat contra vitam*]).

9 The section closes with a proverb and a repetition of the *hebel* formula. The proverb, which is specifically a "better-than" proverb (see 4:2), subtly makes a point that is characteristic of Qohelet. Qohelet prefers *the sight of the eyes* to *roving desire*. The latter is the clearest as to its meaning and harks back to 6:7, where the same Hebrew word, there translated "appetite," appears. This *desire* or "appetite" can never be fulfilled, and therefore it is always *roving*, anxiously seeking the satisfaction that it cannot provide. Some scholars, notably Charles Whitley[140] and R. N. Whybray,[141] dispute this understanding of the phrase on the grounds that the verb *hālak* simply means "to go" or "to depart," not "to rove." They thus take the word *nepeš* as "soul" or "life" and argue that the phrase refers to the departing of life, that is, death. Whitley thus offers the translation: "better the pleasure of the moment than the departing of life," which certainly fits in with some teaching of Qohelet (9:4) but not all (7:1-6). The biggest problem with their approach, however (and one of the reasons why it is not accepted here), is that it requires a different translation of *nepeš, desire,* than it did just two verses before (*desire,* not "life"), and thus Whybray must make the improbable suggestion that "there is no obvious connection between this verse and v. 7."[142]

The first phrase is difficult for another reason. Little doubt attends its

---

139. *the living* means the whole of humanity. In this case, it refers to all other human beings before whom the poor act.
140. Whitley, *Koheleth,* pp. 79-80.
141. Whybray, *Ecclesiastes,* NCB, pp. 108-9.
142. Whybray, *Ecclesiastes,* NCB, p. 109.

translation, though some want to import a later meaning of the word *mar'ēh*, *sight*, rendering it "pleasure."[143] The problem is in Qohelet's commending something as sensual rather than appealing to spiritual realities. However, it is only pietistic commentators who have substantial difficulty with the verse, and I have already characterized Qohelet as a doubting wise man. Nevertheless, in the pietistic tradition we should note the Targum's rendition:

> It is better for a man to rejoice about the world to come, and to do righteousness, and to see a good reward for his labors in the day of the great judgement, than to go into that world with an afflicted soul.

In the same line, Gregory Thaumaturgos basically ignores the "better-than" formula and treats the phrase as denoting something sinful.[144]

The general idea of the proverb is that what is present in hand is much better than what one only desires and does not have. Many commentators have quoted the contemporary proverb: "A bird in hand is better than two in the bush" as analogous, as well as Luther's reference to the Aesop fable that describes a dog snatching at the meat in the mirror and thus losing the morsel in its mouth. This sentiment, of course, fits in with Qohelet's pervasive emphasis on the here and now and denigration of the future.

The concluding *hebel* phrase has occurred many other places (see 1:2 for the fullest comment), and this is the final occurrence of the full form. Once again, the antecedent to *this* is ambiguous. Some believe it refers only to the second half of the proverb, others to the whole. It could even conceivably characterize the whole section. Desire cannot be fulfilled, and certainly the desire or even the attainment of wealth cannot provide satisfaction — it is all *meaningless*.

SUMMARY OF 4:17 (ENGLISH 5:1)–6:9

The section began with Qohelet's advice as to how one should relate to the deity. In a word, he suggests caution. God is not a being whom one should bother or cross. Do not be quick to make a vow, for instance, but if you make one, be sure that you fulfill your obligation.

Next, Qohelet again describes the meaninglessness of wealth. Even if one should attain wealth, its enjoyment is rare. Seldom does it produce contentment. Only in those few cases where God gives not only wealth but also the ability to enjoy it is the person buffered from the harsh pain of real life. In actuality, wealth too is meaningless.

143. See Fredericks, *Qoheleth's Language*, p. 186, for counterarguments.
144. Jarick, *Gregory Thaumaturgos' Paraphrase*, pp. 147-48.

D. QOHELET'S WISE ADVICE (6:10–12:7)

1. The Future — Determined and Unknown (6:10-12)

This short section marks the middle of the book according to Masoretic marginal notation. It also marks a transition in Qohelet's focus. There is overlap between the two halves of the book, but Qohelet here leaves his explicit search for meaning and in the second half of the book focuses on advice and commentary about the future. This short section anticipates the type of advice to come by telling us that it is meaningless and ultimately unhelpful.

A clear connection exists between vv. 10 and 11. The former picks up a thought that was presented before, basically that "there is nothing new under the sun," with the implication that human beings are limited. Thus, humans should not presume to speak against God. Verse 11 follows up the last thought with a saying about the limitations of human language in general. The verse probably has a specific reference to the words of advice to follow in ch. 7 and beyond.[1] The final verse of the section (v. 12) then bemoans the human condition.

10 *Whatever happens[2] has already been named. Also it is known that they are human, so no one may argue with one stronger than they are.*

11 *For there are many words that increase meaninglessness. What advantage is there for people?*

12 *For who knows what is good for people during the few days of their meaningless lives? He makes them like[3] a shadow,[4] so who can tell them what will happen after them under the sun?*

10 The first part of the verse reinforces Qohelet's belief that nothing new ever takes place (see 1:9 and 3:15). Here, though, Qohelet presents a new

---

1. M. Strange, "The Question of Moderation in Ecclesiastes 7:15-18" (D.Sac.Th. dissertation, Catholic University of America, 1969), p. 110.

2. The verb is a qal perfect, which denotes completeness, and thus is usually translated in the past tense in English. The context, though, makes such a translation awkward, so I, along with the versions, most modern commentators, and translations (see Isaksson, *Studies in the Language of Qoheleth*, pp. 85-88, for extended discussion) place the verb in the present.

3. The Septuagint mistakenly read a *beth* here instead of a *kaph, en skia* ("in a shadow").

4. Literally, "like the shadow," but the book of Ecclesiastes uses and omits the definite article in places where it is awkward in English translation (see "Language" in the introduction for comments and bibliography on this phenomenon).

twist by saying that everything has been previously *named,* literally "its name has been called." Turning back to Genesis 1, we see that God calls creation into being by the power of his word, and he also names his creations. Furthermore, it has long been held that Adam's task of naming the animals (Gen. 2:19-20) involved much more than simply giving them a name tag. In the OT, naming captures the essential nature of a person or thing. Thus, to name is to have knowledge and control of something or someone. Qohelet's comment then means that everything that takes place has previously been known.

The next clause is difficult, and its precise meaning has been debated. Disagreement even arises over the Masoretes' decision to associate the word *human,* that is, *'ādām,* with this clause rather than the following one. I will follow the Masoretes because the alternatives are not persuasive. My translation is fairly literal, and in context appears to note human limitation. People are known to be human, that is, finite and relatively weak. That this obscure sentence refers to human limitation seems to be the case in the light of the second part of the sentence, which speaks indirectly of God as *someone stronger than they are.* First, we need to deal with the textual/philological problem of the word *šehtaqqîp.* The root *tqp* is obvious (see note to 4:12) with the meaning "to be strong" or "to prevail." The Qere omits the *h* and makes it clear that this is an adjective, not a verb. Though it is an allusion, it is nonetheless obvious[5] that this is a reference to God (see the Targum, which makes this explicit). The first part of the verse left unstated who the "namer" and "knower" is. Now we find out that it is God, whose knowledge demonstrates his superiority over humans, and thus the uselessness of argument with him when he gives them a fate that they do not like.

11   In the previous verse, it was stated that it was fruitless to argue with someone, presumably God, who was stronger than mere humans, with all their limitations. The present verse draws the implication that a multiplication of words is simply a multiplication of meaninglessness. Thus, there is no benefit for human beings in saying a lot.

The translation *words (dᵉbārîm)* is to be preferred over the alternative possibility "things" (contra the Targum) due to the connection with v. 10, which speaks of arguments (the Vulgate makes this connection explicit). The translation "sayings," another possibility, is also appropriate to the context and would thus draw a close connection with the advice to follow in the coming chapters. Though the prose of the verse is especially cumbersome, it is still clear that an equation of sorts is drawn between a multiplication of words and a multiplication of *meaninglessness.* Since it is fruitless to argue with someone who is stronger, it is a waste of time to make the attempt. R. N. Whybray[6] notes similar teaching in

---

5. Contra Ogden, *Qoheleth,* p. 97.
6. Whybray, *Ecclesiastes,* NCB, p. 110.

Proverbs 10:8, 14, 19. In the context of the book of Ecclesiastes, however, the thought is more radical.

The verse closes with another rhetorical question, which asks about *advantage* (*yōtēr;* see 2:15, 6:8, and 7:16), related to *profit* (*yitrôn;* see 1:3). Once again, Qohelet makes it clear that there is none for anyone.

12 Again Qohelet resorts to rhetorical questions to express his jaundiced view of life. The two questions with which he draws the section to a close throw a curtain of skepticism over both the present and the future. In the first place, he denies that it is possible to know what is *good* in life. Unless he is simply contradicting himself, he must here reject the possibility of knowing the absolute good over against the relative good, which he expresses using the "nothing better than" formula (for the first time in 2:24). Qohelet's problem with life stems from both its being short (*few days,* thus implicitly raising his nemesis, death) and its *meaninglessness.* In the light of my earlier discussion of *meaninglessness* (*hebel;* see 1:2), it is of interest to note that to translate "transitory" or its equivalent in this verse would be awkwardly redundant.

Quite often, translations connect the clause that follows to the first sentence, but this treatment depends here on translating the common Hebrew verb *'śh* as "to spend time" or "to pass" (of time). This meaning, however, would occur only here in biblical Hebrew. The proponents of such a translation[7] point to its use in Mishnaic Hebrew and argue that it is another sign that the Hebrew of Ecclesiastes is late.[8] My own view is that the verb may be translated with its common meaning ("to do, make"), and the antecedent is the "one stronger than they are" in 6:10, that is, God. It makes perfectly good sense and does not require invoking an otherwise unattested meaning for the verb.[9]

Specifically, the verse says that he made people *like a shadow.* The expression occurs elsewhere (1 Chron. 29:15; Ps. 144:4; Job 8:9; 14:12) in contexts that also emphasize the frailty of human beings. The metaphor is one that highlights the brevity of human life, but perhaps even more pointedly its ephemerality. It conveys the fact that humans are so ephemeral, so insubstantial, that they are unable to know the future, what happens after they leave the scene. That Qohelet means the future on earth is clearly established by the key phrase *under the sun* (1:3); Qohelet never seriously entertains the thought of an afterlife.[10]

---

7. And they are many; see Crenshaw, *Ecclesiastes,* p. 132; Gordis, *Koheleth,* p. 264; Whybray, *Ecclesiastes,* NCB, p. 11; as well as the NIV and NRSV.

8. But see Fredericks, *Qoheleth's Language,* p. 248.

9. See Jerome in his commentary (*et faciet eos quasi umbram;* "he makes them like a shadow").

10. M. O. Wise ("A Calque from Aramaic in Qoheleth 6:12; 7:12; and 8:13," *JBL* 109 [1990]: 256-57) appears to misunderstand this verse as applying to the wicked in contrast to the righteous and also the force of the image, leading to his assertion of an Aramaic calque (a literal translation of the Aramaic phrase).

Thus, in this one verse Qohelet raises his two largest problems: death and the future's uncertainty. God has made human beings ephemeral, and that is why they cannot know the future, either theirs or anyone else's. The verse places the responsibility for this sad state of affairs squarely on God.

2. Miscellaneous Advice (7:1-14)

Most recent scholars take 7:1-14 as a separate unit.[11] Graham Ogden is an exception in that he believes that v. 13 begins a new section that extends to the end of the chapter.[12] As my exposition below will demonstrate, however, vv. 13-14 operate as a kind of conclusion to the whole unit.[13]

That 7:1 begins a new section may be observed most readily by the shift in literary form. The first twelve verses of the chapter are proverbs, many constructed according to the "better-than" pattern (see 4:2). While R. N. Whybray[14] is correct in saying that "attempts to see a logical progression of thought throughout the section are probably wasted," there is nonetheless a noticeable change of content in this new section as well. There is a link with the question posed at the end of 6:10-12, "who knows what is good for people during the few days of their meaningless life?" That question was rhetorical, indicating that Qohelet felt that there was nothing absolutely good. By the use of the "better-than proverb," however, Qohelet does indicate that some things are better than others. That is, he gives expression to what he believes are relative values. While some of these values are commonplace in wisdom literature (vv. 1a, 5a, 9), others intend to shock the reader familiar with wisdom orthodoxy (vv. 1b, 2, 3, 11; see the exposition below). Two themes dominate vv. 1-12 and unify the section: death (vv. 1b, 2, 4, and perhaps 8) and wisdom and folly (vv. 4, 5, 6, 7, 9, 10, 11, 12).

Though logical progression is lacking in this section, there is a unity provided by word repetition. Whybray has noted this and has provided the statistics.[15] He notes that *good/better (ṭôb)* occurs eleven times, *wise/wisdom (ḥākām, ḥōkmâ)* six times, *heart (lēb)* five times, *fool (kesîl)* four times, and *sorrow/anger (k's)* three times.

These and a number of other words and sound plays, which will be identified in the verse-by-verse exposition, provide coherence to the first

---

11. Note, for instance, Crenshaw, *Ecclesiastes,* pp. 132-39; and Whybray, *Ecclesiastes,* NCB, pp. 112-19.

12. Ogden, *Qoheleth,* pp. 99-100.

13. Note should be taken of Gordis's argument ("The Heptad as an Element of Biblical and Rabbinic Style," *JBL* 62 [1943]: 21) that the structure of the unit is based on the fact that there is "a collection of seven utterances, each beginning with *ṭobh*."

14. Whybray, *Ecclesiastes,* NCB, p. 112.

15. Whybray, *Ecclesiastes,* NCB, p. 112.

twelve verses. Verses 13 and 14 provide a kind of conclusion to the proverbs that precede them. It should also be noted, along with Roland Murphy,[16] that, as Qohelet ended the previous section with a question about the knowability of the future (6:12), so he concludes this section with reference to the same topic (7:14). Also, the words "good" *(ţôb)* and "day" *(yôm)* serve as an *inclusio* to the opening and the closing of the section.

Murphy points out that vv. 1-12 are a series of prohibitions, but that vv. 13-14 give the whole section the sense of being an instruction.

1 *A good reputation[17] is better than fine oil.*
  The day of death is better than the day of one's birth.[18]

2 *Better to go to a house of mourning than to go to a drinking house,[19]*
  because it is everyone's end, and the living should take it to heart.

3 *Anger is better than laughter,*
  for in a troubled face the heart is made well.

4 *The heart of the wise is in a house of mourning,*
  and the heart of fools in a house of pleasure.

5 *Better to hear the rebuke of the wise*
  than for a person to hear[20] the song[21] of fools.

6 *For like the sound of thorns under the pot,*
  so is the laughter of a fool.
  This also is meaningless.

7 *For extortion makes a fool of the wise;*
  a bribe distorts understanding.

16. Murphy, *Wisdom Literature*, p. 140.

17. The opening *ţôb* is part of the formal idiom of the "better-than" proverb. "Good reputation" translates the Hebrew word *šēm*. The word means more than "name" here because of the context; it indicates one's reputation.

18. The form is a niphal infinitive construct of *yld* with a third masculine singular suffix. The suffix is often overlooked in translations (see NIV, NRSV).

19. A literal translation. A freer rendering would be "house of feasting"; see NIV and NRSV.

20. The construction *mē'îš šōmēa'* is unusual, but not so unusual that an emendation is necessary. Delitzsch (*Proverbs, Ecclesiastes, Song of Solomon,* pp. 316-17) and Podechard (*L'Ecclésiaste,* p. 367) indicate "que la seconde action d'écouter n'est pas faite par le même sujet que la première" ("the second act of hearing is not made by the same person as the first").

21. Zimmermann ("The Aramaic Provenance of Qohelet," *JQR* 36 [1945-46]: 24) and Gordis (*Koheleth,* p. 269) are untypically in agreement that *šîr* means "praise" here and not *song* as it does virtually everywhere else. They believe that it provides a better parallel with *rebuke (ga'arat)* and is supported by an Aramaic cognate. The meaning *song,* however, fits into the overall contrast established in this unit between serious reflection on life and frivolity (see Whitley, *Koheleth,* p. 62).

8 *Better the end of a matter than its beginning.*
    Better patience than pride.

9 *Do not be quick[22] to anger in your spirit,*
    for anger resides[23] in the bosom[24] of fools.

10 *Do not say, "Why is it[25] that the former days were better than these?"*
    For it is not from[26] wisdom that you ask[27] this.

11 *Wisdom is good with an inheritance,*
    a benefit to those who see the sun.

12 *For to be in the shadow of wisdom is to be in the shadow of money.*
    And the advantage of knowledge is that wisdom preserves the life of
    its possessor.[28]

13 *Observe the work[29] of God, for[30] who is able to straighten what he*
    has bent?

14 *On a good day, enjoy yourself. On an bad day, observe: God has made*
    this as well as that, so that no[31] one should find what comes after him.

1   The list of proverbs begins with one that sounds as if it has been transposed directly from the book of Proverbs. Qohelet here extols the importance of *a good reputation*. Indeed, it is more important than fine oil, which was an expensive luxury item to ancient peoples. As a matter of fact, Proverbs 22:1 shows how similar Qohelet is here to traditional wisdom:

22. Concerning the supposed Aramaic origin of this meaning of the root *bhl,* see the references listed in n. 8 on 5:1 (English 2).

23. Ogden (*Qoheleth,* p. 107) suggests that *nûaḥ* may have been chosen as the verb because of its similarity in sound with *rûaḥ.*

24. Or perhaps "lap"; see NIV. It is the "part of the body where one clasps one's beloved, children, animals" (W. L. Holladay, *A Concise Hebrew and Aramaic Lexicon of the Old Testament* [Grand Rapids, MI: Eerdmans; Leiden: Brill, 1988], p. 103). Ogden (*Qoheleth,* p. 107) points out that "deep-seated and passionate feelings are said to lie in one's *ḥêq* (Job 19:27; Ps. 89:50)."

25. For the translation of *hāyâ* in the present tense, see Isaksson, *Studies in the Language of Qoheleth,* pp. 88-89.

26. The Septuagint translates *en sophia,* and thus likely read a *beth* instead of a *mem.*

27. Isaksson (*Studies in the Language of Qoheleth,* pp. 88-89) insists that the verb should be translated in the present tense.

28. Here, the plural noun is an honorific; cf. Waltke and O'Connor, *Biblical Hebrew Syntax,* §7.4.3c.

29. The Septuagint and the Vulgate read the plural, "works."

30. Another option is to read the particle as the asseverative *kî,* "indeed."

31. See Fredericks, *Qoheleth's Language,* pp. 234-35, for arguments against using *so that* (*'al-dibrat*) for a late dating of the book. The Septuagint misread this unusual compound as "concerning speech" (*peri lalias*).

181

> A good name is more desirable than great riches;
> to be esteemed is better than silver or gold.

The only real difference has to do with the comparison. Proverbs compares a good name or *reputation* to precious jewels, while Qohelet chooses another expensive and sought-after item, *fine oil*. The choice may be determined in part by the wordplay of the line, which strengthens its tight syntactic structure. The line is made up of four Hebrew words, the first and the last being the same word *(ṭôb),* though I have varied the translation for contextual reasons *(good/fine).* The two middle words sound alike, *reputation (šēm)* and *oil (šemen).* That oil was highly regarded during the biblical period may be seen in Psalm 45:8 (English 45:7), Psalm 133, Amos 6:6, and Matthew 6:17 and 26:7.

While the first proverb of the verse is traditional, the second is not. In the second, Qohelet states that death is better than birth and seems to express the idea that death is to be preferred over life.

Even if parallels to this proverb might be found in the broader wisdom literature, the appearance of it here, in light of Qohelet's general teaching about death (3:18-21 and 12:1-7), supports an interpretation that this proverb indicates Qohelet's world-weariness.

The connection between the two proverbs is debatable. Attempts have been made, for instance, to consider either the oil of the first proverb as that which is used during burial, or one's reputation as set at the time of one's death.[32] Thus, the righteous rejoice at the time of their death because their reputation is secure (see the Targum).[33]

Whatever the connection between the two proverbs, the best reading of the second is that it expresses Qohelet's relief that life is finally over. In the context of his speech as a whole, this relief arises not because of work completed and well done but because death means escape from life's oppression and meaninglessness.

2 The relative advantage of death over life continues in this verse. In the first half of the verse, Qohelet expresses the opinion that it is better to go to a funeral than a party (as opposed to v. 1, however, it is the death of another that is at issue). The funeral helps remind others that they too will die, and thus they may live their lives in the recognition of their own mortality.

According to Charles Wright,[34] the Talmud struggled to reconcile this verse with the so-called *carpe diem* passages like 2:24-26. Wright himself

---

32. For the connection between oil and reputation, see Crenshaw, *Ecclesiastes,* p. 133.

33. Levine, *The Aramaic Version of Qohelet,* pp. 37-38.

34. Wright, *The Book of Koheleth,* p. 381.

believed that the latter passages encouraged eating, drinking, and pleasure only in the context of the fear of God, while this verse and others like it discourage a frivolous type of pleasure. This harmonization is generated by an unnecessary type of theological approach to the book. Pleasure is never presented as the ultimate good, and furthermore, even the relative good (I would argue, resigned good) presented in 2:24-26 concludes with the statement, "This too is meaningless and chasing wind."

The last clause, *should take it to heart,* is an idiomatic rendering of "gives to his heart" *(yittēn 'el-libbô).* The idea is that the living should remember to live in the light of death, because no one can escape that final destiny.

3   The verse is composed of a brief proverb followed by a motive clause. Qohelet expresses the opinion that *anger is better than laughter,* presumably because it more reliably accords with reality.

Both parts of the verse are enigmatic. The proverb is once again of the "better-than" category. The difficulty is that Qohelet advocates *anger* over *laughter,* whereas Qohelet earlier disparages anger as part of the dark side of life (5:16 [English 5:17]) and advocates pleasure, which on the surface appears coincide with *laughter.* Graham Ogden counters the latter impression by asserting that Qohelet "tries to make a distinction between *śeḥōq* [laughter] that is empty, from *śemaḥ* [gladness] that Qohelet advocates throughout,"[35] but such a distinction does not work out in practice (even as closely as 7:4). Even recent commentators follow Luther in dealing with the first part of the enigma of the proverb. Luther wrote:

> How does it harmonize with what he had said earlier (5:18 [MT 5:17]), that one should not become angry but should find enjoyment in all his toil, whereas here he says that anger is better than laughter? My answer is: He is speaking about sorrow rather than about anger, not about the foolish sorrow which people make up for themselves; but as he speaks about the house of mourning, so he speaks about anger, so that anger is equivalent to sorrow or to trouble which brings sorrow.[36]

Luther's approach is followed in many modern translations (NIV, NRSV), though there is no philological justification for taking *kaʿas* as "sorrow" rather than "frustration" or *anger.*

Such harmonization is only needed if one understands Qohelet to be a perfectly orthodox and consistent wisdom teacher. The reasons for not adopting this approach have been given in the introduction. Qohelet is a wise man who is struggling with the traditions of his people and, thus, contradicts

35. Ogden, *Qoheleth,* p. 103.
36. Luther, "Notes on Ecclesiastes," p. 110.

himself at times. In light of the context, *ka'as,* with the meaning of *anger* or "frustration," is better than *laughter* because it agrees with reality. A frivolous attitude toward life is contradicted by the fact that there is oppression in the present and death in the future.

The motive clause of the verse points us in this direction. R. N. Why-bray has aptly pointed out that the clause is composed of four words that may be broken into two pairs of antonyms.[37] The word *troubled (rōa')* comes from the Hebrew term *ra',* which often has negative moral connotations, while *made well (yîṭab)* is a verb that is a derivative of the root *yṭb,* associated with *ṭôb,* which has positive moral connotations. Then, of course, *face* denotes the external appearance, while *heart* is the internal makeup of humans. The translation *troubled face* is supported by the use of the phrase in Genesis 40:7 and Nehemiah 2:2, and the idiom *the heart is made well* may be found in Ruth 3:7 and Judges 19:6, 9. The point of the passage is that *a troubled face* reflects reality and thus shows that one is not living in denial, or, in the words of John Jarick, "through the contemplation of serious matters such as death, which causes a person to wear a severe or sad facial expression, the mind is improved."[38]

4 Qohelet forcefully repeats the thought of v. 2, though the vocabulary is somewhat varied. In keeping with the previous verses, he states his belief that those who are wise contemplate their ultimate death, while fools are those who blithely live as if there is no end in sight.

In this verse, Qohelet also makes the transition from a predominant emphasis on death to the other major theme of the section, the comparison of wisdom and folly. Only a fool lives a life of pleasure, denying the reality of death. It is important to feel the tension between this verse and the *carpe diem* passages that appear throughout the book. In the latter, Qohelet asserts that there is "nothing better" than the pleasures of eating, drinking, and working, while here he seems to say that such an attitute is the mark of a fool. These tensions lead to the conclusion, argued in the introduction, that Qohelet is a confused wise man who doubts the traditions of his people.

The form of this proverb, as opposed to the similar one in v. 2, is an antithetical parallelism, common in the book of Proverbs.

5 Qohelet directs his reader once again to the somber side of life by the use of a "better-than" proverb. The contrast here guides one to the sphere of wisdom and away from folly. Within the formal structure of a "better-than" proverb Qohelet presents an antithesis between a wise rebuke and foolish songs. Since most people like songs and hate rebukes, this contrast attracts attention since it advocates rebukes. Indeed, Graham Ogden is likely correct

---

37. See Whybray, *Ecclesiastes,* NCB, p. 114.
38. Jarick, *Gregory Thaumaturgos' Paraphrase,* p. 158.

when he points out that a rebuke given by a singular wise person is better than a song sung by plural fools.[39] Once again, Qohelet's attitude is shaped by an attraction to that which, like a rebuke, takes us toward a harsh reality and an aversion to anything that desensitizes us by means of distraction or escape, no matter how pleasant.

Qohelet's teaching, as pointed out by Whybray,[40] reflects that of Proverbs at this point (13:1; 15:31; 17:10; 25:12; 26:9; 29:9), though the type of rebuke Qohelet has in mind may be different. A wise person's rebuke, for instance, may fit in with Qohelet's broader approach to life and be a wake-up call to depressing reality. In other words, Qohelet's own writing may be such a rebuke to those who are living sheltered lives.

6 Qohelet now provides reasons for his evaluation in the verse above (linked by *For* [*kî*]). He presents an image that evokes a vivid picture in our minds by likening a fool's *laughter* to the annoying crackle of thorns in the cooking fire under a *pot*. The point seems to be that a fool's laughter has no connection with reality and is irritating. In regard to this image, James Crenshaw points out, "Thistles provide quick flames, little heat, and a lot of unpleasant noise."[41]

I have not attempted to reproduce the wordplay between *thorns (sîrîm)* and *pot (sîr)*, though it shows Qohelet's concern with literary effect. Christian Ginsburg[42] lists attempts in both English and German to reflect the alliteration. They include August Knobel's "wie das Geräusch der Nettel unter dem Kettle," which Ginsburg translates "as the noise of nettles under the kettle."

The verse concludes with another occurrence of the *hebel* phrase, but there is ambiguity surrounding its referent. What precisely is *meaningless?* While some would restrict the reference to the fool's laughter,[43] it is much more likely that it refers back to v. 5 and the relative superiority of wisdom over folly. In other words, these two verses function similarly to 2:12-16. Both sections assert the relative advantage of wisdom but then throw doubt on its value. In the present case, this is done first by the *hebel* phrase, but also by the content of 7:7.

7 As translated, the verse uncovers the effect of a bribe on one's judgment — even a wise person can be made a fool when money becomes involved. One of the effects of the verse is to show that even wisdom is not foolproof.

39. Ogden, *Qoheleth*, p. 104.
40. Whybray, *Ecclesiastes*, NCB, pp. 114-15.
41. Crenshaw, *Ecclesiastes*, p. 135.
42. Ginsburg, *The Song of Songs and Coheleth*, p. 372.
43. Ogden, *Qoheleth*, p. 104.

There are, however, a number of questions surrounding our understanding of this verse. Though the *For* appears to connect this verse with the preceding, this has been disputed. At least since the time of Franz Delitzsch,[44] it has been felt that there is something radically wrong with the text here. Interpreters could not see the connection between this verse and what preceded, so they resorted to theories such as Delitzsch's that something has fallen out of the text. He argued that a statement similar to Proverbs 16:8 ("Better a little with righteousness than much gain with injustice") was lost at this point.[45] Some modern interpreters have been encouraged because a Qumran fragment has recently attested to a blank space of about fifteen to twenty letters between vv. 6 and 7.[46] However, the versions do not support the supposed "lost" text, and the space on the Qumran manuscript may have been an erasure (as Michael Fox argues). Thus, it is better to work with the text as it stands.

The connective *For* may, thus, be taken as the motive clause of 7:6c, "This too is meaningless," which I have taken as referring to the entirety of 7:5. The wise are not above suspicion. There are factors as to why their advice and/or rebuke may not be reliable, and one is explained in this verse: the wise person's judgment may be affected by *extortion (ʿōšeq)*, that is, blackmail. The term is the same as that rendered "oppression" in 4:1-3, but in this context the more specific rendering is appropriate and attested elsewhere (Lev. 5:23 [English 6:4]). As we will see, this provides a perfectly acceptable parallel to *bribe (mattānâ)*, which we find in the second colon.

The verb in the first colon *(yᵉhôlēl)* provides some measure of difficulty in that there are three different roots listed for *hll* in the dictionaries. However, the context makes it fairly clear that the root in the polel, with the meaning *to make a fool,* is the right choice.

The second colon is parallel with the first and is further linked by an ellipsis of *ḥākām,* supposing the reading *understanding* (of the wise). Much discussion has surrounded the translation of *bribe (mattānâ).* Charles Whitley, on the basis of certain syntactical clues (such as the lack of gender concord between *mattānâ* and the verb) and also with some support of the versions, argues that *mattānâ* is not the subject but rather the object of the sentence. Furthermore, he takes the word not as the common term "gift" in the more specific sense of *bribe,* but rather as "strong," based on a Mishnaic Hebrew word. Thus, Whitley translates "for oppression stupefies the wise man, and destoys his strong heart."[47] Daniel Fredericks, however, properly disputes

---

44. Delitzsch, *Proverbs, Ecclesiastes, Song of Solomon,* p. 317.

45. See Whybray, *Ecclesiastes,* NCB, p. 115.

46. Muilenburg, "A Qohelet Scroll from Qumran," pp. 26-27; Fox, *Qohelet and His Contradictions,* p. 229.

47. Whitley, *Koheleth,* pp. 62-63.

this.[48] Lack of gender concord between subject and verb is not rare in biblical Hebrew, and the meaning *bribe* is well known for this root (Prov. 15:27) and correct for this context. Furthermore, John Jarick points out a more likely scenario for the difficulty in the versions, particularly that the Septuagint translator confused this root with *mtnym* "loins."[49]

The most common meaning of *'ābad* in the piel is "to destroy" or "to perish." With "heart" or, more dynamically, *understanding* as the object, a translation like "clouds," "dissipates," or *distorts* is more to the point.

The verse, thus, throws doubt on wisdom. In the words of James Crenshaw,[50] "Wisdom does not always succeed; it can be nullifed by brute strength or subterfuge." Specifically, wisdom is weakened by *extortion,* on the one hand, and *bribery,* on the other. Extortion requires payment from someone in return for silence, and bribery is the receipt of money from someone in return for some desired action. The former makes the wise person a fool by surrendering control of life to another; the latter clouds one's judgment by introducing bias.

8 Qohelet once again resorts to "better-than" proverbs. He promotes the *end* over the *beginning* of a matter in the first colon. In the second colon, he prefers *patience* over *pride.*

At first glance, this verse has no obvious connection with the broader context. In addition, it is not immediately obvious how the first colon of the verse is related to the second. Closer analysis, however, recognizes a link with the overall theme of death.

In 7:1b, for instance, Qohelet preferred the day of death (the end of life) over the day of birth (its beginning). While v. 8a has a much broader application, it is surely connected with the idea that the *matter* here is life.[51]

The second proverb of the verse gives the relative value of *patience* over *pride.* Literally, the terms are translated "length of spirit" and "height of spirit," respectively, and these spatial terms are used metaphorically here. Bringing this out more explicitly, we might translate, "Better long patience than soaring pride." The expression for *patience (’erek rûaḥ)* is a hapax, but its meaning cannot be disputed. It is synonymous with another expression for

---

48. Fredericks, *Qoheleth's Language,* pp. 187-88.

49. Jarick, *Gregory Thaumaturgos' Paraphrase,* p. 163.

50. Crenshaw, *Ecclesiastes,* pp. 135-36.

51. The word *matter* has been translated in other ways. The Hebrew word *dābār* also is commonly translated "word," and indeed the versions have gone this route (Vulgate [*orationis*] and the Septuagint [*logon*]), as well as a few commentators. Ginsburg (*The Song of Songs and Coheleth,* p. 373) goes so far as to translate specifically "the end of reproof," apparently harking back to 7:5. Most modern translations (see NRSV, NIV, REB, NJB, as opposed to the NAB) follow the context and translate "thing" or "matter." (See similar discussion in connection with 1:8.)

patience, namely *'erek-'appayim* ("long of anger"), found in Proverbs 14:29 and elsewhere. *rûaḥ* substitutes for *'appayim* here because of the parallel with *gᵉbah-rûaḥ*. Also, *rûaḥ* connotes "anger" (Isa. 25:14; Prov. 16:32) and "impatience" (Mic. 2:7; Prov. 14:29).

R. N. Whybray[52] has suggested a plausible connection between the two parts of the verse: "self-control is needed to carry through any project." I would go on to add that no one can know the outcome of anything until it is completed, so *patience,* not *pride,* is called for, the latter presuming to control the future or outcome. Crenshaw[53] quotes the proverb in 2 Kings 20:11: "Let not the person putting on armor brag like the one taking it off."

9 The previous verse called for patience rather than pride, and this verse supports that thought with a prohibition against *anger,* which arises as a result of impatience. This prohibition is accompanied by a motive clause: Do not be angry, for if you are, then you show yourself to be a fool.

An immediate question of context arises when this verse is read in conjunction with 7:3. How can Qohelet prefer *anger* there but warn his listener away from it here? A common recourse is to assert that the word has two different senses. Note, for instance, Whybray's comment that *"ka'as . . .* is used here in a different sense from that which it has in v. 3."[54] Michael Fox puts a twist on this approach when he says that *ka'as* means *anger* in both verses, but in the former it "is applied to the anger of reproof," while in v. 9 it refers "to the anger one feels at unfortunate events that befall him. Neither verse is a statement about anger in all circumstances."[55]

Both of these are admirable attempts to harmonize Qohelet's thought, but the text does not give any indication of these nuances of meaning. I have already commented in connection with v. 3 that Qohelet contradicts himself concerning *anger,* and so we have further evidence of his confusion here (see "Theological Message" in the introduction).

The phrase *in your spirit (bᵉrûaḥᵃkā)* is awkward in English, and the NRSV (as opposed to the NIV) simply omits it as redundant. It also may indicate a kind of deep-seated and perhaps concealed or unexpressed anger, especially in the light of the parallel *in the bosom of.* In other words, it is referring to seemingly uncontrollable anger that has overcome a person.

The motive clause associates anger with fools and thus warns the wise from displaying it. The basic reasoning is that, since anger is a characteristic of fools, if you are angry, then it labels you as a fool.

10 Qohelet departs from proverbial, even poetical, language, to quote

---

52. Whybray, *Ecclesiastes,* NCB, p. 116.
53. Crenshaw, *Ecclesiastes,* p. 136.
54. Whybray, *Eccesiastes,* NCB, pp. 116-17.
55. Fox, *Qohelet and His Contradictions,* p. 230.

a saying as common in his day as it is in our own. The question he cites asks why the past was better than the present. Those who hold this nostalgic view of life believe that their day is worse than any other. He warns his listener against this attitude because its source is not wisdom; rather, it marks the questioner as a fool. For one thing, to believe that the present is worse than the past shows a complete ignorance of history.

Such a question could only be asked by "glorifiers of times past,"[56] and therefore someone who was denying reality. After all, Qohelet has already firmly established that the past, present, and future are all the same (1:9; 2:16; 3:15). There is "nothing new under the sun," and everything is meaningless.

Qohelet had stated in v. 8 that the end is better than the beginning. Thus, it is not surprising that he would admonish those who thought that the early part of life or the early part of history was better than the latter part. Whybray[57] and Robert Gordis[58] were probably correct to say that this longing for the past and dissatisfaction with the present were symptoms of the impatience and pride also spoken of in v. 8.

11 This verse and the next discuss the relative advantage of wisdom over riches. Verse 11, on the surface, appears straightforward with its simple vocabulary and clear syntax. It asserts the belief that wisdom is a good thing, especially when accompanied by money *(with an inheritance)*. This meaning, however, remains somewhat enigmatic. The issue focuses on the meaning of the preposition ʿim (here translated *with*). Two schools of thought dominate the discussion. One approach cites the use of ʿim in the sense of a comparison, yielding a translation along the lines of "wisdom is as good as an inheritance." This is a well-attested meaning of the preposition, and the word has been so used in Ecclesiastes 2:16. Furthermore, the comparison of *wisdom* and riches appears to be echoed in v. 12. Advocates of this approach include Whybray,[59] Graham Ogden,[60] and Michael Fox.[61]

The versions, however, make me wary of this interpretation. Overall, the most common function of the preposition ʿim is to denote accompaniment, and all the major versions[62] understand the ʿim in the present verse in this

---

56. Luther, "Notes on Ecclesiastes," p. 117, quoting Horace.

57. Whybray, *Ecclesiastes,* NCB, p. 117.

58. Gordis, *Koheleth,* p. 272.

59. Whybray, *Ecclesiastes,* NCB, p. 117.

60. Ogden, *Qoheleth,* p. 108.

61. Fox, *Qohelet and His Contradictions,* p. 231.

62. The Peshitta is an exception. It read the preposition as a form of *min* and apparently understood it as a "better-than" form. The Peshitta is not to be given serious consideration, however, since it continues to confuse the verse, translating "Wisdom is better than weapons of war."

way (Septuagint [*meta*], Vulgate [*cum*], and Targum ['*im*]). A number of modern and ancient commentators have so understood the verse, as, for instance, Rashbam:

> A man's wisdom is more respected, and is more advantageous, when it goes together with the patrimony and property bequeathed to him by his father, which will not abide unless he has wisdom to manage his riches; but still better than riches is wisdom for those who lead a public life, for their wisdom assists and maintains them.[63]

If the preposition is taken in this sense, it attributes to Qohelet a rather jaundiced view of wisdom.[64] However, does the adoption of the alternative change the picture dramatically? To say that wisdom is as good as money is a far cry from the exaltation of wisdom in Proverbs and even in Job 28, where jewels and precious metals do not compare with the glories of wisdom.

Thus, it is the combination of *wisdom* with an *inheritance* that is a *benefit* to *those who see the sun.* The latter phrase denotes the living, over against the dead and the stillborn (6:5).

12 This enigmatic verse (both halves have their difficulties) gives the motive for the statement of v. 11. A literal rendition of v. 12a *(kî bᵉṣēl haḥokmâ bᵉṣēl hakkāsep)* is "For in the shadow of wisdom — in the shadow of money." Perhaps this saying was a well-known proverb, but to modern readers it is cryptic. The syntax is certainly drawing an equivalence here, and this equivalence is made explicit by some of the early versions, which smooth out the verse by substituting a preposition of equivalence (= to the Hebrew *kaph;* see Symmachus, the Vulgate, and the Syriac, also the Septuagint in the second preposition) for the preposition *beth.* Perhaps this points to the original text, but it is much more likely an attempt to rid the text of some, but certainly not all, of its difficulty.

As mentioned, it is likely that equivalence is expressed between *wisdom* and *money* in one particular area, their function as a *shadow.* From the use of *shadow* or "shade" imagery elsewhere (Gen. 19:8; Num. 14:9; Jer. 48:45), it is clear that what is meant is protection, presumably from the hard realities of life.[65] Once again, even if Qohelet is throwing this saying in the

---

63. Quoted by Ginsburg, *The Song of Songs and Coheleth,* p. 375. Note that N. D. Osborn ("A Guide for Balanced Living: An Exegetical Study of Ecclesiastes 7:1-14," *Bible Translator* 21 [1970]: 185-96) believes that '*im* was purposely substituted for *min* here in order to "shock" readers.

64. For a particularly tortuous understanding of the verse with the intention of reading Qohelet as a positive, orthodox wise man, see Ogden, *Qoheleth,* pp. 108-9.

65. This is also supported by the parallel in the following sentence, which states that wisdom *preserves the life of its possessor.*

face of those who think that money is the only hope in life, it is still out of keeping with traditional wisdom literature to say that wisdom is on the same level of importance as money.

It is true that the second part of the verse differentiates the two and gives wisdom a more favorable position, but not in a particularly striking way. The syntactical problem of this half of the verse has to do with the relationship between *knowledge* and *wisdom*. Some feel that the whole expression, *the advantage of knowledge (yitrôn daʿat)*, is awkward, and they suggest transposing it to v. 11.[66] Much less radical is the assumption that *knowledge* and *wisdom* are synonyms here. That is the position I have adopted. Thus, in one very important sense *wisdom* does supersede money. In making this point, however, Qohelet does not nullify the importance of money.

13   The last two verses of this unit depart from the proverbial form of the preceding and comprise an instruction on God's work.[67] Qohelet urges his listener to be attentive to the work of God in the world. In conjunction with the next verse it is clear that his advice is not for the purpose of changing what God has done, but to go along with what God has done. After all, no one can influence his actions.

Qohelet begins by calling upon his listener to *observe* what God is doing in the world. In three other places where Qohelet considers God's *work*, he despairs knowing it. Here, he concludes, presumably on the part he can know, that no one can do anything to change what God has done. In the words of John Jarick, Qohelet here asserts "the powerlessness of human beings over against God."[68] He does this by rephrasing the proverb of 1:15a (for a discussion of the key terms, see the commentary on that verse).

Most commentators and translators take note of the pronominal suffix on the verb and attribute it to God — that is, God is the one who has made things *bent*. This interpretation is the most likely since *God* is the closest antecedent to the suffix.

Note should be taken of the Targumic paraphrase that takes *what is bent* as a reference to "the blind, the hunchback, and the lame." It goes on to say that it is only God who is able to make these "bent" individuals straight again. This interpretation likely arose because of an uneasiness over Qohelet's saying, which implies that God is the origin of imperfection.

The term *find* has already appeared in 3:11 but becomes increasingly important in this chapter (see vv. 24, 26, 27, 28 [3 times], 29). These instances will be recalled again in the epilogue (see the discussion on 12:10).

---

66. Whitley, *Koheleth,* pp. 64-65.
67. Murphy, *Wisdom Literature,* p. 140.
68. Jarick, *Gregory Thaumaturgos' Paraphrase,* p. 169.

14 The instruction of this verse follows up the previous one. Qohelet advises his listeners to *enjoy* themselves *on a good day,* while making the best of a *bad day.* God made both, and no one can change what God has done.

The demonstratives, *this* and *that* (both *zeh*), refer to the two types of day. God not only makes the good days, but also the bad. Therefore, Qohelet's advice is to accept life as it comes.

The significance of God's action is that no one can predict what is going to happen in the future. There is disagreement as to whether *what comes after him ('aḥᵃrāyw mᵉ'ûmâ)* refers to the future earthly life or the afterlife. I prefer the former interpretation because Qohelet is nowhere explicit about an afterlife. In either case, however, the situation is bleak. One does not know what to expect in the future. Apparently, not even wisdom can rectify this frustrating fact of life. And what is worse, God has designed it this way. God purposely set up good and bad days in order to hide the future even from the wise.

3. The Limitations of Human Wisdom and Righteousness (7:15-22)

In this section Qohelet imparts some of his most radical-sounding advice. He cautions against exceeding wickedness and folly (v. 17), but also against excessive righteousness and wisdom (v. 16). His advice is based on what he observes as the limits of wisdom and righteousness. These limits have two rationales. First, since wisdom and righteousness do not guarantee prosperity and long life, why bother (v. 15)? Second, while humans are capable of a restricted kind of wisdom and righteousness, perfection is beyond their reach, so why bother (vv. 20-22)?

15 *Both I have observed in my meaningless life: There is a righteous person perishing in his righteousness, and there is a wicked person living long[69] in his evil.*

16 *Do not be too righteous and do not be overly wise. Why ruin yourself?*

17 *Do not be too wicked and do not be a fool. Why die when[70] it is not your time?[71]*

---

69. Podechard (*L'Ecclésiaste,* p. 374) points out that normally *ma'ᵃrik* (the hiphil participle of *'ārak*) is followed by *yammîm,* but he notes analogies to our verse in Prov. 28:2.

70. The temporal use of the preposition *bᵉ;* cf. Williams, *Hebrew Syntax,* §241.

71. Whitley (*Koheleth,* p. 66) cites analogous phrases in Job 22:16, Ahiqar 102, and the Phoenician Eshmunazar inscription.

18 *It is good that you hold on to this and also do not release[72] your hand[73] from that. The one who fears God will follow both of them.*

19 *Wisdom makes the wise person stronger[74] than ten leading citizens[75] who are[76] in a city.*

20 *Surely no one is righteous on the earth, who does good and does not sin.*

21 *Moreover, do not pay attention[77] to all the words that they speak lest[78] you hear your servant cursing you.*

22 *For, furthermore, your heart knows[79] that you also have cursed others many times.*

15 The first verse in the unit sets forth Qohelet's observations concerning the principle of retribution upon which he will base the instructions of the next few verses. To begin with, he states his observations matter-of-factly. Quite simply, he sees good people suffering and evil people thriving.

He starts the new unit with the verb that he characteristically uses to introduce an empirical observation (*rāʾîtî*, from *rāʾâ;* see 1:14). What follows shows that his experience is in tension with at least one strand of thinking in the ancient world, a strict idea that one's actions have a determined and reasonable result.

72. The Septuagint has introduced an interesting scribal error. According to Jarick (*Gregory Thaumaturgos' Paraphrase,* p. 177), "the original LXX equivalent to *nwḥ* hiphil was *aniēmi,* 'to let go, slacken,' but at some point, probably due to a dittographical error arising from the preceding *mē, anēs* becomes *mianēs.*" This verb is a form of the verb *miainō,* "to defile." Thus, pious interpreters like Gregory Thaumaturgos took this as a "warning against 'touching undefiled things with a defiled hand.'"

73. According to *BHS* a number of Hebrew manuscripts read the plural "hands."

74. The Septuagint, a Qumran manuscript, and the Syro-Hexapla evidence a different root for this verb. Instead of a form of *ʿzz* "to be strong," they have a form of the root *ʿzr* "to help." Perhaps the ancient change came about due to the fact that *ʿzz* is rarely used in a transitive sense. However, as many commentators have pointed out, such a transitive use is not unattested (see discussion in Whitley, *Koheleth,* p. 67).

75. Or possibly "officials" (for *šalliṭîm*). See Fredericks, *Qoheleth's Language,* pp. 239-40, for arguments counter to the idea that the root *(šlṭ)* is late.

76. For the translation of *hāyû* in the present, see Isaksson, *Studies in the Language of Qoheleth,* p. 50. He attributes this to its proverbial form (p. 90).

77. *ʾal-tittēn libbekā* is literally "don't give your heart to."

78. For *lest* (*ʾašer lōʾ*), see Whitley, *Koheleth,* p. 68.

79. The Septuagint translators mistakenly read a *resh* for a *dalet* in the verb (thus *yrʿ* [from *rʿʿ*] rather than *yādaʿ*). Furthermore, they were unable to decide which of two ways they were to render it, so they included both, that is, "he will do you harm" (*ponēreusetai se*) and "he will mistreat your heart" (*kakōsei kardian sou*). See the discussion in Jarick, *Gregory Thaumaturgos' Paraphrase,* p. 182. Also note that *pĕʿāmîm (many times)* is rendered twice: *pleistakis* and *kathodous pollas.*

His observation has two sides. There is some ambiguity over what *kōl* refers to, that is, whether it is "retrospective or anticipatory, or both."[80] Nonetheless, since *observed* often begins a unit, it is most likely that it is, primarily at least, anticipatory, and, since the unit deals with the polar opposite of the results of a *righteous* and a *wicked* lifestyle, it is proper to translate the term *Both*. Note as well the initial syntactic position of *Both*, which in this case clearly denotes emphasis.

Another one of Qohelet's favorite words, *meaningless (hebel)*, is also used here, but in an uncharacteristic way. Normally it is used in the phrase "everything is meaningless," but here it modifies the expression "days." Perhaps because it is a time reference, some interpreters who normally translate the word "meaningless" or its equivalent revert to a temporal translation, "brief."[81] This deviation from the normal translation is unwarranted (see the philological discussion at 1:2).

Both refers to the two situations that follow. They are introduced by the existential particle *there is (yēš)*. Qohelet frequently utilizes this particle in order to introduce case studies, the so-called exemplifying function of the particle (see 2:12) that Bo Isaksson[82] attributes to Qohelet's personal style. This particle is ignored by some English translations like the NIV, which then mistakenly format the verse as poetry.

The two case studies present us with a paradox,[83] and Qohelet surely wanted his listener/reader to be shocked by what he said. He saw the *righteous perishing* and the *wicked living long*. This is the polar opposite of what some strands of biblical teaching indicate. For instance, certain legal portions of the Bible teach that observation of the law prolongs life (Exod. 20:12; Deut. 4:40), and the wisdom teachers instructed that righteousness led to life (Prov. 3:1-2), while the wicked suffered and died early (Ps. 1). Although Raymond Van Leeuwen[84] has now shown how the book of Proverbs as a whole does not teach a simple retribution theology, nonetheless, Qohelet's observation cuts across normative biblical expectations.

One of the issues surrounding this verse has to do with the exact force of the preposition *beth* in both parts of the second sentence. Marcian Strange[85] has described three possibilities: (1) the *beth concessivum* ("in spite of"), (2) the *beth instrumentalis* ("through"), and (3) the *beth comitatis* ("in"). While it is difficult to be dogmatic as to the exact force of the preposition

---

80. Crenshaw, *Ecclesiastes,* p. 140.
81. Crenshaw, *Ecclesiastes,* p. 140.
82. Isaksson, *Studies in the Language of Qoheleth,* pp. 46-47.
83. Murphy, *Wisdom Literature,* p. 141.
84. Van Leeuwen, "Wealth and Poverty," pp. 25-36.
85. Strange, "The Question of Moderation."

here, it is to be noted that in all three cases the paradox still stands. The righteous die young and the wicked live long, contrary to expectations.[86] Thus, Qohelet struggled with the same conflict faced by the psalmist in Psalm 73, but without reaching the same resolution. Instead, Qohelet's observation leads him to offer some shocking advice.

16 Qohelet here and in v. 17 advises his readers not to be overly righteous and not to be excessively wise. These verses are structurally related in that both begin with two negated jussives, followed by a question that begins with *why (lāmmâ)*. This syntactic similarity has implications for our understanding of the tone of both verses.

In this regard, there are two main options: (1) Qohelet warns against seeking righteousness and wisdom with too much fervor, or (2) he guards against false pretense in righteousness and wisdom. Interpreters who want to guard Qohelet's piety or orthodoxy have adopted this latter approach.[87] The most formidable defenses of the pretense view, however, are offered by Giorgio Castellino and R. N. Whybray.[88] The focus of the argument is on the force of the hithpael of *ḥkm*.[89] Indeed, there are instances in which the hithpael may indicate pretense (Whybray refers to Num. 16:13 [*śrr*] and 2 Sam. 13:5 [*ḥlh*]), but, as John Jarick[90] points out, this does not establish its use in Ecclesiastes. Indeed, if this were the function of the hithpael in 7:16, then it would be the only such use in the book of Ecclesiastes.[91]

These considerations raise and lower probabilities. Two considerations lead me decisively away from Whybray's viewpoint. The first is the lack of the hithpael in the first part of the verse. The first sentence does not use the hithpael of *ṣdq*, but instead the jussive of *hyh* followed by the noun *ṣāddîq*. The second definitive consideration is effectively presented by Jarick, who notes the verse's syntactical similarity with v. 17. In this verse, pretense is out of the question. Qohelet is writing not about those who pretend to be fools,

---

86. Jerome handles the difficulty by referring to the plight of the martyr. He is someone who dies young in his righteousness. However, Qohelet could not possibly be referring to the martyr since this observation is an ingredient of Qohelet's meaningless life. The same criticism may be made of the Targum's attempt to bring the afterlife into play here.

87. For instance, Gregory Thaumaturgos; see Jarick, *Gregory Thaumaturgos' Paraphrase*, pp. 173-75; and W. Kaiser, *Ecclesiastes*, pp. 85-87.

88. G. R. Castellino, "Qohelet and His Wisdom," *CBQ* 30 (1968): 15-28; R. N. Whybray, "Qohelet the Immoralist (Qoh 7:16-17)," in *Israelite Wisdom: Theological and Literary Essays in Honor of Samuel Terrien*, ed. J. G. Gammie, W. A. Brueggemann, W. L. Humphreys, and J. M. Ward (Missoula, MT: Scholars Press, 1978), pp. 191-204.

89. Note that the vocalization of this verb *(tithakkam)* is influenced by the guttural (Waltke and O'Connor, *Biblical Hebrew Syntax*, p. 426).

90. Jarick, *Gregory Thaumaturgos' Paraphrase*, pp. 339-40.

91. Strange, "The Question of Moderation," p. 80.

but those who are fools in reality. The similarity between the two verses leads us to the same conclusion in v. 16: Qohelet warns those who seek sincere righteousness and true wisdom.

This warning follows hard on the heels of the observation that the righteous receive no special favors. Thus, the question arises, Why exert oneself to attain it?

The warning to avoid extremes of righteousness and wisdom is followed by a question that provides further incentive. The verb here translated *ruin yourself (tiššōmēm)* is difficult to pin down. It may refer to a psychological disturbance (see Septuagint, Vulgate, and Syriac) or to physical injury or death. I have chosen the translation *ruin* rather than "frustrate" or "destroy" in order to reflect this ambiguity. It should also be pointed out that the question does not indicate how *ruin* will come about. Will God cause it, or will a natural process? That is, will God strike down those who attempt to achieve righteousness or will the person simply "burn out"?

17 This verse has a similar syntactical structure to the preceding one, thus highlighting the two poles of the contrast. According to Qohelet, one should avoid not only excessive righteousness and wisdom, but also excessive wickedness and folly.

Qohelet thus evokes four character traits in these two verses: righteousness, wisdom, wickedness, and folly. Of the four only the last is unqualified. That is, he pleads against overweening righteousness, wisdom, and wickedness, but folly is unqualified. This observation leads to two conclusions. First, at least here (Qohelet is not always consistent), he believes that folly is something to be totally avoided. Second he warns against excessive wickedness, which leaves open the possibility of a "reasonable" level of wickedness. This attitude seems far from God's admonition in Leviticus 19:2, "Be holy because I, the LORD your God, am holy."

Interestingly, this verse envisions the possibility of a premature end to the excessively wicked, just as the previous verse warns of a horrible fate for the overweening righteous. Once again the cause of the misfortune is not specified. The point Qohelet is making is not that the wicked always live longer and have fewer problems, but that there is no principle of retribution that assures the righteous that they will be better off than the wicked.

18 After the observation and two lines of advice, Qohelet now provides an evaluation. In the previous verses, he has observed that good people suffer and bad people thrive. He then advised a kind of middle-of-the-road approach to life, not overzealous about wisdom or foolishness, righteousness or wickedness. Here, he observes that the best course is to keep one foot in each world. He further concludes that one who *fears God* will do just that, choose the middle way between extremes.

196

Qohelet often ends sections with such evaluative statements that utilize the word "good" *(ṭôb),* but it is not correct to cite this verse as an example of a *ṭôb*-proverb,[92] since this form requires a comparative *min* that is not present here.

The verse is difficult because the pronouns are indefinite. It is most likely, however, that *this* and *that (zeh . . . zeh)* refer to the two lines of advice given in vv. 16 and 17. That is, Qohelet advocates the avoidance of excessive righteousness and wisdom, as well as folly and excessive wickedness.

The second sentence of the verse also has a troublesome pronoun, the third plural suffix on *both* (see v. 15 for *kōl* as *both*). Once again, it is most likely that the reference to *them* is to the two strands of advice given in the preceding verses. The one who *fears God* will take Qohelet's advice. We should be careful not to interpret this last phrase positively (see "Theological Message" in the introduction). In this I agree with John Jarick, "In Kohelethine usage, this expression . . . should probably be taken as indicating the person who is mindful of human powerlessness over against God (cf. 3:14), and hence in this context the person who will not try to tempt fate by acting in either of the two extremes Koheleth had just mentioned."[93]

The NIV represents a divergent tradition of approach to this verse in its translation of the last sentence as "The man who fears God will avoid all 'extremes.' " In this rendition, the NIV follows older translations such as those of Luther and Coverdale (which translate "escape" rather than *follow).*[94] The NIV further makes explicit what it believes the pronoun refers to when it adds "extremes." Note that the NIV footnote, which indicates that a significant part of the translation committee dissented from the view represented in the body of the text, has a nearly identical translation to mine.

19 The mention of *wisdom* connects this verse with the preceding verses (see v. 16), but the content seems irrelevant to the context. Qohelet here appears to give wisdom great value; he believes that a wise person is more capable and effective than a city's *ten leading citizens.*

Michael Fox proposes that the verse has been moved from its original place following v. 12.[95] While Emmanuel Podechard argues that it was an accidental move,[96] Fox says it was intentional in order to counteract some of the damaging comments Qohelet makes about wisdom. Since there is no textual evidence to support an emendation, I accept the MT.

---

92. Ogden, *Qoheleth,* p. 115.
93. Jarick, *Gregory Thaumaturgos' Paraphrase,* p. 178.
94. See Ginsburg, *The Song of Songs and Coheleth,* p. 381.
95. Fox, *Qohelet and His Contradictions,* p. 232.
96. Podechard, *L'Ecclésiaste,* p. 379.

Indeed, vv. 19 and 20 do have a connection with the preceding verses, particularly v. 16. Verses 19 and 20 are two contrasting quotations[97] that serve to affirm and then to denigrate human possibility. Contrary to Fox, these verses are not too distant from v. 16 to serve this function. As a matter of fact, vv. 15-18 are a unit, and then vv. 19-20 are the very next words from Qohelet.

The point of the saying, which may be a proverb, is simply that wisdom is much more important than other human qualities and abilities. Normally, we think of the political authorities as the most important and significant people in a city. They are invested with power and make important decisions. But Qohelet is countering this claim by stating that a single wise person is stronger, that is, more important and effective, than ten such officials. In this, Qohelet is following the traditional wisdom teaching that wise advisers are significant for the defense of a city (Prov. 24:5-6: "A wise man has great power, and a man of knowledge increases strength; for waging war you need guidance, and for victory many advisers"). Qohelet will later tell a short story to support this view (9:13-16). It is, however, extremely unlikely that Qohelet has in mind a specific historical situation in 7:19;[98] it is more likely that the ten-to-one ratio is hyperbole.

20 As argued in the commentary to v. 19, this verse asserts the limits of human ability. Qohelet sounds like Paul here (Rom. 3:9-20), who is himself quoting a number of OT passages, especially from Psalms. Qohelet denies that anybody on the face of the earth is righteous and without sin.

The force of the conjunction *kî* that begins the verse is a problem, as is the connection between this verse and its context.[99] Some[100] take the conjunction as the causal "for" or "because." They argue that the verse supplies the reason why wisdom is so important, that is, because there is a dearth of righteous people. Since there are no righteous around, the wise must care for the city. This approach strikes me as wrongheaded because of the close association between wisdom and righteousness in other parts of the Bible (see Prov. 8:12-14).

Accordingly, it is much better to translate *kî* as an asseverative conjunction, *Surely.* The verse thus provides a counterbalance to the previous one. Wise people are of immense value, but no one, *not even the wise,* is righteous.

---

97. So Gordis, *Koheleth,* p. 278.

98. See the Targum, which cites Joseph as the wise man and his brothers as the ten officials.

99. The NIV takes the easy route by omitting the conjunction and then isolating the verse from its context.

100. See Ginsburg, *The Song of Songs and Coheleth,* p. 380; Plumptre, *Ecclesiastes; or, the Preacher,* p. 197.

In this way, Qohelet does what he so often does — puts forward a positive value and then relativizes it.[101]

Qohelet does not deny the presence of the righteous. There are righteous people, but these righteous people are not consistently good. They do sin, at least occasionally. This opinion may be found throughout the OT (1 Kings 8:46; Ps. 143:2; Prov. 20:9) and the NT (see especially Rom. 3:10-18, which may even contain an allusion to our verse).

We may even see here the motivation for v. 16. Since Qohelet believes that no one can be consistently righteous, why try for it to the point of frustration?

21-22 This verse and the next go together to provide a concrete illustration of the assertion of the previous verse, the universality of sin.[102] Everyone sins, and here is an example: everyone curses others. Qohelet thus bases his advice on what he knows is common experience. Masters should not listen to their servants too closely, because their servants are speaking poorly of them. After all, everyone, including the masters themselves, curses others. The word *cursing* (from the root *qll*) may have a less extreme sense here, perhaps "slander" or simply "grumble."[103] The Septuagint (though not Alexandrinus), Peshitta, and Targum transform the impersonal construction *that they speak* into "that the wicked speak."

Verse 22 provides the motive clause (note *For* [*kî*]) for v. 21. Qohelet warns his readers against eavesdropping on the conversation of servants, because the former will likely hear things they will not like. But if the masters are honest with themselves, they know that they too speak abusively toward others.

your heart knows (yāda' libbekā) is an idiom for what later would be called the "conscience." That is, the readers know deep inside that they behave this way.

4. Inaccessible Wisdom (7:23-24)

The relationship between this short unit and its context is difficult to determine. The ambiguous demonstrative, *All this (kol-zōh)*, which introduces the section, is of little help. It could refer to what precedes or what follows. I will treat the section as a separate unit, but it is likely that it looks both backward and forward: *All this* summarizes what preceded, but the verb *find (mṣ')* anticipates the unit to follow, which highlights the theme of seeking and following (see 7:25-29).

101. Perhaps this could be another example of what J. A. Loader speaks of in his article "Relativity in Near Eastern Wisdom," *OTSWA* 15-16 (1972-73): 49-58. He provides other examples from Eccles. 7 (vv. 5-7, 11-13).
102. So Lauha, *Kohelet,* p. 135; contra Ogden, *Qoheleth,* pp. 117-18.
103. Gordis, *Koheleth,* p. 279.

23 *All this I tested with wisdom. I said, "I will be wise!" But it was far from me.*

24 *Far away is that which is,*[104] *and deep, deep,*[105] *who can find it?*

23 My introduction observed the ambiguity of the demonstrative, *this (zōh),* making it impossible to be sure how vv. 23 and 24 relate to the context. *All this (kol-zōh)* could refer to what precedes in 7:1-22 (or perhaps even 7:19-22)[106] or what follows, or even could be a separate pericope.[107] As mentioned in the introduction to this unit, it is likely that it looks backward and forward.

In any case, Qohelet reminds the reader that his experiment, his search, is guided by *wisdom.* He is searching for wisdom reflectively and self-consciously, a point he has already made in 1:13 and 2:3.

However, once again Qohelet quickly points out the limits of wisdom, this time on a personal level. He first of all asserts his desire to be wise *(I will be wise).* The verbal form here *('eḥkāmâ)* is unusual for the book in that it is the only occurrence of the cohortative. It lends a sense of determination to the verb,[108] thus the exclamation point. In spite of the determination, however, Qohelet's goal was impossible to attain, a thought he will continue in the next verse.

Michael Fox has difficulty with the logic of the verse.[109] He protests that Qohelet nowhere denies his wisdom status; indeed he affirms it in the first part of this verse. But this presses Qohelet's consistency too far, forgetting that at times Qohelet's words are almost stream of consciousness. It is as if he states his wisdom program, catches himself, and then admits his failings.

24 The connection with the previous verse is obvious since v. 24 begins with the link word *Far away (rāḥôq).* Verse 24 expands upon the reason why Qohelet was incapable of truly achieving wisdom.

Simply stated, wisdom was beyond his human reach. *that which is (mah-šehāyâ)* refers to all things, "reality" according to Fox and Bezalel Porten's interpretation.[110] According to George Barton, though, it refers more

104. Isaksson (*Studies in the Language of Qoheleth,* pp. 90-91) points out that this is an occurrence of *hāyâ* in Ecclesiastes where the context requires that the verb must be translated by the English present tense. See similar syntax in 1:9, 3:15, and 6:10.

The Septuagint read an additional *mem* and thus translated *makran hyper ho ēn,* which Jarick (*Gregory Thaumaturgos' Paraphrase,* p. 185) translates as "[that which is] far beyond what was."

105. For intensificaton by repetition (*'āmôq 'āmôq*), see GKC §133k and Waltke and O'Connor, *Biblical Hebrew Syntax,* p. 233.

106. So Ogden, *Qoheleth,* pp. 118-19.

107. Lauha, *Kohelet,* p. 137.

108. So Crenshaw, *Ecclesiastes,* p. 144.

109. Fox, *Qohelet and His Contradictions,* pp. 239-40.

110. M. V. Fox and B. Porten, "Unsought Discoveries: Qohelet 7:23–8:1a," *Hebrew Studies* 19 (1978): 28.

specifically to "the reality below all changing phenomena."[111] Qohelet is not just interested in the *what* of existence; he desires to know the *why*.

Qohelet intensifies the idea of inaccessible knowledge with a second spatial metaphor — deepness. Here his statement reminds us of Job 28, a moving poem that describes wisdom as more difficult to attain than the precious metals buried deep within the ground.

This verse reintroduces (cf. v. 14) the word *find* (root, *mṣ'*) that will play such an important role in the rest of the chapter.[112] It signals that Qohelet has embarked on a quest for something hard to find, a fact that the following section makes clear.

5. Seeking and (Not) Finding (7:25-29)

This unit is best delimited by its use of three repeated words that express its cental theme: (1) *seek (bqš),* (2) *find (mṣ'),* and (3) the *sum of things (ḥešbôn).* Qohelet sought to find the sum of things, but failed to do so. Along the way, however, "Qohelet searched and kept finding strange things."[113] Specifically, he found three things: (1) women were more bitter than death (v. 26); (2) no females and only an occasional male were virtuous (v. 28); and (3) though God created all people upright, every single one went wrong. Thus, in this section, Qohelet shares his low view of humanity as a whole.

> 25 *I began to devote myself[114] to understand and to explore and to seek wisdom and the sum of things,[115] and to understand the evil of fool-ishness and the folly[116] of madness.[117]*

---

111. Barton, *The Book of Ecclesiastes,* p. 146.

112. See A. R. Ceresko, "The Function of *Antanaclasis (mṣ'* 'to find'//*mṣ'* 'to reach, overtake, grasp') in Hebrew Poetry, Especially in the Book of Qoheleth," *CBQ* 44 (1982): 551-69). His argument that *mṣ'* in 7:23-29 masks two different Hebrew roots and "requires four different English words ('grasp,' 'find,' 'learn,' 'reach')" and thus is an example of *antanaclasis* is totally unnecessary. The translation "find" is used throughout in the present work and is perfectly adequate to the context, and thus it is the most eloquent translation.

113. Fox and Porten, "Unsought Discoveries," p. 38.

114. See comment on the textual emendation of the first part of this verse in the body of the commentary. *myself (libbî)* is literally "my heart." In my translation I stay with the MT and do not follow the tradition of Symmachus, the Targum, and the Vulgate, which prefixes the preposition *beth* onto "heart." If the emendation is not made, then the translation "my heart and I turned to know . . ." is awkward, but defensible (see Crenshaw, *Ecclesiastes,* p. 145).

115. For arguments against the lateness of *sum of things (ḥešbôn),* see Fredericks, *Qoheleth's Language,* p. 198.

116. Note the unusual use of the definite article here *(hassiklût)* in a series of nouns that otherwise do not attest the article (Isaksson, *Studies in the Language of Qoheleth,* p. 146).

117. A number of Hebrew manuscripts, the Septuagint, and the Syriac add the

26 *And I was finding:*[118] *More bitter than death is the woman who is a snare,*[119] *whose heart is a trap*[120] *and whose hands are chains. The one who pleases God will escape her, but the one who is offensive will be captured by her.*

27 *"Observe, this I have found:" Qohelet said, "one thing to another to find the sum of things,*

28 *which I am still seeking but not finding, I found one man out of a thousand, but I did not find a woman among all these.*

29 *Only*[121] *observe this: I have found that God made people upright, but they have sought out many devices.*

25 The opening verb, *I began (sabbôtî 'anî)*, indicates that Qohelet now turns to a new subject (see 2:20 for this translation of *sbb*). I have followed the suggestion of the *BHS* textual apparatus to add a form of the verb *ntn* before "heart" *(lēb)* to yield the idiom *devote myself.* I do this on the basis of the similar verse in 1:17 and because the phrase is awkward without emendation. While it is true that other poetic traditions personify the heart in this way,[122] it is not otherwise attested in Hebrew.

Qohelet, while just admitting the limitations of wisdom in general, and his ability to achieve it in particular (vv. 23-24), nonetheless expresses his eagerness to pursue it. This eagerness is communicated by the piling up of the infinitives construct *to understand (lāda'at), to explore (lātûr)* (see 1:13; 2:3), and *to search (baqqēš),* the last being a key word (see also v. 28) in this section as part of the "seek . . . find" theme. These verbs strongly express Qohelet's diligence in his pursuit.

What are the objects of his pursuit? He first names *wisdom and the sum of things.* The latter word *(hešbôn)* occurs here for the first time (see also

---

conjunction *waw* between the last two nouns. I see no reason to follow this tradition (but see Lauha, *Kohelet,* p. 139).

118. This form *(môṣe')* is the qal participle. The vowel under the second root consonant is the vowel one finds normally associated with *lamed-he* verbs (GKC §75oo).

119. Taking *'ašer* as a relative and *hî'* as a copula. For other options, consult Crenshaw, *Ecclesiastes,* p. 146.

120. The Hebrew accentuation (note the *darga*) indicates that *trap* should be related to the woman, but *BHS,* following the versions and followed by my translation, separates the two.

121. As has been noted before (Podechard, *L'Ecclésiaste,* p. 388; Whitley, *Koheleth,* p. 70), this is the only case when *only (lebad)* is used absolutely in biblical Hebrew. Most translations and commentators, however, render the first part of the verse "I have found only this." This ignores the fact that *only* begins the verse and is separated from *this (zeh).*

122. Plumptre, *Ecclesiastes; or, the Preacher,* pp. 170-71.

7:27, 29, and 9:10). It is an abstract noun formed from the common verbal root *ḥšb* "to reckon, to plan, to calculate," and its nominal form occurs in Ben Sira (6:22; 9:15; 42:3) and the Mishnah.[123] In Ecclesiastes it denotes the explanation that stands behind the world. If Qohelet could discover the *sum of things,* he would be at the end of his quest. But he never achieves this object of his search, and thus we have his harsh conclusion that everything is "meaningless" *(hebel).*

Qohelet also seeks to know *the evil of foolishness and the folly of madness (rešaʿ kesel wᵉhassiklût hôlēlôt).* Most of the terms used in this expression are discussed in 1:17 and 2:12. The syntax in this verse is difficult, and my translation can be debated. Robert Gordis[124] takes the expression as "two sets of double accusatives and translate[s] 'wickedness is foolishness, and folly is madness.'" Michael Fox rightly rejects this approach but then argues that the four are really a series of direct objects: "to understand wickedness, stupidity, and folly [and] madness."[125] This approach, however, necessitates the addition of two *waw* conjunctions. It is possible to simply take the Hebrew text as it stands and to consider the two pairs of words in construct relationship. In this I depart from Christian Ginsburg,[126] who wrongly argues that, if these words were in construct relationship, the second member of the pairs would have a definite article. I do, though, agree with Ginsburg that the words represent abstract terms rather than classes of people, against translations like that of Luther ("the foolishness of the wicked and the errors of the stupid").[127]

26 In v. 25 Qohelet announced his intention to search things out; now he informs the reader what he *was finding (môṣeʾ).* The use of the participle here, rather than the expected suffixed form of the verb, indicates that his conclusions are the result of repeated experience.[128]

The discovery that he first relates is rather surprising and has to do with *the woman (hāʾiššâ).* Is, however, Qohelet speaking of women in general[129] or a particular type of woman?[130] The latter view takes the qualifiers

---

123. Podechard, *L'Ecclésiaste,* p. 384.
124. For instance, Gordis, *Koheleth,* pp. 281-82.
125. Fox, *Qohelet and His Contradictions,* p. 240.
126. Ginsburg, *The Song of Songs and Coheleth,* p. 386.
127. Luther, "Notes on Ecclesiastes," pp. 129-30.
128. Isaksson, *Studies in the Language of Qoheleth,* pp. 65-66.
129. Isaksson, *Studies in the Language of Qoheleth,* pp. 65-66.
130. So Hertzberg, *Der Prediger,* p. 157; and Murphy, *Ecclesiastes,* p. 76. Ogden (*Qoheleth,* pp. 120-21) proposes the bizarre suggestion that the woman here is a metaphor for "untimely death." Over one hundred years ago, Plumptre (*Ecclesiastes; or, the Preacher,* p. 171) already had pointed out that "the suggestion that the writer allegorizes . . . is quite untenable."

that follow *the woman* as circumscribing the referent. That is, only the wicked, seductive woman is *more bitter than death;* all other women are fine. This interpretive approach is fond of citing 9:9 and invoking the wisdom tradition that contrasts the "strange" woman over against the virtuous woman (the climax of which may be found in Prov. 9). Pietist interpreters have been fond of this approach through the ages (see Gregory Thaumaturgos as commented upon by John Jarick).[131] The Living Bible takes this approach most blatantly by translating, "A prostitute is more bitter than death," though the New Living Translation (1996) has changed this for the better to: "I have found a woman who is a trap more bitter than death."

Perhaps if the verse stood alone, this view could be maintained.[132] Verse 28, however, will not allow this interpretation since that verse specifies that not a single good woman could be found among one thousand. As for the contrast with 9:9, it must be remembered that Qohelet is filled with tensions and contradictions since he is a confused wise man. For those concerned that a biblical book appears to support the views of a misogynist, it must also be remembered that the views of Qohelet are not the teachings of the book of Ecclesiastes any more than the speeches of the three friends constitute the normative teaching of the book of Job.

bitter (mar) is oftentimes rendered "strong" by commentators who are influenced by the appearance of the root *mrr* with that meaning in cognate literature.[133] The versions, however, all understood the root as related to "bitter," not "strength," and this meaning fits the context extremely well.

Qohelet ends the verse with an implicit warning to men. Some will be captured by women and others will escape. He differentiates these two classes of men using categories that have already been used and discussed in 2:26. Here, *the one who pleases God* and *the one who is offensive* are not moral categories; the concern is rather "the mysterious actions of

131. Jarick, *Gregory Thaumaturgos' Paraphrase,* p. 188.
132. Even D. A. Garrett ("Ecclesiastes 7:25-29 and the Feminist Hermeneutic," *Criswell Theological Review* 2 [1988]: 309-21), who defends this passage against feminist criticism, admits that Qohelet's object here is women in general and not a specific type of evil woman. He believes that the context is marriage and that Qohelet is simply describing the fact that men have great pain in their marriage relationships. He goes on to say that the text would have been just as true if written from a woman's perspective about men. This attempt to mitigate Qohelet's hard words about women is not helped by this appeal to marriage.
133. Dahood, "Qoheleth and Recent Discoveries," *Biblica* 39 (1958): 308-10; Whitley, *Koheleth,* p. 68; Lohfink, *Kohelet,* p. 112; K. Baltzer, "Women and War in Qohelet 7:23–8:1a," *HTR* 80 (1987): 127-32, who entertains the possibility that both meanings resonate in the text (this is linguistically doubtful); and S. Schloesser, " 'A King is Held Captive in Her Tresses': The Liberating Deconstruction of the Search for Wisdom from Proverbs through Ecclesiastes," *Church Divinity* (1989-90): 205-28.

God."[134] In the words of Jarick, "the former category is the person whom God chooses to bless, for reasons known only to the Deity himself, while the latter category is the person whom God chooses not to bless, for the same inscrutable reasons."[135]

27   This verse introduces what Murphy rightly calls Qohelet's "second finding."[136] The first finding concerned the nature of women; now he will expand upon that observation to evaluate both men and women in vv. 28 and 29.

Qohelet calls our attention to his second finding initially by means of the imperative *Observe (rᵉ'ēh)*. The exact function of the demonstrative *this (zeh)* is somewhat difficult to ascertain, though on analogy with v. 29, it is most natural to take it as a reference to what follows in vv. 28 and 29, namely, his evaluation of men and women.

The verb "to find" *(mṣ')* is used twice in this verse, linking it with its other occurrences in this unit, especially with the next verse, which really completes the sentence begun here. His use of the verb is playful in that he both finds and does not find (see v. 28).

Qohelet speaks in a clipped manner in the second half of the verse. Most translations smooth the syntax by filling out the thought along the lines of the NIV: "adding one thing to another to find the explanation of things." This rendition is certainly in keeping with Qohelet's thought, but perhaps parentheses should have been added in order to indicate that "adding" is not found in the Hebrew. In this phrase, Qohelet indicates that his conclusion does not arise as the result of a single experience, but through a careful analysis of evidence in order to arrive at his goal, *the sum of things (ḥešbôn),* for which see v. 25.

There is a very important interruption of the direct speech in this verse. The frame narrator makes his presence known for the only time in the body of the book by adding the simple phrase, *Qohelet said* (see "Structure" and "Authorship" in the introduction). We are thus reminded that another voice stands behind Qohelet's, the normative voice of the book also heard in the prologue and the epilogue.

28   This verse has generated considerable modern anxiety, and some creative interpretations. Qohelet appears on the surface to make an uncomplimentary remark about humanity in general, and women in particular. The conclusion of the search that he announced in v. 27 is that he found only one man among a thousand, and no women. Of course, the obvious question is, What was he looking for in people that brought him to this conclusion? As I

---

134. Murphy, *Ecclesiastes,* p. 76.
135. Jarick, *Gregory Thaumaturgos' Paraphrase,* p. 190.
136. Murphy, *Wisdom Literature,* p. 142.

will argue below, the context implies that he was looking for virtue, and finding very little.

Older commentators had little problem with this verse, their own cultural biases reflecting Qohelet's attitude. Christian Ginsburg quotes St. Chrysostom on this verse as saying: "What is woman, but a punishment that cannot be driven away, a necessary evil, a natural temptation, a desirable calamity, a domestic danger, one beloved for the colour of good?"[137] Luther, likewise, considers Qohelet's attitude toward women "a divine ordinance."[138]

Many modern interpreters naturally bristle at these interpretations and occasionally attempt to circumvent them by creative, rather fanciful interpretations. Klaus Baltzer, for instance, disputes the translation *a thousand* for *'elep,* arguing that it really means a military unit.[139] Thus, Qohelet is simply saying that he observed "only men" (Baltzer's translation of *'ādām 'eḥād*) and no women in the army! Murphy's approach[140] is less fanciful, but nonetheless unlikely (and he too observes that his suggestion is only a suggestion and not to be taken dogmatically). He argues that Qohelet is quoting a common opinion that he rejects as something he has not found to be true.

But let us examine the verse more closely. While it is possible that the *'ašer* refers to what follows, it is more likely that it is a relative with *sum of things* (v. 27, *ḥešbôn*) as its antecedent.[141] That is, while Qohelet was unable to discover the more profound *sum of things,* he did observe other things, including his conclusion about men and women.

The first comment that I should make about Qohelet's statement is that he speaks elliptically. Many translations (the NRSV is an exception) fill in the gap by importing an adjective before *man* and before *woman.* The NIV is typical as it moves the statement into the realm of morality with the adjective "upright." While perhaps undermining Qohelet's subtlety, the NIV correctly makes explicit Qohelet's meaning, as is clear by looking at the use of "upright" *(yāšār)* in the next verse.

The second comment concerns the force of *man ('ādām).* I have translated it as a gender-specific term, but in the next verse it is gender neutral, as it usually is in Hebrew. The context of the present verse lends support to taking it as *man,* however, since it is in contrast with *woman.* In any case, either translation achieves the same effect.

The conclusion of our study then is that Qohelet indeed expresses himself here as a misogynist. That he elsewhere speaks favorably of women

137. Ginsburg, *The Song of Songs and Coheleth,* pp. 388-89.
138. Luther, "Notes on Ecclesiastes," p. 132.
139. K. Baltzer, "Women and War," pp. 127-32.
140. Murphy, *Wisdom Literature,* p. 142; and *Ecclesiastes,* pp. 75-77.
141. Fox, *Qohelet and His Contradictions,* p. 242.

(9:9) is not surprising. His comments are full of tensions, and thus I have characterized him as a confused wise man whose voice is not to be identified with the teaching of the canonical book (see "Authorship" in the introduction).

29 This verse contains the third and last conclusion *found* by Qohelet. He asserts that God made people virtuous, but they have corrupted themselves.

The word *Only* that begins the verse heightens the importance of the concluding discovery. This is because it is the principle that lies behind the previous points he has made. Why is woman more bitter than death (v. 26)? Why could he not find a woman and only a single man out of a thousand (v. 28)? The answer in the present verse is that, though God made the human race upright, they have all gone astray.

The verse is an obvious reflection on the first few chapters of Genesis,[142] though the vocabulary is different. For instance, as God completed his acts of creation, including the creation of humanity, he pronounced the results "very good"; there were no problems with the work of his hands. This, I would argue, relates to Qohelet's statement that humanity was created "upright," and the connection with the creation lends strong support to the usual understanding that *upright* here is a moral and not an intellectual characteristic.[143]

However, while God created humanity without moral blemish, men and women *sought out many devices (biqšû ḥiššᵉbōnôt rabbîm)*. We hear in this phrase verbal echoes that remind us of Genesis 6:5: "The LORD saw how great man's wickedness on the earth had become and that every inclination of the *thoughts* of his heart was only evil all the time." The italicized word is related to the word translated *devices* here in Ecclesiastes in that both are words formed from the verbal root ḥšb ("to think, to calculate").

The form of the word in Ecclesiastes does present some difficulties, however. It is a plural form of the word that appears twice in this context (vv. 25 and 27), but not with the same meaning that those contexts demand, "sum of things." Here there is an obvious contrast with *upright,* which determines the morally negative tone of the word. This is confirmed by the versions (see Septuagint *logismous pollous* "many arguments," and Vulgate *infinitis quaestionibus* "infinite questionings"). Otherwise, it appears that these contexts (further including 2 Chron. 26:15) have in common only the verbal root "to think, calculate."

142. Contra Ogden, *Qoheleth*, pp. 124-25; note the explicit connection with Genesis in the Targum (cf. Levine, *The Aramaic Version*, p. 40).
143. Contra Fox, *Qohelet and His Contradictions*, p. 243.

SUMMARY OF 6:10–7:29

The first unit (6:10-12) of this part of the book provides an important transition from the search for meaning to the giving of advice. However, this is not a radical division. Qohelet will occasionally allude to his search in these last few chapters (e.g., 7:25-29).

The section really provides a miscellany of materials. It begins with a reflection on the divine determination of the future and the human inability to know that future (6:10-12). Qohelet then continues with a series of proverbs, a number of which reverse one's expectations. For instance, Qohelet prizes death and sorrow over life and laughter (7:1-2).

Chapter 7 continues with two reflections on wisdom. The first (vv. 15-22) points out that wisdom and righteousness do not guarantee blessing, and so he advises a moderate approach to wisdom. The second (vv. 23-24) indicates that no matter how much one desires wisdom, it is ultimately beyond human grasp.

Finally, the section concludes (7:26-29) with the confession that Qohelet's search yielded no major breakthroughs. He looked diligently, but all he found was a corrupt humanity seeking its own desires.

6. No One Is Like the Wise! (8:1)

Opinion differs over the placement of this verse in its context. Some[1] feel that it (or at least 8:1a) concludes the previous section. Others[2] rather believe it introduces the advice that follows concerning behavior before the king. Everyone struggles over the issue, sometimes to the point of believing that it is a gloss.[3] My interpretation understands the verse as a sarcastic exclamation of frustration that stands between two larger units.

> 1 Who is like[4] the[5] wise person? And who knows the interpretation[6] of

1. Whybray, *Ecclesiastes,* NCB, p. 128.
2. For instance, Crenshaw, *Ecclesiastes,* p. 149.
3. Lauha, *Kohelet,* p. 144.
4. The Septuagint tradition adds the verb "to know" *(oiden)* to the first sentence, yielding the meaning "Who knows the wise person?" This verb is read back from the second sentence.
5. The article is not elided before the prefixed preposition, which is rare but not unattested (GKC §35n, and Waltke and O'Connor, *Biblical Hebrew Syntax,* p. 239).
6. While *interpretation (pēšer)* has been called an Aramaism since it appears in the Aramaic part of Daniel (2:4, 5, etc.; cf. Whitley, *Koheleth,* p. 71), Fredericks (*Qoheleth's Language,* p. 236) rightly points out that this root occurs earlier in Akkadian *(pāšaru),* and both the Aramaic and Hebrew roots may be cognate to it.

*a matter? The wisdom of a person brightens his face and changes[7] its
stern expression.[8]*

1 Qohelet raises two questions concerning the wise. He asks if anyone is like
a wise person. He then asks who can know how to interpret a matter. Finally, he
asserts that someone who is wise can change a stern expression into a smile.

In the previous unit Qohelet informed his readers that wisdom was
ultimately beyond their reach (7:23, 24) as was the "sum of things." What he
did discover was the deep depravity of mankind and the even deeper depravity
of womankind. In the light of the end of ch. 7, the only possible answer to the
rhetorical questions that begin ch. 8 is, "No one!" There are no wise, and no one
knows the *interpretation,* or perhaps "solution," *of a matter.*

If this is the proper understanding of the first part of the verse, then
the second part must be sarcastic. Of course, this interpretation of the verse
must remain hypothetical because it is the context, rather than anything explicit
in the text, that signals the sarcastic tone. However, can one imagine a cheery,
happy-faced Qohelet at this point in the book, rejoicing in the blithe expression
of others who claimed to be wise?

7. The Word of the King Is Supreme (8:2-9)

Qohelet gives advice concerning behavior before the king. The tenor of his
advice is strong evidence that Qohelet himself is not a king (see "Date" and
"Authorship" in the introduction) and that his intended addressees are young
courtiers who have occasion to interact with the king in the normal course of
their occupation.

Like a typical wise man, Qohelet gives advice so that his students may
get along in the world. The person so instructed stays out of trouble (vv. 5-6a),
or so it seems at first. In vv. 6b-9 Qohelet admits that in the final analysis no
one has the power or the knowledge to act correctly in every situation. The
world is an unpredictable and dangerous place.

2 *I say: Observe the king's command, and do not rush into a vow to God.*

3 *You should leave his presence and not persist in an evil matter, for he
will do whatever he wants.*

7. *y^ešunne'* is an example of a *lamed-he* verb that acts like a *lamed-aleph* verb
(GKC §75rr). A similar phenomenon occurs in 8:12, 9:2, 12 *(hōṭe'),* and 7:26 *(môṣe').*

8. By understanding the verbal root to be *šānā'* "to hate" rather than *šānā'* "to
change," the Septuagint understood that the last clause of the verse contrasts rather than
continues the description of the wise person: "a person of shameless countenance will be
hated" (*anaidēs prosōpō autou misēthēsetai;* cf. Jarick, *Gregory Thaumaturgos' Paraphrase,* p. 196). Luther ("Notes on Ecclesiastes," p. 134) follows this translation.

4 *For[9] the word of the king is supreme,[10] so who will tell him, "What are you doing?"*

5 *The one who observes his command[11] experiences no evil thing. A wise heart[12] knows a time and custom.[13]*

6 *For there is a time and a custom for every matter, but people's troubles lie heavily upon them.*

7 *For no one knows what will happen,[14] because who can say when[15] it will happen?*

8 *No one has power over the wind to restrain the wind. No one has power over the day of death. There is no discharge during battle. Evil[16] will not rescue those who practice it.[17]*

9 *All of this I observed, and I devoted myself[18] to all the acts that are done under the sun at a time when people have power over other people to harm them.*

9. The force of *ba'ᵃšer* is causal (see also 7:2). The Septuagint mistook the preposition *beth* as a *kaph* and thus translated "just as" *(kathōs)*. The Septuagint also understood *dbr* as a verb *(lalei)* rather than a noun.

10. This noun *(šilṭôn)* occurs only here and in 8:8 in biblical Hebrew. Some have pointed to its occurrence in Aramaic in Dan. 3:2, 3 and Ben Sira 4:17 and have argued that it is a late word. Whitley (*Koheleth,* p. 72) makes this argument and begins by citing only an Arabic cognate to the term. This type of approach neglects the older cognates. Fredericks (*Qoheleth's Language,* pp. 239-40) argues that it is a preexilic word. See the use of the verb in 2:19; 5:18 (English 19); 6:2; 8:9.

11. In the Hebrew the noun occurs without pronominal suffix or definite article, thus leading some to believe this to be a traditional wisdom saying (e.g., Murphy, *Ecclesiastes,* p. 83). Context, however, suggests the connection with the king in the previous verses (see Isaksson, *Studies in the Language of Qoheleth,* p. 146).

12. Without the article on *wisdom (ḥākām),* it is unlikely that this is in construct with *heart* (contra the versions).

13. Some Hebrew manuscripts and the Septuagint omit the conjunction before *custom (mišpāṭ)* and understand it to be in a genitive relationship with the preceding noun, hence "time of judgment" *(kairon kriseōs).*

14. For the expression *what will happen (mah-šeyyihyê),* see 3:22 and 10:14.

15. Symmachus, the Vulgate, and the Syriac all emend *when (ka'ᵃšer)* to "what" *('ᵃšer),* but this change is unnecessary and unsupported.

16. Some (K. Budde, *Der Prediger* [Tübingen: Mohr, 1923]; K. Galling, "Der Prediger," in *Die fünf Megilloth,* 2d ed., HAT 18 [Tübingen: Mohr/Siebeck, 1969]; W. Zimmerli, "The Place and Limit of Wisdom in the Framework of the Old Testament Theology," *SJT* 17 [1964]: 146-58; and Whitley, *Koheleth,* p. 74) argue that *reša'* should be emended to *'ōšer* "wealth," but this is unsupported and unnecessary.

17. *bᵉ'ālāyw,* literally, "its owner."

18. The infinitive absolute here *(nātôn)* has the effect of continuing the previous verbal tense. The idiom is explained in 1:13.

2 Qohelet begins his section on the word of the king by warning that his
hearers should be careful to obey the king and slow to enter into a vow with
God. What appears in translation to be a basically straightforward verse
actually has a number of difficult issues. The first word in the MT is the
independent personal pronoun *I (ʾᵃnî),* which has no obvious connection with
the context. It appears to hang in midair, and thus emendations have been
proposed. Some have suggested that the verb *ʾāmartî* "I say" has dropped
out; others believe that the *I (ʾᵃnî)* should be emended to the direct object
marker *ʾet.*[19] One of the more creative suggestions is based on an analogy
with a similar line in the Aramaic tale of Ahiqar and results in a form of *ʾnpy
mlk* (in the presence of the king).[20] None of these emendations finds support
in the versions. While it is true that neither the Septuagint nor the Peshitta
reflects the word, that does not mean the direct object was there instead,
because the Septuagint would likely have reflected its presence with *syn*
(characteristic of the Septuagint of Ecclesiastes). My translation simply follows the MT for lack of evidence to do otherwise, and treats the presence of
I as a "short-hand way of saying 'I would give the following advice' or '*my*
view is as follows.' "[21]

   The second issue surrounding the text of this verse has to do with the
force of the prepositional phrase *ʿal dibrat,* which could either have a causal
sense ("because") or else reflect the sense of "concerning." Most (note the
NIV and NRSV, besides the standard commentaries) take it the former way
and follow the verse division of the Masoretes. Thus, the *vow to God* is the
vow that a king's subjects take to be loyal to their king. This then is the reason
why they should follow the king's command.[22] The difficulty with this rendering is that it makes the next verse syntactically and semantically awkward
(though not impossible). According to my treatment, the verse echoes the
sentiment already expressed in 5:1 (English 5:2).

   Thus, in this verse Qohelet gives his advice concerning proper behavior
in the presence of authority, both divine and human. This advice continues in
the next few verses.

   3 Qohelet continues his instruction concerning behavior in the presence of the king. After asserting the necessity of obeying the monarch's

   19. Murphy, *Ecclesiastes,* p. 80.
   20. For instance, Whitley, *Koheleth,* pp. 71-72.
   21. So Jarick, *Gregory Thaumaturgos' Paraphrase,* p. 196. See also C. Rabin's
remark: "the MT phrase could possibly be translated 'As far as I am concerned, it [the
rule of conduct] is "watch the king's mouth!" ' " in "Lexical Emendation in Biblical
Research," in *Focus: A Semitic/Afrasian Gathering in Remembrance of Albert Ehrman,*
ed. Y. L. Arbeitman (Amsterdam: John Benjamins, 1988), pp. 391-92, quoted in Waltke
and O'Connor, *Biblical Hebrew Syntax,* p. 680, n. 28.
   22. See the treatment by W. A. Irwin, "Ecclesiastes 8:2-9," *JNES* 4 (1945): 130-31.

command, Qohelet says that it is prudent not to argue with the king, but just leave his presence and carry out his will. After all, he is the king. He is sovereign and his desires will be accomplished no matter what.

The decision has been made above to go against the Masoretic verse division and the majority of commentators. By moving "do not hasten" to the previous verse, one avoids having to argue that there are two finite verbs in a single sentence in asyndetic relationship (and no verb in v. 2b). The syntax is not impossible if left alone but is much smoother in both vv. 2 and 3 if one changes the verse division. Furthermore, unless one makes the emendation to the Masoretic versification, then v. 3 appears to advise the reader both against (v. 3a) and in favor of (v. 3b) leaving the king's presence.

As I have translated it, Qohelet's advice is "to leave the king's presence when he is angry."[23] The scenario that Qohelet envisions is that of a courtier who has presented an idea or given advice to a ruler, and the ruler has rejected it. Qohelet advises the courtier against pushing his idea once the king has rejected it, and by way of justification of his advice he reminds the courtier that the king is all-powerful *(he will do whatever he wants)*.

evil matter (dābār rāʿ) has a wide semantic range. In my opinion, though, it is probably closer to a "bad idea" than it is to a full-blown political conspiracy.[24]

4 Verse 4 adds yet another reason for the reader to obey the king quietly: the king's word is *supreme;* no one can gainsay him. Thus, it is fruitless, even dangerous, to question his actions, and better just to do whatever he wants.

Interestingly, Job (9:12) posed the same rhetorical question as Qohelet, but in Job's case it was a question about God, not the human king: Who can gainsay God? The similarity may be the simple coincidence of a common question, or perhaps Qohelet is subtly drawing a comparison and implicitly saying that the king's authority is virtually godlike. In either case, pietistic interpreters took this as a clue to the proper reference of the passage and identified the *king* as God himself.[25] Other passages that similarly ascribe power to God are Isaiah 45:9 and Daniel 4:32.

5 This verse begins by reaffirming what has already been taught in v. 2, namely, people are safe if they obey the royal command. The connection may be seen also in the repetition of the verb "to observe" *(šmr)*. It is true, however, that the two sentences are not as close in the Hebrew as the English

<hr>

23. So Fox (who adopts the same versification that I follow here), *Qohelet and His Contradictions,* p. 246.

24. Contra N. Waldman, "The *dābār raʿ* of Eccl 8:3," *JBL* 98 (1979): 407-8.

25. So the Targum and Gregory Thaumaturgos; cf. Jarick, *Gregory Thaumaturgos' Paraphrase,* p. 200.

translation indicates, because "command" in v. 2 is a translation for the idiomatic "mouth of the king." In any case, though, the similarity between the two verses confirms the interpretation that reference is to the *king's* command and not the divine command (favored by the pietistic tradition evidenced by Gregory of Thaumaturgos and the Targum).

Those who do obey the king will avoid unpleasant consequences *(evil thing)*. This expression is a verbal echo of v. 3. Those who understand *evil thing* as a reference to a political conspiracy (see v. 3) could understand this verse as a description of a courtier who obeys commands and is not intent on mutiny, though Nahum Waldman[26] does not make this point.

The last half of the verse sounds like a typical wisdom admonition that highlights the importance of appropriate timing in an action or a word. Qohelet comments that a wise person should know the proper time and the right customs.

Ecclesiastes 3:1-8 illustrates the principle that there is a time for everything, and its following pericope (3:9-15) indicates the frustration of the wise because of their limitations. This pattern is echoed here; thus 8:6-7 will nuance the statement here in v. 5b.

The last word of the verse is *mišpāṭ*, a term usually translated "judgment," but here taken as *custom*. The broader meaning of the Hebrew term is "standard of behavior." In our present context it has the sense of *custom*, "procedure," or perhaps even "assessment."[27]

6 In the previous verse Qohelet described the wise person as one who knows the "time and custom." Now, while he reaffirms that there is a *time and custom for everything*, he states that it is of no real benefit to anyone. Humankind is rather beset by trouble and unable to know what the future will bring (v. 7).

The first half of the verse not only calls to mind v. 5 but also 3:1 and its context. There we read that there is "a time for every activity under heaven" (see comments on that verse for philological discussion). There, as here, Qohelet tells us that, though there is a " 'right time' for everything, it is known only to God, who has concealed it from his creatures, so rendering them helpless and unable to plan or exercise control over events."[28]

Human limitations are the subject of the second part of the verse (and continue into v. 7). One matter of difficulty is the force of the conjunction *kî*, here translated *but*. *kî* actually occurs four times in vv. 6 and 7. The *kî* that opens the verse is clearly causal, in that it supplies the motivation for the previous verse. While some take this second occurrence as concessive ("though"), the contrast with the first part of the verse suggests the adversative.

26. Waldman, "The *dābār raʿ*," pp. 407-8.
27. Ogden, *Qoheleth*, p. 131.
28. Whybray, *Ecclesiastes*, NCB, p. 132.

We have already encountered the noun *trouble (rā'at)* , most often with a strong moral connotation. Indeed, a minority of commentators[29] render it as "evil" here as well. However, I agree with Whybray[30] that in the context "Qoheleth is here worried about man's ignorance and not his sin," taking our cue from v. 7. I should also point out that the Septuagint and Theodotion read "knowledge," but this results from a confusion of the letter *resh* with a *dalet* (thus producing *da'at*).

7 Now we come to the crux of the matter. Above, Qohelet stated his belief that there is a time for everything. Now he is admitting the countervening truth: no one can know that proper time. It is beyond human ability.

While a number of commentators believe that the thought of this verse is to be applied to the king, John Jarick is certainly correct when he states: "Koheleth appears to have been referring to the ignorance of Everyman concerning the future."[31] A shift of focus takes place in v. 5 when attention is directed away from the king to the wise person. This verse is a further admission of the limitations upon human wisdom begun in the last half of v. 6. The specific limitation here is the wise person's ignorance concerning the future. A wise person is someone who is able to make competent decisions that fit a particular situation. An important component of this ability is an intuition concerning the future results of a decision. But here such a possibility is denied.

8 The previous verse addressed human ignorance; now Qohelet enumerates four further instances of human impotence. They are human inability to control the wind, to prevent death, to get out of a battle, and, for someone who is evil, to be rescued.

The first two are related by the use of the expression *no . . . power* (*'ên* with the root *šlt*). The first points out that no one, presumably even the king (who is characterized by the word *šlt* in v. 4), has the ability to control the wind. Some ambiguity attends the exact force of the word here translated *wind*. Some[32] take it as a reference to the "breath of life." Support is gained for this interpretation by the third sentence in the verse, which specifically mentions human impotence in the face of death. The second colon does assert that no one can predict, put off, or delay the time of their death.

The third and fourth sentences are a little more difficult to understand. The word *discharge (mišlaḥat)* occurs only in one other place (Ps. 78:49) and with a different meaning ("band, company"). The context here in conjunction

---

29. Delitzsch, *Proverbs, Ecclesiastes, Song of Songs,* p. 342; Crenshaw, *Ecclesiastes,* p. 148.
30. Whybray, *Ecclesiastes,* NCB, p. 132.
31. Jarick, *Gregory Thaumaturgos' Paraphrase,* p. 206.
32. Gordis, *Koheleth,* p. 290; Eaton, *Ecclesiastes,* p. 120.

with the base meaning of the root (*šlḥ,* "to send") leads to my present translation. Some have questioned this meaning when comparing the verse with the teaching of Deuteronomy 20:5-8 that allows for discharge from the army.[33] However, close study shows that the discharge there is before, not during, a battle, the situation envisioned by Qohelet.

The fourth and last sentence highlights the evil person. It is somewhat ambiguous as to what exactly is meant here. Perhaps it speaks to the attitude that wickedness or evil gives prosperity to people (Ps. 73).

9 Qohelet concludes this unit with a summary statement. He asserts that his comments are based on the results of his observations on life. He again reminds us that he was a devoted student of the full range of human activity. We are already familiar with much of Qohelet's language in this verse from previous uses (e.g., 1:14).

Most scholars believe that *All of this* introduces a summary statement that concludes the previous unit. A few others, for instance, Ernst Hengstenberg[34] and Roland Murphy,[35] dissent from this view and believe that the phrase is looking forward to the verses that follow. It is somewhat unclear. Nonetheless, the previous use of the phrase as well as the verbal link between *have power* and words with the root *šlṭ* in the previous verses tip the scale in favor of the view that v. 9 is a conclusion, not an introduction.

Beginning with some ancient versions, dissatisfaction has been expressed about the Hebrew of the last clause of the verse, resulting in the suggestion that *ʿēt* should be emended to *ʾet,* the direct object marker (the Septuagint has *syn* at this point). Nonetheless, the Hebrew text makes perfectly good sense once *ʿēt* is recognized as an accusative of time. The clause is dependent (marked by *ʾašer*) and not an independent sentence (see, for instance, the NIV).

The final issue of the verse concerns the referent to the concluding pronominal suffix. It is unclear whether the *harm* befalls the perpetrators or the receivers of the abuse. It is likely that Qohelet has in mind the latter, which fits in with his major theme that the powerful oppress the vulnerable (most notably 4:1-3).

8. Are the Wicked Really Punished? (8:10-15)

Qohelet once again (see 3:16-22) raises the issue of retribution. Are the wicked punished or not? From Qohelet's perspective, it does not seem so (vv. 10-12a); wickedness thrives because there is no apparent punishment for it.

---

33. Ogden, *Qoheleth,* p. 133.
34. Hengstenberg, *A Commentary on Ecclesiastes,* p. 199.
35. Murphy, *Ecclesiastes,* pp. 84-85.

There is an interesting clash with the thought expressed in vv. 12b-13, where Qohelet gives expression to an orthodox sentiment. It is almost as if Qohelet changed his mind in mid-thought. However, whatever the dynamics of his thinking, it is clear that he did not long dwell on an orthodox view of divine retribution since he proceeds with a statement that once again questions justice (v. 14). The final verse is another expression of the *carpe diem* theme, which in this context can only be understood as the expression of resignation.

10 *Thus,*[36] *I observed the wicked buried and departed.*[37] *They used to go out of the holy place,*[38] *and they were praised in the city where they acted in such a way. This too is meaningless.*

11 *Because*[39] *the sentence*[40] *for an evil deed is not quickly carried out,*[41] *therefore the human heart is filled with evildoing.*[42]

36. Thus translating *ûbᵉkēn*, which is composed of the conjunction *waw*, the preposition *beth*, and the particle *kēn*. Waltke and O'Connor (*Biblical Hebrew Syntax*, p. 221; see also GKC §119ii) cite this as an example of a "complex preposition [that] functions as an adverbial."

37. This verb *(bā'û)* is problematic in the verse. For one thing, the verb usually means "to go to, to enter, to arrive," not "to depart." It is possible (see discussion at 1:4) that *bô'* is used in this way earlier in the book of Ecclesiastes. The Septuagint, though, emends the text to "the wicked are brought *[mwb'ym]* to the tombs" (*eis taphous eisax-thentas*), suggesting that the *mem* prefixed to the verbal root *bw'* was lost by haplography. Note should also be taken of a line of interpretation that emends tomb *(qᵉburîm)* to a form of the verb *qrb* "to approach." See, in particular, the article by J. J. Serrano, "I Saw the Wicked Buried (Eccl. 8,10)," *CBQ* 16 (1954): 168-70, where his interpretation leads to the following translation: "And then I saw the wicked approach, they entered and went out of the holy place, and they were praised in the city because they acted thus. Indeed this is vanity."

38. The exact referent here is ambiguous. Jarick (*Gregory Thaumaturgos' Para-phrase*, p. 344, n. 21) summarizes the positions: Gordis (*Koheleth*, p. 295) and C. W. Reines ("Koheleth viii, 10," *JJS* 5 [1954]: 86-87) believe that this is a reference to a cemetery; Barton (*The Book of Ecclesiastes*, p. 153), the temple; and Eaton (*Ecclesiastes*, p. 122), Jerusalem.

39. While some translate the *'ašer* with a temporal force ("when"), it is best to take it as causal here, due to the conjunction (*'al-kēn*) that begins the main clause of the sentence (Podechard, *L'Ecclésiaste*, p. 401).

40. The word *sentence (pitgām)* has occasioned much discussion because it is one of two possible Persian loanwords in the book (see the discussion of *pardēs* at 2:5). Many have argued that it came to the book via Aramaic. After all, while it also occurs in the late biblical book of Esther (1:20), it occurs often in the Aramaic portions of Daniel and Ezra. Thus, the conclusion has been drawn that this Persian loan is a sign of linguistic lateness (Barton, *The Book of Ecclesiastes*, p. 52). Fredericks (*Qoheleth's Language*, pp. 242, 244-45), however, argues that Persian influence may have been earlier.

In connection with the meaning of *pitgām*, it should be noted that the Septuagint apparently misunderstood the word when it translated "controversy" or "counterstatement."

12 *For*[43] *sinners do evil a hundred times*[44] *and their days are lengthened*
   — although I know that it will be well for those who fear God because
   they fear him,

13 *and it will not be well for the wicked, and their days will not lengthen*
   like a shadow,[45] *because they do not fear God.*

14 *There is another example of meaninglessness that is done on the earth:*
   There are righteous people who are treated[46] *as if they did wicked*
   deeds.[47]

Jarick (*Gregory Thaumaturgos' Paraphrase*, p. 213), who brought this problem to my attention, also points out that the Targum, Symmachus, and the Syriac translated it correctly.

41. There is some confusion about the verb *is carried out (naʿăśâ)*. The form is a niphal perfect, but this strikes many as unusual in that they believe that the negative particle *not (ʾên)* occurs only before participles (e.g., Ogden, *Qoheleth*, p. 136). However, Ginsburg (*The Song of Songs and Coheleth*, p. 201) had long ago answered this objection that *ʾên* may indeed be "used with finite verbal forms (Jer. 38:5; Job 35:15)." For a full discussion of the problem, though he leaves it unsolved (since a further problem involves gender concord between subject and verb), see Isaksson, *Studies in the Language of Qoheleth*, pp. 73-74.

42. I leave untranslated the prepositional phrase with its pronominal suffix *(bāhem)*, because I agree with Murphy (*Ecclesiastes*, p. 81) that it "can be construed with *mlʾ* and is in itself redundant."

43. *For (ʾăšer)* once again (see v. 11) opens the verse. Here, as there, the force of the relative is causal. Many translations render the verse concessively, but according to Ginsburg (*The Song of Songs and Coheleth*, p. 407) "Gesenius . . . and Ewald, . . . who assign to it this concessive signification, have not adduced a single instance to justify this unnatural sense." Whybray (*Ecclesiastes*, NCB, p. 137), Delitzsch (*Proverbs, Ecclesiastes, Song of Solomon*, p. 348), and Gordis (*Koheleth*, pp. 296-97) also say that the relative cannot have the sense of "although" (contra NIV).

44. The Hebrew text has the word *hundred* in the construct state *(mēʾat)*. Perhaps a form of the word "time" *(paʿam)* fell out of the text or was simply understood by the reader. Another possibility is that the form in the text is an "archaic absolute" (Gordis, *Koheleth*, p. 297). The textual history of the verse indicates that some early readers struggled with it. For instance (see Jarick, *Gregory Thaumaturgos' Paraphrase*, p. 215, for a helpful discussion of the text), the Septuagint read "from that time" *(apo tote*, presumably reading *mēʾāz)*. The other Greek translations (Aquila, Theodotion, Symmachus) departed from both the Hebrew and the Septuagint, understanding a form of the root *mût*, "to die," to be in the text *(apethanen)*. The Syriac and Targum preserve the MT.

45. The Septuagint read "in a shadow" *(en skia)*, apparently confusing the preposition *kaph* with *beth*.

46. According to Ogden (*Qoheleth*, pp. 138-39), the semantic development is as follows: "The hiphil participle, *maggîaʿ*, from *ngʿ* 'to reach,' carries the idea of 'extend as far as,' thence 'befall.' "

47. Here and in the second colon of the parallelism *maʿăśēh* is given its normal meaning "deed(s)," but some take it as "recompense" or "reward" (e.g., Gordis, *Koheleth*, p. 298; Crenshaw, *Ecclesiastes*, p. 156).

and there are wicked people who are treated as if they did
righteous deeds.
I say that this too is meaningless.

15 *Then I commended pleasure, for there is nothing better for people*
under the sun except to eat and to drink and to have pleasure. It will
accompany them in their toil during the days of their life that God
gives them under the sun.

10 This verse vies for the most difficult in the book, and thus I begin its
exposition by admitting that certainty eludes every honest interpreter, even
though the problems are often hidden behind smooth English translations. Since
it is impossible to summarize all the suggested approaches, I will present my
rendering along with a description of some of its major contenders.

It is clear that the verse does speak of the *wicked* and of *the holy place,*
and since it concludes with the "meaningless" formula, there must be some
anomalous connection between the holy place and the wicked that contributes
to Qohelet's feeling that the wicked do not get what they deserve. This starting
point, however, is at odds with the most natural reading of the verse as it
stands in the MT, a reading represented by the following paraphrase (I am
paraphrasing here because even this reading involves emendation, which
signals to me that the verse is problematic from a textual point of view):
Qohelet observes that wicked people die and their deeds are forgotten (the
verb in the MT is the hithpael of *škḥ*) in the city where they were active in
the holy place. On a surface level that sounds like good news to the righteous:
What could be better than to have the wickedness of the evil slide into
oblivion? But Qohelet surprises us and concludes, "This too is meaningless."

Scholars have taken two approaches to the problem. Christian Ginsburg,[48] Franz Delitzsch,[49] and Roland Murphy[50] retain the verb "were forgotten" *(yištakᵉḥû)* but understand the whole clause to read: "But those were
forgotten in the city who acted justly" (supplying the adverb at the end; it is
not in the Hebrew text).[51] These scholars understand this phrase to indicate
the actions not of the wicked but, with a subtle shift in the focus of the verse,
of the righteous. The shift is too subtle, however. It is not signaled by the text
at all, so I find the argument tenuous.

The other approach is adopted here and argues on the basis of the
ancient versions[52] for a slight emendation from the hitpael of *škḥ* "to forget"

---

48. Ginsburg, *The Song of Songs and Coheleth,* pp. 398-99.
49. Delitzsch, *Proverbs, Ecclesiastes, Song of Solomon,* p. 346.
50. Murphy, *Ecclesiastes,* pp. 79-80.
51. Murphy, *Ecclesiastes,* p. 79.
52. Specifically the Septuagint, Aquila, Symmachus, Theodotion, and the Vulgate.
Note Jerome as well.

to the hithpael of *šbḥ* "to praise." With this reading (see also NIV, NRSV, and numerous modern commentators), the verse clearly pinpoints a logical cause behind Qohelet's frustration. The wicked may indeed die, but even then they are buried and praised in the city where they did their evil deeds and religious posturing. It is the fact that the wicked continue to receive the praise owed to the righteous that frustrates Qohelet and leads him to utter his conclusion that "this is meaningless."

11 My interpretation of the difficult preceding verse indicated that the absence of retribution was at the heart of Qohelet's frustration. He now formulates the problem and states why it is a problem. In this verse, Qohelet asserts that when there is no apparent punishment for evil, then it will flourish. If people do not observe negative consequences for bad actions, they will be encouraged to do even more evil.

It is true that Qohelet never says that evil always prospers, or that it is never punished. But he does argue that the lack of a quick and clear punishment is enough to encourage wicked people to foster new evil plans.

It is (intentionally?) unclear whether Qohelet refers to human or divine retribution here, but perhaps it is both rather than one or the other. However, only theological, not exegetical, considerations could lead pious interpreters such as Gregory Thaumaturgos to see in this verse a testimony to God's saving patience.[53]

12 The first part of the verse continues the thought of v. 11. Qohelet notes that there are gross sinners who may live for a very long time, thus once again providing evidence against a doctrine of retribution. After all, a long life was taught to be the result of God's blessing (Prov. 3:2, 16, 18, and throughout the book of Proverbs).

The second half of the verse at first seems to move in a different direction, and, unless close attention is given to the wording and the flow of the passage, it might mistakenly be believed that Qohelet is going back in the direction of what is thought to be traditional wisdom instruction. In seeming contradiction to the first half of the verse, Qohelet states that things will go well for those who fear God.

Qohelet, however, gives us a signal that he is stating an argument that is not his own, and thus he is not contradicting himself. His unusual use of the participle of the root *yd'*, *know*, is out of keeping with his usual use of the word — the finite form of the verb is typical of Qohelet and is used by him when he is giving the results of his empirical investigations. Thus, the participle here, in the words of Bo Isaksson, show us that Qohelet is imparting "the kind of knowledge that represented the *comme il faut* teaching of the sages."[54] This

---

53. As in 2 Pet. 3:9; see Jarick, *Gregory Thaumaturgos' Paraphrase,* pp. 213-14.
54. Isaksson, *Studies in the Language of Qoheleth,* p. 67.

continues into the next verse. In any case, v. 15 will once again revert to Qohelet's typical skepticism concerning retribution.[55]

13 Qohelet here flatly contradicts what he stated in v. 12a and continues the line of thought he began in v. 12b. In v. 12a he expressed his frustration that sinners live a long time. Here he states just as baldly that the wicked will not live a long time, and that they will not live long because they do not fear God. It is difficult to tell whether Qohelet thus exposes his own conflicting thoughts or else is quoting traditional wisdom, perhaps because he knows it is the right thing to do. In any case, as v. 14 confirms, Qohelet continues to question the doctrine of retribution, thus showing that vv. 12b-13 are out of keeping with the mainstream of his thinking. Graham Ogden is wrong when he concludes from this verse that "Qoheleth basically supports the traditional view about divine justice."[56]

The image of the *shadow* is appropriate here because as the day ends the shadows gradually lengthen. Thus, the lives of the wicked will not grow longer as they approach the end of their days. Alternatively, the image of the *shadow* could point to the brevity of life, but this interpretation would presuppose a reading of the verse that might be paraphrased "their days will not be lengthened, (but they will be) like a shadow (that is short-lived)."[57] While the use of the image of a shadow for brevity may be more traditional, the syntax of the verse suggests the former approach.

14 Qohelet follows vv. 12b and 13, which sound quite traditional, with a statement that profoundly questions divine retribution. The heart of this verse is an antithetically parallel line that points to the same truth — no one gets what they deserve! The righteous do not get rewarded; they get punished. The wicked do not get punished; they get rewarded. Once again we are back to the teaching of vv. 10-12a.

The verse opens with the existential particle *yēš (There is),* which Qohelet characteristically uses to introduce an example story (see my comment at 2:21). Thus, though the text has just the word *meaningless (hebel)* here, it seems awkward in context, and so I translate *another example of meaninglessness.* This example takes place *on the earth,* which is simply another way of saying "under the sun" (see 1:3).

Though the text does not name God as the one who ignores or frustrates the moral order, it would be no other.[58] The context has to do

---

55. See Crenshaw, *Ecclesiastes,* p. 155.
56. Ogden, *Qoheleth,* p. 137.
57. This is the approach of the Targum.
58. Jarick (*Gregory Thaumaturgos' Paraphrase,* p. 218) recognized this when, in comparing the Hebrew text to the paraphrase by the pietistic interpreter Gregory Thaumaturgos, he says, "The sage of Jerusalem was accusing God of treating people unjustly, but the bishop of Neocaesarea is accusing people of appraising their fellows falsely."

primarily with death. To treat the righteous and the wicked according to their deserts would mean that the former would die old and the latter young, but this is not the case in Qohelet's experience. Thus, he is thrown into a quandary of doubt, so much doubt, indeed, that he repeats his conclusion that the situation is *meaningless*.

15   The section is brought to a close in a familiar manner, a new turn on the *carpe diem* theme. Once again, Qohelet advocates the simple pleasures of eating and drinking in the light of meaningless existence.

Qohelet speaks in the first person and *commends pleasure*. The verb was already encountered in 4:2 (in that context translated "praised") where Qohelet envied the dead in the light of oppression. I observed at that time that Qohelet could advocate both death and pleasure because they both anesthetized people from the harsh realities of life. Qohelet himself saw through the surface of things, and so pleasure could not keep him from frustration (see 2:2). But as the second part of this verse states, God gave some people the ability to actually enjoy pleasure.

R. N. Whybray argues that Qohelet speaks with increasing confidence with each of the positive *carpe diem* passages. He points to the addition of the verb *I commended* before the now characteristic *there is nothing better than* formula (see 2:24; 3:12 and 22).[59] When read in the light of the previous context (particularly 8:14), however, it takes on a tone of strident desperation, or perhaps resignation.

The second sentence of the verse begins with a third-person independent pronoun that clearly refers to *pleasure*. The verb, a qal of *lwh,* occurs in this meaning only in Ecclesiastes, though Daniel Fredericks guards against arguments that this indicates a late date for the language of the book.[60]

9. Not Even the Wise Know (8:16-17)

Qohelet here restates the goal of his intellectual labor (vv. 16-17a). He wants to *know wisdom* (v. 16), but his conclusions are extremely disappointing. What he discovers is the limitation of knowledge. No one, not even the wise, can understand what is going on in the world. As in 7:25-29 Qohelet admits that no one can find *(māṣā',* here translated *comprehend)* the world. This admission is extremely important for our understanding of the frame narrator's perception of Qohelet's work (see 12:10).

---

59. This is the gist of the argument in Whybray, "Qohelet, Preacher of Joy," pp. 87-98.

60. Whitley (*Koheleth,* pp. 66-67) argues that the verb is late. Fredericks (*Qoheleth's Language,* p. 174) points out that the verb occurs in a similar form in Gen. 29:34, which is usually associated with J and is thus early.

16 As[61] *I devoted myself[62] to know wisdom and to observe the task[63] that is done on the earth, for no one sees sleep day or night,*

17 *I observed all the work of God. Clearly[64] no one is able to comprehend the work that is done under the sun, on account of[65] which he toils in order to seek, but he does not comprehend. Even if the wise man says he knows, he is not able to comprehend it.*

16 Qohelet again describes his goal, using language reminiscent of 1:13 and 2:12. He states his devotion to the pursuit of wisdom and his observation of what is going on in the world. This verse is connected to the next verse as a protasis to an apodosis.[66]

The difficult part of the present verse is the second half, which seems awkwardly connected to the first. Woodenly literal, the verse would be rendered (ignoring for the moment the opening conjunction) "in day and in night sleep in his eyes not seeing." Among other problems, the antecedent to "sleep" is not clear and the idiom of "seeing sleep" is foreign to both Hebrew (it is a hapax here) and English.[67]

The general sense seems clear enough, though. As Graham Ogden puts it, "presumably people are so preoccupied with their business that they never have the chance to sleep or rest properly."[68] The idea is related to that expressed in 2:23.

While some think that Qohelet refers only to himself,[69] the pronoun likely anticipates the *hāʾādām* in the next verse.[70] And though *seeing sleep* is unusual, it is certainly understandable.

The remaining issue is the phrase's connection within the verse (and

---

61. Translating *kaʾᵃšer* in its temporal sense. The Septuagint apparently read *ba* instead of *ka* prefixed to the relative. Such an emendation, however, is unnecessary.

62. For this expression, see the commentary at 1:13.

63. See comments on this word at 1:13 and 3:10.

64. So rendering the *kî*, which is understood in its asseverative function.

65. *on account of which* is an unusual form in biblical Hebrew *(bᵉšel ʾᵃšer)*. Whitley *(Koheleth,* p. 77) is typical in taking it as an Aramaism. Fredericks *(Qoheleth's Language,* p. 220), citing Ewald before him, attempts to argue against this by offering an emendation based on the versions to "in all that" *(bᵉkōl ʾᵃšer).* He remarks on the repetition of the MT. This argument is weak, however, since repetition is a well-known characteristic of Qohelet's style. Thus, I stay with the MT.

66. Isaksson, *Studies in the Language of Qoheleth,* pp. 16-17.

67. Many commentators are quick to point out parallels in Latin poetry, though no significance is made of it (e.g., Gordis, *Koheleth,* p. 298; Murphy, *Ecclesiastes,* p. 81).

68. Ogden, *Qoheleth,* pp. 140-41.

69. Fox, *Qohelet and His Contradictions,* p. 255, even emending to "my eyes."

70. Crenshaw, *Ecclesiastes,* p. 157.

with the next). It is true that *kî gam* may signal a parenthetical remark,[71] but it may also be understood simply as *for,* a common understanding of the particle *kî.*

17   The chapter concludes on a note of skepticism. In spite of hard labor, no one may figure what God is up to in the universe. Qohelet first remarks on people in general, and then, in specific, points out that not even the wise, noted for their insight, can really understand the *work of God.*

The verse is the apodosis of v. 16. I have broken up v. 17 into separate English sentences for ease of understanding and reading. The teaching of the verse — that no one can fathom God and his ways — is a major theme in Qohelet's speech (3:11; 7:25-29; 9:12; 11:5).

Aarre Lauha is correct to see that the answer to Qohelet's frustration is divine revelation. He cites Matthew 16:17, Romans 1:19-20, and 1 Corinthians 1:21 as the NT solution to Qohelet's problem. Of course, God also revealed himself, accurately though not fully, during the OT period, so even from an orthodox OT perspective Qohelet's frustration is hard to understand. But as Lauha notes, "For Qohelet there are no means of revelation. History, nature, and cult are all silent in this regard according to him."[72]

SUMMARY OF CHAPTER 8

In this chapter Qohelet seriously questions some of the assumed tenets of wisdom theology. In the first place, he continues a line of thinking from the previous chapter as he expresses skepticism concerning the power of wisdom (8:1). No one can know the future, not even the wise (8:16-17).

In 8:2-9 Qohelet gives typical wisdom advice concerning how one should act in the presence of a king, but then he undermines his advice as he admits the limits of wisdom once again. The skepticism of the chapter is also directed toward divine retribution as Qohelet questions whether the wicked are really punished (vv. 10-15).

71. So Delitzsch, *Proverbs, Ecclesiastes, Song of Solomon,* p. 352.

72. Lauha, *Kohelet,* p. 162, "Nur für Kohelet gibt es keine Offenbarungsmittel. Geschichte, Natur und Kult sind für ihn in dieser Hinsicht stumm."

10. One Fate for All (9:1-10)

As a survey of different commentaries indicates, the next two chapters are especially difficult to subdivide. Fortunately, our interpretation of the text does not depend on the exact division of the text into subunits.

The message of the first ten verses of Ecclesiastes 9 is among the most clearly pessimistic of the entire book, though its thought has already been encountered: Death comes to all and is the definitive end. Acting righteously or religiously does not save anyone from death, which, according to Qohelet, is a fate worse than life. The only recourse for human beings is to eke out whatever enjoyment life offers (vv. 7-10), because there is nothing beyond the grave.

Thus, once again we may observe that Qohelet's command to enjoy life *(carpe diem)* occurs in a context that demands we read it with a note of resignation.

> 1 Indeed,[1] I devoted myself[2] to all this and to examine[3] all this: the righteous and the wise and their works[4] are all in the hand of God. However, no one knows whether love or hate awaits them.[5]

1. Taking the *kî* as an asseverative (Schoors, *The Preacher Sought to Find Pleasing Words*, pp. 107-8), though there may be a weak connection with the previous unit that would argue for the causative, "for" (Fox, *Qohelet and His Contradictions*, p. 256).

2. The MT has the preposition *'el* where we would expect the direct object marker *'et*. It might be best to emend on the basis of normative usage, though if the MT is the result of a textual error, it is an early one since it is reflected in the Septuagint *(eis)*.

3. This verb *(lābûr)* is difficult. Some take it as a form of the root *bwr*, in the sense of "to examine," but if so, then it is a hapax. More likely it is related to a similar verb *brr*, perhaps as a by-form with the same meaning ("to test"; see 3:18). It should be noted that many versions attest to a variant, which stems from a form of the verb *rā'â* "to see."

4. This word *('ăbādêhem)* is pointed like an Aramaic noun (see Whitley, *Koheleth*, p. 78; Crenshaw, *Ecclesiastes*, p. 159; Schoors, *The Preacher Sought to Find Pleasing Words*, pp. 60-61), but for arguments against using this as evidence against a late date, see Fredericks, *Qoheleth's Language*, pp. 233-34.

5. Literally, "all are before them" *(hakkōl lipnēhem)*. The end of the verse is very awkward in the MT, leading many to suggest an emendation. The most common follows the Septuagint, which connects the phrase with the beginning of v. 2 and emends *hakkōl* to *hebel*, "meaningless." Thus, the emended phrase would read "all before them is vanity." I have retained the MT and take the "all" as a reference to love and hate, thus perhaps better rendered, even in the literal rendition, as "both." The "before" is taken in a temporal and not in a locative sense. The translation *awaits them* is thus an idiomatic translation of the MT.

2   *Everything is the same for everybody:*[6] *there is one fate for the righ-*
teous and the wicked[7] *and for the clean and the unclean, and for the*
one who sacrifices and for the one who does not sacrifice; as it is for
the good, so it is for the sinner; as it is for the one who swears, so it
is for the one who is afraid to swear.

3   *This is evil among all that is done under the sun. For there is one fate*
for all, and furthermore the human heart is full of evil, and madness
is in their hearts during their lives, and afterward[8] — *to the dead!*

4   *Indeed,*[9] *there is hope*[10] *for whomever is joined to all the living. For*
it is better for a live dog[11] *than a dead lion.*

6. This opening phrase *(hakkōl ka'ašer lakkōl)* is extremely difficult. For part of the discussion, consult the comment on the previous verse, where I review the reasons and arguments in favor of emendation. However, I feel (along with many others; see Plumptre, *Ecclesiastes; or, the Preacher,* p. 184; Gordis *Koheleth,* p. 300; Whybray *Ecclesiastes,* NCB, p. 141; and Jarick, *Gregory Thaumaturgos' Paraphrase,* p. 225) that the MT makes sense as it stands. My translation is closest to that of Crenshaw, *Ecclesiastes,* p. 158.

7. The MT has "for the good" *(lattôb).* It is awkward in the text, however, because it stands alone in a context where each word is paired with another. One solution is to suggest scribal haplography and emend (primarily on the basis of the Septuagint "and for the wicked" [*kai tō kakō*]). Fox (*Qohelet and His Contradictions,* p. 257) supports this alternative by saying that the Septuagint is too literal in Ecclesiastes to believe that the translator added it. More persuasive, however, is the fact that *tôb* appears later in the verse in a pair, raising the question whether the word would have appeared in two pairs in the verse. In the words of Ogden (*Qoheleth,* p. 146), "the first and solitary *tôb* represents a later intrusion into the text." I thus omit it from my translation.

8. Literally, the MT has "after it" *('aḥᵃrāyw).* However, along with Murphy (*Ecclesiastes,* p. 89), I understand the phrase in an adverbial sense here. The singular suffix has perplexed some since it follows a series of plural suffixes (cf. *their hearts* and *their lives*). Thus, it is not surprising that the Septuagint and the Syriac have plural suffixes. Note should be taken as well of Symmachus, who translates "their end" *(ta de teleuteta autōn).*

9. Taking the *kî* in its asseverative rather than its causal function, since the verse does not appear to provide a motivation for the preceding.

10. It is often (e.g., Gordis, *Koheleth,* p. 309; Whitley, *Koheleth,* p. 80) argued that *biṭṭāhôn* with the meaning *hope* is late, since in its only other biblical occurrence its meaning is "trust" or "confidence" (see 2 Kings 18:19 = Isa. 36:4). Fredericks (*Qoheleth's Language,* p. 179), though, correctly points out that the semantic range between *hope* and "trust/confidence" is too narrow to posit such a strong chronological distinction.

11. The force of the *lamed* prefix before *dog* is a vexed question, but it fortunately does not affect the interpretation of the verse. Some understand it to mark the emphatic (Waltke and O'Connor, *Biblical Hebrew Syntax,* p. 212; Wright, *The Book of Koheleth,* p. 409; and Whitley, *Koheleth,* p. 80), while others believe it marks *dog* as a *casus pendens* (GKC §143e). I prefer to follow Fox (*Qohelet and His Contradictions,* p. 258), who treats it as a preposition.

5 *For the living know they will die, but the dead know nothing. There is no longer any reward[12] for them, for the memory of them is forgotten.*

6 *Their love, their hate, and their jealousy have already perished. They have no portion any longer in anything that is done under the sun.*

7 *Go, eat your food with pleasure, and drink your wine with a merry heart, for God has already approved your deeds.*

8 *Let your clothes be white[13] at all times, and do not spare oil on your head.*

9 *Enjoy life[14] with the wife whom you love all the days of your meaningless life, that is, all the meaningless days[15] he has given you under the sun, for it[16] is your reward in life and for the toil that you do[17] under the sun.*

10 *All that your hand finds to do, do with your power,[18] for there is no action or thought or knowledge or wisdom in the grave where you are going.*

1 Qohelet begins with an assertion of the intensity of his search for meaning in life. Once again he returns to the thought that people do not automatically get what they deserve; indeed, the possibility exists that they may get the opposite of what they deserve through their actions (see 3:17-22 and 8:10-15).

12. This word *(śkr)* may have been chosen in this context because of its assonance with *memory (zkr)*.

13. According to A. Brenner (*Colour Terms in the Old Testament* JSOTSup 21 [Sheffield, England: JSOT Press, 1982], pp. 90-91), this word is "a property of brightness more than hue." She also points out that "white clothes" is a hapax in the OT, though it does occur in Mishnaic Hebrew.

14. Compare similar expressions in 2:1 and 3:13.

15. Some Hebrew manuscripts and the Syriac omit this repetitive phrase *(kol yᵉmê ḥayyê heblekā)* as a dittography. A few Hebrew manuscripts and the Targum omit the entire subordinate phrase (see *BHS*), but the text makes sense as it stands.

16. So Furkovitch (L) and the Qere of Oriental manuscripts. The Ketib of Oriental manuscripts reads "she" *(hî')*, thus drawing a closer connection with the woman in the first part of the sentence.

17. This is the verb and its cognate *(ûba'ᵃmālᵉkā 'ᵃšer-'attâ 'āmēl);* see n. 14 to 1:3.

18. The Masoretic accents would indicate that *with your power (bᵉkōḥᵃkā)* should go with the first clause of the verse. Ginsburg (*The Song of Songs and Coheleth*, p. 417) thus renders the verse: "Whatever thine hand findeth to do, whilst thou art able, do it." However, there are some Hebrew manuscripts as well as most versions that divide the line in the manner that I have. It should also be noted that the Septuagint apparently misunderstood the preposition *beth* as a *kaph*, thus rendering *hōs,* and the whole clause is then translated "as you can"; see Jarick, *Gregory Thaumaturgos' Paraphrase*, p. 346, n. 16.

Qohelet does not doubt that the *righteous* and the *wise* are in God's control — *the hand of God* is certainly an image of God's power and control — but he does doubt whether God is concerned to reward them or is well disposed toward them. In the context it is clear that the *love* and *hate* are divine and not human.

2 This verse is closely associated with the previous verse and carries forward its thought. It repeats the point that Qohelet has already made (2:14) that everyone, no matter what their character or lifestyle, will meet the same end: death.

Qohelet makes his point here by citing five pairs of opposites. While some of the pairs may have general application (*the righteous and the wicked; the good person . . . the sinner*), others are clearly from a cultic setting (*the clean . . . the unclean; the one who swears . . . the one who is afraid to swear*). The latter probably has to do with the taking of religious oaths. It is difficult, though, to tell which is the negative and which the positive. In other words, is it good or bad to be afraid to swear an oath? In the previous pairs, the first unit was good, the second, bad. Following this pattern, those who are afraid to take an oath would be those who were hesitant to accomplish things for God. However, Qohelet had earlier (though using a different vocabulary) warned against taking a vow too hastily (5:3-4 [English 5:4-5]). In addition, we might have a climactic reversal to the good-bad pattern, supporting the variance in the line in terms of syntax.

3 The *this (zeh)* that opens the verse refers to that which is expressed in vv. 1-2: everyone, regardless of merit, will die! The translation of this opening sentence is awkward in English and may actually have the force of the superlative. This view is shared by the Vulgate *(pessimum)* and Ibn Ezra and is best articulated by Christian Ginsburg, who states: "the preposition b^e in $b^ek\bar{o}l$ gives to $r\bar{a}^\cdot$ the force of the superlative, making it stand forth prominently as evil in the midst (b^e) of all other evils; none of all those by which it is surrounded can eclipse it."[19]

The remainder of the verse reasserts the tragedy that death is the end of everyone in spite of the way they live or conduct themselves in the cult. It adds the moral dimension that human beings are thoroughly sinful while they live. The use of $r\bar{a}^\cdot$ here must be moral, thus supporting the moral translation of it in its first occurrence in the verse.[20] The course of one's life is characterized by *evil* and *madness,* and what can a person expect at the end? Death. The abrupt syntax at the end of the verse is intentional and reflects the suddenness of death in the midst of life.

4 The theme of death continues. Qohelet surprisingly begins by say-

---

19. Ginsburg, *The Song of Songs and Coheleth*, p. 325.
20. Contra Ogden, *Qoheleth*, pp. 146-47.

ing that the living have hope, even though in the previous verse he described life as full of evil and madness. However, as wisdom is better than folly, but only on a relative scale (2:12-16), so life is better than death. Indeed, the *hope* mentioned here is a false one. Though there may be some pleasure, it all ends up in death, which is the end of all knowing and feeling (9:7-10).[21]

The phrase *for whomever is joined to all the living (kî-mî ʾašer yᵉbuḥar ʾel kol-haḥayyîm)* is awkward in Hebrew as well as in English. A more idiomatic rendering might be "for whoever is among all the living." Even this translation depends on rejecting the Ketib and following the Qere (supported by about twenty Hebrew manuscripts, the versions, and a number of modern commentators) in understanding a textual error (metathesis) and restoring a form of the verb ḥbr "to join" in place of the verb bḥr "to choose." A plausible rendering has been suggested by Ginsburg, who connects the first phrase in v. 4 with the end of v. 3 and translates "yet, after it, they go to the dead; for who is excepted?"[22] In this he is followed by James Crenshaw[23] and Roland Murphy.[24]

The short proverb that ends the verse makes it clear that Qohelet is favoring life over death here, but it is a sarcastic or bitter preference. While modern Western cultures prize their canines, the OT imbibes the ancient Near Eastern attitude that they are dirty, horrible animals. They are wild, live on garbage, and will eat cadavers if given an opportunity. "Le chien, animal impur, est en Orient un objet de mépris (I Sam. xvii,43; xxiv,15; II Sam. iii,8; ix,8; xvi,9; Math. xv,26; Apoc. xxii,15)."[25] Yet the *lion* is a noble beast, "le symbole de la force (Gen. xlix,9; Is. xxxviii,13; Lam. iii,10; Os. xiii,7; Job x,16)."[26] Thus, life may be preferred to death, but it is a miserable business, and those who are living also know that they too will die.

5 In this verse, Qohelet presents another reason why the living have a relative advantage over the dead, and an advantage that should probably be connected with the "hope" of the previous verse. That advantage is, simply, consciousness. The living are self-aware, the dead are not.

The sarcasm seems obvious to most.[27] What are the living aware of? Death. Thus, while the living may be better off than the dead, they are nonetheless pitiable.

---

21. Another alternative to the problem is to translate *biṭṭāḥôn* as "confidence" or "trust," an attested biblical meaning (2 Kings 18:19). Qohelet could be saying that the only thing that is certain and that one can have confidence will take place is death (Fox, *Qohelet and His Contradictions*, p. 258).

22. Ginsburg, *The Song of Songs and Coheleth*, pp. 411-12.

23. Crenshaw, *Ecclesiastes*, pp. 160-61.

24. Murphy, *Ecclesiastes*, pp. 88-89.

25. Podechard, *L'Ecclésiaste*, p. 412.

26. Podechard, *L'Ecclésiaste*, p. 412.

27. But see Whybray, *Ecclesiastes*, NCB, pp. 142-43.

Furthermore, the second half of the verse comments on the oblivion of the dead. *reward* likely refers to the end of all earthly wages or benefits, and thus Qohelet is not leaving open the possibility of heavenly rewards. The thought does not even cross his mind.

Pious interpreters have difficulty with this verse. The Targum assumes that it refers to the lack of eternal rewards for the wicked, while Gregory Thaumaturgos believes that Qohelet is quoting a mistaken opinion.[28]

6 The previous verse highlighted awareness as the advantage of life over death. Here, Qohelet is more specific in his listing of three emotions: *love, hate,* and *jealousy.* These three are not all pleasurable emotions, but they certainly are intense. On the one hand, it does appear that Qohelet believes that even unpleasurable emotions are better than no emotions at all. On the other hand, the relative advantage of life is really a double-edged sword: To live is to love, yes, but it is also to hate and envy, not an unmixed blessing.

But at death even these come to an end, and there is nothing left for the person. We have already seen that one's *portion* is limited to this life (2:10, 21; 3:22; 5:17, 18 [English 5:18, 19]; 9:9; 11:2).

7 In the light of death, Qohelet urges his reader/hearer to seek pleasure, specifically, to eat and drink. Graham Ogden is correct to see here a "move from advice to imperative"[29] in this fifth of the so-called *carpe diem* passages (see also the earlier 2:24-26; 3:13-14; 5:17-19 [English 5:18-20]; 8:15). In spite of R. N. Whybray's arguments to the contrary,[30] Qohelet is not moving from doubt to certainty but rather to urgency in the light of death.[31]

Qohelet's motivation clause *(for God has already approved your deeds)* jars the reader. It sounds as if he believes that God gives people unlimited approval for their actions. The possibility of this interpretation is too much for some, so they take great pains to avoid this impression. The Targum gives the verse an eschatological twist by having Solomon as simply the divine spokesperson for this command. The ultimate speaker is the Lord himself, who speaks to the righteous as they enter eternal bliss. They will enjoy food and drink because they had given to those who were in need. Thus, since they are righteous and since their lives are over, God can approve their deeds. By contrast, Gregory Thaumaturgos places this verse in the mouths of those who hate the Lord.[32] This, then, is bad advice.

Ogden further argues that the context restricts God's approval to what

---

28. Jarick, *Gregory Thaumaturgos' Paraphrase,* pp. 229-30.
29. Ogden, *Qoheleth,* p. 151.
30. In Whybray, "Qoheleth, Preacher of Joy."
31. So Crenshaw, *Ecclesiastes,* p. 162.
32. See Jarick, *Gregory Thaumaturgos' Paraphrase,* p. 233.

God's will allows.[33] This is not at all obvious, as the struggles and strained interpretations of the Targum and Gregory indicate.

8 Qohelet continues his call to enjoy this life. He admonishes his hearers to waste no opportunity or expense to seize whatever good things life has to offer. He tells them to put on their best clothes and refresh themselves with oil.

Athalya Brenner, in her study of OT color terms, synthesizes the biblical evidence on white garments and concludes that they can symbolize "purity, festivity, or elevated social status."[34] While pietistic interpreters have gone with purity,[35] the context makes it clear that joy is the reason for white here (compare 2 Chron. 5:2; Esth. 8:12, among other places).

This conclusion is bolstered by the second part of the verse in which Qohelet advises his listeners to pour oil on their head. The hot, dry climate of Palestine is the reason for both the white clothes, which reflect rather than absorb the heat, and the oil, which protected against dry skin (Ps. 23:5; 45:8 [English 45:7]; Prov. 27:9; Isa. 61:3).

9 The commands to enjoy life continue, but with a steady reminder that this is not the ultimate solution to the question of meaning. Specifically, Qohelet tells his listeners to enjoy life in the company of their wives. That is their reward, though life is ultimately meaningless.

It is difficult to tell from the verse whether Qohelet advocates a strong, vibrant marital relationship or promiscuity. The point at issue is the referent of *'iššâ*, here translated "wife" but arguably simply "woman." The strongest argument in favor of the latter is the lack of a definite article, "enjoy life with *a* woman whom you love," thus encouraging going from one infatuation to another like the legendary Solomon. However, Charles Whitley cites Genesis 21:21; 24:3; and Leviticus 20:14 as examples of *'iššâ* without the definite article referring to a wife.[36] While James Crenshaw is correct in his counter that these verses refer not to a married woman but to one who will be taken in marriage — not a wife per se[37] — we still have to reckon with the rather unpredictable way in which the definite article is used in this book. Although the "promiscuous" view has had strong advocates, including Jerome, Ibn Ezra, and Ginsburg,[38] the view that Qohelet refers to a wife has an even older and perhaps stronger history (see the comment on this verse by the Midrash *Koheleth Rabbah:*[39] "A man who has no wife lives without good, help, joy,

---

33. Ogden, *Qoheleth,* p. 152.

34. Brenner, *Colour Terms,* p. 90.

35. Compare the Targum and Hengstenberg, *A Commentary on Ecclesiastes,* pp. 214-15.

36. Whitley, *Koheleth,* p. 80.

37. Crenshaw, *Ecclesiastes,* p. 163.

38. Ginsburg, *The Song of Songs and Coheleth,* p. 416.

39. Quoted by Jarick, *Gregory Thaumaturgos' Paraphrase,* p. 235.

blessing, and atonement"). This view also seems more in keeping with its ancient setting. The command to enjoy a promiscuous lifestyle sounds like a postsexual revolution statement and not like one an Israelite wise man, no matter how confused and questioning, would make to his students.

Yet the important point of the verse is not changed whether Qohelet refers to a wife or to an unmarried woman: enjoyment may be found in this life. It is not an enjoyment, however, that overrules his assessment of life as a whole: it is *hebel, meaningless.*

Such enjoyment too is a momentary respite from the tragedy and evil of the present world, no more and no less. Where do these *meaningless days* come from? The text leaves it implicit, *he has given you.* The context makes it quite clear that the *he* is God. After all, who else could do it? Thus, this verse fits in with the others that speak of God giving things to humans.

10 This verse climaxes Qohelet's appeal to enjoy life in the present, especially in view of death. He urges his listeners to act now, because death brings everything to a stop.

Disagreement exists over exactly what Qohelet is asking his reader to *do.* Some think this argues for complete license to do whatever one can and wants. Others say that it is a call to work hard. The reference probably cannot be restricted to either. A comparison with other uses of the idiom (Judg. 9:33; 1 Sam. 10:7) indicates that the issue is opportunity.[40] If you have a chance to do something, do it now, because who knows what the future will bring.

Indeed, it might bring death, and in death there are no opportunities at all. The second half of this verse is one of the clearest indications that Qohelet had absolutely no concept of life after death. Those who wish to argue otherwise are reduced to special pleading of the most obvious kind, like Ernst Hengstenberg, who remarks, "there are forms of knowledge and work which belong only to the present life, and he who does not employ them has buried his talent in the earth, and thus committed a heavy sin, — a sin, the consequences of which will stretch into eternity."[41] John 9:4 is not parallel here[42] because the night referred to there is not death in general but Christ's death, and the work is specifically his redemptive work.

The list of things absent after death, *actions, thought, knowledge,* and *wisdom,* suggest both physical and mental processes coming to a complete end. For Qohelet death is the absolute end. We thus see that "under the sun" entails the entirety of human possibility; it is no wonder that ultimate meaning eluded him.

40. Hengstenberg, *A Commentary on Ecclesiastes,* p. 216.
41. Hengstenberg, *A Commentary on Ecclesiastes,* p. 216.
42. So Delitzsch, *Proverbs, Ecclesiastes, Song of Songs,* p. 364.

11. Time and Chance (9:11-12)

The previous section urged the enjoyment of the present in the light of death, but now Qohelet admits that the present may not be easily manipulated and is subject to frustration and disappointment.

Qohelet's main point is that there is no way one can prepare for victorious living. Human ability is prey to the ravages of chance. Aarre Lauha compares and contrasts Romans 9:16: "It does not, therefore, depend on man's desire or effort, but on God's mercy."[43] In other words, human inability drives Paul to divine grace, while Qohelet ends up in frustration.

> 11 *Then I turned and observed[44] something else under the sun. That is, the race is not to the swift, the battle not to the mighty, nor is food for the wise, nor wealth to the clever, nor favor to the intelligent, but time and chance happen to all of them.*

> 12 *Indeed, no one knows his time. Like fish that are entangled in an evil[45] net and like birds caught in a snare, so[46] people are ensnared[47] in an evil time, when it suddenly falls on them.*

11 Qohelet now looks at life and concludes that time and chance determine who prospers and who does not. It is not necessarily those who are more able or gifted that reap the benefits of life.

The opening idiom, *I turned and observed*, starts a new subject, but it is related to the previous topic. In the previous section the fact of death compelled Qohelet to encourage enjoyment in the present. However, vv. 11-12 warn that the present cannot be manipulated in one's favor because ultimately *time and chance* rule the outcome of one's life, not any ability.

---

43. See Lauha, *Kohelet*, p. 174.

44. This idiom *(šabtî werā'ôh)* occurs in 4:1, where it is explained. See also 4:7. The only difference is that here the verb "observe" is an infinitive absolute *(rā'ōh)*, whereas in its earlier occurrences in the idiom it was a regular finite verb. However, there is no significant difference in meaning.

45. The Vulgate and the Targum do not have the adjective *evil*, and on this basis Lauha *(Kohelet*, p. 172) omits it. But this seems slim evidence to remove something that strengthens the analogy of the verse (see the Septuagint *kakō*).

46. Literally, "as these, people . . ." *(kāhēm . . . benê hā'ādām)*, but this sounds awkward in English. It should be noted that the Peshitta translated "thus . . . ," apparently reading *kōh*, and presumably took the *mem* as the prefix on the following participle (see n. 47).

47. The two previous verbs *entangled* and *caught* have the same verbal root *('ḥz)*, but this verb *ensnared*, while in the same semantic domain, is different *(yqš)*. Further, its form is somewhat unusual. The vocalization leads me to think that it is a pual participle without the *mem* prefix. This is an unusual but not unattested form (see GKC §52s for other examples).

The verse lists five lines of evidence that demonstrate that things do not always turn out as we might presume. We would expect the fastest person to win a footrace, the most seasoned and powerful warriors to win a battle — that is, the most physically capable are expected to come out on top in a physical contest. But Qohelet reminds us that this is not always true.

We might also expect that the most mentally competent would have the best parts of life as well, but here we learn that being *wise, clever,* or *intelligent* assures people of absolutely nothing. Everyone is subject to the vicissitudes of time, over which they have no control. We need to feel the shock of Qohelet, a wise man, telling his hearers that, though wisdom may be better than folly, it is irrelevant when disrupted by death (2:12-17) or if chance does not give the wise person the opportunity to thrive.

12 The issues surrounding chance, the unpredictability of life, are brought into explicit connection with death. No one knows when they are going to die. The two images from wildlife support this idea. Fish may swim blithely along and birds may fly effortlessly through the air, and then in a moment they are struggling in a trap that will lead to the end of their lives.

Qohelet believes that *no one* is aware when his end will come. This, of course, includes the wise, who once again have no ultimate advantage over other humans.

The emphasis in the verse is on the suddenness of calamity. People remain unaware until the last moment that the end is upon them, and this colors their enjoyment of the present.

12. Limitations of Wisdom: An Example Story (9:13-16)

Once again, Qohelet uses an anecdote (cf. 4:7-8) to suggest that, though wisdom has a short-term effect, it amounts to nothing over the long run. The story incarnates Qohelet's point that wisdom in the final analysis is meaningless.

13 *Moreover I observed this example of wisdom[48] under the sun, and it made a big impression on[49] me.*

14 *There was a small city and there were a few people in it. A great king invaded and surrounded it. He built huge siegeworks[50] against it.*

---

48. Literally "I observed wisdom under the sun" *(rāʾîtî ḥokmâ taḥat haššāmeš),* which is adequate but somewhat awkward in English. Some alternative approaches include the suggestion to emend by dropping *wisdom (ḥokmâ;* cf. *BHS),* but this is unnecessary. There is no evidence of a textual problem. For the problem that what follows is not an example of wisdom, see the commentary on the verse. I add *example* generally on the basis of context and specifically because this verse introduces an example story.

49. *ʾēlāy* is perhaps to be emended to *ʿālî* on the basis of 6:1.

50. This word *(mᵉṣôdîm)* is translated "snare" in 7:26 and "net" in 9:12. Thus,

15 *A poor but wise man was found*[51] *in it, and he rescued the city by means of his wisdom, but no one remembered that poor wise man.*

16 *And I said, "Wisdom is better than power." But the wisdom of the poor man was despised! His words were not heeded.*

13 This line serves as an introduction to the example story that follows (vv. 14-16). Qohelet simply announces that he has an example of wisdom that made a large impact on him. The story actually demonstrates the limitations of wisdom, and some have felt that this introduction does not serve the story well. However, according to my translation there is no doubt that what follows is an example of wisdom, but wisdom that is not appreciated or rewarded in the end, and it is this fact that makes such a *big impression (g*e*dôlâ)* on Qohelet.

14 The example story begins by setting the scene. The action takes place in a *small city,* which only had a *few people.* The emphasis on size in these first clauses serves to contrast with what is coming, namely a <u>great</u> *king* and <u>huge</u> *siegeworks.* In other words, Qohelet imagines a tremendously lop-sided battle. From the perspective of manpower and resources the city does not stand a chance.

15 Although it appears the city has no chance, against all expectations it is rescued, and by a surprising source, *a poor but wise man.* Though his plan is unspecified, the poor man saves the city through the use of his wisdom. This story, thus, highlights the value of wisdom. By commenting on the man's economic status Qohelet makes it clear that it was the man's wisdom that effected the city's deliverance, not his financial resources. Qohelet is not interested in how he did it (a subject on which he remains silent), but that he did it, thus illustrating wisdom's benefits. Note too that this part of the story incarnates the truth that "the battle [is] not to the mighty" (v. 11).

However, as Qohelet has done so often before, he praises wisdom only to turn around and eviscerate it. The climax of the story is that, though the wise man has accomplished this great feat, *no one remembered that poor wise man.* In the short run, the wise man's actions were significant, but in the long run they disappeared in the oblivion of passing time.

There is an alternative interpretation of the concluding clause, one that

---

some want to emend to *m*e*ṣûrîm* on the basis of two Hebrew manuscripts and the versions. After all, it is a simple confusion of two commonly mistaken letters. However, the emendation is unnecessary since the word can clearly mean *siegeworks* as it stands, the meaning that the context demands.

51. This verb *(māṣā')* has been the occasion of some controversy in interpretation. One grammatically acceptable reading would take the *great king* as the subject (Wright, *The Book of Koheleth,* p. 416; Fox, *Qohelet and His Contradictions,* p. 262). However, this does not make sense in the context. How could the king have found a wise man in the city when he was besieging it from outside? Furthermore, what significance would the statement have?

understands the verb *rescued* as having "a potential meaning."[52] Bo Isaksson translates, "Now there lived in that city a man poor, but wise, and he alone might have saved the city by his wisdom, but no one thought of that poor man."[53] However, the verb *remembered (zkr)* works better with an actual event in the past. Also, the fact that he saved it and was not remembered heightens the pathos of the verse.

In either case, Qohelet's main point is clear. Wisdom is fine in the short run, but meaningless in the long run.

The Targum provides an interesting point in the history of the interpretation of vv. 14 and 15. It takes an allegorical approach, which understands the city to be a person's body. This body is invaded by a great king, which is an evil spirit. The poor wise man stands for a good but humble spirit that wages war against the evil spirit. Thus, the verse is a description of the spiritual struggle that goes on in a person.[54]

16 Qohelet then evaluates the situation presented in the previous verses. Once again, he begins by giving the relative advantage to wisdom, this time over something as significant as *power.* (Compare, for instance, the relative advantage accorded to wisdom over folly in 2:12-16.) Yet wisdom is once again attenuated by the rest of the verse. Some interpreters believe that the reaction[55] to the poor wise man's advice as described in the last part of the verse indicates that he was unable to save the city because no one listened to him. This interpretation flies in the face of v. 15. The best understanding of v. 16 is that, after he saved the city, no one remembered him or paid any attention to him.[56] Thus, Qohelet reiterates that, though wisdom is better in the short run, it makes no difference in the long run (see also 4:13-16).

13. Assessments of Wisdom (9:17-18)

The theme of wisdom continues in these two verses, but there is no obvious connection with the preceding example story. Here the assessment of wisdom is positive, at least relatively and initially.

Two better-than proverbs (*ṭôb* proverbs) conclude the chapter (vv. 17-18a), promoting wisdom over folly and physical power. The section is not unalloyed praise of wisdom, however, since the concluding half verse (18b)

52. Crenshaw, *Ecclesiastes,* pp. 166-67.
53. Isaksson, *Studies in the Language of Qoheleth,* p. 97.
54. Levine, *The Aramaic Version of Qohelet,* p. 43.
55. Expressed by two participles, *was despised (bᵉzûyâ* — qal passive) and *were not heeded ('ênām nišmā'îm* — a negated niphal participle). According to Ogden (*Qoheleth,* p. 160), the participles have "the effect of stressing the perennial nature of this rejection of wisdom by so many."
56. Fox, *Qohelet and His Contradictions,* p. 264.

admits that it takes very little to spoil the gains of wisdom. The attenuation of wisdom continues into the next chapter.

> 17 *The quiet words of the wise are better heeded*
> *than the shouts of a leader among fools.*
> 18 *Wisdom is better than instruments*[57] *of war,*[58]
> *but one person who messes up destroys a whole lot of good.*

17 Qohelet now prizes the quiet words of wisdom over the loud words of fools. The force of this verse is achieved through the use of well-placed contrasts. On the one side, there are *quiet words,* and on the other, *shouts (za‘aqat).* The former are associated with the *wise (ḥᵃkāmîm),* while the latter, with *fools (kᵉsîlîm).* The relative advantage of the *quiet words of the wise* over the *shouts* of *fools* is expressed through the use of the better-than proverbial form. Indeed, the contrast is heightened by the asymmetrical elements of the verse as well. On the positive side we have simply the *wise,* and this is contrasted not only with *fools* but with *a leader among fools.* In other words, there is a relative advantage to any words from the wise, even when compared with a *leader* of fools.

Some ambiguities in the verse have been noted, as well as tensions with other parts of Ecclesiastes. First, note that, while our present verse talks about *heeding* the words of the wise, v. 16 concluded that the words of the wise are not heeded. However, it is likely that Qohelet is here saying something to the effect that the words of the wise are "worth hearing,"[59] not that they are always heeded.[60]

Second, in the first part of the verse the Hebrew is unclear[61] as to whether it is the words of the wise that are *quiet* or whether those who hear those words should hear them in quiet. It seems, though, that the contrast is with the *shouts* of the leader of the fools, so it would be best to attribute the quietness to the wisdom teacher himself. In other words, the teachings of the wise appeal by virtue of their content, not by their volume.

18 The positive assessment of wisdom continues in this verse with yet another better-than proverb. Here Qohelet evaluates wisdom as superior to weapons. Then he notes that it takes very little to destroy something that is essentially good.

---

57. In this context, "weapons" may be a justifiable translation of the Hebrew word *kᵉlê* (NRSV, NIV).

58. This word for *war (qᵉrāb)* is often taken as an Aramaism (Whitley, *Koheleth,* p. 149), but see Fredericks, *Qoheleth's Language,* pp. 237-38, for counterevidence.

59. So Whybray, *Ecclesiastes,* NCB, p. 149.

60. Isaksson, *Studies in the Language of Qoheleth,* p. 98.

61. A literal translation of the colon *(dibrê ḥᵃkāmîm bᵉnaḥat nišmā‘îm)* would be "the words of the wise in quietness are heard."

This proverb may very well be placed here because of the anecdote in vv. 13-16. After all, the relative advantage here is given to *wisdom* over *instruments of war,* just as the above-mentioned anecdote illustrated.

Qohelet, however, once again attenuates his high praise of wisdom by throwing a wrench into the works. The contrast in v. 18b emphasizes the *one* (*'eḥād*). It takes only one person to cause *a whole lot of* trouble. In other words, it takes only one person to spoil the work of the wise.

This thought continues into the next chapter. Indeed, Aarre Lauha[62] actually transposes v. 18b to a position right after 10:1a. As Roland Murphy has pointed out,[63] however, this is both unnecessary and violates an *inclusio* (based on *ṭôbâ*) in v. 18.

The basic meaning of the Hebrew root *ḥṭ'* is "to miss (a goal)." It may be used in either a moral sense, "to sin," or a nonmoral sense. Qohelet uses it in both ways (see 2:26 and 7:26 for the nonmoral use and 7:20; 8:12; and 9:2 for the moral use). It is conceivable that a moral sense is meant here, but the contrast in this section is with the fool (which of course does have moral connotations).

SUMMARY OF CHAPTER 9

In ch. 9, Qohelet gives advice in the context of statements of deep skepticism. Indeed, this chapter might be judged the most depressing of the entire book.

Qohelet begins the chapter with a powerful evaluation of life (9:1-10). He states that it does not matter who one is or what one does, death renders everything meaningless. After all, death is the end of everything for an individual (vv. 6, 10). From this basic, though sad, truth, Qohelet advises his readers to seize the joy of the day.

The next unit (9:11-12) continues the depressing thoughts of the previous one by asserting that time and chance rule the lives and the deaths of all people. Qohelet once again puts an emphasis on death — that is, no one knows when the end is going to come. There is absolutely nothing that anyone can do to prevent or predict one's death.

This appropriately leads to two further units that question the effectiveness of wisdom. First, wisdom has its limits (vv. 13-16). A wise man may save a city, but he will not be remembered. Second, wisdom has power and is, on a surface level, to be preferred to foolishness, but it does not take much to spoil the good that it might produce (vv. 1-18).

62. Lauha, *Kohelet,* p. 181.
63. Murphy, *Ecclesiastes,* p. 92.

14. Miscellaneous Proverbs on Wisdom and Folly (10:1-4)

Chapter 10 opens with additional proverbs on the subject of wisdom. Indeed, 10:1 continues the thought of 9:18, and perhaps the unit should be defined to include 9:17–10:4. The principle is that a little of a bad thing like folly spoils much of a good thing like wisdom. The next two verses (vv. 2-3) also deal with the themes of wisdom and folly. The fourth verse departs from the pattern of proverbs on wisdom. However, it does have a proverbial form and imparts wisdom to the reader. Verse 5 begins another example story and thus is the introduction to the next unit.

1 Dead flies[1] make a perfumer's[2] oil stink and ferment;[3]
   a little folly is weightier[4] than wisdom and glory.[5]

1. Numerous issues surround the translation of *dead flies* (*zᵉbûbê māwet*). First, the Hebrew most naturally means "flies of death," indicating either "poisonous flies" (and is taken as such by the Septuagint; Targum; Delitzsch, *Proverbs, Ecclesiastes, Song of Solomon*, p. 371; and Wright, *The Book of Koheleth*, p. 417) or perhaps "doomed flies" (2 Sam. 12:5 is suggested as support for this interpretation by Fox [*Qohelet and His Contradictions*, p. 264]). But, as Fox points out, these translations make no sense in the context, which demands "dead flies." It is possible to suggest emendations to this effect (thus Fox, who suggests an emendation to *zbwb ymwt*), but these are just guesses. Perhaps it is best simply to take the construct as attributing death to the flies.

Second, there is the lack of number concord between the verbs *(make stink* and *ferment)* and *dead flies*. This is often cited as evidence for the need for emendation, but number discord is not so rare as to always necessitate a textual change (Ogden [*Qoheleth*, p. 164] mentions Eccles. 1:16 and 2:7 as two of a number of examples of such discord in Ecclesiastes).

2. See 1 Sam. 8:13 and Neh. 3:8. Some English versions simply drop this in their translation (see NIV; contrast NRSV). The Septuagint mistakenly translated "sweetened oil" *(elaiou hēdysmatos)*.

3. Many commentators note that this is a verbal asyndeton. Most versions add a conjunction between the two. Indeed, some believe that the second verb is an intrusive gloss or the result of a textual error. The most thorough case for the latter is presented by Fox (*Qohelet and His Contradictions*, p. 264), who argues that the verbal root *nbʿ* "to bubble" makes no sense here and then suggests that the Septuagint and, in particular, the Peshitta give evidence that Hebrew *gābîaʿ* "vessel" stood there originally. Thus, his translation of the colon as: "A fly dies and spoils a chalice of precious perfumer's ointment." However, it seems as reasonable a hypothesis to argue that "ferment" is an appropriate extension of the verb's basic meaning, making sense in the context.

4. Controversy surrounds the meaning of this word *(yāqār)*. Its more typical meaning in biblical Hebrew is "precious" or "rare," whereas either "heavy" or "weighty" is more appropriate to the context. The latter meanings are known in Aramaic and have been used to argue for a late date of the book. Fredericks (*Qoheleth's Language*, p. 227), though, marshals evidence to conclude that "both meanings are viable and probably EBH [Early Biblical Hebrew]."

Jerome understands the word as "precious," translating "precious above wisdom

2 *A wise heart (goes)[6] to the right;*
   a foolish heart to the left.

3 *Even when the fool[7] walks on the road he lacks sense and says to*
   everyone he is a fool.

4 *If the leader's anger falls[8] on you, do not leave your place! For*
   gentleness appeases[9] great offenses.

1   Though this verse is filled with textual and philological issues (see footnotes), its basic meaning is clear. It takes only a little of something bad to spoil
something good. Qohelet moves from the mundane, dead flies making perfume
stink, to the more serious, a bit of foolishness spoiling wisdom and glory.

Qohelet constructs this proverb by setting two cola in parallel to one
another, thus creating an analogy between them. Some translations make this
explicit (NIV) by adding "as" to the first colon and "so" to the second. Even
without this aid to understanding, though, it is obvious that the mundane
illustration in the first colon serves to concretize the more abstract truth in
the second. We can envision how a small fly can wreak such havoc and spoil
so much good when it flies into something as sweet smelling and precious as
perfumed oil. It takes only a little bit to spoil something worthwhile, which
is exactly the point of the second colon. *wisdom* and *glory* are wonderful and
highly valued, but it just takes a touch of *folly* to spoil them.

---

and glory is a little folly" (quoted by Ginsburg, *The Song of Songs and Coheleth,* p. 424).
However, to accept such a translation necessitates understanding Qohelet to be speaking
with a sarcastic tone or, like Jerome, to understand wisdom here in the sense of crafty. See
also Lauha (*Kohelet,* p. 181): "The word *yqr* 'precious' in 10:1b must here be understood
as ironic," that is, "Das Wort *yqr* 'wortvoll' in 10:1b muss hier ironisch verstanden
werden."

5. A nominal asyndeton, the conjunction being added to make the English less
awkward.

6. No verb appears in the verse. It is possible that a simple copula is appropriate:
"A wise heart is to the right, a foolish heart is to the left," but this seems awkward. In the
light of the following verse, with which it is closely connected, I understand the verb
"goes" and add it for smoothness of translation.

7. The Ketib seems strange because the noun has a direct object even after the
temporal *ke* and the relative pronoun *(še)*. Thus, the Qere is without the article, *kešessākāl.*
However, "the difference is merely euphonic" (Crenshaw, *Ecclesiastes,* p. 170), and we
have already observed how the definite article breaks the rules in the book of Ecclesiastes.

8. The Hebrew idiom is literally "ascends on you," but I have transferred the
thought into the appropriate English idiom.

9. Both *leaves* and *appeases* are hiphil from the same verbal root *(nwḥ),* though
their respective contexts demand different English translations. We should not, however,
lose sight of the wordplay. *BHS* suggests an emendation of the second occurrence of the
verb to a form of "to prevent" *(nw'),* but this spoils the wordplay.

2 This verse has a typical proverbial form; it is an antithetic proverb that looks at the same truth from two different perspectives. The basic truth is that wisdom and folly go in two different directions. The wise go to the right and fools to the left.

Even apart from any special significance to *right* and *left,* there is no doubt that this verse prizes wisdom and demeans folly. However, it is likely true but not provable that these two directions carry connotations of good and bad. John Jarick states that these connotations are "universal."[10] More to the point is the idea that the *right* is the locus of "power and strength"[11] and the *left* is apparently devoid of these.

3 The preceding verse described the different directions that the wise and the fool take. Now Qohelet furthers the image by evoking the picture of the fool walking on a road. While it may well be true that the *road* here is an actual road and not a metaphor for life, the two are intimately connected. The verse does not specify the precise behavior of the fool on the road, but the point is clearly that when one sees him one will know he is a fool. Specifically, the verse says that the fool *lacks sense* (for which see Prov. 6:32, 7:7).[12]

My translation attempts to capture the ambiguity inherent in the last phrase,[13] *he says to everyone he is a fool.* It is unclear in the original whether *lakkōl* should be taken as "to all," in the sense that he is proclaiming his folly to everyone who sees him, or as "concerning all," in the sense that he thinks everyone he sees is a fool.[14] In either case it is an uncomplimentary view of the fool. The fact that a fool cannot conceal his folly but exposes it every time he speaks and acts is found also in Proverbs (12:23; 13:16).

4 This verse is not closely connected with the first three verses of the chapter. It has a weak word link with 9:17, which contains the only other occurrence of *leader (môšēl).* It also has links with the next three verses in which Qohelet talks also about civil authorities (though the Hebrew term is *šallîṭ*).

Qohelet here gives advice to his reader about how to deal with an irate superior. In that it imparts advice on how to deal with a ruler, this verse is similar to court wisdom found in Proverbs and other wisdom literature. Qohelet advises those who serve the king to counter the king's anger with gentleness. In this way, the problem will be smoothed over.

At first sight, Qohelet seems to contradict the advice that he gave in

---

10. Jarick, *Gregory Thaumaturgos' Paraphrase,* p. 251.
11. Ogden (*Qoheleth,* p. 165), who cites Gen. 48:18 and Isa. 41:10 in support.
12. Wright, *The Book of Koheleth,* p. 420.
13. Murphy, *Ecclesiastes,* p. 98.
14. Plumptre, *Ecclesiastes; or, the Preacher,* p. 194.

8:2-9, where he advises those who serve the king to get out of the king's way, but the present verse is dealing with a specific situation: what to do when the king is angry with you.

The second half of the verse gives the motive for the first half. The courtier is not to leave because his calm demeanor will soothe the king. Apparently, if he left the scene, the king could suspect him even more, and his anger would increase. The word *gentleness (marpē')* has been debated in terms of its etymology. Some argue that its form is the result of a confusion of roots: It looks like it is from *rp'* "to heal," while its contextual meaning is closer to *rph* "to relax." Thus, Charles Whitley among others argues that this confusion between *lamed-he* and *lamed-aleph* verbs is a sign of lateness.[15] Daniel Fredericks,[16] though, has a quick and persuasive rejoinder to this when he says, "the judgment of BDB 951 is more appropriate, where the semantic relationship of physical health and mental/spiritual health (composure) is subsumed under *mrp'*."

Pietistic interpreters (see the Targum and Gregory Thaumaturgos) spiritualize the verse by interpreting the *rûaḥ* of the ruler here as an evil spirit.[17] The verse thus becomes an exhortation to fight a spiritual battle.

15. An Example Story: The World Upside Down (10:5-7)

Qohelet offers another example story with the purpose of illustrating again the fact that it takes only a small problem to wreak havoc in the world. An incidental error results in the placement of fools in positions of authority and power, thus resulting in a topsy-turvy society. Other wisdom texts (Prov. 19:10; 30:21-22; the Admonitions of Ipu-Wer and apocalyptic texts (Isa. 24:2; the Marduk Prophecy; and the Šulgi Prophecy)[18] give similar descriptions of a world gone awry.

    5 *There is an evil that I have observed under the sun, an error indeed[19] that originates[20] from the ruler.*

---

15. Whitley, *Koheleth,* p. 84.

16. Fredericks, *Qoheleth's Language,* p. 203.

17. See the discussion in Jarick, *Gregory Thaumaturgos' Paraphrase,* p. 254.

18. For the Admonitions of Ipu-Wer, see *ANET,* pp. 441-44. On the apocalyptic texts, see Longman, *Fictional Akkadian Autobiography,* pp. 132-36, 144.

19. In the Hebrew, this reflects the asseverative *kaph* that is prefixed to the noun *error (kiš^egāgâ).* Some take the preposition as a comparative, but this seems slightly awkward (NRSV).

20. A feminine participle, once again illustrating the book's tendency to treat *lamed-he* and *lamed-aleph* verbs alike (GKC §75qq).

6 *The fool*[21] *is placed in important positions,*[22] *while the rich sit in low places.*

7 *I observed slaves on horses and nobles walking on foot*[23] *like slaves.*

5 Qohelet introduces yet another illustrative anecdote with the characteristic *there is (yēš;* see the discussion at 2:21). The situation he narrates is described ahead of time as an example of something *evil* in the world (see 5:12 [English 5:13]).

The *evil* arises from an *error.* The Hebrew word here normally designates a mistake that comes about through negligence, forgetfulness, or by accident. This *error,* however, has very serious repercussions. After all, it is an error committed by someone in authority, namely, a *ruler.* While there is an idiosyncratic view that understands the *ruler* to be God,[24] it is much more likely that the *ruler* in this verse is the "leader" in the previous one. The ruler's error will be specified in the next two verses.

6 In this and the next verse, Qohelet now tells his hearer/reader what the "error" of the ruler is. He turns the world upside down by placing the wrong people in the wrong positions. The *fool,* who should be given no responsibility and avoided at all costs, is given positions of authority and responsibility. The *rich* are placed in subordinate positions. It is interesting to note the contrast between the *fool* and the *rich* in this verse, the latter standing in a place where we normally find the wise. It does indeed appear that Qohelet favors the privileged classes of Israel. It grates on him that people so blessed do not have their rightful positions in society.

7 This thought continues as he presents us with a vivid picture of societal upheaval. Usually, the most important and privileged individuals are those who ride horses (see 2 Chron. 25:28; Esth. 6:8, 9), while slaves or servants walk alongside to tend to their masters' needs. Here, however, we have the exact opposite, and the ruler's simple error of judgment results in a totally chaotic society.

21. The noun *sekel* is a hapax; normally we encounter *sākāl* in the book of Ecclesiastes (cf. 2:19). Most understand the segolate to be an abstract and, on the basis of the versions and the context, translate it as a concrete noun, that is, *fool* rather than "foolishness" (contra Crenshaw, *Ecclesiastes,* p. 171).

22. There is some discussion about the force of *rabbîm* in this verse. Most take it as an adjective that modifies *mᵉrômîm* (as in the above translation). However, some are disturbed by the lack of an article on *rabbîm* and take the word with the next clause and translate "the mighty and the rich." But the lack of an article is more easily explained in the light of the rather eccentric use of it throughout the book.

23. *'al-hā'āreṣ* is literally, "on the ground/earth."

24. Jerome, quoted and supported by Hengstenberg, *A Commentary on Ecclesiastes,* p. 225.

16. The Disastrous "Accidents" of Life (10:8-11)

Qohelet may indeed believe in divine providence, but it is no source of comfort to him as he faces the unpredictable chaos of life (9:1). Much effort has been expended in order to find a strong connection between this pericope and those around it, but it seems that these verses are collected here more as different lines of evidence to demonstrate the difficulty and lack of fairness in life.

8 *The one who digs a pit[25] may[26] fall into it;*
   the one who breaches a wall may be bitten by a snake.

9 *The one who quarries stones may be injured by them;*
   the one who splits trees may be endangered[27] by them.

10 *If the axe is blunt[28] and the edge[29] is not[30] sharp, then he must increase his efforts. But the advantage of wisdom is success.*

11 *If the snake bites without a charm,[31] there is no advantage to having a charmer.[32]*

25. Whitley (*Kohelet,* p. 86) calls *gûmmāṣ* an "Aramaic word," and even Hengstenberg (*A Commentary on Ecclesiastes,* p. 227) refers to it as "a pure Aramaic word." However, Fredericks (*Qoheleth's Language,* pp. 188-89) attempts to bring evidence to argue that this does not indicate late language.

26. The use of the perfect twice in this verse and twice in the next indicates potentiality here (see GKC §107r; cf. Lauha, *Kohelet,* p. 186; Delitzsch, *Proverbs, Ecclesiastes, Song of Solomon,* p. 378). To translate these verbs as simple futures makes no sense of experience.

27. This is the only use of the niphal of *skn* in the Hebrew Bible. Whitley (*Koheleth,* p. 86) once again argues that its use in this stem in the Mishnah and the Targum indicates that it is a late word, but Fredericks (*Qoheleth's Language,* pp. 188-89) disputes this interpretation of the evidence, citing the work of E. Lipiński ("*Skn* and *sgn* dans le sémitique occidental du nord," *UF* 5 [1973]: 191-203) in support. Note too the arguments of I. Kottsieper ("Die Bedeutung der Wz. *'ṣb* und *skn* in Koh 10,9," *UF* 18 [1986]: 213-22) that the verb means "cut" *(schneiden)* here.

28. While the verb *qēhâ* occurs in the qal in three other places (Jer. 31:29, 30; and Ezek. 18:2) with the meaning "to be numb," it occurs only here in the piel and means "to be blunt." The Septuagint simply misunderstood the verb and translated "if the axe should fall" *(ekpesē).*

29. The best guess is that *pānîm* (literally, "faces") in this context is a reference to the *edge* of the axe. However, if so, it is likely a hapax usage, since the edge is normally referred to as the "mouth" *(peh)* of the sword. Ezekiel 21:21 is often cited as another such usage, but L. C. Allen (*Ezekiel 1–20,* WBC [Dallas: Word, 1990], p. 20) disputes this. The main alternative, which has been suggested at least since Jerome, has been to treat it as *lepānîm* "beforehand" (Gordis, *Koheleth,* p. 322), but this seems equally awkward in translation and has no support of the versions.

30. Some Oriental Hebrew manuscripts, as well as the Septuagint and the Syriac, have *lô* "to him" rather than *lô'* "not."

31. It is possible to construe the clause *(belô'-lāḥaš)* temporally on analogy with

8 In this verse, Qohelet warns that people might fall into a pit that they dug or get bitten by a snake as they tear down a wall. The thought, though not the motivation, is similar to Psalm 7:16 (English 15):

> He who digs a hole and scoops it out
>   falls into the pit he has made.

The context of the Psalm is clearly one of just retribution. The enemy tries unjustly to trap an innocent person, but ends up in his own trap. Qohelet's use of this image is the opposite. Here an innocent person is simply engaged in his occupation, and he is accidentally injured. This is the first of four illustrations of people who are simply doing their jobs and who fall prey to the dangers that are inherent in their occupations. Their injuries are simply accidental. They are not punishments for bad behavior,[33] and they are not mentioned so that the wise person can avoid them; they are unavoidable accidents. No matter how careful people are they may fall into the pit they dug, and they might be surprised by a snake on the other side of the wall they are demolishing.

9 Two more occupations are listed here, the stonecutter and the logger. Qohelet does not feel it necessary to say how the stonecutter will be *injured* by the stones or how the logger will be *endangered* by the wood that he is cutting. The point once again is that life is prey to accidents even in the midst of our common, everyday experiences.

10 Though it has been over a century since he made this judgment, Charles Wright is certainly correct when he states, "this, linguistically speaking, is confessedly the most difficult passage in the Book of Koheleth."[34] The

---

similar syntactical structures in Eccles. 7:17 and Job 15:32, thus "before it is charmed." The noun comes from a verb *(lḥš),* which means "to whisper" and in certain contexts "to charm by whispering." For a similar use of the noun, see Jer. 8:17.

32. Literally, "master of the tongue" *(baʿal hallāšôn).* This has been taken as a reference to a slanderer. Thus, the Vulgate understands the verse to draw an analogy between a sly serpent and a slanderer: "If a serpent bites silently, he is nothing better than he who slanders in secret" *(si mordeat serpens in silentio nihil eo minus habet qui occulte detrahit).*

Admittedly, this verse could be translated along the lines of the NIV: "If a snake bites before it is charmed, there is no profit for the charmer." The major difference with my translation is the treatment of the preposition *lᵉ* on the last clause. However, the verse then would have no obvious connection with the context, unless it is the charmer who is imagined to be bitten, but this treatment seems too subtle.

33. Contra Crenshaw, *Ecclesiastes,* p. 172, who says that they are examples of retributive justice here though not in the next verse, an unsupported and unsupportable division between the two verses. Not surprisingly, the Targum and Gregory Thaumaturgos (Jarick, *Gregory Thaumaturgos' Paraphrase,* pp. 258-60) also take this moral approach to these two verses.

34. Wright, *The Book of Koheleth,* p. 423.

problems are ancient, as the translations of the various ancient versions attest.[35] Some of these issues are treated in the footnotes, and some will be treated here, with as much resolution as they permit. Though it may sound somewhat overly optimistic, it is my feeling that we can come away from this verse with the general idea that it intends to convey.

The protasis and apodosis of the verse are fairly certain in their translation and state the simple truth that if an axe is not sharp then the person wielding it has to exert himself a lot more to make it effective.

It is the last three words that are difficult to understand, and by their position they seem to draw the moral of the truism just stated. Semantically, there is little problem with the phrase. The first word *(yitrôn, advantage)* is common in Ecclesiastes (see 1:3), and the third word *(ḥokmâ, wisdom)* is common throughout the OT. It is the middle word and the syntax that frustrate interpreters. The middle word has a common Semitic root *kšr*, which normally means "to succeed," though some want to argue that the root has a late meaning "to keep prepared, to be fit."[36] Anthony Frendo[37] presents a persuasive argument that we have here an example of a "broken construct chain," thus yielding the above translation.

If my translation is correct, then the meaning of the verse is that success is the fruit of wisdom, and the inference must be that a wise person would have sharpened the axe in the first place, saving himself a lot of wear and tear. Thus, as Roland Murphy argued, we are dealing with a "saying about the wise use of one's abilities."[38]

11 Once again Qohelet describes the limits of wisdom by means of a striking example. Snake charming was a mysterious occupation that needed a special and esoteric expertise, but the skill was of no use after the snake bit someone. It was too late then to charm the snake; the damage had been done.

At first reading, the verse appears to urge the wise to apply their wisdom or else it will be of no use. According to James Crenshaw, the verse's moral is "unused skill is wasted,"[39] while Murphy summarizes the verse with "even the experts fail if they do not apply their skill."[40]

---

35. The Septuagint may be translated, "If the axe falls and it troubles a face, then he will strengthen his strength. The advantage of man is wisdom." The Vulgate reads, "If the iron is blunt and it is not as before, but if it is dull, it can be sharpened with much labor. And after industry follows wisdom." And finally the Peshitta, "If the axe be blunt, and it troubles the face and increases the slain, and the advantage of the upright is wisdom" (these are Ginsburg's translations [*The Song of Songs and Coheleth*, p. 424]).

36. Whybray, *Ecclesiastes*, NCB, p. 154.

37. A. Frendo, "The 'Broken Construct Chain' in Qoh. 10:10b," *Biblica* 62 (1981): 544-45.

38. Murphy, *Ecclesiastes*, p. 102.

39. Crenshaw, *Ecclesiastes*, p. 173.

40. Murphy, *Ecclesiastes*, p. 102.

However, the verse is not about unused skill; it is about wisdom that is useless in practical situations. In order to prevent snakebite, the charmer needs to work his wisdom before the bite takes place; afterward is too late since he is not able to reverse the effect of the poison. Yet in most situations a snake bites without warning, as for instance in v. 8, when the worker is going about his occupation and accidentally disturbs a snake. Basically, the skill of a snake charmer is good for shows but not for practical everyday living, where snakebites are a matter of life and death.

17. Fools (10:12-15)

This section has no obvious connection with the previous one. It is a collection of proverbs that denigrate folly. Qohelet elsewhere has stated his belief in the relative superiority of wisdom over folly, though such sentiments are usually accompanied by an indication that wisdom itself is not ultimately to be prized. Such qualifications are not found here; these proverbs are remarkably similar to those found in the book of Proverbs (10:8, 21; 15:2; 18:7).

12 *The words of the mouth of the wise bring favor;*
    and the lips of the fool swallow[41] him.
13 *The beginning of the words of his mouth is folly,*
    but the end of (the words of)[42] his mouth is wicked madness.
14 *And the fool multiplies words:*
    No one knows what will happen.[43]
        Who can tell anyone what is going to happen after him?
15 *The toil of fools wearies[44] them,*
    for[45] they do not know how to get to the city.

41. For the lack of number concord between the singular verb and its plural subject, see Whitley, *Koheleth,* p. 86. For the meaning of the verb, consult A. Guillaume, "A Note on *bl'*," *JTS* 13 (1962): 320-22.
42. The words in parentheses are not in the Hebrew, but are understood by ellipsis, and the English makes no sense without them.
43. The Septuagint, Symmachus, and the Peshitta read the past *(mah-šehāyâ)* here rather than the future. In other words, they thought this colon denied knowledge of the past, while the next colon denied knowledge of the future. However, it is likely that these early versions simply tried to erase what they thought was a redundancy in the translation.
44. The syntax of this verse is anomalous and has led to a number of explanations and attempts at emendation. The verb (piel of *yg'*) is feminine singular with a masculine singular pronominal suffix, but the subject is masculine and the antecedent to the suffix is plural.
    More than one explanation is available for both of these grammatical anomalies. For the feminine/masculine problem, other cases of a lack of gender concord are available in biblical Hebrew, as are the more systematic occurrences in Ugaritic (Whitley, *Koheleth,*

246

12   Qohelet begins his section on fools by comparing their speech to that of the wise. While the latter brings favor, the former brings harm.

My rather literal translation of the verse intends to show some of Qohelet's wordplays. Besides the obvious contrast between the *wise* person and the *fool*, there is also the focused contrast between the former's *mouth* and the latter's *lips*. This contrast is often obscured by translations. A more idiomatic translation might be:

> Speaking wisely brings approval;
> a fool's words invite destruction.

In the Hebrew original it is not obvious whether Qohelet means that the *words of the mouth of the wise (dibrê pî-ḥākām)* dispense favor or effect favor for the wise person. It may be that both are meant, but the parallel with the second colon, in which the fool's words harm him, shows that the latter sense is definitely intended. Thus, that meaning is reflected in the translation.

The second colon is masterful in its imagery. While the words of the wise result in positive effects, the fool's speech culminates in destruction. The verb chosen to convey this thought *(swallow: blʿ)* is perfect in that it is the fool's own *lips* that engulf him. In this verse, Qohelet does not question the relative advantage of wisdom over folly as he does elsewhere (e.g., 2:12-16).

13   The verse is linked by the pronominal suffix *(his mouth: pîhû)* to v. 12b. In other words, v. 13 focuses in on the speech of the fool, who is contrasted with the wise in v. 12. This verse also is constructed by antonyms, though here the subject remains the fool. *Beginning (tᵉḥillat)* mirrors *end (ʾaḥᵃrît)*, not providing a merism, but rather describing a process. While the fool's speech might seem inane or silly to start, the end result is insanity.

---

p. 87). For the lack of number concord, it may be that we have a case of the distributive singular here (Whybray, *Ecclesiastes,* NCB, p. 156), or that the *mem* on the end of the plural noun could originally have been an enclitic *mem* misunderstood as a plural by the Masoretes. Then, of course, we can always appeal to the fact that Ecclesiastes as a book is full of anomalous grammatical and syntactical forms (see "Language" in the introduction).

Nonetheless, some scholars are not convinced (e.g., Fox, *Qohelet and His Contradictions,* pp. 269-70) and suggest a textual solution. *BHS* preserves a suggestion of Hertzberg (*Der Prediger,* pp. 193, 196) that the first part of the verse originally read *haksîl mātay yᵉyaggᵉʿennû* "the toil of the fool — when will it weary him." Yet it is inappropriate to press the textual issue with a book that has such a well-know propensity to depart from what we consider normative biblical Hebrew.

45. Taking the *ᵃšer* as a causative, though it is difficult to rule out a simple relative or a purpose clause.

14 There is the possibility that v. 14a is the conclusion to a tricolon that begins in v. 13 (see NIV), and there are verbal links with *words* and *fool* (both words occur in vv. 13a and 14a). It is more likely, however, that v. 14a is an introduction to the next two cola, v. 14b.[46]

In other words, the *fool* is going on and on about something for which he has no information and about which he can gain no knowledge: the future. *The fool multiplies words,* more idiomatically "the fool talks a lot" *(hassākāl yarbeh dᵉbārîm)* about what is going to happen in the future, a subject about which Qohelet has already told us there is no knowledge (6:12; 7:14; 8:7). Thus, Qohelet adds another stroke to his caricature of the fool: he talks incessantly about subjects that he knows nothing about.

15 This verse continues the fool bashing of the previous ones. It is somewhat different than those that immediately precede it since it speaks of the fool's actions and not his speech. Apparently the fool is so stupid that he loses his way back to the city. Graham Ogden[47] attempts to stretch a contextual argument in his effort to understand the fool's toil as that of talking too much.

The exact force of the verse eludes us because the idiom of the second part is foreign to us. Literally it should be translated "they do not know to go to the city" *(lō'-yādāʿ lāleket 'el-ʿîr)*. It has been argued, since it is the best that we can do with it, that it must refer to some action that points out the stupidity of the fool. Thus, the verse is like 10:3 in pointing to the truth that the fool demonstrates his folly by his public, silly actions. It is likely that the verse says that the reason why fools are so tired after a long day's work is that they are so stupid that they get lost and walk a longer distance than necessary to return to their homes in the evening.

18. The King: Blessing or Curse? (10:16-17)

Some commentators[48] argue that these verses should be combined with 10:18-20, as if all the verses concern the king. Close study, however, shows that the royal theme is found in vv. 16-17 and 20, but not vv. 18-19; thus, I treat these verses under three rubrics.

Verses 16-17 first present a dirge over a land whose king is immature, and they follow this with a blessing upon a land whose king is responsible and fit for rule.

46. So the NRSV and Lauha, *Kohelet,* pp. 190-91. Also consult the commentary on the next verse.

47. Ogden, *Qoheleth,* pp. 174-75.

48. For instance, K. A. Farmer, *Who Knows What is Good? Proverbs and Ecclesiastes,* ITC (Grand Rapids, MI: Eerdmans, 1991), pp. 188-89.

16 *Woe[49] to you, O land[50] whose king is immature*
   and whose leaders feast in the morning.

17 *Blessed are you, O land whose king is a noble[51]*
   and whose leaders eat at the appropriate time —
   for strength, and not to get drunk.

16 The new section begins with a dirge[52] directed to a land that is ruled by an *immature (nāʿar)* ruler. Such a land is in deep trouble. The Hebrew word *nāʿar* is a relative term designating youth and/or subservience. The designation can refer to a "servant" (so NIV and NRSV) on the basis of the parallel with *noble,* and if that is the case, then the thought is similar to that in 10:7 (where *ʿabādîm* is used). Yet the expression probably means "youth," and in more than a chronological sense (cf. 4:13-16, where Qohelet preferred a wise, youthful *[yeled]* king to an old foolish one). Thus, I opt for the translation *immature.*

It is not only the king who lets the nation down, however, it is also the secondary *leaders (śar).* The text says literally that they "eat in the morning" *(babbōqer yōʾkēlû).* However, the context, which includes the parallel with v. 17b, leads me to believe that this eating is inappropriate for the time of day, and thus most translations understand that this is excessive, riotous eating (so the translation *feast;* cf. Isa. 5:11-13; 21:5 for the denigration of early morning indulgence).

17 The first two cola of the verse parallel v. 16, but instead of a woe oracle the verse begins with a beatitude on the land whose king is a *noble.* Such a land, in Qohelet's opinion, is blessed. This verse supports the view that Qohelet is somewhat of an elitist (see also 10:6) since he prizes and trusts the upper classes of his society.[53]

49. The verse begins with a shortened form of the word *woe (ʾî).* The common biblical form is either *ʾôy* or *hôy.* For more, see n. 41 to 4:10.

50. The Septuagint has "city" *(polis)* for "land" here, but this is likely an attempt to specify the political boundary of the vague term *land* by an association with *ʿîr* in 10:15. Note that the Targum not unexpectedly specifies the *land* as the "land of Israel." It further concretizes what it takes to be historical references by naming Jeroboam (I) as the wicked king in v. 16 and Hezekiah as the good king in v. 17.

51. Literally, *ben-ḥôrîm* is "a son of nobles." Gordis (*Koheleth,* pp. 326-27) identifies the phrase as an Aramaism, but it occurs a number of times in biblical Hebrew (cf. 1 Kings 21:8, 11; Neh. 2:16; 5:7).

52. See T. Longman III, "Nahum," in *The Minor Prophets,* vol. 2, ed. T. McComiskey (Grand Rapids, MI: Baker, 1993), pp. 811-13, for a discussion of the "woe oracle." This oracle does not precisely fit the pattern of those found in the prophets, but nonetheless, like them, it finds its origin in a funeral dirge.

53. Hengstenberg (*A Commentary on Ecclesiastes,* p. 233) represents those who try to soften this: "ʿA noble' not merely by birth, but in disposition and customs."

In contrast to the gluttonous *leaders* in v. 16, this blessed king's officials eat at the right time and for the right reasons. The verb *eat* is the same
as that translated *feast* (from the root *'kl*) in the previous verse, and thus the
contrast is quite intentional. I have varied the translation in English to eliminate
awkwardness.

The most difficult part of the verse is the third colon, which seems
added because it is not parallel to anything in v. 16. However, since we
frequently get such intensifying additions in poetic parallelism, it is better to
treat the colon as original.

The colon has its difficulties, though. The dictionary meaning of the word
gᵉbûrâ is *strength,* and I understand its meaning in this context to be that they
eat to sustain them through the day. Some, though, take their key from the related
word *gibbôr* "manly," with the result that they "eat like men."

Further, this happy land's rulers avoid drunkenness. The MT has a
noun from the root "to drink" *(šth).* It should be noted that the Septuagint
took the word as a form of the root *bôš* "to be ashamed."

19. Miscellaneous Wisdom (10:18-19)

No obvious connections link these two verses with the preceding. Some[54]
argue on the basis of context that the neglected house of v. 18 is the "land"
of vv. 16-17. Specifically, the immature king and drunken leaders ignore their
responsibilities and the kingdom disintegrates.[55] Michael Fox believes that
v. 19 "applies to the banqueters most recently mentioned (v. 17) as well as
to the dissolute nobles of v. 16."[56] In agreement with R. N. Whybray,[57] I
observe nothing within vv. 18-19 that lends support to such a connection.

There is the further question of the verses' relationship to each other.
Once again, there is nothing obvious. In the analysis to follow we will see
that v. 18 denigrates laziness in good wisdom fashion, and that v. 19 extols a
life of material enjoyment. The relationship between the lines depends on the
tone of the second. Is Qohelet serious in his promotion of a materialistic
lifestyle? On the one hand, support could be garnered from the *carpe diem*
passages throughout the book. On the other hand, Qohelet has criticized a
lifestyle of excessive and blind enjoyment (in the case of national leaders as
recently as 10:16; note also 2:2). Qohelet throughout has been an inconsistent
thinker, particularly on the topic of enjoyment.

---

54. Farmer, *Who Knows What is Good?* p. 189.
55. Plumptre, *Ecclesiastes; or, the Preacher,* p. 201; Ginsburg, *The Song of Songs
and Coheleth,* p. 442.
56. Fox, *Qohelet and His Contradictions,* p. 272.
57. Whybray, *Ecclesiastes,* NCB, p. 157.

18 *Due to laziness*[58] *the roof*[59] *sags,*
    and due to inactivity[60] *the house leaks.*[61]
19 *One makes*[62] *a feast*[63] *for laughter;*
    wine makes life even merrier,
    and money answers everything.

18 In good practical wisdom fashion Qohelet warns against laziness by pointing out its consequences. People who sit around doing nothing will end up with a disaster on their hands. Specifically, if they do not attend to the regular upkeep of their houses because of laziness, then after a time the houses will begin to fall apart. The book of Proverbs considers such sluggards at least implicitly to be fools (Prov. 6:6; 26:16; see also 10:4; 12:27; 26:15).

19 If v. 18 gives the impression that the reader should go out and work diligently, the next verse, at least on the surface, seems to encourage a sensual lifestyle of eating, drinking, and the use of money to satisfy one's needs and luxuries. We have seen above that the relationship between these two verses is ambiguous, in part because Qohelet's tone is uncertain. However, the most natural reading of the words in the verse would understand Qohelet to be sincere in his praise of feasting, laughter, wine, and money.

The last clause presents the most difficult problems in translation. Most vexing is the meaning of the verb (*'ānâ*). The difficulty is that *'ānâ* could derive from several roots with many possible meanings in Hebrew: specifically for this verse, "answer, obey, submit, hear, testify, afflict." We can add

58. *Laziness* (*'aṣaltayim*) is a dual form of the adjective used as a substantive (GKC §88b). The dual nature of the word has perplexed scholars for years. Some take as an intensive dual; the reference is to extreme laziness. Others adopt a text critical solution, believing that the final *ym* are a dittography of the first two consonants of the following verb. A less likely explanation is that the dual here is anticipating the dual *hands* in the second colon. Thus, there are explanations for the dual form, but none is so persuasive that I can settle on it to the exclusion of others.

59. *roof* (*meqāreh*) is a hapax, though there is little doubt about its translation. The more common expression is *qôrâ* "beams of a house."

60. An idiomatic translation of *šiplût yādayim* ("lowering of hands").

61. M. J. Dahood ("Three Parallel Pairs in Ecclesiastes 10:18," *JQR* 62 [1971-72]: 84-87) argued that there were three parallel pairs in this verse similar to the pairs found in Ugaritic. However, with the exception of the first (*mkk//dlp*), the pairs are either mistakenly identified (Hebrew *meqāreh* "roof" with Ugaritic *qryt* "city") or based on a syntactical construction (causal *beth*), which presupposes no special relationship with Ugaritic. In terms of the first parallel, the root *dlp* may have a different meaning in Ugaritic than it does in Hebrew.

62. *makes* (*'ōśîm*) is a participle, used without a subject. This is a classic way of expressing an impersonal subject.

63. Literally, "bread," a synecdoche for "food" or excessive food = a *feast*. A comparable expression to Qohelet's *makes a feast* may be found in the Aramaic expression *'abad leḥem* (Dan. 5:1).

to this list "to occupy, to provide for."[64] Some manuscripts of the Septuagint and Vulgate take the verb from *'ānâ* "to obey, submit." The Peshitta differs with its translation "to afflict, humble." The Targum, according to Levine's translation, renders "will proclaim," being thus closest to "answer." We can therefore see that the confusion entered early in the history of interpretation.[65]

I cannot be dogmatic about my translation, but it makes sense in the context. The idea is that money is necessary to buy the food and the wine and other enjoyments of this world.

20. Advice Concerning the King — Once Again (10:20)

This verse returns (see vv. 16-17) to advice concerning the king and other powerful figures. The wise person is to take extraordinary precautions in dealing with such people.

> 20 *Moreover, do not curse the king even in your thoughts;*
> *do not curse the rich even in your sleeping chamber,[66]*
> *for a bird may carry the message*
> *or some winged creature[67] may tell the matter.*

20 The chapter concludes with Qohelet's advice that his reader/student not even think about cursing the *king (melek)* or the *rich ('āšîr)*. The danger is too great; the repercussions too grave. After all, the king is sovereign (8:2-4).

Unlike much of the book, this verse is in poetic parallelism. This has led some scholars to question the translation of *your thoughts (maddā'ᵃkā)*, arguing that this provides a poor parallel for *sleeping chamber (miškābᵉkā)*. There have been many alternative suggestions, the most frequently cited being (1) "in your night lodging" (emendation to *bᵉmaṣṣā'ᵃkā)*;[68] (2) "in your bedroom" (based on the verbal root *yd'* in its sexual meaning);[69] (3) "in your

---

64. Whybray, *Ecclesiastes*, NCB, p. 157.

65. See R. B. Salters, "Text and Exegesis in Koh 10:19," *ZAW* 89 (1977): 423-26, for full and detailed discussion of the textual history of this verse.

66. The Hebrew is plural, though a singular room is surely meant. Some Hebrew manuscripts, supported by the Syriac, Targum and Vulgate, attest the singular.

67. Literally, "lord of wings." The compound use of *ba'al* is similar to Akkadian *bēlu*, which occurs in compound with a variety of words (*agê, kakki*, etc.). According to *CAD* (vol. 2B, p. 198b) it can be used in compounds to signify "holder of, responsible for, entitled to." The MT attests a definite article prefixed to "wings" (the Ketib), but the Masoretes did not point it and thus did not want it read (Qere). Gordis (*Koheleth*, p. 329) notes that the Qere was "not a correction but a variant reading."

68. Lauha, *Kohelet*, p. 196.

69. KB, p. 497b.

repose" (based on the meaning "to rest, to be still" of *ydᶜ* in Hebrew and Arabic);[70] (4) "in the presence of your messenger" (based on an Ugaritic word *mndᶜ*);[71] and (5) "with your friends" (based on an Akkadian word found at Ugarit).[72]

In the final analysis, however, all of these suggestions are quite unnecessary and are based on a faulty understanding of parallelism. In the first place, the word's meaning as "knowledge" and thus "thought" is not disputed, though it is attested in late biblical texts (2 Chron. 1:10, 11, 12; and Dan. 1:4, 17).[73] In the second place, all the major ancient versions translate in this semantic range (Targum, Septuagint, and Vulgate).

The parallelism is indeed more powerful when efforts are not made to make the two cola strictly synonymous. The first colon speaks of the king, and Qohelet warns his hearers not to speak ill against him even in the secret recesses of the mind. Qohelet then goes on to advise against cursing the rich, who are powerful but not quite as dangerous, in the secret recesses of the house.

The motive clause follows in the last two clauses of the verse, which are also parallel to one another. As has been frequently pointed out, this is analogous to our own saying that "the walls have ears." Perhaps stirred by the expression "bird of heaven" *('ôp haššāmayim),* the Targum had a spiritual understanding of the verse and believed that this bird was in actuality the angel Raziel.

SUMMARY OF CHAPTER 10

Chapter 10 is difficult to summarize in a connected fashion because the units seem relatively isolated from one another, only occasionally and briefly interacting with their context. However, they are united by form and general topic. There are a number of proverbs in this chapter (see vv. 1-4, for instance), and certainly a lot of advice (vv. 18-20) as well as insight into how the world does and should work (vv. 8-9, 15-17). Also, the topics of wisdom and foolishness (vv. 1-3, 12-15), as well as the king (vv. 16-17, 20), seem to be in the forefront. Qohelet continues to raise some of the same deep issues that he has before, most notably the lack of human ability to know the future.

70. D. W. Thomas, "A Note on *bᵉmaddāᶜᵃkā* in Eccles. x.20," *JTS* 50 (1949): 177.

71. Dahood, "Qoheleth and Recent Discoveries," p. 306.

72. M. J. Dahood, "The Phoenician Background of Qoheleth," *Biblica* 47 (1966): 270.

73. And for this reason alone Fredericks (*Qoheleth's Language,* pp. 230-31) wants to argue for "repose."

21. Risk and Uncertainty (11:1-6)

This section contains some of the more difficult, though provocative, verses in the book. The first verse, debated in meaning, is yet well known even in popular idiom. All six verses question the possibility of certainty in one's endeavors. Indeed, Roland Murphy identifies the unit as composed of "sayings about the uncertainty of human industry."[1] Nonetheless, Qohelet urges action, not inactivity.

1 Send[2] your bread upon the surface of the waters, for after many days you may find[3] it.

2 Give a portion[4] to seven, even to eight, for you do not know what evil may[5] occur in the land.

3 If the clouds are full, they will empty rain on the earth; and whether a tree falls south or north, the place where the tree falls, there it is.[6]

4 Those who watch the wind do not sow, and those who observe the clouds do not harvest.

5 In the same way that you do not know what is the way of the wind or how the bones[7] are formed in the mother's womb, so[8] you do not know the work of God, who does all things.

---

1. Murphy, *Wisdom Literature*, p. 147.

2. Not "throw" or "cast" (so NIV), meanings that are not attested for the piel of *šlḥ*.

3. The imperfect *(timṣā'ennû)* can have a modal aspect *(may find)* rather than represent the future tense (see Murphy, *Ecclesiastes*, p. 106).

4. Sometimes *ḥēleq* is better translated "reward." See 2:10 for comment.

5. Once again (see v. 1), the force of the imperfect (here *yihyeh*) is likely modal *(may occur)*.

6. The form of the verb that concludes the verse *(yᵉhû')* has perplexed interpreters, though its meaning is not in dispute. The fullest discussion of the options is given by Fredericks *(Qoheleth's Language*, pp. 222-23). He lists four options: (1) the MT in *BHS* is corrupt and the evidence of four Hebrew manuscripts should be followed by emending to the third-person masculine pronoun *(hû')*, functioning as a copula (GKC §75s; Zimmerli, *Das Buch des Predigers Salomo* [Göttingen: Vandenhoeck und Ruprecht, 1962], p. 239); (2) it is the jussive of *hyh* with final *aleph* (GKC §23i; Barton, *The Book of Ecclesiastes*, p. 193; Lauha, *Kohelet*, p. 199); (3) it is an imperfect of the Aramaic verbal root *hwh* (Whitley, *Koheleth*, p. 93); or (4) it is cognate with an Arabic root *hwh*. Fredericks does not decide among these since his concern is to show alternatives to an Aramaic cognate with its supposed chronological implications. As mentioned, this discussion does not affect the sense of the verse, because in each case the meaning of the verb is a form of "to be."

7. Or "body," taking the Hebrew *bones* *(ʿᵃṣāmîm)* as a synecdoche.

8. The main conundrum of the verse is whether there are one or two illustrations given. The MT supports two, with the second introduced by *kaʿᵃṣāmîm* (literally, "like/as bones"). However, the MT as it stands is admittedly awkward: one might naturally expect

6 *In*[9] *the morning plant your seed and do not let your hand rest at*[10] *evening. For you do not know which*[11] *will succeed, whether this or that, or whether both will do equally well.*

1   The translation of this verse is simple from a philological perspective, but its proverbial and metaphorical nature makes it difficult to understand. What does it mean to *send your bread upon the waters?* Even if one could find it after many days, what value would waterlogged bread be anyway? In spite of its uncertain interpretation, the image finds use even in twentieth-century American language, registering a kind of vague hope for a risky investment.

A popular interpretation understands the verse to refer to charity, a view that has been espoused from antiquity to modern times.[12] The Targum, for instance, reads "Give your nourishing bread to the poor who go in ships upon the surface of the water, for after a period of many days you will find its reward in the world-to-come."[13] In support, modern scholars cite other ancient texts like "The Instructions of 'Onkhsheshonqy" (19:10)[14] and the Arabic proverb: "Do good, throw your bread on the waters, and one day you

---

a *waw* to begin the clause. The Targum, *BHS,* a number of Hebrew manuscripts, as well as Gordis (*Koheleth,* pp. 331-32), Fox (*Qohelet and His Contradictions,* p. 276), Ogden, (*Qoheleth,* p. 120), and the NSRV accordingly opt for one illustration. The NSRV renders the verse: "Just as you do not know how the breath comes to the bones in the mother's womb, so you do not know the work of God, who makes everything." Though this is a possible understanding and does not change the main point, I stay with the MT, the Septuagint, the Vulgate, the NIV, and a number of modern commentators (e.g., Ginsburg, *The Song of Songs and Coheleth,* p. 302; Barton, *The Book of Ecclesiastes,* p. 179). Lauha (*Kohelet,* p. 199) admits that the MT is very difficult but also notes the possibility of an asyndetic relationship between the first two clauses and concludes that the MT is not impossible.

9. Hebrew prepositions have a wide semantic range, and thus there is oftentimes confusion concerning their exact nuance in a sentence. It is conceivable (based especially on the Ugaritic evidence) that the preposition *b^e* prefixed to *morning* could be translated "from," and the preposition *l^e* prefixed to *evening* could be translated "until." Qohelet would thus admonish his reader to be ever active. This is certainly the gist of the passage, but it is more likely that Qohelet uses *morning* and *evening* as two discrete moments since he goes on to refer to the two plantings as *this* and *that.* It could be that *morning* and *evening* are parts of a merism that simply means "all the time in between."

10. See n. 9.

11. See Waltke and O'Connor, *Biblical Hebrew Syntax,* p. 327, n. 25, on *'ê-zeh.* It is used elsewhere only at Eccles. 2:13.

12. This view was held by the Talmud, Gregory Thaumaturgos, and Jerome in antiquity and by D. W. Staerk ("Zur Exegese von Koh 10:20 und 11:1," *ZAW* 59 [1943]: 216-18) and Fox (*Qohelet and His Contradictions,* p. 274) in modern times.

13. Levine, *The Aramaic Version of Qohelet,* p. 45.

14. Crenshaw, *Ecclesiastes,* pp. 178-79.

will be rewarded." However, there is nothing in the verse itself that hints that Qohelet had charity in mind. The Arabic proverb could be influenced by the early charitable interpretation of Ecclesiastes.

A similar structure associates v. 1 with v. 2, which, though it has its own difficulties, seems to be concerned with business transactions. Such a connection is the strongest argument in favor of those who understand v. 1 to refer to the calculated risks of business. In other words, it is saying that, in spite of the risks of loss involved, one should go ahead and engage in maritime trade. This view seems most likely in the context. *bread (lehem),* thus, stands for any kind of commodity of trade. The idea of the verse, then, is that, as people engage in trade, profits may flow back to them. Risk is involved, but reward may come. This view is widely held.[15]

Even if we are unable to come to a definitive understanding of the verse, Podechard is certainly correct that this verse fits in with the teaching of 3:11, 8:17, and 9:11 that, according to Qohelet, the future is uncertain.[16]

2 The theme of uncertainty about the future continues in this verse, which is also associated with the first verse by virtue of its close syntactical structure (initial imperative and concluding motive clause [marked by initial *kî*]). As with the preceding verse, Qohelet's statement is somewhat elliptical to a modern reader. We are left with questions about the nature of the *portion (ḥēleq)* that is to be given to seven or eight. It is surely to be connected with "bread" in the preceding verse, but there is disagreement over what that word means in context. Further, Qohelet does not explicitly tell the reader to whom to *give* the *portion.*

Thus, those commentators who understand v. 1 to refer to charitable giving continue that theme into the present verse. Distribute your charity to many people. However, I prefer to understand the verses as referring to business activities. Thus, the force of the advice is to diversify one's financial risks. If one or two go under, there are other investments that will come through.

In terms of the message of the book as a whole, Qohelet has consistently maintained the uncertainty of life in the present world. No one can *know* what will happen. Furthermore, given Qohelet's jaundiced view of the world, it is fitting that he would suggest that the result will be *evil,* that is, tragic.

The use of the x/x+1 pattern (here *seven, even to eight*) is well known in Hebrew literature (see, for instance, Prov. 30:15, 18, 21, 29; Amos 1:3, 6, 9, 11, 13; 2:4; Mic. 5:4) as well as in the literature of the ancient Near East. Wolfgang Roth identifies two functions: (1) when the second number is the

15. For example, see Deltizsch, *Proverbs, Ecclesiastes, Song of Solomon,* pp. 391-93; and Gordis, *Koheleth,* pp. 329-30.
16. Podechard, *L'Ecclésiaste,* p. 198.

will be rewarded." However, there is nothing in the verse itself that hints that Qohelet had charity in mind. The Arabic proverb could be influenced by the early charitable interpretation of Ecclesiastes.

A similar structure associates v. 1 with v. 2, which, though it has its own difficulties, seems to be concerned with business transactions. Such a connection is the strongest argument in favor of those who understand v. 1 to refer to the calculated risks of business. In other words, it is saying that, in spite of the risks of loss involved, one should go ahead and engage in maritime trade. This view seems most likely in the context. *bread (lehem),* thus, stands for any kind of commodity of trade. The idea of the verse, then, is that, as people engage in trade, profits may flow back to them. Risk is involved, but reward may come. This view is widely held.[15]

Even if we are unable to come to a definitive understanding of the verse, Podechard is certainly correct that this verse fits in with the teaching of 3:11, 8:17, and 9:11 that, according to Qohelet, the future is uncertain.[16]

2 The theme of uncertainty about the future continues in this verse, which is also associated with the first verse by virtue of its close syntactical structure (initial imperative and concluding motive clause [marked by initial *kî*]). As with the preceding verse, Qohelet's statement is somewhat elliptical to a modern reader. We are left with questions about the nature of the *portion* (*hēleq*) that is to be given to seven or eight. It is surely to be connected with "bread" in the preceding verse, but there is disagreement over what that word means in context. Further, Qohelet does not explicitly tell the reader to whom to *give* the *portion.*

Thus, those commentators who understand v. 1 to refer to charitable giving continue that theme into the present verse. Distribute your charity to many people. However, I prefer to understand the verses as referring to business activities. Thus, the force of the advice is to diversify one's financial risks. If one or two go under, there are other investments that will come through.

In terms of the message of the book as a whole, Qohelet has consistently maintained the uncertainty of life in the present world. No one can *know* what will happen. Furthermore, given Qohelet's jaundiced view of the world, it is fitting that he would suggest that the result will be *evil,* that is, tragic.

The use of the x/x+1 pattern (here *seven, even to eight*) is well known in Hebrew literature (see, for instance, Prov. 30:15, 18, 21, 29; Amos 1:3, 6, 9, 11, 13; 2:4; Mic. 5:4) as well as in the literature of the ancient Near East. Wolfgang Roth identifies two functions: (1) when the second number is the

---

15. For example, see Delitzsch, *Proverbs, Ecclesiastes, Song of Solomon,* pp. 391-93; and Gordis, *Koheleth,* pp. 329-30.

16. Podechard, *L'Ecclésiaste,* p. 198.

who does all things [ma'*ᵃśēh hā'*ᵉlōhîm '*ᵃšer ya'*ᵃśeh 'et-hakkōl]) to refer to God's creative activity (NIV), but it is much more likely that this generic phrase refers simply to what God is doing in the world. James Crenshaw rightly points out that Ecclesiastes 3:11, 8:17, and 9:12 have anticipated Qohelet's statement about human inability to know of God's activity on earth.[21]

6 On the basis of the uncertainty of human endeavor (note the repetition in this verse of *you do not know, 'ênᵉkā yôdēʿ;* the other occurrences are found in 11:2, 5), Qohelet now gives his advice, and, as we might expect after 11:4, he tells his readers to go ahead and act anyway. Though he uses agrarian language here *(plant your seed),* he likely intends this to stand for all human activity. Since we do not know whether the seed we planted in the morning will germinate and produce the food that we need, we had better plant twice with the hope that one, or with good luck that both, will come to fruition. Qohelet thus once again expresses a skeptical attitude toward life, though not a skepticism that leads to inactivity.

The Targum understood the verse to refer to the seed of sexual intercourse, perhaps under the influence of v. 5: "In the days of your youth take a wife to beget children, and in the time of your old age do not leave the wife of your lot so as not to bear children, for you do not know which of them is destined to be good, one or the other, or whether both will be good."[22]

22. Youth, Old Age, and Death (11:7-10)

Qohelet concludes his teaching with a reflection and instructions on youth, old age, and death. Indeed, death may be the theme that unites this section since youth is ultimately seen from the perspective of old age, from the threshold of death.

Some discussion attends the beginning of this final section, since a few scholars argue that 11:7-8 actually concludes the preceding section. Though I cannot be dogmatic, the verses read more smoothly as the introduction to a section that extols the joys of youth, while living under the shadow of old age and death.

7 *Truly,*[23] *sweet is the light, and it is pleasant for the eyes to see the sun.*

8 *Indeed,*[24] *if someone lives many years, let him enjoy all of them.*[25] *But*

---

21. Crenshaw, *Ecclesiastes,* p. 180.

22. Levine, *The Aramaic Version of Qohelet,* p. 46.

23. Gordis (*Koheleth,* p. 334) lists the passages in Ecclesiastes (3:16; 4:4; 7:26; 8:10; 12:1) where a *waw* begins a new section. Here it is best to translate as an emphatic.

24. *kî 'îm,* which begins the verse, usually has an exceptive force, but the majority of scholars take it either as a causal or, as I have, an asseverative.

25. An example of the lack of gender concord. The suffix on *all of them (bᵉkullām)* is masculine, while the antecedent *(years)* is feminine.

*he should remember the days of darkness, for they will be many. All
that which is coming is meaningless.*

9 *Rejoice, young man, while[26] you are young. Let your heart be merry
in days of your youth.[27] Follow the ways of your heart and the sight[28]
of your eyes. But[29] know that God will bring you into judgment concerning all these things.*

10 *Put away anger from your heart and turn away evil from your body,
for youth and vitality[30] are meaningless.*

7   The last section of Qohelet's speech begins with an exclamation that extols
life. Qohelet says that consciousness, indeed life itself, is *sweet.* This attitude
seems at variance with that expressed in 4:2 and elsewhere that life is not
worth living and death is preferable. However, the contrast may be between
the attitude of a youth (11:9) versus an older person who has experienced
disappointment and tragedy in the fallen world. It is true that Qohelet prizes
life over death elsewhere in the book (9:4-6), but this verse is the most
optimistic. As we will see, Qohelet's enthusiasm will once again be tempered
by his awareness of death.

Graham Ogden[31] betrays his literary insensitivity when he argues that
sweet (mātôq) is an awkward attribute of *light ('ôr).* Indeed, it is a powerful
metaphor, highly estimating the value of life itself.

8   Qohelet begins with the advice to enjoy life as long as one lives.
He does this by encouraging his pupils to make the most of all the days of
their life. However, he immediately notes the impossibility of his own counsel.
People will remember that the light of life (11:7) will be followed by the
darkness (haḥōšek) of old age and death. Furthermore, the dark days of one's

---

26. Treating the preposition as a temporal *beth* (Williams, *Hebrew Syntax,*
§241).

27. The feminine plural form of *your youth (beḥûrôtekā)* likely indicates an abstract
(Whitley, *Koheleth,* p. 93). It appears only here and in 12:1.

28. The Ketib form of the word is plural and unique *(mar'ê).* The Qere is singular
and probably the correct form *(mar'ēh).*

29. The context determines an adversative meaning for the *waw.*

30. This word *(haššaḥarût)* occurs only here and in Mishnaic Hebrew (though note
a similar root in Lam. 4:8). The root means "to be black" and is in some way connected
with the noun "dawn" *(šaḥar).* Fredericks *(Qoheleth's Language,* pp. 136, 191, 199)
provides counterarguments to the belief that this word is a Mishnaism, over against Barton
(The Book of Ecclesiastes, p. 195). Schoors *(The Preacher Sought to Find Pleasing Words,*
p. 218) and Lauha *(Kohelet,* p. 209) suggest that the word is in a hendiadys with *youth.*
The latter translates the clause "die Jugend mit ihrer Blüte," or "in the bloom of youth."
The Septuagint misunderstood the word and translated "folly" *(ha anoia).*

31. Ogden, *Qoheleth,* p. 194.

259

life are many. Thus, Qohelet concludes with his characteristic view of the value of life: it is *meaningless*.

Many commentators and translations argue that the verb here translated *he will remember (wᵉyizkōr)* is a second jussive, "let him remember," and thus continues Qohelet's advice. From a morphological point of view this is possible, but it really does not make sense in the context, for Qohelet would then be giving contradictory advice that his reader should both enjoy life but also remember that he is going to die.

It is interesting to note the approach of Gregory Thaumaturgos, who represents an early Christian pietistic interpretation. This verse worries him because he reads passages like 1 Corinthians 15:55, which indicates that death is not a problem for the Christian. They are not dark days, but days of joy and celebration. Thus, he puts the thoughts of vv. 7 and 8 in the mind of the non-Christian.[32]

R. N. Whybray, in order to support his claim that Qohelet is a preacher of joy, unjustifiably reverses his thought when he argues that "Qoheleth's intention here is not to introduce a note of gloom to negate or qualify the cheerful note struck in v. 7, but to use the backdrop of inevitable death to highlight the positive opportunities for joy in this life."[33]

9 Verses 7 and 8 have established a pattern repeated here. First, we had a call to enjoy life (vv. 7-8a), then the warning about darker days ahead (v. 8b). In verse 9 Qohelet begins with encouragement to enjoy life in the first two parts. He first encourages the young to rejoice, and then advises them to enjoy themselves while they are young. After this positive advice, however, he imparts a somber reminder of the coming judgment. Specifically, he will judge them for their youthful enjoyment!

Indeed, the contrast is so great that some commentators treat v. 9c as a redactional gloss added by a later pious reader to tone down Qohelet's harsh rhetoric.[34] Yet there are other ways to deal with the apparent contradiction. Pious interpreters have prized v. 9c to the denigration of vv. 9a and b. Gregory Thaumaturgos, for instance, felt that the first part of the verse was the viewpoint of another whom Qohelet critiques in v. 9c.[35]

The tension between the two parts of the verse is also compounded by the apparent tension between v. 9ab and other parts of the OT. Since the earliest time, Qohelet's canonicity (see "Canon" in the introduction) has been contested on the basis of the contrast between 11:9 and Numbers 15:39 ("you may obey them and not prostitute yourselves by going after the lusts of your own hearts and eyes").

---

32. See Jarick, *Gregory Thaumaturgos' Parphrase,* p. 285.
33. Whybray, *Ecclesiastes,* NCB, p. 161.
34. Lauha, *Kohelet,* p. 205; Crenshaw, *Ecclesiastes,* p. 184.
35. Jarick, *Gregory Thaumaturgos' Paraphrase,* p. 286.

Early attempts at smoothing the tension may also be seen in the rendition of Codex Vaticanus of the Septuagint, which adds two words to produce the following rendition: "walk in the ways of your heart *blameless,* and *not* in the sight of your eyes."[36] More recently it has been argued that, though the same words are used, Qohelet and Numbers are really talking about "two different kinds of desire."[37]

However, all of these attempts are based on the supposition that Qohelet is offering a single coherent point of view. It has been the contention of this commentary that it is better to understand Qohelet as a confused, skeptical wise man who vacillates between the traditional doctrine in which he was trained and the harsh realities of life (see the introduction). Thus, these tensions do not surprise us.

In sum, his advice to the young is to pursue whatever they want to do, not to wait or it will be too late. He specifically mentions the *heart* and the *eyes* because these are the "organs of desire."[38]

At the end Qohelet remembers the *judgment (mišpāṭ),* but is this remembrance any more than a theological reflex? He has already denied that there is equity in earthly judgments (3:16), and he leaves no room for a heavenly, eschatological judgment since he denies the existence of an afterlife.

10   This verse's structure parallels that of the previous verse. It begins with admonitions to live a joyful and apparently carefree life, but then concludes with an observation that deflates enthusiasm.

Qohelet admonishes his reader to live a happy life by using two verbs of removal (*put away* [*hāsēr,* a hiphil of *sûr*] and *turn away* [*ha'ǎbēr,* the hiphil of *'br*). From the heart, which is the seat of the emotions as well as the intellect, Qohelet calls on his reader to put away *anger (ka'as),* which can also be translated "frustration" in certain contexts (see earlier in 1:18; 2:23; 5:16 [English 5:17]; 7:3). From the *body (bāšār,* literally "flesh") Qohelet advises the removal of *rā'ā,* which literally means "evil" but in this context likely means *pain,* a kind of evil that afflicts the body.

The basis for Qohelet's advice is that *youth and vitality are meaningless:* that is, *anger* (frustration) and *pain* are characteristics more frequently found among the aged. Thus, enjoy a life relatively free of these traits while you can. I have rendered *hebel* as *meaningless,* as has been the case throughout the book. Qohelet, from his vantage point of old age, observes the meaninglessness of youth. This may, however, be the one verse where the temporal

36. Lauha (*Kohelet,* p. 205) gives the misimpression that the Septuagint (rather than simply one manuscript of the Septuagint) supports this reading.
37. Ginsburg, *The Song of Songs and Coheleth,* p. 455.
38. Gordis, *Koheleth,* p. 335.

aspect of the root is emphasized. In other words, the verse may be saying: "for youth and vitality are transient."

SUMMARY OF CHAPTER 11

Chapter 11 is the shortest chapter in the book and contains two sections. The first deals again with uncertainty and emphasizes the risk involved in an ambiguous future (vv. 1-6). Some of the most memorable imagery comes from this section of the book (e.g., the bread returning on the water [v. 1]).

The second unit (vv. 7-10) begins the transition into the last topic that Qohelet will address in the book: youth, old age, and death. In the four verses that end this chapter, Qohelet tells his young audience to enjoy their youth. However, he reminds them that the future hangs like a dark cloud over their heads.

23. Approaching Old Age and Death (12:1-7)

The chapter division obscures the integrity of the larger unit that begins in 11:7. In other words, 12:1-7 is a subunit of the larger pericope of 11:7–12:7 that deals with youth and old age. The section 11:7-8 dealt with the joy of youth, but already in 11:9-10 there was the spectre that something horrifying was on the horizon. "Youth is fleeting," and what follows is now made clear by 12:1-7 — death. Thus, as Roland Murphy points out, 12:1-7 flows naturally from the preceding unit.[1] Furthermore, there is continuity of genre between the sections since 11:7-10 and 12:1-7 are both instructions, though 12:1-7 also has elements of a reflection on death.[2]

Nonetheless, 12:1-7 is a subunit and as such has its own integrity. The cohesiveness of this unit is marked by the repetitive before ('ad 'ašer, vv. 1b, 2a, 6) that follows the initial imperative, remember (zᵉkōr, v. 1a).

Much discussion attends the proper understanding of the images (the storm [v. 2], the house and its inhabitants [vv. 3-5], and the precious utensils [v. 6]) presented in these verses. The oldest attested interpretations[3] take an allegorical approach that is still popular in some forms today. This approach takes as its departure point apparent connections between the image of the house and its inhabitants and specific body parts. As one illustration (more will be drawn in the

---

1. Murphy, *Ecclesiastes*, p. 114.
2. Murphy, *Wisdom Literature*, p. 148.
3. For instance, the Targum (see Levine, *The Aramaic Version of Qohelet*, pp. 46-47); *Qohelet Rabbah* 12; *b. Shabbat*, 151b.

commentary to follow), Qohelet notes that the grinders (female servants in the household) cease because they are few. The connection with the deterioration and loss of teeth during old age is too close to overlook, and I will argue that such connections are not impossible. The problem with this type of allegorical interpretation of the passage is the arbitrariness of many of the associations that are made and the fact that there are often multiple possibilities for association. The whole approach is thus extremely subjective and, therefore, suspicious.

Nonetheless, a less arbitrary symbolic understanding of the poem is invited by the strange collocations of the poem itself. For instance, why did Qohelet describe the inhabitants of the house as being composed of four classes of people? Michael Fox and John Sawyer provide helpful guidelines to the proper interpretation of these verses.

Fox's approach[4] takes account of three levels of meaning: literal, figurative, and symbolic. He followed the literal approach of C. Taylor,[5] who argued that the poem as a whole describes a funeral. However, the connection with 12:2 makes me think that the reaction to follow in vv. 3-6 finds its setting in the onset of a powerful and destructive storm. This understanding will be explained in the commentary to follow.

Sawyer calls Fox's second level of meaning metaphoric. He notes, for instance, that the descriptions of the house and its inhabitants in v. 3 are strange when understood literally.[6] Sawyer points out that this verse operates as a metaphor. The house and its inhabitants represent the body; the decline of the house in the midst of the encroaching storm[7] communicates the body's physical decline during advancing old age.

Then lastly, as Sawyer also argues, there is an allegorical level of meaning intended by Qohelet.[8] This level is signaled by one or two obvious connections. Who but the most hardened exegetes can resist the association between the "grinders" and teeth? This is hard to make sense of on the literal level; the difficulty drives us to the allegorical interpretation. The allegory reminds us that old age is often accompanied (especially in the days before extensive dental care) with the loss of teeth.

4. Fox, "Aging and Death in Qohelet 12," *JSOT* 42 (1988): 55-77; and *Qohelet and His Contradictions,* pp. 281-98.

5. C. Taylor, *The Dirge in Ecclesiastes 12* (Edinburgh: Williams and Norgate, 1874).

6. See J. F. A. Sawyer's helpful study, "The Ruined House in Ecclesiastes 12: A Reconstruction of the Original Parable," *JBL* 94 (1974): 519-31.

7. Sawyer reads the house image in the context of the storm image of v. 2.

8. It may, with Fox (*Qohelet and His Contradictions,* pp. 294-96), be more appropriate to call this literary phenomenon figuration rather than allegory. Though I have learned much from Fox's interpretation of this passage, nonetheless, I find myself extending the concept beyond Fox's conservative approach.

The problem with the allegorical approach is extent. Is the whole an allegory? If only a few verses of the poem are allegorical, then where do we stop making connections? The fact that the answer to the first question is likely negative and the answer to the second is not clear lead many to shy away from an allegorical understanding of any part of the passage. I will identify those parts of the poem that I believe make allegorical associations in the commentary below, but I readily admit that I may be either over- or underextending the allegory. This is not a matter of scientific precision.

1 *Remember[9] your creator[10] in the days of your youth before the evil days come and the years approach when you will say, "I have no delight in them,"*

2 *before the sun and the light and the moon and the stars grow dark, and the clouds return after the rain,*

3 *on the day when[11] the house guards[12] tremble[13] and the landowners[14]*

---

9. The verse actually begins with a *waw* that is not translated here. In Ecclesiastes the *waw* often simply serves to introduce a new section (Schoors, *The Preacher Sought to Find Pleasing Words,* p. 206), for example, 2:18; 3:16; 4:1; 4:4; 4:7; 8:10; 11:7; 12:1.

10. The translation of this enigmatic reference to God, the creator, will be treated in the body of the commentary. Here, however, I raise the issue surrounding its morphology. The difficulty is that the word is in the plural, literally "your creators." However, the plural makes no sense in this context and has been explained in several ways. Baer (in 1886; see reference in Whitley, *Koheleth,* p. 95) and Lauha (*Kohelet,* p. 205) note that the versions (*creatoris* [Vulgate] and *ktisas* [Septuagint]) and a few Hebrew manuscripts show the singular. Perhaps the translations of the versions were based on these Hebrew manuscripts, though we must leave open the possibility that they "corrected" the text for theological reasons. Gordis (*Koheleth,* pp. 340-41) approaches the issue by arguing that a *lamed-aleph* is treated as a *lamed-he* verb (the form is a participle with suffix). A third option is to understand that the plural is used as an emphatic rather than as indicating plurality (Schoors, *The Preacher Sought to Find Pleasing Words,* p. 24). While it is impossible to decide among the options, their availability undermines the necessity of an emendation.

11. The temporal expression *on the day when (bayyôm še-)* that opens the verse associates its contents with v. 2 (so Fox, *Qohelet and His Contradictions,* p. 301). Thus, the approaching storm (12:2) is the day when the inhabitants of the house react in the way described in the verse.

12. Or perhaps more broadly, "keepers of the house" (*šōmᵉrê habbayit)*, so NIV and Fox, *Qohelet and His Contradictions,* p. 302. The important points for the following interpretation are their male gender and their relatively low social position.

13. The qal of *zwʿ* occurs only one other place in biblical Hebrew (Esth. 5:9), and this late occurrence has been used to date the book. However, the pilpel (Hab. 2:7) and the noun (Isa. 28:19) are also attested in earlier books. Indeed, there are so few occurrences of this word that its appearance in two late books may simply be coincidental.

bend, and the women grinders cease[15] *because they are few, and those women who look through the window grow dim;*

4 *the doors in the street*[16] *are shut,*[17] *when*[18] *the sound of the mill decreases, and one rises*[19] *at the sound of a bird, and all the daughters of song are brought low.*

5 *Moreover,*[20] *they are afraid*[21] *of heights and the terrors*[22] *in the path.*

14. The exact translation of this phrase is not certain. The determinative word is *ḥāyil,* which indicates wealth, power, or prestige. In any case, in contrast to the male servants, these are the male occupants and probably owners of the house (for this meaning see Holladay, *A Concise Hebrew and Aramaic Lexicon of the Old Testament,* p. 102).

15. It is understood that they cease their labors and thus are idle. The verb *bṭl* is often taken as a late form since it occurs only here in biblical Hebrew and often in Aramaic (see M. Wagner, *Die lexikalischen und grammatikalischen Aramaismen im alttestamentlich Hebräisch,* BZAW 96 (Berlin: de Gruyter, 1966), p. 34. However, Fredericks *(Qoheleth's Language,* pp. 173, 179-80, 219) argues that its Semitic, particularly Akkadian, cognates indicate that it has an early history and may not be used for late dating the book.

16. This word *(sûq)* occurs only two other places in biblical Hebrew (Prov. 7:8 and Song of Songs 3:2). It occurs frequently, though, in Aramaic and has been used as evidence for a late date. Besides its well-attested use in Arabic (for marketplace), a cognate is also found in Akkadian *(šuqu),* and thus it is not necessarily a late form (so Fredericks, *Qoheleth's Language,* pp. 238-39).

17. The Septuagint attests an active verb, but I stay with the Masoretic pointing, which is a pual perfect.

18. Understanding the *beth* prefix on the infinitive construct of *spl* to have a temporal force.

19. This clause is the focus of syntactical issues in this verse. The problem arises because of the lack of an antecedent for the verb. I understand it as an impersonal subject (Schoors, *The Preacher Sought to Find Pleasing Words,* pp. 155-56), and thus I reject the necessity of textual emendation (for instance, that suggested by Symmachus, who substitutes the Greek equivalent of Hebrew *qml* "to be thin").

20. Here *gam* has an "associative function," that is, it links vv. 4 and 5 (Schoors, *The Preacher Sought to Find Pleasing Words,* p. 129).

21. The text-critical history of this verb is interesting, due to the close similarity between the conjugated roots of the verbs "to see" *(rā'â)* and "to be afraid" *(yārē').* The context (see the following noun *terrors)* leads one to expect the latter, but if so, we would expect the imperfect form to be pointed *yîr'û* rather than *yirā'û,* since normally the initial *yod* of the root is preserved in the imperfect form. However, this is not always the case (Schoors, *The Preacher Sought to Find Pleasing Words,* p. 28), and so the MT is a perfectly appropriate form of the verb *yāre'* "to be afraid." I should note that other support for some form of the verb "to see" comes from the versions (Septuagint and Symmachus). However, over against this reading is the witness of the Vulgate and Syriac, which support the MT and read a form of "to fear." On the basis of context, then, I stay with the Masoretic reading and understand the verb to be from *yārē'.* With Schoors, we argue that the Masoretic form is simply an unusual vocalization of *yārē'* "to be afraid."

22. This word is a hapax legomenon. However, its meaning is easily derived from its base root *ḥtt* "to be filled with terror."

The almond tree blossoms[23] and the grasshopper[24] drags itself along[25] and the caperberry is useless.[26] For humans go to their eternal home[27] and mourners walk about in the street,

6[28] *before the silver thread is snapped,[29] and the golden bowl is crushed, and the jar is broken[30] by the well,[31] and the wheel[32] is crushed at the cistern,*

23. The verb is difficult. All ancient translations and the majority of modern commentators believe that the root is *nṣṣ* ("to bloom"), and that the form found in this verse is a full writing or else a "scribal error" (Schoors, *The Preacher Sought to Find Pleasing Words,* p. 42). This view is adopted here. The alternative is that the root is *n'ṣ* "to despise," the idea being that in old age even delicious almonds are hated, since the sense of taste is gone.

24. Or perhaps *ḥāgāb* is some type or stage of development of the "locust."

25. The verb *sbl* in the qal means "to carry, to bear." I here take the hitpael in a reflexive sense. Some of the versions indicate that the verb might mean "to become fat" or "to swell," and thus be more explicitly allegorical (Targum, Vulgate [*pinguabitur*], Septuagint [*paxynthē*]).

26. The verbal root is *prr,* which can mean either "to burst forth" or "to break." I take it in the latter sense and, when speaking of the quality of the caperberry as an aphrodisiac, find the translation "is useless" suitable to the context.

27. Many commentators have noted that the extrabiblical evidence indicates that *eternal home (bêt 'ôlāmô)* refers not to heaven (of which Qohelet shows no awareness) but to the grave. Quoting J. L. Crenshaw ("Youth and Old Age in Qohelet," *HAR* 10 [1986]: 9, n. 33), "The expression 'eternal home' refers to the grave in a Palmyrene inscription from the end of the second century B.C.E., a Punic inscription, Egyptian usage; the Targum on Isa. 14:18; and Sanhedrin 19a; cf. Tobit 3:6." R. F. Youngblood's argument that *'ôlām* should here be associated with the proto-Semitic root *ǵlm* and the phrase translated "dark house" is unnecessary and very unlikely (see his "Qoheleth's 'Dark House' (Eccl. 12:5)," *JETS* 29 [1986]: 397-410, reprinted in *A Tribute to Gleason Archer: Essays on the Old Testament,* ed. W. C. Kaiser, Jr., and R. F. Youngblood [Chicago: Moody, 1986], pp. 211-28).

28. Lauha (*Kohelet,* pp. 204-5) rather subjectively argues that this verse should be placed between vv. 2 and 3, but he is not generally followed in this.

29. The Ketib is a niphal imperfect from *rḥq* with the meaning "to be removed." In isolation from the rest of the verse, "the silver thread is removed" makes sense, but the translation does not fit very well with the other clauses of the verse, each of which describes something being broken. The Qere is *yērāṭēq,* which is the niphal of *rtq* with the meaning "be joined." This too makes little sense in the context, so the vast majority of commentators (J. E. Bruns, "The Imagery of Qoh 12,6a," *JBL* 84 (1965): 428-430, who accepts the Qere, is an exception) and contemporary and ancient translations understand it as "is snapped," niphal of *rtq* (see Nah. 3:10; cf. Septuagint, Symmachus, Vulgate, Syriac, *BHS,* NIV, NRSV).

30. It appears that the Masoretes understood this verb as derived from the root *rwṣ,* "to run." Context, especially the appearance of *nārôś* in v. 6d, suggests that the verb is a form of *rṣṣ,* "to break." Thus, I emend the text to *tērōṣ,* a niphal from *rṣṣ.*

31. On the basis of Prov. 28:47 and Isa. 14:15; 38:18, Fox (*Qohelet and His Contradictions,* p. 307) provocatively suggests that *well (bôr)* is used here because of its metaphoric associations with the tomb.

32. This noun is debated. While many believe the reference is the wheel-like pulley of a well, others dispute this and suggest rather that the word refers to some kind of jar, jug, or

7 *and the dust returns*[33] *to the earth as it was, and the spirit returns to God, who gave it.*

1 Once again we have a contrast between youth and old age. Youth is a time of life, enjoyment, and the possibility of connection with God (11:7-10). Old age faces death, does not have the possibility of enjoyment *(I have no delight in them),* and is a time when it is not propitious to establish a relationship with God. Old age is characterized as *evil days.* We find out why as we read the next few verses.

Some scholars (see James Crenshaw below) have questioned what is, to them, the abrupt appearance of God as creator in the verse. Their concerns are heightened by what seems to be an anomalous plural form (see n. 10). Thus, they present alternatives to the MT. Some argue that we should read *bôreʰkā* "your pit," a reference to the grave. Thus, once again Qohelet calls on his readers to meditate on death in the time of youth (11:9). Others (most recently Crenshaw)[34] prefer *beʾerʰkā,* literally "your well," but metaphorically "your wife." Lastly, others repoint the Hebrew text to either *berûʾeykā* or *boryʰʾākā* "your health." Such changes, while appealing in that they too fit in with Qohelet's message, are not necessary since the Hebrew text makes perfectly good sense as it stands. It is also not necessary to excise v. 1a as the contribution of a pious redactor.[35] We have already witnessed Qohelet's ambivalent attitude toward God (most recently in 11:7-10). Michael Fox appropriately points out that if this clause is removed, the remaining Hebrew is extremely difficult syntactically.[36]

That these alternatives are attested in antiquity is shown by a quote from Rabbi Aqiba, who synthesizes all the possibilities into a single statement that the verse is understood well by the following paraphrase, "know whence you came [*bʾrk,* your source], whither you are going [*bwrk,* your grave], and before whom you are destined to give an accounting [*bwrʾyk,* your Creator]."[37]

---

bowl. For a discussion, see Fox, *Qohelet and His Contradictions,* pp. 307-8. Fox disputes the idea that we have two images associated with light and water in this verse and rather postulates that the cord held up three objects, each of which was broken when the cord snapped.

33. The form is jussive, but the context demands an indicative sense. Most commentators and grammarians point out that there are a number of cases in the Hebrew Bible where the shortened form has an indicative force (GKC §109k; Isaksson, *Studies in the Language of Qoheleth,* p. 27, n. 102). In the most recent analysis of the language of Ecclesiastes, Schoors (*The Preacher Sought to Find Pleasing Words,* p. 28) agrees and adds his opinion that in this case the shortened form is preferred to keep it grammatically parallel to *weⁿārōṣ* in the previous verse.

34. Crenshaw, *Ecclesiastes,* p. 185.

35. So Lauha, *Kohelet,* pp. 204-5.

36. Fox, *Qohelet and His Contradictions,* p. 300.

37. Crenshaw, *Ecclesiastes,* p. 185.

These alternatives are attractive because Qohelet's reference to God as creator seems odd, and even forced, as he draws his teaching to a close, especially since he has just finished telling his hearers to enjoy their youth. This awkwardness is intensified by the fact that his remaining few verses go on to describe death as the end of it all — God does not have a prize waiting for those who remember him at the end of their lives. However, it is too easy to do away with the problem by the tour de force of emendation. I understand the reference as a pious, but fairly empty, impersonal, and objective reference to God as he introduces the real subject of his concluding section — God.

2 Verse 2 continues the long sentence that began in 12:1. The main clause is found there, "Remember your creator in the days of your youth. . . ." Here we get the second of the temporal clauses that begin with *before* (*ʿad ʾªšer lô*).[38] The description that follows is metaphoric.

The first half of the verse describes the time when the heavenly lights become obscured. Four are mentioned, three of which are quickly understood: *the sun, the moon,* and *the stars.* The other, which appears second in the list, is more difficult: *the light.* It has commonly been understood as forming a hendiadys with the following words: "and the light of the moon and the stars."[39] Fox, however, points out that this would be the only instance of this type of three-member hendiadys.[40] He also notes, along with many others,[41] that Genesis 1:3-5 describes a light that existed independently of the sun. However, the view that this light is independent of the sun is tenuous, depending as it does on the supposition that Genesis 1 gives a chronological description of creation. Also it presupposes that "the light" was an entity that continued to function or exist after the creation of the sun. In any case, it would be surprising that only Genesis 1 and Ecclesiastes would mention this astral phenomenon. Though we cannot be certain exactly what is meant in this context by *the light,* our lack of knowledge does not interfere with our interpretation of the passage.

The second half of the verse is relatively easy to translate with one possible exception. The preposition *ʾaḥar* is normally translated "after," but this is difficult from the standpoint of weather patterns. Why does Qohelet describe the *clouds* as coming after the rains? One argument[42] is that Ruth 1:15-16 and Ugaritic support the idea that the idiom means that clouds come

---

38. Schoors, *The Preacher Sought to Find Pleasing Words,* p. 145.

39. Gordis, *Koheleth,* p. 341.

40. Fox, *Qohelet and His Contradictions,* p. 300.

41. Including Ginsburg, *The Song of Songs and Coheleth,* p. 457.

42. R. B. Y. Scott, *Proverbs. Ecclesiastes,* AB (Garden City, NY: Doubleday, 1965), p. 255.

along with the rain. However, from a psychological viewpoint, the idea that clouds are coming after rain evokes even more pathos. It is, after all, the darkness created by the clouds that make a rainy day so depressing. Thus, I stay with by far the most common translation of the preposition.

One centuries-old interpretive approach understands the various elements of the verse in an allegorical fashion, though there is nothing in the verse itself to encourage such an understanding. The Targum translates as follows:

> Before the glorious brightness which is like the sun be changed, and before the light of thy eyes be darkened, and before the beauty of your cheeks becomes black, and before the centers of your eyes, which are like stars, be dim, your eyelids drip tears like clouds after rain.[43]

Franz Delitzsch finds himself in continuity with the allegorical interpreters of the past,[44] when, among other connections, he associates the sun with the male spirit, the moon with the soul, and the stars with the five senses.

Such an approach is much too eisegetical and arbitrary. The metaphors of the darkening of the cosmic lights and the encroaching rain clouds are understood readily enough on a psychological plane as communicating Qohelet's belief that old age is a catastrophe that engenders sorrow. As one grows old, one grows weak, having less control over body and mind. Finally, death comes, and, in Qohelet's thinking, that is the end of the story. Ernst Hengstenberg understood that "in Old Testament delineations of adversity we so often read of the destruction of the heavenly lights," and "dark clouds are often used as an image of troubles."[45] In sum, the passage presents images evoking dread and sorrow in the light of encroaching old age and impending death.

3   The focus now shifts to the inhabitants of a house. The four classes of people mentioned indicate that we are to think of a rather elaborate structure, perhaps a palace, though it really makes little difference to the metaphoric story.

The four groups are carefully chosen. The first two are male and the second two are female. The first and the third are lower-class servants; the second and the fourth are upper class. I will discuss them in order. The first group, *the house guards (šōmᵉrê habbayit)*, are male servants. As the storm approaches (see n. 28, which describes the relationship between vv. 2 and 3), they react in fear; they *tremble*. The second group is male and upper class,

---

43. Levine, *The Aramaic Version of Qohelet*, p. 46.
44. Delitzsch, *Proverbs, Ecclesiastes, Song of Solomon*, pp. 402-5.
45. Hengstenberg, *A Commentary on Ecclesiastes*, p. 245, citing Ezek. 13:11-13; 38:22; Song of Songs 2:11.

the landowners ('anšê hehāyil*).* They are said to *bend.* It is hard from the context to be specific about the significance of this action, and the choice of the verb may have more to do with its figurative meaning (see below) than its literal sense. The bending may be out of fear or consternation. The third group is lower class and female, *the women grinders (hattōhᵃnôt).* They are the women who do the daily grinding of the grain and provide the household with flour for food.[46] Once again, problems arise in understanding the line on a literal level, for it is hard to see why their numerical decrease would require their idleness; if anything, their labors would increase. One might speculate that it indicates their despair; they just give up. Once again, however, it is likely that this difficulty is presented to us because of Qohelet's interest in the figurative meaning, to be explained below. The last and fourth group is female, but upper class, *women who look through the window (hārō'ôt bā'ᵃrub-bôt).* These are the women of leisure. They are not grinding or doing any other toil; rather they look out of the window, perhaps at the approaching storm described in v. 2.

The verse speaks of a deteriorating household facing a devastating storm. On a symbolic level, Qohelet thus describes the deterioration of old age. Everything falls apart.

It is hard to resist the next step. Whether we call it allegorical or figurative, there is a strong likelihood that the author intended his readers to think of specific body functions. The main signals are the difficulties presented by a straight literal reading of the verse. For instance, what is the logic behind the decreasing number of grinders? If we understand the grinders to represent teeth, then it is clear that their diminution is the result of loss of teeth, a frequent occurrence in old age particularly in antiquity. Why are the women who look through the window said to grow dim? This is an allegorical reference to the loss of eyesight in old age.

Such an interpretation of the verse is often resisted on the basis of the apparent arbitrariness of the associations. However, it must be pointed out that there has been no variation in these two identifications. Both ancient (Targum) and modern (Delitzsch)[47] interpreters go in this direction. It must be admitted, though, that the first two groups (i.e., the house guards and landowners) are not as universally identified. Robert Gordis indicates some of the variation when he points out that the house guards have been identified as knees or ribs or legs or arms, while the landowners have been associated with arms or thighs.[48] Though a precise identification cannot be made, there

46. See Plumptre, *Ecclesiastes; or, the Preacher,* p. 215, for a list of passages that indicate the servant status of such women.
47. Delitzsch, *Proverbs, Ecclesiastes, Song of Songs,* pp. 405-7.
48. Gordis, *Koheleth,* pp. 342-43.

is no doubt that trembling and bending are actions that characterize the elderly. Such a figurative approach cannot be denied.

4   The description of the household threatened by storm (v. 2) continues at least in the first half of the verse. In anticipation of the storm *the doors* are closed. Also, the daily grinding operation stops (as seen above in v. 3).

There is more than one suggestion for v. 4a by advocates of an allegorical/figurative approach to the poem. The closing of the doors cannot help but suggest the blocking or disability of all or some bodily orifices. After all, the doors provide entrance to and exit from the house (the body) from the *street* (the outside world). Significantly, *doors* is in the dual (*delātayim*), encouraging an identification with some body part that has two parts. While some (e.g., Ibn Ezra) have argued that the doors are the lips, the remainder of the verse points strongly to the ears.

The lowering of the grinding sound could simply describe the effect of hearing loss or possibly, but less probably, refer back to the loss of teeth (v. 3). The next two clauses confirm the former understanding, though, since they both concern hearing.

There is a surface contradiction with the next clause *(one rises at the sound of a bird),* since it indicates that the elderly hear too well, so well that a bird disturbs their sleep (cf. Targum). However, hearing loss and restlessness are both characteristics of old age.

The phrase *daughters of song (benôt haššîr)* is unusual to modern ears. Interestingly, it is strikingly similar to a phrase *(bnt hll)* used to describe the *ktrt,* female singers, in Ugaritic literature. Thus, some understand Qohelet to refer to female singers or possibly songs.[49] It could also conceivably be a poetic description of the birds. The best guess is that the clause once again remarks on loss of hearing.

5   As Charles Whitley has remarked, "obscure allegory and textual uncertainty combine to make this line one of the most difficult in Qoheleth."[50] Much of the difficulty is philological and textual and is dealt with in the footnotes that accompany the translation. The uncertainty of translation compounds the difficulty of determining when and if Qohelet speaks allegorically/figuratively as well as literally.

Qohelet speaks very straightforwardly about the fears of old age in the first sentence, *they are afraid of heights and terrors in the path.* Due to decreased physical abilities, the elderly fear to venture out in public. Michael Fox questions whether the fear of heights is a typical characteristic

---

49. Whybray, *Ecclesiastes,* NCB, p. 165.

50. Whitley, *Koheleth,* p. 41, quoted also by Schoors, *The Preacher Sought to Find Pleasing Words,* p. 41.

of old age,[51] but his question is beside the point since Qohelet is painting an extreme picture of the mental and physical deterioration that comes with advanced years.

It is in the next sentence that most of the difficulty is registered. I have presented my best educated guess along with alternatives in the footnotes, so I will here simply concentrate on the possible meaning. My philological choices demonstrate that I am moving in the direction of a figurative understanding of the verse.

There are three parts. Before treating them individually I should point out that all three describe events outside the house (vv. 3 and 4). The almond tree, the caperberry, and the grasshopper go on as if the deterioration of the house is not taking place. Perhaps this signifies the indifference of the surrounding world to the decline and eventual death of the individual.[52] Furthermore, the possible allegorical/figurative associations continue. First, the white blossoms of the almond tree may represent the white hair of the aged. Second, the verb used to describe the movement of the grasshopper, which has lost its spring *(yistabbēl)*, could conceivably (though this is much more tenuous) describe the painful and labored movement of old age. In the third part, the focus is on the well-known qualities of the caperberry as an aphrodisiac. Later Jewish literature made this connection explicit.[53] If this is true, then the uselessness of the caperberry highlights the loss of sexual potency.

If 12:1-5b describes old age,[54] then v. 5c climaxes the section by talking about death. Eventually, everyone goes to their *eternal home,* the grave.

6 In this verse, Qohelet presents us with four more metaphors. Here there is no doubt that their referent is death and not old age, on which vv. 1-5 focus. In this way vv. 6 and 7 climax the poem begun in v. 1.

The first metaphor is the *silver thread* that is *snapped;* the second describes the *golden bowl* that is *crushed.* In both cases we have an object of significant value, and in both cases the object is destroyed, rendered useless. Qohelet makes an implicit comparison with human life. Indeed, it is something of value, but it is rendered valueless at the time of death.

It is possible, though difficult to be certain, that these two images are connected. The word *bowl (gullat)* occurs in Zechariah 4:2-3, where it is the bowl that holds the wicks of candles. Thus, some commentators argue that the silver cord holds the golden bowl, and when the cord is severed, then the

---

51. Fox, *Qohelet and His Contradictions,* p. 305.
52. Sawyer, "The Ruined House in Ecclesiastes 12," pp. 519-31.
53. Whitley, *Koheleth,* p. 99.
54. And this is disputed; see Ogden, *Qoheleth,* pp. 197-208.

bowl containing the lamp is smashed with the result, in the words of Christian Ginsburg, that the "light of the lamp is gone."[55] This lamp is the light that symbolizes life.

The third metaphor is a broken jar; the fourth is a wheel. Both of these are associated with a *well* or *cistern*. There is a dispute over the meaning of *wheel,* but with few exceptions[56] it is thought that it refers to the pulley that would lift a jar out of a well. If so, then the second two images go together as well. The jar and the pulley connected with a well are destroyed, with the result that "the water of the well is unavailable."[57] Water, absolutely essential to sustaining life, symbolizes life. Thus, the verse describes death as the cessation of light and water.

7 In conclusion to his meditation on death Qohelet makes allusion to Genesis 2:7 and 3:19, particularly the former. God created Adam, the forefather of all human beings, by forming his body from the dust of the ground and endowing it with his spirit. Genesis 3:19, in the context of the judgment that is the result of the fall, describes death as the return of the body to the dust to the ground. Thus, what Qohelet describes is a reversal of creation, the dissolution of human creation. This is true as well of the last part of the verse, which states that *the spirit returns to God who gave it.* This is not an optimistic allusion to some kind of consciousness after death, but simply a return to a prelife situation. God temporarily united body and spirit, and now the process is undone. We have in this verse no affirmation of immortality. According to Qohelet, death is the end.

We might ask whether there is a contradiction here with Ecclesiastes 3:21 ("Who knows whether the breath of humans goes up above and the breath of animals goes down to the depths of the earth"). That is, in ch. 3 Qohelet raises a question about life after death, about which he is unsure, and now in 12:7 he dogmatically states what happens.

As has already been stated, Qohelet, being a confused wise man, is not above tensions and contradictions. However, whether this is a true tension or not (the rhetorical question in 3:21 may serve the purpose of dogmatic denial), the important point to bear in mind is that in neither context is there an affirmation of the afterlife.[58]

---

55. Ginsburg, *The Song of Songs and Coheleth,* p. 378.
56. See Fox, *Qohelet and His Contradictions,* pp. 307-8.
57. Ginsburg, *The Song of Songs and Coheleth,* p. 379.
58. Contra Ogden, *Qoheleth,* p. 207; and Ginsburg, *The Song of Songs and Coheleth,* pp. 468-69.

III. FRAME NARRATIVE: EPILOGUE (12:8-14)

A. THE EVALUATION OF THE FRAME NARRATOR (12:8-12)

A change of narrative voice signals the change from Qohelet's meditation to the epilogue; we move from first-person speech by Qohelet (in v. 7) to third-person speech about Qohelet (in v. 8). Early tradition concerning Solomonic authorship has obscured this rather dramatic shift. It saw not a change of speaker but a change in the speaker's perspective, the epilogue representing an aged, repentant Solomon, who comments on the speech of the young, confused Solomon.[59] However, as already discussed in the introduction, nothing in the book of Ecclesiastes or in the historical books of the Bible lends support to the idea that Solomon repented.

The NIV and NRSV use a rubric to divide vv. 8 and 9, but it is clear from the shift in narrative voice that vv. 8-14 must be treated as the final unit of the book. The most natural reading of this shift from first-person to third-person speech, I believe, is to recognize an actual shift in speaker. A second person is now commenting on Qohelet's speech. Further, I see no indication in the text that there is more than one hand involved in the writing of vv. 8-14. In this, I disagree with historical-critical analyses of the epilogue.

James Crenshaw represents a typical historical-critical assessment of the epilogue.[60] He recognizes two hands in it, both to be distinguished from the words of Qohelet. The division within the epilogue is signaled by $w^e y\bar{o}t\bar{e}r$, which begins vv. 9 and 12. The first epilogue (vv. 9-11) is sympathetic to Qohelet and probably was written by a disciple. The second epilogue (vv. 12-14) is critical and written by someone who wants to question and undermine Qohelet's perspective. My own view notes that the epilogist both affirms and critiques Qohelet's views, and it does not resort to the more complicated hypothesis of two glossators. Unlike the shift of narrative voice that indicated a shift in speaker between the body of the book and the epilogue, no shift of narrative voice appears within the epilogue itself.

Within this section we encounter some of the most significant disputes concerning translation and interpretation of the text.

---

59. Whybray (*Ecclesiastes*, NCB, p. 169) asserts that it is "universally agreed that this final section of the book is the work not of Qohelet but of one or more persons who were familiar either with the book in its present form or at least with its contents." By attributing global assent to his historical-critical assumption, thus neglecting virtually all conservative opinion on the matter, Whybray exemplifies critical myopia and scholarly chauvinism.

60. Crenshaw, *Ecclesiastes*, pp. 189-90; see also Whybray, *Ecclesiastes*, NCB, p. 169.

8   *"Completely meaningless," Qohelet said. "Everything is meaningless."*

9   *Furthermore, Qohelet was a wise man. He also[61] taught the people knowledge. He heard,[62] investigated, and put in good order[63] many proverbs.[64]*

10   *Qohelet sought to find words of delight and to write[65] honestly[66] words of truth.*

61. At first it appears awkward to say that Qohelet taught people in addition to being a wise man, since we would assume that every wise person functioned as a teacher. Yet we really know little about the function of wisdom teachers in ancient Israel, and it may very well be the case that some did not teach. I find it even more doubtful to imagine Qohelet as one who "constantly" taught (the alternative translation of *'ôd;* cf. Schoors, *The Preacher Sought to Find Pleasing Words,* p. 116).

62. Typically this verb is taken as a hapax legomenon, a piel from *'zn* II "to weigh." There is an Arabic cognate and a noun *m'znym* "scales," from which the verbal root is supposedly derived. However, there is a more common root *'zn* I that means "to hear, listen to," which is also appropriate to the context. This meaning is reflected in almost all the versions, though the Septuagint *(ous),* followed by the Syro-Hexapla and Coptic, takes it as a noun, while Aquila, the Peshitta, and the Targum translate it as a verb. The Vulgate's *enarravit quae fecerit* ("and he declared what he had done") seems a rather free translation. The difficulty with my understanding of the verb is that this would be the only place in the Hebrew Bible where *'zn* I would be in the piel, all other occurrences being in the hiphil. Note that the three verbs *'izzēn, ḥiqqēr,* and *tiqqēn (heard, investigated,* and *put in good order)* are all in the piel, perhaps for aural reasons.

63. Consult M. Fishbane (*Biblical Interpretation in Ancient Israel* [Oxford: Clarendon, 1985], p. 32) for the argument that this is a technical scribal term that means "to edit." For other comments, consult 1:15 and 7:13.

64. The Septuagint apparently had difficulty with this last sentence. It understood both the first and last verbs as nouns, thus *kai ous exichniasetai kosmion parabolōn* ("the ear will trace out the order of the parables"; see commentary by Jarick [*Gregory Thaumaturgos' Paraphrase,* p. 301]).

65. The grammatical difficulties of *to write (kātûb)* are well recorded. The word is a qal passive participle, but that is awkward in the verse, though the NKJV appears to defend the text as it stands: "The Preacher sought to find acceptable words; and what was written was upright — words of truth." However, many emend the text to either the perfect form *(kātab)* or the infinitive absolute *(kātôb).* Since the latter involves only a vocalic change, it is to be preferred. Nonetheless, once the syntax of the Hebrew is established, there are still disagreements about the translation. The infinitive absolute can stand in the place of other forms of the verb; it functions like a verbal wild card (GKC §113d). The NRSV, for instance, understands the infinitive absolute to function like a perfect: "The Teacher sought to find pleasing words, and he wrote words of truth plainly." I, though, understand the infinitive absolute to be parallel to the infinitive construct *to find* and to act as a second verbal complement to *sought,* the main verb of the verse. The reasons for my choices are driven by the context (discussed in the body of the commentary). In this I agree with Fox ("Frame-Narrative and Composition in the Book of Qohelet," p. 97), who provides grammatical analogies in Deut. 28:56 and Isa. 1:17; 42:24.

66. *yōšer* functions here as an adverb rather than a noun (so Schoors, *The Preacher Sought to Find Pleasing Words,* pp. 45-46).

11 *The words of the wise are like goads, and like firmly implanted nails are the masters of collections.*[67] *They are given by a shepherd.*

12 *Furthermore,*[68] *of these, my son, be warned! There is no end to the making of many books, and much study*[69] *wearies*[70] *the body.*

8 This verse mirrors 1:2 (see comments). Together they form an *inclusio* around Qohelet's speech, and in this way the frame narrator indicates that he understands this typically Qohelethine expression to be a proper summary of his message. That message is: there is no ultimate meaning in this world. Once all is said and done, Qohelet's conclusion is that *everything is meaningless.*

Two deviations from 1:2 are worthy of mention but do not significantly change the meaning of the verse. 12:8 is actually a shorter form of 1:2 since the earlier reference repeats *completely meaningless* a second time. Also, here *Qohelet* is prefixed by the definite article. From this, we understand that Qohelet is a type of professional designation since proper names do not appear with the article — proper names are inherently definite. The appearance of the definite article also reminds us of the rather irregular use of the definite article in the book of Ecclesiastes, and it is also rather arbitrary as to when the article appears with *Qohelet* and when it does not.

67. *ba'ǎlê 'ǎsuppôt* is a difficult phrase that has elicited much discussion. It occurs only here in the Bible, though it does occur in later Jewish literature (see below). Parallelism has been used to support the translation "collected sayings" (NIV, NRSV). In other words, most commentators have felt the need to come up with a term that is closely synonymous with *words of the wise.* Philological evidence (especially that provided by the Talmud) would lead most naturally to a translation like "masters of collections" (see especially the reference in *Sanhedrin* 12a, quoted by Crenshaw [*Ecclesiastes*, p. 191]). Recent studies of parallelism (Kugel, *The Idea of Biblical Poetry;* R. Alter, *The Art of Biblical Poetry* [New York: Basic Books, 1985]; and Longman, *How to Read the Psalms,* pp. 95-110) have successfully challenged the idea that parallelism is based on true synonymity, noting that the second colon always sharpens or progresses the thought of the first colon. This implies that it is unreliable to use parallelism as a means of determining the meaning of a word.

68. See the comment on *yōtēr* in the commentary section on 12:9.

69. While the meaning of *lāhag (studied)* is not disputed, its form is. Most take it as a nominal form from a root *(lhg)* otherwise unattested in Hebrew. The meaning is derived from context and from an extension of the definition of the Arabic cognate, "to be devoted." For some, however, this is too much of an journey, and, since the word bears close enough resemblance to a more common Hebrew root that also fits the context (*hgh* "to meditate"), they assume some kind of textual corruption in order to posit an infinitive construct form (*lhgwt* would be expected). The versions (Septuagint: *meletē;* Vulgate: *meditatio*) may support this, but it is hard to say for sure. As mentioned, the meaning is secure in either case.

70. Literally, "to study is weariness to the body." "Weariness" is actually a noun whose pattern has been identified by some as a late form, but arguments against this use of the word for dating have been presented by Fredericks (*Qoheleth's Language,* p. 183).

276

9 After summarizing Qohelet's teaching in v. 8, the frame narrator begins his evaluation. He starts with a description of Qohelet's work that is somewhat complimentary but very reserved. He refers to him as a *wise man,* to be sure, and one that has worked hard at his task. By piling up the verbs *(taught, heard, investigated, put in good order),* the frame narrator describes an industrious person. Nontheless, this description of Qohelet's task lacks any honorifics or terms of respect. It reminds me of student recommendations to a highly competitive academic program in which the recommending professor writes, "Mr. X is industrious; he works hard." When accompanied by mediocre grades, this is the "kiss of death"; the student is usually rejected.

There is an important disagreement concerning the translation of the opening word complex (*weyōtēr šehāyâ qōhelet,* which I translate *Furthermore, Qohelet was*). The NIV and NRSV mistake *yōtēr* as an adverb and translate: "Besides being wise, the Teacher also taught . . ." (NRSV) and "Not only was the teacher wise, but also he imparted knowledge . . ." (NIV). Th NIV translation ignores the Masoretic punctuation (disjunctive *zaqeph gadol*), but more importantly misunderstood *weyōtēr šehāyâ* for *weyōtēr miš-šehāyâ. yōtēr* must be understood here in its nominal, not adverbial, sense,[71] literally "and this is remaining. . . ." I understand it as a conjunction, "and furthermore."[72]

The frame narrator reminds us that Qohelet was a *wise man.* We must be careful not to read moral overtones into this expression. It is true that in the book of Proverbs wisdom is inextricably bound with righteousness and godliness (e.g., Prov. 8:12-21), but this is not true throughout the canon. In this usage it is clear that the frame narrator simply identifies Qohelet's profession. There are, as Michael Fox[73] reminds us, good sages as well as evil ones (Jonadab [2 Sam. 13:3]; Ahithophel [2 Sam. 16:15–17:29]).

The frame narrator in rather neutral terms expands upon the description of Qohelet's legacy by saying that *he taught the people knowledge.* As mentioned in n. 61, it is impossible to say whether Qohelet is going above and beyond the call of duty in instructing the masses, or whether this is once again simply a description of his role as wisdom teacher.

The last sentence of the verse lists three activities that Qohelet performed during his career, and there is some disagreement over the precise nature of these actions (see footnotes). However, it appears that he studied proverbs and did not invent new ones. This coincides with what we encounter in 1:12–12:7. He occasionally quoted proverbs, but it is at best disputable that he actually created proverbs.

71. Schoors, *The Preacher Sought to Find Pleasing Words,* p. 115.
72. See also Fox, "Frame-Narrative and Composition in the Book of Qohelet," p. 98.
73. Fox, "Frame-Narrative and the Composition in the Book of Qohelet," p. 97.

10 In the previous verse the frame narrator commented respectfully on Qohelet's diligence; here he begins his evalation of his conclusions. In doing so, he chooses words that cast doubt on Qohelet's success.

The evaluation begins with rather lukewarm comments, and then in the following verses it becomes more openly negative. In this verse the frame narrator acknowledges that Qohelet's intention was to discover the truth. In the following words, he will cast doubt on his success.

The key to understanding this verse comes in the phrase *sought . . . to find (biqqēš limṣō'),* already encountered a number of times in Qohelet's section. Many times Qohelet seeks something, but he never finds what he is after (7:24-29; 8:17). Those things he does claim to find are undesirable, for instance, the "bitterness of women" (7:26). Qohelet's entire life was spent seeking for meaning in life but coming up empty.

Indeed, this verse subtly calls Qohelet a double failure. After all, what did Qohelet seek to find? In the first place, *words of delight.* The word *delight* always refers to something pleasing or pleasant. This expression, therefore, likely refers to artful expression, that is, words that elicit delight when read. If so, though there are some nice turns of phrase, the book is better characterized as difficult and problematic. Though admittedly a subjective judgment, I would argue that Qohelet's speech is not one of the most literary books in the canon. If the expression is understood as words that evoke delight, the problem is even more obvious. His words are troublesome, not pleasant or delightful. In the second place, the frame narrator says that Qohelet sought to write *words of truth.* Is the frame narrator ready to admit this? I think not. Qohelet truly describes the world as it really is under covenant curse, but is this the ultimate perspective from which life should be viewed? Not from a normative OT perspective, it isn't. That Qohelet's perspective is considered inadequate by the second wisdom speaker is indicated by the fact that he turns his son's attention away from Qohelet at the end by directing it toward the foundational truths of his faith (12:13-14). By using the expression *sought . . . to find,* then, the frame narrator falls far short of commending either Qohelet's literary skills or his truthfulness.

11 The frame narrator proceeds from his description of Qohelet's intentions to his characterization of the writings of wisdom teachers generally. Though he may be quoting a well-known proverb in the first part of the verse,[74] he certainly intends it to apply to Qohelet's writings as well.

In brief, the frame narrator likens wisdom teaching to the goads that prod cattle into line and nails that are firmly fixed in their place. He also names their source as coming from a shepherd. In other words, the frame narrator uses figurative language to describe the origin and effects of wisdom

---

74. Murphy, *Wisdom Literature,* p. 148; Lauha, *Kohelet,* pp. 218-19.

teaching. One of the major tasks for the interpreter of this verse is to unpack the meaning of the images.

In my translation I have tried to capture the chiastic relationship between v. 11a and b, though the resultant English syntax is a little odd. The chiasm is formed by the occurrence of the images *(goads* and *firmly implanted nails)* in the middle while the objects of comparison *(words* and *masters)* are found first and last.

The imagery, which began with the mention of goads and nails in the first part of the verse, is continued in the third part of the verse *(given by a shepherd),* which I treat as an independent sentence (there is no relative). There is much confusion about the identity of the shepherd. In the first place, the word *'eḥād* occurs before *shepherd.* This has led many to understand the word to be a metaphoric reference to God; thus the NIV and the NKJV capitalize the word. It is true that the Bible refers to God as a shepherd on occasion (Ps. 23:1 is the most notable), but this would be a unique reference in the wisdom literature and a startling affirmation of the divine origin of wisdom.[75] It also seems to put stress on the oneness of God, which seems totally out of place since this issue has not been raised in the book.[76]

The proposed identification between the shepherd and God misleads some commentators,[77] who assert that all of Qohelet's observations and advice are positive and optimistic, if not downright orthodox.[78] This results in extremely strained exegesis in order to harmonize what Qohelet actually says with this evaluation.

The history of interpretation has presented alternatives to the divine identification. Moses, Solomon, and Qohelet himself have all been proposed. The best understanding is to see the reference as part of the metaphor of the verse. A *goad,* which is a long rod with one or more points on the end of it and is used to stir cattle into motion, has already been mentioned. This is part of the shepherd's trade. The best interpretation of the verse is to understand the *shepherd* as a reference to wisdom teachers in general, the numeral *'eḥād* being a late form of the indefinite; thus, I translate *a shepherd.*[79]

In order to understand the nature of the frame narrator's evaluation of wisdom teachers, we must unpack the images of *goad* and *firmly implanted nails.*[80] At least as early as the Targum to the book it has been suggested that

75. Fox, "Frame-Narrative and Composition in the Book of Qohelet," pp. 102-3.
76. Fox, *Qohelet and His Contradictions,* p. 325.
77. For instance, Ogden, *Qoheleth,* p. 210.
78. This is the position of W. Kaiser, Jr., *Ecclesiastes;* see especially pp. 122-25.
79. Fox, "Frame-Narrative and Composition in the Book of Qohelet," p. 102.
80. F. Baumgartel's suggestion ("Die Ochenstachel und die Nägel in Koh. 12," *ZAW* 81 [1969]: 98) that these are references to wisdom written in cuneiform is far-fetched and has not been seconded.

279

the images are positive: "The words of the wise are like inciting goads and forks, which incite those who are destitute of knowledge to learn wisdom as the goad teaches the ox." The paraphrase of Gregory Thaumaturgos states: "I know that the mind is roused and spurred by the instructions of wise people just as much as the body is by an ox-goad being applied or a nail being driven into it."[81] Thus, the *goad* prods to greater wisdom and the *nail* refers to the firm establishment of good teaching. Christian Ginsburg calls this a statement of "liberal" and "conservative" tendencies![82]

Michael Fox, though, has recently and rightly pointed out that the images are united in one regard — they both "sting" when applied.[83] If the frame narrator wanted to focus on the positive aspects of the shepherd's function, he would have more likely written of the rod and staff (Ps. 23:4). Thus, I believe that the frame narrator uses the image of the shepherd and his tools to emphasize the dangerous and painful aspects of wisdom teaching, a very appropriate image after presenting the skeptical and pessimistic teaching of the wise man Qohelet.

12 The frame narrator makes the recipient of his teaching (the book as a whole) explicit for the first time, *my son (b^enî)*. The father-son dialogue is common in ancient Near Eastern wisdom, as the book of Proverbs abundantly attests (cf. Prov. 2:1; 3:1; 4:1, etc.). Nonetheless, it remains unclear whether the "son" is a biological or a vocational designation[84] — that is, rather than one's literal son, a disciple or student might be meant. The same uncertainty attends its occurrence here at the end of the book of Ecclesiastes.

The frame narrator issues a warning to his son. He warns the student *of these (mēhēmmâ)*, the context making it difficult to determine the exact reference of the demonstrative pronoun. Perhaps the proper interpretation of the verse understands the warning to exclude Qohelet's speech since, according to this interpretation, the "words of the wise" (v. 11) include Qohelet's. The Targum, which takes the view that Qohelet is optimistic and orthodox, solves the difficulty in another way by translating: "And more than these, my son, take care to make many books of wisdom without end; to study much the words of the Law, and consider the weariness of the body."[85] Thus, the Targum reverses the meaning of the Hebrew text. Rather than a warning of the danger of books, it gives an exhortation to produce more of them!

I think the Hebrew text of the first part of the verse *(w^eyōtēr mēhēmmâ*

---

81. Jarick, *Gregory Thaumaturgos' Paraphrase*, p. 303.

82. Ginsburg, *The Song of Songs and Coheleth*, p. 381.

83. Fox, *Qohelet and His Contradictions*, p. 325.

84. See R. N. Whybray, *Proverbs*, NCB (Grand Rapids, MI: Eerdmans, 1994), pp. 37-38.

85. Levine, *The Aramaic Version of Qohelet*, p. 47.

bᵉnî hizzāhēr) should be rendered *Furthermore, of these, my son, be warned!* The opening *yōtēr* is taken as a conjunction as in v. 9, and the point of the sentence is that the frame narrator intends to include Qohelet as worthy of warning. *these* would comprise all the wisdom writings, including Qohelet's. In essence, he says to his son, "Qohelet's thinking is dangerous material — be careful."

For those in academics, the second part of the verse *(There is no end to the making of many books, and much study wearies the body)* needs little explanation. There are too many books, and people exhaust themselves by trying to keep up with them. The sentence certainly presents a jaundiced view, but we understand the statement as appropriate after reading the strange and challenging words of Qohelet.

B. THE CONCLUSION: FEAR GOD (12:13-14)

The last two verses are a continuation of the words of the frame narrator, but here he turns from a critique of writings like those of Qohelet to what he believes the reader of his book (the book of Ecclesiastes) should learn. The second wise man turns to his son and concludes with a series of commands with their accompanying motivations.[86]

13 *The end of the matter. All has been heard. Fear God and keep his commandments, for this is the whole duty of humanity.*

14 *For God will bring every deed into judgment, including[87] every hidden thing, whether good or evil.[88]*

13 The last two verses comprise the ultimate conclusion to the book of Ecclesiastes. They are composed of a declaration and a motive clause.

The Hebrew of the declaration is brief, even abrupt, and thus emphatic *(sôp dābār)*. I have tried to capture this by translating the sentence without a verb *(The end of the matter)*. Some translations try to incorporate what I have

---

86. Murphy, *Wisdom Literature,* pp. 148-49.

87. See also Eccles. 11:9, where "*'al* introduces what one is judged for" (Fox, "Frame-Narrative and Composition in the Book of Qohelet," p. 99; cf. Williams, *Hebrew Syntax,* §293).

88. The Masoretes repeated 12:13 (unpointed) after 12:14, apparently because they did not want the book to end with the word *evil.* A similar principle is at work in Isaiah, the Minor Prophets, and the book of Lamentation (see T. A. Perry, *Dialogues with Kohelet: The Book of Ecclesiastes* [University Park, PA: Pennsylvania State University Press, 1993], p. 174, for the textual evidence for Ecclesiastes).

taken as two sentences into one sentence, "Let us hear the conclusion of the whole matter" (NKJV), but this obscures the emphatic nature of the verse.[89]

The abruptness of the first sentence perhaps reflects the impatience of the frame narrator. The effect may be: "Enough of Qohelet, let's get on with what is really important."

In any case, we are left in no doubt as to what is of greatest significance for the frame narrator. His statement is brief and to the point, utilizing key words in order to invoke major concepts and also the three different parts of the canon.

First, the frame narrator's son must *Fear God*. It is true that Qohelet has stated the same words (3:14; 5:6 [English 5:7]; 7:18; 8:12), but with doubtful conviction (see the commentary at those places). Here there is no doubt that the intention of the speaker/writer is to lead his listener/reader to a right relationship with God, one in which he is properly subservient to the deity. To *fear God* in this sense means to respect, honor, and worship the Lord. The motto "fear God" also invokes the book of Proverbs (1:7 in particular), a book which has received implicit criticism throughout Qohelet's writings.

Second, the frame narrator exhorts his son to *keep his* [God's] *commandments*. Qohelet never so admonished his students, and the juxtaposition of the command to fear God and to keep his commandments is one of the major contextual items that signals that the frame narrator advocates orthodox worship, that is, worship in keeping with the normative teachings of the rest of the OT. With his call to obey God's commandments, we see the frame narrator's interest not only that his son establish a right relationship with God, but that he maintain it in the proper way. Also, this language evokes the legal material of the OT canon, which is made up of numerous commandments (*miṣwôt*).

The verse ends with the first of two motive clauses: *for this is the whole duty of humanity*. Literally, the Hebrew (*kî zeh kol-hā'ādām*) reads "for this is the whole of humanity," which may be an idiom in Hebrew, but it does not communicate well in English. The difficulty was felt early in the history of exegesis since even the Talmud (*Berakot* 6a) raises the question of its interpretation. Rabbi Eleazar answers the question and asserts that the phrase meant that the commands to fear and obey God were the most important things in life. Robert Gordis believes that it is a "pregnant" saying that implies one's "whole duty."[90] The general meaning of the statement is fairly clear: fearing God and obeying his commands is the most important thing a man or a woman can do.

---

89. Note that the NKJV also follows the Vulgate in understanding the verb (*nišmā'*, which it translates "let us hear") as a jussive, which is possible but not likely.

90. Gordis, *Kohelet*, p. 355.

14 The section, and the book, concludes with a second motive clause. Why fear and obey God? Because God will judge you. Qohelet talked about God's judgment earlier (most recently in 11:9), but it was never linked with his law. Indeed, it is hard to know exactly how Qohelet thought God's judgment would work in practice since he never admits to justice in the present or to the possibility of judgment in the future (see the discussion in connection with 3:16-22). Qohelet looked for a time when God would give the righteous their reward and the wicked their just punishment, but he did not discover evidence that God would make things right. For Qohelet, the righteous suffered and the wicked prospered (7:15-18; 9:1-12), but here the second wise man asserts his understanding that God will indeed make things right through judgment.

The frame narrator anticipates a judgment that will take place in the future rather than the present, and one that includes *hidden,* or "secret," acts. Thus, it is likely that he had an eschatological judgment in mind.[91]

The book thus ends on a strong orthodox note, one that is in keeping with the dominant teaching of the rest of the OT, and one that is positive, at least for the faithful. It is thus correct to characterize the book as positive and orthodox, while maintaining the dubious nature of Qohelet's own thinking.

SUMMARY OF CHAPTER 12

Qohelet's speech ends with a section that calls for people to remember God. The bulk of this concluding unit meditates on the aging process, which ultimately culminates in death. The tone is depressing, not uplifting.

Qohelet uses three metaphor clusters to describe the aging process. First (v. 2), he likens the aging process to a coming storm. Second (vv. 3-5), he compares the aging body to a house with four types of inhabitants, each of which is flagging in energy and strength. The idea is that as people grow old, they slowly deteriorate like a neglected building. Third (vv. 6 and 7), life is compared to precious objects, which at death are smashed and rendered useless.

On this depressing note, Qohelet's speech ends and the unnamed frame narrator speaks up. His voice has not been heard since the prologue in 1:1-11.[92] In the prologue the frame narrator simply set the mood and introduced Qohelet's speech. Here he concludes and evaluates what has been heard. He also points the hearer in what he considers to be the proper direction.

91. So Ginsburg, *The Song of Songs and Coheleth,* p. 478.
92. With the exception of 7:27, where he briefly surfaces in the narrative: "Qohelet said."

In this section the frame narrator addresses his son (v. 12) and begins by summarizing Qohelet's conclusion, which he does by simply citing Qohelet's most common refrain, "Everything is meaningless."

Nonetheless, as the frame narrator goes on, he respectfully commends Qohelet, a professional wise man who worked hard and had good intentions. The narrator also afffirms that Qohelet sought to find truth, although nowhere does he ever clearly state that Qohelet found truth. What truth Qohelet found was truth "under the sun." Indeed, apart from God, which is one of the meanings I believe this phrase has, there is no meaning, no reason to do more than to pursue the simple pleasures of life (eat, drink, and enjoy work).

However, the frame narrator is unhappy with this ultimate conclusion. In vv. 11-12, he becomes more openly critical, warning his son of the dangers inherent in a writing like the one they just looked at together. Finally, in the last two verses of the book, he turns his son toward the central truths of revealed religion: the fear of God, obedience to his commandments, and an awareness of the coming judgment.

A FINAL WORD

The book of Ecclesiastes must in the final analysis be understood by the modern reader in the light of the full context of the canon. For the Christian that context includes the NT. For this reason, now that we have looked through the book as a whole, I commend the rereading of the introduction, particularly the sections that concern the theological message of the book. The idea is presented there that Jesus Christ is the ultimate answer to Qohelet's conclusion of meaninglessness under the sun. Jesus emptied himself of his divine prerogatives to subject himself to the world "under the sun" in order to free us of the chaos to which God subjected the world after the fall into sin (see Gal. 3:3 and Rom. 8:18-27).

INDEX OF SUBJECTS

INDEX OF SUBJECTS

Wealth, 159-60, 165-66, 168, 170-71, 173, 175, 189-91, 242

Wisdom, 79-80, 84, 89, 93, 94, 96-97, 99-100, 104, 110, 132, 145, 150, 172-74, 179, 181, 186-87, 189-92, 196-201, 206, 208-9, 213-14, 219, 221, 223, 231, 234-39, 245-48, 250-51, 277-79

Women, 92-93, 203-6, 230-31, 238-41, 270

Work, 65, 100, 102-4, 106-8, 136, 139-40, 142, 148, 152

INDEX OF AUTHORS

INDEX OF AUTHORS

291

INDEX OF SCRIPTURE REFERENCES

292

INDEX OF SCRIPTURE REFERENCES

INDEX OF FOREIGN WORDS

INDEX OF FOREIGN WORDS

qml	265	šûb	60	**ARAMAIC**	
qin'â	136, 137	šbḥ	134, 219		
qn'h	137	šābîm	71	'illu	140
qrb	216	šabtî	232	'im	190
qᵉrāb	236	šᵉgāgâ	155	sdy	92
qryt	251	šd	92		
rā'â	193, 224, 265	šdd	92	**PERSIAN**	
rᵉ'ēh	205	šᵉhāyâ	277		
rā'ōh	232	šehtaqqîp	177	pair:daēza	91
rᵉ'yôn	81	šāw'	63		
rᵉ'îyat	160	šaḥar	259	**GREEK**	
rᵉ'ît	160	šeyyihyû	163		
rᵉ'ôt	160	šeyyōlēk	161	aiōn	121
rō'š	145	škb	140	anaidēs	209
ri'šōnîm	75	škḥ	218	aniēmi	193
rā'îtî	193, 233	šlḥ	215	anēs	193
rābab	165	šāllît	240	anoia	259
rabbîm	207, 242	šālliṭîm	193	apethanen	217
ragleykā	149	šlt	214, 215	apo tote	217
raglᵉkā	149	šilṭôn	162, 210	gnōseōs	78
rādap	81	šām	69, 125	doulou	166
rûaḥ	69, 81, 130, 181,	šēm	182	egkopos	71
	188, 241	šemen	182	eis	224
rōa'	184	šm'	150	eisathentas	216
rwṣ	266	šōmēa'	180	ekklēsia	1
rḥq	266	šmr	212	ekklēsiastēs	1
rāḥôq	200	šōmēr	158	ekpesē	243
rḥq min	116	šōmᵉrê	264, 269	elaiou	238
rē'a	150	šemeš	164	en andreia	104
ra'	80, 139, 151,	šn	102	en skia	176, 217
	184, 212, 227	šānā'	209	en sophia	181
r'h	81, 104, 105	šeni	140	erei	74
rᵉ'ût	80	šeqer	63	exichniasetai	275
r''	81	šîr	180	hēdysmatos	238
ra'at	214	šth	250	helkei	69
rp'	241	šṭyp	69	hos	74
rph	241	tᵉbû'a	160	kai	74
rṣṣ	266	tᵉhillat	247	kairon	210
rîq	63	taḥat	233	kairos	121
rᵉqôd	116	taḥat haššēmeš	163	kakō	232
rāš	145, 146	timṣā'ennû	254	kathōs	210
reša'	203	tiqqēn	275	kakōsei	193
rtq	266	tqp	140	kardian sou	193
śᵉḥōq	183	tûr	79	kosmion	275
śkr	226	tērōs	266	kriseōs	210
śemaḥ	183	tiššōmēm	196	ktisas	264
śimḥâ	88, 168	tithakkam	195	lalei	210
śmk	89	tittēn	193	lalēsei	74
śar	249			logismous	207
še	60, 102, 239			logon	187
šā'ap	69				
šāb	69				

305